T R A V E L L E R S
S U R V I V A L   K I T

Madagascar,
Mayotte & Comoros

TRAVELLERS
SURVIVAL KIT

Madagascar,
Mayotte & Comoros

James & Deborah Penrith

Published by Vacation Work, 9 Park End Street, Oxford
www.vacationwork.co.uk

**TRAVELLERS SURVIVAL KIT: MADAGASCAR,
MAYOTTE & COMOROS**

by James & Deborah Penrith

Editor: Ian Collier

Copyright © Vacation Work 2000

ISBN 1-85458-241-0

Cover Design: Miller Craig & Cocking Design Partnership

Maps by Andrea Pullen

Illustrations by Beccy Blake

Cover Photograph
Courtesy of Air Madagascar

Typesetting by Worldview Publishing Services

Printed by William Clowes Ltd., Beccles, Suffolk, England.

Contents

MADAGASCAR AND ITS PEOPLE

Geography – Geology – Topography......................................17
Climate – Best Times to Visit – Average Temperatures........................21
History..22
Politics – Legal System 25
The Economy – Tourism..28
The People – Population – Ethnic Groups – Origins – Education........30
Languages – Getting it Right – Useful Words and Phrases................34
Religion..38
National Anthem and Flag..40
Further Reading 40

MADAGASCAR: PRACTICAL INFORMATION

GETTING THERE 43
  By Air – Air Madagascar Offices Around the World – Other
  Airlines Serving Madagascar – Airport 43
  By Sea – Malagasy Shipping Company Offices – Cruise Ships –
  Shipping Lines in Madagascar 45
  Tour Operators 47
  Travel Safely 48
RED TAPE 48
  Entry Requirements – Passports and Visas – Health Documents
  – Customs Regulations..49
  Malagasy Embassies and Consulates Abroad 50
MONEY 50
  What Money to Take..50
  Money in Madagascar – Exchange Rates................................50
  Banks and Banking – Credit Cards and ATMs – Tipping................51
  Emergency Cash..52
HEALTH AND HYGIENE 52
  Before You Leave – Medical Advice – Jet-Lag – Useful Addresses...52
  When You Return..54
  Medical Services – Medical Centres...................................54
  Everyday Health 55
  AIDS 56
  Health Hazards – Bilharzia – Cholera – Malaria – Tetanus
  – Typhoid – Viral Hepatitis 57

Sensible Precautions..59
Natural Hazards – Sun – Humidity 59
First-Aid Hints – Tips...60
CLOTHING 61
What to Wear & When 61
COMMUNICATIONS 61
Mail..61
Telephones – Charges – Access Code – Area Codes – Mobile
Phones – Call Boxes 61
Media – Television – Radio – Newspapers and Magazines 63
GETTING AROUND 64
Maps and Guides...64
By Air – Domestic Flights – Regional Links – Local Air
Madagascar Offices – Charter Flights 64
By Sea 67
By Rail...67
By Road – Buses – Taxis..68
DRIVING 68
Licences 68
Roads – Vehicles – Fuel 69
Vehicle Rental – Car Rental Agencies – Hazards....................69
ACCOMMODATION 70
Camping..71
EATING AND DRINKING...71
Cuisine – Some Useful Words..71
Drinking 74
ENTERTAINMENT..75
Song and Dance 75
Music..76
SPORT AND RECREATION 76
Diving 77
Hiking – Other Activities..77
SHOPPING 77
Gifts and Souvenirs...77
Handicrafts – Markets – Boutiques and Designers........................78
Red Tape 79
CRIME AND SAFETY 79
Crime – Photography – Tips 79
Drink, Drugs and the Law – Drugs – Hookers – The Police..........81
HELP AND INFORMATION 81
Tour Operators in Madagascar..81
Tourist Information Centres...82
Foreign Embassies and Consulates..82
Gay Travellers 82
Disabled Travellers 83
Useful Information – Time Zone – Electrical Appliances – Weights
and Measures – Useful Addresses and Telephone Numbers 83
PUBLIC HOLIDAYS 84
Fixed Dates – Variable Holidays..84

SOLAR ECLIPSE 2001 84

FLORA AND FAUNA

Introduction 87
Flora 88
   Central Madagascar 89
   The North 89
   The East 89
   The West 90
   The South 90
   Notable Flora 90
Fauna 91
   Lemurs – Lemur Sub-Species and Genera – Aya-Aye – Sifakas
   – Mouse Lemurs – Bamboo Lemurs – Ring Tailed Lemurs
   – Black Lemurs – Crowned Lemurs – Red-Bellied Lemurs
   – Mongoose Lemurs – Ruffed Lemurs – Family Megaladapidae 92
   Chameleons...101
   Bats 101
   Small Mammals –Tenrecs – Rodents Carnivores...........102
   Reptiles – Geckos – Crocodiles – Turtles – Snakes 102
   Others – Amphibians – Insects 103
Bird-Watching..103
National Parks and Reserves – National Parks – Special Reserves
   – Strict Nature Reserves – Private Reserves 107
Conservation...110
Proof from the Past – Fossils 116

EXPLORING MADAGASCAR

Tourist Attractions...118
ANTANANARIVO AND THE CENTRAL HIGHLANDS 120
   Antananarivo – Local Attractions – Excursions 120
   Mantasoa – Manjakatompo Forestry Station 123
   Antsirabe – Further Afield – Ambositra – Ranomafana 124
   Fianarantsoa – Ambalavao...................................125
   Accommodation – Antananarivo – Mantasoa – Antsirabe
   – Ambositra – Fianarantsoa – Ranomafana 126
   Eating Out – Antananarivo....................................128
   Entertainment..129
NORTHERN REGION...130
   Antsiranana/Diego Suarez – How to Get There 130
   National Parks and Reserves – Montagne d'Ambre National
   Park – Analamera Special Reserve – Ankarana Reserve
   – Tsaratanana Strict Nature Reserve – Marojejy National Park.......131
   Nosy Bé...133
   Hell-Ville – Places of Interest – Djamandjary – Smaller Islands 135
   Sport and Recreation – Diving – Dive Sites – Fishing
   – Sailing – Caving 136

Accommodation – Diego Suarez – Ambanja – Sambava – Nosy
Bé – Belle Vue – Other Areas of Nosy Bé – Nosy Komba
– Nosy Sakatia – Nosy Mitsio 137
Eating Out and Entertainment 140
WESTERN REGION 140
Mahajanga – Further Afield 140
Morondava – Tsingy de Bemaraha 143
Accommodation – Mahajanga – Katsepy – Morondava 143
Eating Out 144
SOUTHERN REGION 145
Toliara – Anakao 145
Isalo National Park – Sapphires – Beza-Mahafaly Special Reserve
– Zombitse National Park 147
Taolagnaro – Further Afield 148
National Parks and Reserves – Berenty Private Reserve
– Andohahela National Park 150
Accommodation – Toliara – Ifaty – Isalo National Park
– Taolagnaro – Berenty 150
Eating Out 152
Entertainment 152
EASTERN REGION 152
Toamasina – Canal des Pangalanes – How to Get There
– Further Afield 152
The Masoala Peninsula 155
Maroantsetra 156
Nosy Boraha (St Mary's Island) – Ambodifotatra 156
Accommodation – Toamasina – Canal des Pangalanes
– Andasibe – Nosy Boraha 158
Eating Out 160

MAYOTTE AND ITS PEOPLE

Geography – Topography...161
Climate – Temperatures 162
History..164
Politics...166
The Economy – Exports – Tourism 167
The People – Women 167
Languages – Useful Words and Phrases.......................................169
Religion – National Anthem and Flag...171
Further Reading 172

MAYOTTE: PRACTICAL INFORMATION

GETTING THERE...173
By Air – Flights from France to Réunion – Airport..........................173
Inter-Island Ferry – Tickets – Times..175
Tour Operators 176

By Sea – Contact Details...176
RED TAPE..177
    Entry Requirements – Passports and Visas – Health
    Documents – Customs Regulations....................................177
    French Embassies Abroad...178
MONEY...178
    What Money to Take – Banks and Banking 178
HEALTH AND HYGIENE..178
    Before You Leave...178
    Medical Services..179
    Everyday Health..179
    AIDS...179
    Health Hazards..180
    Natural Hazards – Seasickness 180
    First Aid Hints...181
CLOTHING..181
    What to Wear and When...181
COMMUNICATIONS 182
    Mail..182
    Telephones 182
    Media – Radio and Television – Newspapers and Magazines 183
GETTING AROUND 183
    Maps and Guides..183
    By Sea..183
    By Road 184
DRIVING 184
    Licences...184
    Roads – Fuel...185
    Vehicle Rental – Petite Terre – Grande Terre – Hazards..............185
ACCOMMODATION 186
    Hotels on Petite Terre – Cottages/Guest Houses/Furnished
    Apartments..186
    Hotels on Grande Terre – Cottages/Guest Houses/Furnished
    Apartments – Gîtes – Camping...187
EATING AND DRINKING 188
    Cuisine – Vegetarian and Self-Catering.........................188
    Restaurants – Petite Terre – Grande Terre....................190
    Drinking 191
ENTERTAINMENT...192
    Nightlife – Cinema and Theatre 192
FLORA AND FAUNA 193
    Flora 193
    Fauna – Birdlife – Wildlife...193
    Sealife – Turtles – Whales and Dolphins – Rarities – Excursions...194
SPORT AND RECREATION..195
    Diving and Snorkelling – Dive Centres – On Petite Terre – On
    Grande Terre – Alternatives – 196
    Fishing – Charter Companies 198
    Hiking 198
    Other Activities – Swimming and Surfing – Aerial Trips – Golf 199
SHOPPING..200

Gifts and Souvenirs..200
CRIME AND SAFETY 201
    Crime...201
    Drink, Drugs and the Law – Drink – Drugs – The Law..................201
HELP AND INFORMATION 202
    Tourist Information Centres...202
    Mayotte Tourist Offices and Representatives Abroad...............202
    Useful Information – Useful Telephone Numbers.........................203
    Public Holidays – Festivals – Public Holidays 204

EXPLORING MAYOTTE

Tourist Attractions – Petite Terre – Grande Terre 206
PETITE TERRE...206
GRANDE TERRE..207
    Mamoudzou – The North – Central – West Coast – The South
    – The East...207

COMOROS AND ITS PEOPLE

Geography – Topography..213
Climate – Average Temperatures – Average Rainfall 215
History 216
Politics 217
The Economy – Exports 220
The People – Women...222
Languages – Useful Words and Phrases..223
Religion 225
National Anthem and Flag 226
Further Reading 227

COMOROS: PRACTICAL INFORMATION

GETTING THERE 228
    By Air – The Best Route – Other Routes – Airlines Serving
    Comoros – Airport 228
    By Sea 231
    Tour Operators 232
    Travel Safely 232
RED TAPE...232
    Entry Requirements – Passports and Visas – Health
    Documents – Customs Regulations – Caution 232
    Comoros Embassies Abroad 234
MONEY 234
    What Money to Take – Exchange Rates – Banks and Banking
    – Credit Cards and ATMs – Tipping 234

HEALTH AND HYGIENE...235
    Before You Leave – Cholera – Malaria – Polio – Rabies
– Tetanus – Typhoid – Viral Hepatitis – Yellow Fever 235
    Medical Services 237
    Everyday Health...238
    Health Hazards – Diving – Barotrauma – Rupture of Lung Tissue
– Air Embolism – Decompression Sickness – Diving and Flying:
Caveat..238
CLOTHING...240
What to Wear and When..240
COMMUNICATIONS 240
    Mail..240
    Telephones 240
    Media – Radio and Television – Newspapers and Magazines 241
GETTING AROUND 241
    Maps and Guides..241
    By Air – Comores Aviation Timetable..242
    By Road 243
    By Sea 243
DRIVING 243
    Licences – Roads – Fuel 243
    Vehicle Rental – Hazards 244
ACCOMMODATION..244
    Accommodation on Anjouan – Accommodation on Mohéli
– Budget Accommodation 246
EATING AND DRINKING 246
    Cuisine..246
    Drinking 248
ENTERTAINMENT..248
FLORA AND FAUNA 249
    Flora 249
    Fauna – The Coelacanth – Fruit Bats – Marine Turtles.................249
    Bird Watching – Grande Comore – Anjouan – Mohéli 252
    National Parks...252
SPORT AND RECREATION...253
    Diving – The Best Dive Sites – Other Dive Sites 253
    Fishing – Other Watersports 257
    Hiking and Scrambling 258
SHOPPING..259
    Gifts and Souvenirs...259
CRIME AND SAFETY 260
    Crime..260
    Drink Drugs and the Law...261
HELP AND INFORMATION 262
    Tourist Information Centres 262
    Foreign Embassies and Consulates 262
    Disabled Travellers 262
    Useful Information – Electrical Appliances – Useful Addresses
and Telephone Numbers...263
PUBLIC HOLIDAYS 263
    Fixed Dates – Religious Festivals..263

EXPLORING COMOROS

GRANDE COMORE 265
    Moroni – Around Moroni..265
    Mitsamiouli – Further Afield...268
    The East Coast – Chomoni – Foumbouni.....................269
    The South Coast – Iconi..270
    The Central Region 270
    Excursions – Perfume Island Tour – Moroni-Chomoni – Three
    Craters Nature Walk – Karthala Rainforest.......................271
ANJOUAN 272
    Mutsamudu...272
    Around Anjouan – Domoni..273
MOHÉLI 275
    Privateers and Pirates...275
    Fomboni..275
    Around Mohéli..276
    Nioumachoua Marine Reserve.....................................276

Index..279

MAPS

Location of Madagascar, Mayotte & Comoros...........................14
Madagascar 19
Air Madagascar Network 65
Antananarivo 119
Nosy Bé Island 134
Mayotte 163
Mamoudzou 208
The Comoros Archipelago 214
Moroni...266
Grande Comore..267
Anjouan & Mohéli...273

Acknowledgements

Many people have helped us in one way or another to put together this guidebook, but without the contributions of the following we would have truly been up the *crique* without a *pagaie*.

Marc Lubert, Director, Comité du Tourism de Mayotte, Mamoudzou, and statistician François Perrin; Greta Jeanne Du Bois, manager for South Africa, Air Austral; Bruno Ranarivelo, Consul-General of Madagascar for the Republic of South Africa; Colin Ainsworth Sharp, Honorary Vice-Consul for Madagascar, Johannesburg; Fara Andrianiazy Bonneville of Air Madagascar, St Denis, Réunion; Thompson A Andriamanoro, Director of Communications and Promotions, La Maison du Tourisme de Madagascar, Antananarivo; Sonja Ranarivelo and Ony Haja of Boogie Pilgrim Tours, Antananarivo; Jean-Marc Heintz, General Manager and Chief Pilot, Comores Aviation; and Pauline Byrom for helpful assistance. To these and all others we say *misàotra, merci beaucoup, marahabha,* and thanks.

Sources of Information

British Foreign and Commonwealth Office; US State Department; Air Madagascar and its in-flight magazine *Orchid;* Air Austral magazine *Escale;* Duke University's Primate Center; British Airways Travel Clinics; Medical Advisory Services for Travellers Abroad (MASTA); *Habitat* magazine, Johannesburg; *Proceedings of the International Congress on Madagascar,* edited by Sandra Evers and Marc Spindler; the Federal Research Division of the US Library of Congress Country Studies Series; *Les Etats d'Afrique, de l'Océan Indien et des Caraïbes* (Institut National de la Statisque de Madagascar, Antananarivo).

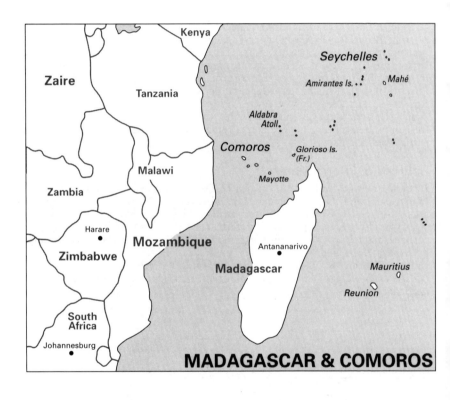

MADAGASCAR & COMOROS

Preface

Every traveller dreams of visiting somewhere that has not yet been discovered by the masses, or ruined by hordes of lager louts in search of curry and chips. The great island continent of Madagascar and the little tropical islands of the neighbouring Indian Ocean archipelago, Mayotte and Comoros, together make up such untouched destinations. They are among the last places on earth that are only now going into tourist mode.

Madagascar is an exciting destination, starting to open up its bounty to tourists. This island, said to be a remnant of the legendary continent of Atlantis, is a natural time capsule whose geological past has ensured the development of a vast array of unique animals, birds, trees, plants, flowers and fish. This is what is drawing visitors in increasing numbers, but like many other Third World countries Madagascar can be maddening if you expect hot water always to pour out of the shower and cold water to run out of the tap; likewise if you need to make an urgent international call, or think the names or at least the spellings of places should always match up on maps and road signs, as they do in Europe and America. These, and many other irritations, are a small price to pay for the natural treasures this land that time forgot has to offer the traveller. Madagascar is truly a unique country, difficult to imagine and impossible to forget once you have sampled its magic. It's a place where the capital is called the Citadel of a Thousand Warriors and a town of scholars is known as the Place of Good Learning, and where even the rivers have poetic names – the Tsiribihina, or Unfordable One; the Mania, or Straying One; the Morondava, or Long-Shored One; the Ihosy, or River of Goats; the Mananjara, or Happy River, the Manakara, or River of Shells; and the Mahajamba, or River of Blindness. The ancient Malagasy name for Madagascar itself was simply *Ny Anivon Riaka,* or 'That which is in the midst of the moving waters.' You need time and patience to make the most of a trip to Madagascar. A couple of nights in Antananarivo, the capital city, and a visit to some of the highlights listed in the following pages can comfortably be handled in a short two-week visit, but this will only whet your appetite and make you keen to see more of this fascinating island, with its vast lakes, soaring peaks, great waterfalls, caverns full of bats and crocodiles, forests of fantastic beauty, hot mineral springs and tropical islands like none on earth.

Mayotte is geographically an island in the same archipelago as the three which form the Islamic Republic of Comoros, but the resemblance tends to end there. This delightful place is an outpost of metropolitan France and this, as much as its distance from the USA, Australia and countries of Europe, has preserved it from all except the odd cruise ship visit and a trickle of tourists from that other French possession in the Indian Ocean, Réunion. You've got to do a bit of island hopping by air and sea to get to Mayotte, but the island will amply repay you for the effort.

Take away the bikes and taxis, the transistor radios and TV sets, and the three sleepy islands of Comoros look more or less the same now as they did when the Arabs arrived centuries ago from the north in their dhows to convert the heathen islanders. Where there are buildings and mosques they largely echo the style of Zanzibar; on the smallest of the trio of islands sun-dried mud and palm thatch predominate. These islands have had a chequered modern history. Since it shrugged off French rule the Republic has had so many mini-revolutions that it is sometimes jokingly known as Cloud Coup-Coup Land, although the coups have usually been so discreet that visitors have been unaware that anything out of the ordinary has happened. The only intimation that a government has been toppled is when the radio replaces its usual strident music with a sombre classical piece prior to the official announcement. The Comoros remain gem-like islands known in the main to divers and others who like to travel far from the beaten track.

Taken singly or together the sun-drenched islands of Madagascar, Mayotte and Comoros are very much the coming thing among savvy travellers from the northern hemisphere and, happily, these islands can all still be caught at their pristine peak.

James and Deborah Penrith
Mamoudzou, Grande Terre, Mayotte

Madagascar

Ring tailed Lemur

GEOGRAPHY

Madagascar is known with good reason throughout the south-west Indian Ocean as the Great Red Island. It is the fourth largest island in the world after Greenland, New Guinea and Borneo and vast areas of its red lateritic soil cover have been exposed by years of thoughtless deforestation and now appear from the air to incoming travellers like gigantic red wounds in the landscape. As you descend to the airport outside Antananarivo, the capital city, you can't miss these gaping scars. What you're seeing is some of the world's worst erosion, the result of centuries of such destructive agricultural methods as slash and burn (known locally as *tavy*). This is still practised, and nearly 20% of Madagascar's land is torched annually to provide fresh greenery for the vast herds of near-sacred zebu cattle. The impression is further strengthened when torrential tropical downpours scour the red blanket and wash more soil into streams and rivers to turn them into blood-red tributaries of the ocean.

Like Australia, Madagascar is an island continent created by aeons of continental drift. It stretches 981 miles (1,580 km) from top to bottom and is 360 miles (580 km) at its widest point, giving it a surface area of 226,656 sq miles (587,041 sq km), or more than the combined size of Germany and the United Kingdom, and almost the size of Texas. The highest point is Mt Maromokotro, in the volcanic northern Massif du Tsaratanana, at 9,442 ft (2,877 m). North of this is volcanic Montagne d'Ambre; just south of Cap d'Ambre is the excellent natural harbour at Diego Suarez. The island lies almost entirely between the Equator and the Tropic of Cancer, its east coast open to thousands of miles of rolling ocean and its west coast 310 miles (500 km) from the shores of Mozambique on the African mainland and about 186 miles (300 km) from the islands of Comoros in the Mozambique Channel. A number of smaller islands surround Madagascar and are part of the Republic. The larger and more important are the holiday resort of Nosy Bé, off the north-west corner, which is the largest (124 sq miles/321 sq km) of the surrounding islands, and Nosy Boraha (Ile St Marie or St Mary's Island) off the east coast, which was notorious as an infamous pirate stronghold in the 17th and 18th centuries.

Geology

Madagascar was once part of the ancient super-continent of Gondwanaland which broke up to form Africa, South America, India, Australia and Antarctica. The island in turn broke away from the African continent some 165 million years ago and this gave it the isolation which has turned it into a living museum of plants, animals and birds found nowhere else on earth, an astonishing biodiversity that makes Madagascar a unique destination for travellers in a world where very little is truly unique.

TOPOGRAPHY

The island is dominated by the *Hautes Terres* (highlands), which form a massive central mountainous backbone, a plateau at an elevation of 2,600-4,900 ft (800-1,500 m) and 80 miles (129 km) long by 60 miles (97 km) wide. The plateau is a high granite moorland, burnt bare and treeless, and drenched often by heavy rainfall, which further erodes the fan-shaped gullies known as *lavaka*. The mountainous central spine separates the permanently damp east from the drier west, and the semi-desert south.

The central highlands are full of rounded and eroded hills, massive granite outcrops, extinct volcanoes, alluvial plains, and marshes which have been converted into irrigated rice paddies. The highlands extend from the Tsaratanana Massif in the north to the Ivakoany Massif in the south and include the Anjafy High Plateaux, the volcanic formations of Itasy – Lake Itasy itself is in a volcanic crater – and the Ankaratra Massif, reaching a height of 8,747 ft (2,666

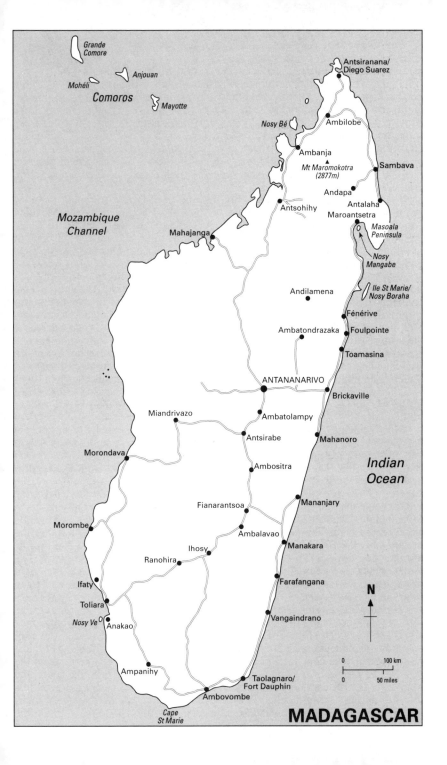

Grande
Comore

Anjouan

Mohéli

Comoros

Mayotte

Antsiranana/
Diego Suarez

Nosy Bé

Ambilobe

Ambanja

▲ Mt Maromokotra
(2877m)

Sambava

Andapa

Antalaha

Antsohihy

Antalaha
Maroantsetra

Masoala
Peninsula

Mozambique
Channel

Mahajanga

Nosy
Mangabe

Andilamena

Ile St Marie/
Nosy Boraha

Fénérive

Ambatondrazaka

Foulpointe

Toamasina

ANTANANARIVO

Brickaville

Miandrivazo

Ambatolampy

Antsirabe

Mahanoro

Morondava

Ambositra

Indian
Ocean

Fianarantsoa

Mananjary

Morombe

Ambalavao

Manakara

Ihosy

Ranohira

Farafangana

Ifaty

N

Toliara

Vangaindrano

Nosy Ve

Anakao

Ampanihy

0   100 km

0   50 miles

Taolagnaro/
Fort Dauphin

Ambovombe

Cape
St Marie

MADAGASCAR

m). The Isalo Massif lies between the central highlands and the west coast. Antananarivo, the capital city, sits 4,816 ft (1,468 m) above sea level in the northern part of the central highlands. A prominent feature of the central highlands is a north-south rift valley, east of Antananarivo and including Lake Alaotra, which with a length of 25 miles (40 km), is the largest stretch of fresh water on the island. The lake is 2,497 ft (761 m) above sea level. The highest elevations of the central highlands run parallel to the east coast, which is a band of lowlands only 31 miles (50 km) wide and bordering an escarpment of about 1,640 ft (500 m) which gives access to the highlands. The land slopes more gradually down to the west coast.

The coastal region extends roughly from north of Baie d'Antongil, the most prominent feature on the east coast of the island bounded by the Masoala Peninsula, to the far south of the island. A feature of the east coast is the Canal des Pangalanes (Lakandranon' Ampalangalana), some 435 miles (700 km) of interlinked lagoons and lakes formed by Indian Ocean currents washing up sand on the island, by the silting of rivers, and linked by artificially created waterways. This enormous canal is used as a fishing ground and for transportation and runs nearly half the length of the east coast. The entire island coastline runs for 3,000 miles (4,828 km) and on the east is remarkable for being virtually straight and without natural bays, ports and indentations of any size, except for the massive Baie d'Antongil and the Baie de Diego Suarez, at the north-eastern tip of the island. The west coast doesn't have this problem and is full of splendid little bays, inlets and coves, especially on the north-western stretch. These deep bays and well-protected harbours have attracted explorers, traders, and pirates from Europe, Africa, and the Middle East since ancient times and this area has long been an important link between Madagascar and the rest of the world. The land is very fertile along the coast and in the riverine valleys of the plateau.

Most principal rivers and streams emptying into the Indian Ocean are not navigable because of the steeply contoured terrain they traverse. Rivers are short and boisterous, and many descend to the east coast in scintillating cascades and foaming rapids. The Mananara and Mangoro rivers flow from the central highlands to the east coast, as does the Maningory, which flows from Lake Alaotra. Other rivers flowing east into Indian Ocean include the Bemarivo, the Ivondro, and the Mananjary. Rivers flowing to the west coast and emptying into the Mozambique Channel tend to be longer and slower, because of the more gentle slope of the land. The major rivers on the west coast are the Sambirano, the Mahajamba, the Bestiboka (the port of Mahajanga is located at the mouth), the Mania, the North and South Mahavavy, the Mangoky, and the Onilahy. The Ikopa, which flows past Antananarivo, is a tributary of the Betsiboka. Important lakes, aside from Alaotra, include Lake Kinkony in the north-west and Lake Ihotry in the south-west.

Inland Madagascar is roughly divided into four major habitat regions separated by the chain of mountains running the length of the island. Rain-forest covers the eastern slopes of the mountains, patches of what was once an enormous deciduous forest are to be found in the west, while grasslands typical of the high plateau now dominate the island's scenery. At the southern end of the island is an area known as the spiny desert. The principal river in the south, the Mandrare, has an enormous 4,801-sq mile (12,435 sq km) basin, but even this dries up during certain months. Weathering of Madagascar's sedimentary rocks has created some wild and wonderful scenery, from the Isalo mountains in the south-west, where sandstone outcrops have been carved into a spectacular landscape of weird formations and winding canyons, to the labyrinthine limestone karst or *tsingy* massifs of Bemaraha, Namoroka and Ankarana, which can be even more impressive. Poet Flavien Ranaivo aptly sums up Madagascar, calling it 'the land at the end of the earth.'

CLIMATE

Madagascar is situated in the tropical zone of the southern hemisphere and basks in more than 300 days of sunshine a year. It has two fairly distinct seasons: a dry season from May to October when you can expect cloudless, warm days, and a hot rainy, summer season from November to April. Altitude and latitude, however, can result in notable differences. Nosy Bé and the north-western islands enjoy a fairly stable temperature through the year of 77-86°F (25-30°C) and in spite of the sudden tropical downpours the atmosphere there is usually clear and dry. Conversely, the highlands of the interior offer a mountainous barrier to the trade winds and thus in summer attract the rain-bearing monsoon. On the highlands themselves, frost is not unknown in winter, and in Antananarivo the average temperature is 59°F (15°C) because of the capital's altitude (4,816 ft/1,468 m). Even summer nights can be quite cool in Antananarivo. Above 4,900 ft (1,500 m) frost may occur in mid-winter, although snow is rare and has been recorded occasionally only on the Andringitra massif. The east and north-west around Montagne d'Ambre are the wettest areas of the island. The east coast generally gets most of the rainfall, anything from 59-118 inches (1,500-3,000 mm) a year, while the northern part of the island is rainy mainly during the monsoon season. The semi-desert south-west is much drier, with a lengthy dry season broken by meagre and fitful rains.

The interior escarpment and eastern plateau region get more than 59 inches (1,500 mm) of rain a year, with a dry season of between one and four months. The western plateau region, which has a longer dry season of five to six months, gets 37-59 inches (950-1,500 mm) of rain a year and summer days here can be very hot and the nights swelteringly humid. The dry season can last up to seven months in the western plains, with rainfall reaching only 20-59 inches (500-1,500 mm) a year. Temperatures of 104°F (40°C) and above are not uncommon. The semi-desert of the extreme south-west has an average rainfall of 14 inches (350 mm) a year. Madagascar is battered by cyclones from time to time, usually between January and March. In February 1994, Cyclone Geralda was the worst cyclone to strike the island in nearly 70 years. The cyclone killed 70 people and destroyed enough property to leave about 500,000 homeless, including 30,000 in Antananarivo and 80,000 in Toamasina. In February 2000, Cyclone Eline struck the island, to be followed a month later by Cyclone Gloria, leaving in all several hundred people dead and causing widespread floods which left an estimated 600,000 people displaced or homeless.

Best Times to Visit

October and November are the best times to travel in Madagascar. The best time to visit the eastern rainforests is from late August to January. In the arid south the climate is ideal all year round, except for Fort Dauphin (Taolagnaro), which can be extremely windy in September. Some parts of western Madagascar are not accessible in the summer months of December to March after rain. In the popular Nosy Bé archipelago the climate is ideal all year except for February, when cyclones may occur.

Average Temperatures

January	68°F (20°C)
February	68°F (20°C)
March	66°F (19°C)
April	65°F (18°C)
May	61°C (16°C)
June	57°F (14°C)
July	57°F (14°C)
August	59°f (15°C)
September	61°F (16°C)
October	66°F (19°C)
November	68°F (20°C)
December	68°F (20°C)

The temperature of the ocean is tropically mild throughout the year right round the island.

HISTORY

Folk tales and old Malagasy chronicles regard a race of hairy dwarfs known as *vazimba* as the first inhabitants of the island and islanders still consider these mysterious aboriginal settlers as the ancestral guardians of their land. Ethnographers admit the possibility that pygmy-like people did once inhabit Madagascar but vanished along with the flightless giant 'elephant bird' and other monster animals that once roamed the island before also becoming extinct within the past 1,000-2,000 years. More conventional historians believe that the island continent was settled between 1,500 and 2,000 years ago by skilled navigators and fishermen from Indonesia or other areas of south-east Asia who sailed their ocean-going outrigger canoes there either in a series of long coastal hops or in one single epic voyage of discovery. The Merina and Betsileo peoples who live in the uplands of the interior show strong physical Asiatic features to this day and are the most likely descendants of those early settlers from the east. Many of present day Madagascar's customs and traditions seem to have their roots in Indonesia and Polynesia, as does its historical preference for rice, its fishing methods, the design of its pirogues, or dug-out outrigger canoes, and the Malagasy language.

According to Arab records, their wide-ranging merchant dhows reached Madagascar in the seventh century AD and established trading posts along the north-west coast, the final ports of call along a trade route they had gradually pushed south along and off the east coast of Africa from the Red Sea and the Persian Gulf. Ruins of Arab fortifications dating back to the ninth century have been found at several places along the coast. Chinese chronicles indicate that in the 15th century renowned navigator Admiral Cheng Ho made port in Madagascar on his vessel *Three Jewel Eunuch*, accompanied by a large fleet of ocean-going junks. Madagascar was unknown to Europeans until 1500 when, on 10 August, Portuguese navigator Diego Dias stumbled on the east coast of the island while sailing to India, and thought it was the African mainland. While the Portuguese were consolidating their dominance of the 'Spice Route' to India in the 16th century the Merina chief Andrianjaka was busy in the highlands of Madagascar founding the 'town of a thousand warriors,' Antananarivo, and turning surrounding marshland into paddies for the cultivation of rice, still the island's staple crop. Antananarivo became the hub from which the Merina kingdom was to spread over more than two thirds of the country by the early 19th century. The first Europeans to make a determined effort to settle on Madagascar were the French. In 1642, a party which had earlier rejected Réunion island as a suitable base for a French way station in the Indian Ocean landed at the south-eastern tip of Madagascar and founded Fort Dauphin – now Taolagnaro – at the extremity of a peninsula commanding the entrance to a commodious anchorage. Like the Dutch, French navigators preferred the east coast or Outer Passage to the Indies, while the British favoured the Inner Passage up the Mozambique Channel between Africa and Madagascar's west coast. Shortly after the French established themselves at the foot of Madagascar a number of hare-brained schemes were floated or mooted in England with the object of securing for the crown what was held to be 'the chiefiste paradise this day upon earth.' In 1644, one scheme actually came to fruition and 144 unlucky settlers arrived at St Augustine's Bay, on the south-west coast, and quickly found the touted paradise to be unbearably hot and full of fever and hostile tribesmen. After an unhappy 13 months only nine surviving settlers made it back to Britain. Another doomed British attempt at settlement – the last – was made on the beautiful island of Nosy Bé, off the north-west coast, in 1649. This also failed after settlers gave up the battle against searing heat, fever and treacherous locals. One settler later recalled: 'I set sail from ye island of Noosa and my desire is never to see it again any more.' The French at Fort Dauphin fared better, although the history of the settlement there is one of endless quarrels, insubordination, mutiny, and defection. It all ended in 1674, when 15 teenaged orphan girls on their way from France to Réunion to marry batchelors there were shipwrecked off Fort Dauphin and decided that local settlers would serve as husbands just as well. During their mass wedding festivities at the fort jealous, discarded Malagasy mistresses of the new bridegrooms opened the gates at the fort to waiting Malagasy warriors who poured in and massacred virtually the entire garrison and all the merrymakers.

For the next century or so the chastened French contented themselves with sporadic trading expeditions to Madagascar and botanical forays to gather specimens for the gardens of the Ile de France (Mauritius), which were nurseries for potentially useful and commercial plants and trees from all over the southern hemisphere. The absence of any significant naval power in the region made the waters of the south-west Indian Ocean a happy hunting ground for pirates and corsairs during the closing years of the 18th century and the first quarter of the 19th century and along with the islands of Comoros, Madagascar became a prime haven for these buccaneers – particularly St Mary's Island, off the east coast. One English pirate, Thomas White, even married a Malagasy princess, Antavarata Rahena, and fathered a king, Ratsimilaho, who made a present of St Mary's Island to his daughter Bety when she in turn married a French corporal known as *La Bigorne.* On the island mainland during this period the highland Merina tribe was nearing completion of its conquest of most of Madagascar under a king with arguably the longest name in history. This was *Nampoina,* short for *Andrianampoinimerina*, which in turn was the shortened version of his official name, *Andrianampoinimerinandriantsimitoviaminandriampanjaka*, meaning 'The Beloved Prince of Imerina Who Surpasses the Reigning Prince.' Nampoina died in 1810 and his son and successor Radama I was helped in the expansion of the Merina kingdom by the support and firepower provided by weapons supplied by the British and French interests he adroitly played off against each other. In 1817, the British governor of Mauritius, Robert Farquhar, concluded a treaty with the Merina monarch, one of whose provisions was the abolition of the slave trade. In return, Radama received British military and financial assistance. For a few years British interests were in the ascendant and during Radama's reign were prime movers in helping to modernise royal institutions along Western lines. Due to British influence the London Missionary Society was allowed to establish churches and schools from 1820 and its Welsh missionaries devised a written form of the Malagasy language which their printing press helped to spread, laying the foundation for Madagascar's present day high 80% adult literacy rate.

The next Merina monarch was not so benevolent. Radama's widow Queen Ranavalona came to the throne in 1828 to begin a 33-year reign still remembered for her excesses and cruelty. Thousands died hideous deaths at her whim and caprice, among them hundreds of her subjects who had embraced Christianity. The missionaries who had converted them were also martyred with their flock when she declared Christianity illegal. In 1831, Queen Ranavalona met a young European adventurer whose talents helped to change the course of Madagascar's history by placing his considerable mechanical and engineering skills at her service – and by becoming her lover. This was Jean Laborde, the son of a French blacksmith, who was shipwrecked on the east coast of the island while on his way to Bordeaux from India, where he had made a modest fortune as an inventive jack of all trades. Queen Ranavalona seized on his skills to build up the arsenal she needed to keep her kingdom subdued, and in 1841 he also built her a palace on the highest hill of Antananarivo, while developing a vast agricultural estate stocked with imported livestock and numerous species of plants. Laborde fled the country to Réunion in 1857 after the ageing Queen accused him of plotting against her. On her death in 1861, she was succeeded by her son who, as Radama II, instituted a more enlightened and liberal rule and recalled Jean Laborde, his old teacher, as an advisor. The reign of Radama II was brief; he was murdered in 1863 by Malagasy nobles alarmed by his cordial relations with the West, particularly France. His widow was the first of three queens to rule ineffectually between 1863 and 1896. During this time Laborde was active as French consul, promoting the influence of his homeland, which led after his death in 1878 to the resumption of missionary work in 1880 by French Roman Catholics, resulting in new mass conversions to Christianity. In 1885, the British finally waived their interest in Madagascar, accepting the imposition of a French protectorate over Madagascar in 1890 in return for France's recognition of British control of Zanzibar. The French had set the stage for this carve-up establishing future spheres of influence in the region by attacking Madagascar in 1883 and occupying the main ports and centres of power after a lengthy and enervating campaign. Madagascar's pre-colonial independence finally came to an end in 1896 when it became a fully-fledged colony a year after Antananarivo's capitulation to the French, who had invaded the island in force. By 1897, the last Malagasy ruler, Queen Ranavalona III, had packed her bags and gone into exile to die in obscurity in Algeria, French was declared the official language of Madagascar, and General Joseph Galliéni was installed to administer the new colony along strict military lines. In 1912, the nearby islands of Comoros were also proclaimed French colonies and administered as extensions of Madagascar until 1947.

Nationalist opposition to French colonial rule began to emerge in the years leading to the First World War and was strengthened by the return of Malagasy soldiers who had served with French military forces during the war. Throughout the post-war years, the increasingly vocal nationalists called for labour reforms and demanded equality of civil and political rights with France. It was not until after the Second World War that France indicated its willingness to accept any form of Malagasy self-rule, starting with the election of two Malagasy representatives to the Constituent Assembly of the Fourth Republic in Paris. During the war Madagascar had been wrested by British and South African troops from its Vichy French rulers and later handed over to the Free French forces of General Charles de Gaulle, who subsequently firmly placed it on the road to sovereign independence. In 1946, France declared Madagascar a *Territoire d'Outre-Mer* (Overseas Territory) and extended full French citizenship to all Malagasy. Despite ongoing reforms, the political scene in Madagascar remained volatile. In March 1947, Malagasy nationalists revolted against French rule and although the insurrection spread over a third of the island, it was suppressed after months of bitter conflict ending with an estimated 60,000-80,000 casualties. The military leaders of the uprising were tried by French military courts and 20 of them were executed. Other trials produced 5,000-6,000 convictions, with penalties ranging from short jail sentences to death. France's socialist government renewed the French commitment to greater autonomy in Madagascar and other colonial possessions in 1956, providing for universal suffrage and parliamentary government in each colony. Universal suffrage in Madagascar meant the end of the highland Merina's dominant influence in the political process and the rise of the *côtiers*, or coastal ethnic groups, who outnumbered the Merina. The close of the 1950s saw growing debate over Madagascar's future relationship with France. The newly created Democratic Social Party of Madagascar (*Parti Social Démocrate de Madagascar* – PSD), led by Philibert Tsiranana, wanted self-rule while maintaining close ties with France. The PSD rapidly extended its power base by absorbing most of the smaller parties organised by the *côtiers*. The Merina-led Congress Party for the Independence of Madagascar (*Antokon'ny Kongresy Fanafahana an'I Madagasikara* – AKFM) wanted nothing less than complete independence from France, the nationalisation of foreign-owned industries, collectivisation of land, the rejection of French values, customs and language, international non-alignment, and withdrawal from the *Communauté Financancière Africaine* (CFA) franc zone. In 1958, the government of General de Gaulle gave the go-ahead for an island referendum on the independence issue, in which Madagascar voted overwhelmingly to become an autonomous republic within the French community of nations. Unlike many other overseas possessions breaking the bonds of colonial European control around this time Madagascar trod the path to full independence over the next two years in an atmosphere of peace and calm expectancy.

POLITICS

Madagascar became a fully independent sovereign republic on 26 June 1960 under President Philibert Tsiranana and his Democratic Social Party of

Madagascar (PSD), bringing to an end more than six decades of French colonial administration. One of the first things Tsiranana did was to sign a series of agreements and conventions further strengthening Madagascar's ties with France before entrenching the PSD in a constitutional framework that effectively stifled opposition to his party's rule. Both moves set the stage for increasing agitation from his left-wing critics, but it was 11 years before the first outright revolt. In April 1971, hundreds of peasants were killed in the Toliara province after they took part in an anti-tax protest that turned into armed insurrection. Their leaders were exiled to the island of Nosy Lara, but the simmering discontent boiled over again early in 1972 with a general strike in the capital fomented by students calling for an end to ties with France, freer access to secondary education for the underprivileged, and the replacement of French teachers and a Francophile educational system by one emphasizing national culture and values and taught by Malagasy teachers. The government's response was to close the schools, ban demonstrations and banish hundreds of student leaders to Nosy Lava. Far from quelling the opposition, these actions stoked the fire and gained it support from civil servants, peasants, workers and the unemployed young, all disenchanted with Tsiranana and his First Republic and the government's failure to halt the general economic decline. After security forces killed and wounded a number of rioters, Tsiranana declared a national state of emergency and dissolved the government in May 1972. The army was called in to restore order and its Merina aristocratic commander, General Gabriel Ramanantsoa, took power to give Madagascar its first military regime. Madagascar began to turn its back on France and the West, revoking Tsiranana's agreements and eventually nationalising without compensation all French banks and insurance companies, moves which hastened the drain of French aid and skills.

Ramanantsoa governed a nation racked by economic and ethnic problems for less than three years – surviving a coup attempt by fellow officers in the process – and for the sake of unity handed over power in February 1975 to Colonel Richard Ratsimandrava, another Merina army officer, but one from a more acceptable background. Ratsimandrava was assassinated five days after taking over from Ramanantsoa. The ensuing leadership crisis was resolved in June 1975 when the military chose former foreign minister Lieutenant-Commander (later Admiral) Didier Ratsiraka, a dedicated Marxist, as Madagascar's new head of state and president of the ruling Supreme Revolutionary Council. Ratsiraka ushered in the Second Republic at his election as President on 21 December 1975 by adopting a new Constitution allowing only one political organisation, the *Front National pour la Défence de la Révolution* (FNDR), a coalition of the six main political parties, in which his party, the Vanguard of the Malagasy Revolution (*Arema*) played the dominant role.

Taking a leaf from the book of Red China's leader Mao Zedong, Ratsiraka produced *Boky Mena*, his own version of Mao's Red Book, detailing the *Charter of the Malagasy Socialist Revolution* which he declared was 'the only possible choice' for Madagascar to achieve rapid economic and cultural development. Only parties endorsing the revolutionary tenets in Ratsiraka's little Red Book were allowed to take part in the political process. The effect was to give Madagascar a Marxist one-party state in everything but name. Ratsiraka finished dismantling French involvement in the economy and wound up by nationalising major financial, transportation, marketing, mining and manufacturing enterprises. Within two years of the implementation of Ratsiraka's 'only choice'

economic policies severe shortages of food and other essentials saw
demonstrators take to the streets of Antananarivo again. Popular pressure in the
face of famine conditions was compounded by the tough economic liberalisation
measures Ratsiraka was obliged to institute to sustain the foreign aid he needed
to keep the stuttering economy functioning. By late 1978 Ratsiraka was
resorting to the mailed fist to stifle dissent. His waning support was charted in
the space of a few years by election results. The 95% of the popular vote
Ratsiraka gained in the 1975 presidential elections fell to 80% in 1982 and to
63% in the 1989 elections, when his electorally suspect victory in the year the
Berlin Wall fell was the signal for massive demonstrations and violence that left
at least 75 dead and injured. Calls for Ratsiraka's resignation then mounted
month by month as government policies plunged the country deeper into the
economic mire against a background of crippling strikes and protests inspired by
the *Comite des Forces Vives* ('Vital Forces Committee') of Albert Zafy, an
umbrella group for opposition political parties. Discontent led in August 1991 to
a demonstration by more than 400,000 people at the President's ostentatious
North Korean-built palace in the capital. This protest ended tragically when
Ratsiraka's Presidential Guard opened fire on the peaceful marchers, killing and
wounding hundreds. This, and the tactics of the street, had the desired result – a
leadership crisis. In October 1991, Ratsiraka agreed to a transition to
democracy, along with a new pluralist Constitution and the staging of free and
fair multiparty elections. Zafy shared power with Ratsiraka during the brief
transitional process, but roundly trounced him in both rounds of presidential
elections, held in August 1992 and February 1993. Zafy was sworn in as
president in March 1993, officially inaugurating Madagascar's Third Republic.
Once the restrictions of Ratsiraka's old regime on the formation and activity of
political parties were scrapped under the new Constitution parties proliferated in
the democratic and liberal Third Republic, helped by a new proportional
representation system determining election to the National Assembly. Their very
number gives an indication of how tribal, factional, and sectional national
politics are. In the first free legislative elections in 1993 more than 120 parties
put up some 4,000 candidates to contest the then 138 seats in the National
Assembly. Once translated, many party names give weird and wonderful
inklings of their political platforms, among them the Pillar and Structure for the
Salvation of Madagascar; the Renewal Faction of the Congress Party; Acting
Together; Living Forces Rasalama; Agreement, the Christian Action of Regional
Cadres and Businessmen for Development; Flower of Madagascar; and one
party known simply as Measures and Weights.

    In contrast to Ratsiraka's policy of predominantly establishing ties with
socialist and radical regimes, such as Cuba, North Korea, Libya, and Iran, Zafy
broadened foreign relations to include more democratic countries of the West.
Within its first year in office the Zafy regime found itself entangled in the
economic, political and ethnic problems that had bedevilled the country since
independence. Madagascar had long experienced tensions arising from the
dominance of the central highlanders, largely the Merina, historically the
aristocratic ruling class. Many ethnic groups from among Madagascar's 18
recognised tribes favoured a federalist decentralised government with greater
power for each of the six provinces. The Merina bloc and its supporters naturally
wanted the seat of power to remain in the highlands, in Antananarivo. While
reconciling these opposing factions within his coalition government, Zafy also had
to deal with increasing pressure from the IMF and donors of foreign aid urging

him to undertake economic reforms and cut both the budget deficit and the bloated civil service he had inherited from Ratsiraka. In the end it was all too much for Zafy, whose attempt to juggle and keep so many conflicting balls in the air was abruptly halted in September 1996 when he was impeached and removed from office on charges of abusing his authority and exceeding his constitutional power. Zafy (National Union for Development and Democracy – UNDD) contested the presidential election held three months later but in a surprise bounce-back Ratsiraka (Arema) narrowly defeated him by winning 50.7% of the votes to Zafy's 49.3%, although nearly three-quarters of eligible voters showed their lack of interest in the process by staying away from the polling stations. Ratsiraka officially became Madagascar's president again in February 1997. The next presidential elections are scheduled for 2002. The president appoints the Prime Minister from a list of candidates nominated by the 150-member *Antenimieram-Pirenena*, or National Assembly.

Legal System

Madagascar's Penal Code affords the accused most of the rights and protections granted under French and Western law and the legal system is based primarily on French penal codes and procedures, influenced by Malagasy customary law. The most severe punishments are death and forced labour for life. There are three levels of courts: Lower courts are responsible for civil and criminal cases carrying limited fines and sentences; the Court of Appeals includes a criminal court for cases carrying sentences of five years or more; and the Supreme Court functions as the highest court in the land. There is also a separate and autonomous Constitutional High Court which reviews laws, decrees, and ordinances and monitors elections and certifies their results. A special military court has jurisdiction over all cases involving national security. Each province has a central prison for inmates serving jail sentences of less than five years. At the locations of the various courts are at least 25 lesser prisons for offenders serving jail terms of less than two years and for prisoners awaiting trial. Courts at the local (sub-prefecture) level have jails for offenders serving minor sentences of up to six months. Women normally serve long sentences in the *Maison Centrale* (Central Prison) in Antananarivo.

THE ECONOMY

In sharp contrast to the natural riches found on Madagascar the people of this huge island make up one of the 10 poorest nations on earth. To remedy this, the country has shed the centralised Marxist policies that dominated the economy for decades and has adopted the free market model. The task of liberalising the economy has ironically fallen to President Didier Ratsiraka, the man whose misguided communist economic policies led to Madagascar's drastic economic slump during his previous 17-year dictatorship. Ratsiraka's government is concentrating on developing the private sector and privatising the parastatals which helped to run the country into the ground. The privatisation programme involves numerous leading companies, including major state-owned banks, Air Madagascar, the oil parastatal Solima, and telecommunications company Telema. The leader who once committed Madagascar to 'revolutionary socialism' is today leading a new revolution, reforming an agrarian-based economy, heavily reliant on subsistence production and the export of cash crops, such as coffee, cotton, cloves, vanilla, pepper, rice, ylang-ylang, sugar, cassava and peanuts. Agriculture employs 88% of the workforce drawn from the island's 14.6-million people and generates around 43% of GDP and, with fishery products, brings in the bulk of Madagascar's export earnings. Prawns now rival coffee, vanilla, and tourism as a foreign exchange earner. Total exports in 1998 were worth US$796-million, while the value of imports was nearly double this amount, with capital goods, fuel, consumer goods, and foodstuffs accounting for the bulk of the inflow. Major trading partners are France, South Africa, USA, Germany, and Japan.

Madagascar's current annual GNP per capita is just $270 (about £179), and about 65% of the rural population lives at subsistence level. Between 1990-97, real per capita GNP shrank by 1.6% a year, as it was outstripped by a high population growth rate of 2.8% over the same period. While the economy might still be in poor shape, things are improving. The country at last appears politically stable, and bustles with economic activity. Since 1996, the government has broadly adhered to reforms suggested by the International Monetary Fund (IMF) and the World Bank, including agricultural liberalisation and currency convertibility. The IMF has called, however, for more action on tax collection, including the recovery of arrears, an upgrading of the customs administration and the broadening of the value-added-tax, along with steps on privatisation and civil service reform. In 1995, the economy expanded in real terms by 1.7%, in 1996 by 2.1%, and in 1998 by close to 4%, although the World Bank has pointed out that even to return to its 1971 per capita income level Madagascar needs an annual growth rate of at least 6% by 2003. Inflation fell from 60% in 1994 to 8.6% in 1999.

The establishment of Export Processing Zones (known locally as Free Zones) utilising imported capital and (cheap) local labour is also proving successful, and Mauritian companies now investing in zonal schemes are contributing 35% of all direct foreign investment. The government is also hoping to encourage the exploitation of Madagascar's mineral resources, especially chrome, graphite, marble, gold, semi-precious stones, titaniferous sands, and nickel-cobalt. Most mineral deposits exist in scattered and relatively inaccessible locations and lack of adequate infrastructure is the main obstacle to this development.

Tourism

The island's full tourist – and particularly eco-tourism – potential has yet to be realised, although its growth has been steadily increasing at an average rate of 13.5% for the past few years, and latest annual figures show arrivals have, at 130,000, more than doubled since 1994. More than half of all tourists visiting Madagascar come from France, followed by Réunion (10%), Germany (4%), Switzerland (4%), and the UK (3%). A report financed by the World Bank cites eco-tourism as the principal attraction of Madagascar and says that 67% of visitors give eco-tourism and the environment as their reason for choosing to holiday in Madagascar. The government's efforts to improve its tourism are supported by such international organisations as Conservation International, the World Wildlife Fund, and US AID. To make the most of its tourism potential Madagascar must expand its air transportation and tackle its limited hotel capacity. The country currently has around 6,600 rooms spread through hotels, hostels, and lodges, many of which are of dubious quality. Projected increases in the tourist influx will require the addition of at least another 3,500 international-class hotel rooms in eco-lodges, seaside resorts and better-class hotels. The government has already established a National Institute of Tourism and Hotel Training School to help make the most of the island's human resources and prepare future staff for the tourism industry. The overriding requirement is an improvement in the infrastructure. Telecommunications have taken huge strides since the introduction of cellular (mobile) phones, although there are only 60,000 land telephone lines serving a bare 10% of the island. The roads are generally poor, but they do connect some of the dots on the map of Madagascar, although there are no east-west all-weather land links and only one narrow, meandering and overburdened north-south artery.

A relative newcomer to the tourism industry, Madagascar expects to rapidly become a major destination. It is a democratic and peaceful country with no external or domestic problems and the people have a long tradition of hospitality. Tourism has already had a positive effect on conservation. The island's natural treasures have become valuable economic assets rather than purely environmental concerns, and this emphasis has become much more understandable to local people faced with short-term survival issues. Efforts to promote natural reserves and open them to visitors have already proved effective. Several new reserves and parks have been added to the national list, including the Masoala Peninsula on the east coast. Preservation of this huge forested tract on the Indian Ocean has been widely acclaimed by conservationists. Growth in the number of package tours for eco-tourists, divers, and sun-worshippers is bringing in a stream of foreign exchange and proving that conservation pays. While the chance to see or touch undreamed of animals and flowers is Madagascar's main attraction for tourists, the diversity of its culture also fascinates visitors.

THE PEOPLE

Population

Madagascar has an estimated population of 14.6 million spread over the island at an average density of 65 to the sq mile (25 per sq km), although the density is higher in the rural areas, where there are around 1,000 people to the sq mile (400 per sq km). The population is growing at 3.2% a year and has seen a fivefold increase in less than a hundred years, a growth rate that is one of the highest in Africa, with 60% of the population under the age of 25. One contributory factor to this high growth rate and its concomitant growth in poverty levels was the appeal made to the people by Madagascar's first president after independence, Philibert Tsiranana. He said: 'Our country has plenty of uncultivated plains and valleys, it is manpower we lack. I want every Malagasy to have at least 12 children.' It seems many took him at his word. Helped by improved and more accessible healthcare services Madagascar has seen a sharp decline in infant mortality from 177 per 1,000 live births in 1981 to 87 per 1,000 in 1999 in a region where the comparable average for the period was about 103. Average life expectancy (1998) is 58, and only 5.1% of the people live beyond 60.

ETHNIC GROUPS

The noun and adjective for all indigenous islanders and their language is Malagasy. The people are divided into 18 officially recognised tribes, or ethnic groups, each with distinctive characteristics shaped largely by historical, geographical and topographical factors. By and large the ethnic groups break down into Malayo-Indonesian (Merina and related Betsileo), and *cotiers*, or coastal people of mixed African, Malayo-Indonesian, and Arab ancestry, such as Betsimisaraka, Tsimihety, Vezo, Bara, Antandroy, Antaisaka, and Sakalava. Many of these ethnic groups, but not all, have descriptive tribal names. There are also French, Indian, Creole, Comorian, Chinese, and Arabic communities. The *Merina* ('those from the country where one can see far') live in the central highlands and form the largest ethnic group, making up more than a quarter of the total population. Not only are they the most numerous of the Malagasy people, but since the early 19th century they have been the most cohesive and organised group in terms of social, economic, and political structures. Before French colonisation, they almost succeeded in unifying the whole of Madagascar under a succession of their monarchs. Although their influence has declined they are still a force to be reckoned with among the island's socio-economic and political elite. Many Merina have left the highlands to settle in other parts of the island as government officials, professionals, and traders, and all the major cities have sizeable Merina populations. The Merina – also known as Hova – are considered the most Asian of the ethnic groups, having relatively light complexions and straight black hair, as well as agricultural practices based on wet-rice cultivation. They generally exhibit the characteristics of the peoples of South-East Asia, where their ancestors are thought to have originated. Merina are sensitive to physical differences and distinguish among themselves between people who are *fotsy* (white), with relatively light complexions and descended from freeborn members of the 19th century Merina kingdom, and those who are *mainty* (black), or descendants of slaves or captives. The *Betsileo* ('the unconquerable'), who account for more than 12% of the population also live in the central highlands, south of the Merina. They have a culture similar to that of their aristocratic northern neighbours. They are regarded as the best farmers in Madagascar, building rice terraces on steep hill slopes similar to those common in Indonesia and the Philippines. The Betsileo provide a significant portion of Madagascar's official, professional, and skilled artisan classes and share something of the Merina's privileged position. The *Bara* (3.3% of the population), live to the south of the Betsileo in the dry regions of the uplands. They keep large herds of hump-backed zebu cattle and are Madagascar's main pastoralists. The *Tsimihety* ('those who do not cut their hair') live in the north-central part of the island and are noted for an exploding population (7.3%). Primarily raisers of cattle, they are looked on as the individualists of the island, opting where possible for a life in the unsettled hinterlands free of government restrictions.

The second most numerous (about 15%) are the *Betsimisaraka* ('numerous and inseparable') who live mainly on the east coast. They are divided into the northern Betsimisaraka, the Betanimena ('people of the red land'), and the southern Betsimisaraka. They have traditionally been traders, seafarers, and fishermen, as well as cultivators of the tropical lowland areas, and trace their origins back to the tribal confederacy founded on the coast in the 18th century by the son of a British pirate and a Malagasy princess. South of the Betsimisaraka are ethnic groups who trace their origins to Islamic traders of mixed Arab, African, and Malayo-Indonesian blood who settled on the coast after the 14th century, and are known as *Antalaotra* ('people of the sea'). The *Antambahoaka*, whose name simply means 'the people,' make up 0.4% of the population and live around the Mananjary River, south of Betsimisaraka territory. The *Antaimoro* ('people of the shore') constitute 3.4% of the population and also live to the south of the Betsimisaraka. They were the last historically significant immigrants, arriving around the end of the 15th century, possibly from the Arabian Peninsula by way of Ethiopia or Somalia. Before the 19th century they were the only Malagasy people to use a system of writing, based on Arabic script. Along with the Antambahoaka, the Antaimoro are noted throughout the island for their medical skills and knowledge of the supernatural. Among other groups around the southern end of the Canal des Pangalanes are the *Antaifasy* ('people of the sands'), who constitute 1.2% of the population. To the south, the *Antaisaka* (5.3%) are found in large numbers around the valley of the Mananara River. The *Antanosy* ('people of the island') who live in the extreme south-east make up 2.3% of the population. On the escarpment separating the east coast from the central highlands are the *Sihanaka* ('people of the lake'), who make up 2.4% of the population and live around Lake Alaotra; the *Bezanozano* ('many little braids'), living south of the Sihanaka and representing 0.8%; and the *Tanala* ('people of the forest') who make up 3.8%.

On the west coast, are the *Sakalava* ('people of the long valley'), who constitute 6.2% of the population. They were among the most dynamic and expansionist of the Malagasy peoples from the 16th to the early 19th centuries, when they were conquered by the Merina. With the Bara, the Sakalava are regarded as having the most African features of the ethnic groups. The Sakalava are pastoralists and those who live in the hinterland keep large herds of zebu cattle. They are also well known for their seafaring skills. During the late 18th and early 19th centuries large fleets of Sakalava outrigger canoes went on seasonal slaving raids among the islands of the Comoros archipelago and along the East African coast. The *Vezo* fishing communities of the south-west coast are a clan of the Sakalava. A group known as the *Makoa*, the descendants of people brought from Africa by such slave raiders, also live along the north-west coast and account for about 1.1% of the population.

The *Antankarana* ('people from the rocks') live on the Tsaratanana Massif and the northern tip of the island and are isolated from other Malagasy groups by the topography of the region. These cattle herders and horticulturalists make up 0.6% of the population. The major ethnic groupings in the arid south-west region of the island are the *Mahafaly* ('bringers of joy') and the semi-nomadic *Antandroy* ('people of the thorns') making up 1.6% and 5.4% of the population respectively. Both tribes depend upon the raising of cattle, although limited cultivation is also practised. Along with cattle, the prickly pear cactus dominant in the area is vital to the people's survival. The spiny plants serve as a source of water and nourishment and as a means of defence.

As well as the official 18 different tribal groups there are other ethnic communities, among them European (mainly French), Creole, Indian, Arabic, Chinese, Comorians, Malaysian, and Indonesian. These minority groups account for less than 2% of the total population, with French expatriates forming one of the largest groups of non-indigenous residents. As a former French colony Madagascar still has among it resident expatriates many former French colonial administrators and officers, as well as French professionals, business executives, plantation managers, and *colons*, small farmers. The Muslim Comorian population is another notable group which, until 1976, formed 10% of the populations of the port cities of Mahajanga and Antsiranana where they worked on the docks or as unskilled farm labourers in rural areas. Nearly 1,400 of them were killed in anti-Comorian riots in December 1976 and soon after a further 17,000-20,000 were repatriated to Grande Comore. Indo-Pakistanis are another large minority group, descendants of immigrants from the Gujarat and Bombay regions of India. They are mainly merchants and small business entrepreneurs and their communities tend to be concentrated in the cities and larger towns of the west coast. The Chinese are also a major minority group and like the Indo-Pakistanis are primarily in commerce, mostly along the east coast and around Antananarivo, but unlike them they are not averse to working in rural areas where they operate as small traders, often marrying indigenous Malagasy. Nearly 80% of the island's inhabitants live in the rural areas, eking out a living as subsistence farmers and fishermen. Approximate populations of the main towns are Antananarivo (2-million), Antsirabe (2.5-million), and Fianarantsoa (2.6-million).

ORIGINS

There are several theories about the origins of the people of Madagascar. One is that their ancestors migrated along the coast of south Asia, across the Arabian Peninsula to East Africa and, finally, across the Mozambique Channel to Madagascar. This migration is believed to have taken place over several generations and, because of the gradual interaction between Asian and African populations, led to the arrival and settlement of a distinct Malagasy people and culture. Another is that Malayo-Polynesian people arrived after direct ocean voyages of up to 6,000 miles (9,650 km), and another is that the Malagasy are the result of migrations by different peoples over the centuries, beginning with those from the Indonesian archipelago, who settled in the central highlands, and were followed by a succession of African and other races as a result of historical migrational trends and the rise of the slave trade. At bottom, the theories are generally regarded as complementary. Although there are significant variations, important cultural elements unify the Malagasy people and give them a national identity. These include a common language, a system of kinship in which descent can be traced through either the paternal or the maternal line, respect for dead ancestors (*razana*), and division of society into aristocrats, commoners, and the descendants of slaves. Society is further divided into *cotiers*, or people living in the coastal areas, and those who live in the central highlands, and this has long decided the Malagasy *Who's Who*. Ethnic group identities have begun to blur in recent years but this division between the highland tribes and the coastal people continues to dominate social standing and political affiliation. The division and its effects are the result of the historical ascendancy of the Merina kingdom originally founded in the central highlands around the city of Antananarivo. The life of the Malagasy people is lived in a complex social and religious web, but the lasting impression of most visitors is of their gentleness, charm, conduct and hospitality. Author and conservationist Gerald Durrell has summed them up, saying 'they are just the nicest people.'

EDUCATION

Education in the modern sense first appeared in Madagascar when David Jones of the London Missionary Society established a school in Antananarivo in 1820, sponsored by King Radama I, and attended by children of the royal family. Literacy spread and by 1835 the Bible has been translated and some 15,000 Malagasy knew how to read and write the newly compiled language. Today, the government claims an 80% literacy rate for all Malagasy over 15, although the national average including schoolchildren is probably nearer 50%. Education is free and compulsory for children between the ages of six and 14, with primary schooling from ages six to 11 and secondary education for seven years, divided into four years at junior secondary level, and senior secondary level from ages 16 to 18. The University of Madagascar established in 1961 in Antananarivo, is the main institute of higher education, with five other separate, independent branches in Antsiranana, Fianarantsoa, Toamasina, Toliara, and Mahajanga. A report by the United Nations Children's Fund (Unicef) says that in spite of the expansion of educational opportunities it considers Madagascar's educational system a failure, pointing out that in contrast to a decade earlier when education was allocated about 33% of the national budget, education in the mid-1990s received less than 20% of the budget, and 95% of this amount was devoted to salaries. During their rule the French established a two-level system of public schools: elite schools, modelled after those of France and reserved for the children of French citizens, and schools for indigenous Malagasy, offering practical and vocational education but not designed to train students for positions of social responsibility or political leadership. Education is often a controversial political issue in Madagascar, especially as the system has long been characterised by unequal distribution of resources among the different regions. The central highlands with its long history of formal education going back to the early 19th century, has given the Merina and Betsileo groups more schools and higher educational standards than the people of the coastal areas. This proved to be a major divisive factor in national life following independence, as the Merina and Betsileo tended to dominate the administration and the country's professions, although this is slowly changing. For example, it is now usual where the president is a central highlander for the Prime Minister to be a *cotier*.

LANGUAGES

In spite of the numerous ethnic groups and races which make up the island nation the indigenous people all speak Malagasy. Although different dialects of the language are spoken in the different regions each can be understood by all islanders, no matter where they come from, and the language is therefore a significant unifying force in a national cultural identity. Malagasy, originally the dialect of the Merina, is one of the two official languages of Madagascar. The other is French, although its use outside the cities and larger towns is limited. The use of English is growing in areas frequented by tourists and in services catering for them, but is by no means widespread. This is not a problem if you are on a package tour but other travellers without a smattering of French or a good Malagasy dictionary will usually have to rely on sign language. Like many other things in this fascinating country the Malagasy language is, if not downright unique, definitely unusual. In a region where the roots of language are buried in Africa, Arabia, or both, Malagasy traces its origins to the Malayo-Polynesian language family, now more fashionably known as Austronesian, from the Latin for southern and the Greek for island. This group of languages is made up of 600-1,000 tongues spoken in a vast area bounded by Hawaii, the Tuamotu and Madagascar. Two of the world's major languages, Indonesian-Malay and Javanese, belong to this grouping. Linguists believe that Malagasy shares a common origin with and is most closely related to Ma'anyan, a language spoken in south-east Borneo, on the island of Kalimantan, and Malagasy is classified by linguists in the east

Kalimantan coastal language category. Both Malagasy and Ma'anyan have a close affinity with other languages of the western Indonesian archipelago, although the language of Madagascar has over the centuries absorbed an enriching mixture of Arabic, Swahili, African, English, and French words and phrases. The names of the days of the week and the months of the year, for instance, are taken from Arabic, and the names of animals come from a Swahili dialect of East Africa. English and French words entered the language in the 19th and 20th centuries. The result is a lyrical language of complicated intonations which lends itself admirably to one of the Malagasy's favourite pastimes – oratory. No conversation is regarded as worthy of the name unless it is liberally sprinkled with clever euphemisms and time-worn proverbs, *ohabolana*, most of them incomprehensible in translation. Oratory, known as *kabary*, was developed to a high degree in the absence of a written language and good practitioners can hold an audience enthralled for hours on end, either with speeches or stories. Such oratory has become an entertaining art form and competitions are held to choose the most popular exponents. Before the 19th century, the only Malagasy people with a written language were the Antaimoro, who used an Arabic script. Written Malagasy using Roman characters was first developed by members of the London Missionary Society (see *History*) and the result was the almost perfectly consistent phonetic language still used today. With his gift for diplomatic compromise the monarch of the time, Radama I, instructed the missionaries to ensure that the consonants were pronounced as in English and the vowels as in French. The language gets by with an alphabet of only 21 letters; the characters C,Q,U,W and X are not used. French became the dominant language during the colonial period and Malagasy was relegated to an inferior position. Although the government of the independent First Republic adopted an official policy of bilingualism (French and Malagasy), French continued to predominate until the first inauguration of President Ratsiraka in 1975. He set about removing all vestiges of colonial rule by promoting education in the national language and undertook the more radical excision of French culture and influence from the economy and from the political system. In power once more since 1997 Ratsiraka has gone into reverse and is now active in the international francophone community. French remains important in Madagascar not only because of its wide currency in international diplomacy, commerce, and industry, but because most members of the political and social elite, including Ratsiraka, have benefited from a French education. All government publications are issued in French and Malagasy.

Getting It Right

Malagasy (noun and adjective) is the name of the people and of the language.
Madagascar is the name of the island in English, French, and a number of other
    languages.
Madagasikara is the name of the island in Malagasy.

Repoblikan'i Madagasikara	are the official names of the country in Malagasy,
Republic of Madagascar	English,
République de Madagascar	and French.

Malgache is French for Malagasy.
Just as shaking hands is very important to Malagasy people, they also appreciate it

if you greet them in their own language, so you should make an attempt to learn at least a few civilities. While some words can look quite daunting, especially the length, just remember that the letter **a** is always short (as in watch), the letter **e** sounds like a long a (as in pace), the letter **i** is pronounced like a long e (as in bean), the letter **j** sounds like dz, and the letter **o** sounds like oo. When they greet you the Malagasy say *Manao ahoana tompoko* ('How are you?'). You should reply *Tsara fa misaotra* ('Fine, thank you'), and when you leave don't forget to say *Veloma* ('Goodbye').

USEFUL WORDS AND PHRASES

English	Malagasy
Hello	*Manao ahoana*
My name is	*Ny anarako*
What's your name?	*Iza no anaranao?*
Excuse me	*Azafady*
Pardon me	*Ombay lalana*
Go away!	*Mandehana!*
I don't understand	*Tsy azoko*
I don't know	*Tsy fantatro*
Thank you	*Misaotra*
When?	*Rahoviana?*
Today	*Androany*
Tomorrow	*Rahampitso*
Yesterday	*Omaly*
Morning	*Maraina*
Evening	*Hariva*
Where is...?	*Aiza...?*
Road	*Lalana*
Village	*Vohitra*
River	*Ony*
Sea	*Ranomasina*
Sand	*Fasika*
Swim	*Milomano*
Swimming pool	*Dobo-filomanosana*
Toilets	*Fidiovana*
Near	*Akaiky*
Far	*Lavitra*
Small	*Kely*
Big	*Lehibe*
To arrive	*Tonga*
What time is it	*Amin'ny firy izao*
To be late	*Tara*
Long	*Ela, lava*
Quick	*Vetivety*
Money	*Vola*
How much?	*Ohatrinona?*
How much is that?	*Ohatrinona ity?*
Money	*Vola*
Expensive	*Lafo*
Too expensive	*Lafo be*

Inexpensive	*Mora*
(I have) nothing	*Tsy Misy*
I'm tired	*Vizako aho*
Hot, warm	*Mafana*
Cold	*Mangatsiaka*
Very nice	*Tsara be*
Bad	*Ratsy*
One	*Iray*
Two	*Roa*
Three	*Telo*
Thousand	*Arivo*
Man	*Lehilahy*
Woman	*Vehivavy*
Baby	*Zaza*
Foreigner	*Vazaha/Vahiny*
I love you	*Tiako ianao*
To go fishing	*Manjono*
Canoe	*Lakana*
Boat	*Sambo*
Wet	*Lena*
Insect	*Bibikely*
Hair	*Volo*
Sick	*Marary*
Doctor	*Dokotera*
Blood	*Rè*
Medicine	*Fanafody*
Hurt	*Maratra*
Island	*Nosy*
Big/plenty	*Bé*
To walk	*Mandeha an-tongotra*
Which is the way to...?	*Aiza ny lalana mandeha any...?*
Where is the post of office?	*Aiza ny paositra?*
There is nobody	*Tsy misy alona*
It is closed	*Mihidy*
It is open	*Misokatra*
Dirty	*Maloto*
Clean	*Madio*
Feet	*Tongotra*
Hands	*Tanana*
Eyes	*Maso*
Head	*Loha*
Mouth	*Vava*
Nose	*Orona*

While the correct words for yes and no are *eny* and *tsia* you'll rarely hear them used in ordinary conversation. Instead, Malagasy usually say something that sounds like *yoh* for yes and something that sounds like *ah* for no. One phrase you can expect to hear wherever you go is the expression *Mora Mora* 'easy, easy' which in effect means tomorrow is another day'. This can be said to be the very kernel of island philosophy and neatly encapsulates the Malagasy concept of time and urgency.

RELIGION

Madagascar is a land where ancient customs, traditions and superstitions co-exist quite happily with Christianity and other major religions, and animist practices intermingle with the more orthodox rituals of the established churches. Although rather a latecomer to the island – more than a thousand years after the first Muslims arrived – Christianity found fertile ground in Madagascar after being welcomed to Antananarivo in the shape of the London Missionary Society by King Radama I in 1820. Despite subsequent setbacks that included persecution and martyrdom (see *History*) Christianity flourished to the point where today more than 40% of all Malagasy are adherents, more or less evenly divided between Catholics and Protestants, with the remainder of the population being made up of those holding traditional beliefs (52%), Muslims (5%) and Hindus. Religious freedom is guaranteed under the Constitution. The Malagasy traditionally believe in *Zanahary*, the sole creator of the universe. Ancestor worship permeates all levels of Malagasy society. Malagasy never speak of the dead because for them death does not exist. Death is the passage to another life, when ancestors pass to a higher state where they become known as spirits (*fanahy*) and are near to the Creator. The wisdom and the knowledge acquired by ancestral spirits enables them to guide and protect their relatives. They can, however, also punish anyone who does not respect traditions and rituals. Ancestors are constantly consulted or evoked and to ensure their protection of descendants they have to be buried in appropriate tombs. As the ancestors will inhabit them for all eternity these tombs must be built to last. The size and decoration are an indication of the wealth and prestige of the family that built them, and it is common for the dead to rest in costly, substantial mausoleums while their descendants live nearby in relatively humble dwellings. For the most ornate burial tombs, visit the south-west, inland from Toliara. This area is the tribal land of the Antandroy, Masikoro, Mahafaly and Bara peoples. The tombs and funerary art of the Antandroy and Mahafaly are the most impressive. Mahafaly tombs are decorated with the horns of the zebu cattle eaten at the funeral feast and surmounted by tall carved wooden posts depicting human and animal figures, called *aloalo*, which look like the totem poles of the American Indians. Tombs were traditionally built of stone but more modern ones, especially those built by wealthy families, are often made of concrete, with glass windows, and jazzy coloured designs and they often have amazing models of aircraft, taxis, and other modern novelties mounted on the roof. The Menabe Sakalava are noted for the erotic carvings they placed on their tombs. In the past it was custom of the Sakalava living around the Morondava River on the west coast to decorate their tombs with carvings of explicit sexual activity, representing the life-giving force, or fertility, of the ancestors. Not many of these carvings now exist outside of museums, most having found their way into the hands of private art collectors.

All Malagasy exhibit a profound veneration for their ancestors (*razana*), for those from the distant past to those only recently buried, and this respect is integral to everything they do. The best-known tradition is that of *famadihana*, or 'turning of the bones,' which is practised by the Merina and Betsileo peoples of the highlands and which echoes some Asian ceremonies where ancestral spirits are invited to a feast organised by their descendants. *Famadihana* is a graphic example of the way the Malagasy regard their dead ancestors, and it is considered a serious violation of religious and social tradition for a family financially able to bear the considerable cost of the ritual not to do so. This burial rite requires families practising it to remove the body or bones of a deceased relative from the tomb, usually in the dry winter months between June and September, and wrap it in a new shroud before re-burial. This ceremony is a festive occasion, something akin to an Irish wake, and those taking part speak and sing to the corpse or bones of the departed ancestor to ensure good luck for the living. The dead are exhumed early in the morning and are laid out on the grass side by side throughout the day, where everyone can touch them and speak to them. At the end of the day, they are wrapped in new silk shrouds and carried on the shoulders of their relatives in procession seven times around the tomb before being replaced. Not many foreigners have the experience of attending a *famadihana* and to be invited is a rare honour. Malagasy customs and traditions can be complex in the extreme and are hedged around by taboos (*fady*) and superstitions and very few *vazaha* (white foreigners) have ever come close to understanding all of them. Taboos cover a bewildering variety of things regarded as sacred or forbidden and, depending on the tribe and region, can include such taboos as a girl not being allowed to wash her brother's clothes, or a son not being permitted to mention his father's name, to diggers opening a tomb having first to remove all their clothes, and fish being taboo food for pregnant women. A more understandable one is the *fady* which says you should not deny hospitality to a stranger, nor should you ever refuse any hospitality offered. Some tribes, such as the Betsimisaraka, believe in ghosts and other spirits, mermaids, and long-haired, two-foot high gnomes who live in the forest and steal cooked rice, and who could be an ancestral echo of the vanished *vazimba*. The Sakalava people, however, believe the *vazimba* are still alive and well and hiding out in the caverns which honeycomb parts of the island. As well as respecting immemorial taboos Malagasy are also governed by the *vintana*, a sort of universal astrological calendar which lists what can be done at different times on each day of the week. This lays down the law on such things as days which are lucky or unlucky, which colours are favourable for defined occasions, and what food should be eaten and when. Monday, for example, is regarded as a black day, so don't expect to get much done on this day. Space is also believed to be subject to the forces of *vintana*, with east being superior to west, north superior to the south, and the north-east regarded as the most favourable direction. People build their houses on a north-south axis and reserve the north-eastern corner for prayers; guests are always seated on the northern side of a room, and chickens are confined to the south-western corner. The concept of *vintana* relates to fate, and the different values and forces attributed to different times and days are best defined for important occasions by *ombiasy* and *mpanandro*, who combine the functions of diviners, healers and astrologers. Even a highly educated Merina would not think of building a house without consulting one of these to ascertain a favourable day to start construction, and when a marriage is being arranged the parents of both families consult these seers to make sure that the prospective partners will be well matched. Anthropologists see rituals as something giving structure and meaning to social life, providing people with a sense of purpose in life and a feeling of security. From birth to death and beyond in Madagascar life is marked by identification rituals that give it such meaning and in some cases, such as *famadihana*, they are similar to rituals followed in South-East Asia. All these traditional rituals, beliefs and animist superstitions are comfortably accommodated with Christian and whatever other religions the people profess.

NATIONAL ANTHEM AND FLAG

The music for Madagascar's national anthem was written by Norbert Raharisoa in 1958 and the lyrics were added by Pasteur Rahajason in the same year, when it was officially adopted.

Ry Tanindrazanay Malala O	**O, Our Beloved Country**
Ry Tanindrazanay malala ô!	O, our beloved Fatherland,
Ry Madagasikara soa	O, fair Madagascar,
Ny fitiavanay anao tsy miala,	Our love will never decay,
Fa ho anao doria tokoa	But will last eternally.

Chorus

Tahionao, ry Zanahary	O, Lord Creator, do Thou bless
Ity Nosin-dRazanay ity	This island of our Fathers,
Hiadana sy ho finaritra He!	That she may be happy and prosperous
Sambatra tokoa izahay.	For our own satisfaction.
Ry Tanindrazanay malala ô!	O, our beloved Fatherland,
Irinay mba hanompoana anao	Let us be thy servant
Ny tena sy fo fanahy anananay,	With body, heart and spirit
'Zay sarobidy sy mendrika tokoa.	In dear and worthy service.

Chorus

Ry Tanindrazanay malala ô!	O, our beloved Fatherland,
Irinay mba hitahiana anao,	May God bless thee,
Ka ilay Nahary izao tontolo izao	That created all lands;
No fototra ijoroan'ny satanao.	In order He maintains thee.

The Flag. This has two equal horizontal bands, with red at the top and green at the bottom, edged with a vertical band of white of the same width on the hoist side.

FURTHER READING

Robert Drury's Journal is an early personal narrative by a sailor who was shipwrecked off Madagascar on the East Indiaman *Degrave* in 1703 and at 16 became a slave to the Antandroy royal family for 10 years, and then to the Sakalava, before escaping and returning to England.

Indian Ocean: Five Island Countries edited by Helen Chapin Metz (1994). This book is one in a continuing series of books prepared by the Federal Research Division of the US Library of Congress under the Country Studies/Area Handbook Program sponsored by the Department of the Army. The information is close to exhaustive but relevant only to mid-1994.

Madagascar, A Natural History by Ken Preston-Mafham (Struik, Cape Town 1991), presents a detailed review of Madagascar's flora and fauna, and some of its more important reserves. Illustrated by 300 superb colour photographs. Foreword by David Attenborough, author of *Journeys to the Past* (Lutterworth Press, Guildford 1981) and *Zoo Quest to Madagascar.*

Madagascar: A World Out of Time by Frans Lanting, Alison Jolly, and Gerald Durrell (Aperture 1990). A book that reveals not only the astonishing beauty of this unique and diverse island continent, but also examines the conflicts going on between changing cultures and the effect on its fragile ecosystems.

Famous wildlife conservationist Gerald Durrell recounts his search for a rare mammal in *The Aye-Aye and I – A Rescue Mission in Madagascar* (Arcade Publishing 1993), following his *Ark on the Move* (Coward-McCann Inc, New York 1983).

A World Like Our Own, Man and Nature in Madagascar by Alison Jolly (Yale University Press 1980). Widely regarded as one of the best general books about Madagascar and its conservation issues.

Madagascar, Island of the Ancestors by John Mack (British Museum of Natural History 1986). An interesting, scholarly paperback about Malagasy culture.

Field Guide to the Birds of Madagascar by Olivier Langrand (Yale University Press 1990). The definitive text on the island's birdlife, with an overview of some reserves and recommended top spots for visiting twitchers.

Field Guide to the Sharks and Rays of Southern Africa by LJV Compagno, DA Ebert, and MJ Small (Struik, Cape Town 1989) will give you a good idea of what might be patrolling off the coast.

A Field Guide to the Amphibians and Reptiles of Madagascar by Frank Glaw and Miguel Vences will do the same as the above for dry land and freshwater.

Madagascar, the Red Island by Arlette Kouwenhoven (WINCO Publishing 1996).

Madagascar: Profil de L'Environment edited by MD Jenkins (published by World Wildlife Fund for Nature).

The Palms of Madagascar by Dr John Dransfield and Dr Henk J Beentje (published by the Royal Botanic Gardens, Kew, and the International Palm Society). The first time all 175 species of Madagascar's known palms have been described in English. Palms are of great importance in rural Madagascar, where they are used in house-building, arts and crafts, medicine, and magic, as well as providing food. Many are now under threat, and several species are in immediate danger of extinction. In this profusely illustrated book, local names and uses are listed, and conservation status is indicated for each species.

Plant Collectors in Madagascar and the Comoro Islands by Laurence J Dorr (The Royal Botanic Gardens 1997). A botanical and travel book rolled into one, with fascinating stories about the sort of dedicated (or cuckoo) people whose braving of the rigours of Madagascar helped to put some lovely potted plants on your window-sill.

Iles des Espirits by Jacques-Yves Cousteau.

The Eighth Continent: Life, Death, and Discovery in the Lost World of Madagascar by Peter Tyson (HarperCollins 2000).

Madagascar: Politics, Economics, and Society by M Covell (Frances Pinter, UK 1987).

Distant Shores: By Traditional Canoe from Asia to Madagascar by Sally Crook (Impact Books, UK 1990). This recounts a seven-week voyage by traditional outrigger undertaken to prove that the first settlers of Madagascar could have come from South-East Asia.

Dancing with the Dead: A Journey through Zanzibar and Madagascar by H Drysdale (Hamish Hamilton, UK 1991).

Madagascar. A World Out of Time by F Lanting (Robert Hale, UK 1991).

The Possessed and Dispossessed by Lesley A Sharp (University of California Press, Berkeley, Los Angeles, London). An enquiry into spirits, identity, and power in a Madagascar migrant town, which assesses the impact and importance of the supernatural on aspects of Malagasy life.

The African Cookbook by Diane and Leo Dillon (Carol Publishing Group, New York 1993). Everything you've ever wanted to know about whipping up an authentic Malagasy meal, as well as other interesting titbits.

PRACTICAL INFORMATION

Getting There

BY AIR

Air Madagascar, the national carrier, operates international flights to and from Paris. Two flights from Charles de Gaulle are non-stop (Sunday and Wednesday) and the others fly via Munich and Nairobi, and Rome and Nairobi. There is also a weekly flight on Saturday from Singapore. Air France fly direct to Antananarivo from Charles de Gaulle airport on a Monday, Wednesday and Friday, and via Réunion on a Tuesday, Thursday and Sunday. If you combine your trip to Madagascar with a holiday on one of the other Indian Ocean islands you can also get there via Mauritius, Seychelles, Réunion, Mayotte, and Comoros. Air Madagascar has twice weekly flights from Johannesburg, Interair, a privately-owned South African-based airline, flies to Antananarivo every Tuesday, and Air Austral flies there from Johannesburg every Thursday. Another alternative is to fly Air France from Paris to Réunion and then by Air Austral to Madagascar; or Air Mauritius from London or Rome to Mauritius. From there you can fly Air Mauritius from Sir Seewoosagur Ramgoolam International Airport to Antananarivo every Tuesday and Friday. There is no direct commercial air service from the US but American travellers can fly with Virgin Airways to London and then connect with Air Mauritius to Madagascar via Mauritius; or via Virgin to Johannesburg and on from there with one of the local carriers. Madagascar is about 5,595 miles (9,000 km) from France and the average flight duration from Europe is 10-12 hours, 3¹/₂ hours from Singapore, and three hours from South Africa. Air Madagascar services are often subject to delays and occasional breakdowns and changes are often made to flight schedules with little or no warning to passengers – which is probably why it is lightheartedly known as Air Mad. The best thing is to contact the airline's nearest office for the latest information.

From Paris connecting flights can be arranged that result in fares between £1,640-£1,681 ($2,310-$2,368) in May, and £1,678 and £1,682 ($2,448-$2,456) in November; these trips reach the island via Johannesburg or Réunion. Depending on the route taken and time of year flight prices from London to Madagascar will vary between £4,144 in May and £1,733 in November ($6,050-$2,530), to Mauritius and £2,317 to £1,191 ($3,382-$1,739) respectively to Johannesburg, with fares onwards from these locations adding to your flight cost.

AIR MADAGASCAR OFFICES AROUND THE WORLD

Australia: Tony Knox & Associates, 19-31 Pitt Street, Sydney NSW 2000 (tel 2-9252 3770; fax 2-9247 8406).

Britain: Aviareps Airline Management Group, Premiere House, 3 Betts Way, Crawley, West Sussex RH10 2GB (tel 01293-596666; fax 01293-596665).

Comoros: Travel Service International, Bâtiment DHL, rue Oasis, Moroni (tel 73 3044; fax 73 3054).

France: 29-31 rue des Boulets, Paris (tel 1-53 27 31 10; fax 1-43 79 30 33; e-mail air-madagascar@filnet.fr).

Germany: Aviareps, Schwanthaler Strasse 26, D-80336 Munich (tel 89-5525 3310; fax 89-5450 6839).

Italy: International Tourist Representative, Via Bissolati 76-00187 Rome (tel 64-77 1318; fax 64-82 5711).

Kenya: Island Air Service, Hilton Hotel, PO Box 45170, Nairobi (tel 2-22 5286; fax 2-25 2347; e-mail mdnbo@africaonline.co.ke).

Mauritius: Ireland Blyth Limited (IBL), 10 Dr Ferriere Street, Port Louis (tel 208 2811; fax 208 3766).

Réunion: 2 rue Victor MacAuliffe, St Denis (tel 21 0521; fax 21 1008).

Singapore: Rhianfa, N90 Club Street, 069458 Singapore (tel 224 0557; fax 223 5736).

South Africa: Travel Directions, Holiday House, 158 Hendrik Verwoerd Drive, Randburg (tel 11-289 8222; fax 11-289 8072; e-mail madagascar@ traveldirections.co.za).

Switzerland: Aviareps, Schanzeneggstrasse 1, 8002 Zurich (tel 1-286 9950; fax 1-286 9951; e-mail zurich@aviareps.com).

Once you have arrived in Madagascar it is essential that you reconfirm your return flight, as well as any connecting flights on Air Madagascar, as soon as possible. The office is at 31 Avenue de l'Indépendance, Analakely, Antananarivo (tel 20-22 22222; fax 20-22 33760; e-mail airmad@dts.mg).

OTHER AIRLINES SERVING MADAGASCAR

For information on flight schedules and rates for the other airlines flying to Madagascar you can contact them at their offices in Antananarivo or other major cities around the world:

Air Austral:

France: 2 rue de l'Eglise, 92200 Neuilly, France (tel 92-0133; fax 92-0137).

Madagascar: Ario 77 Lalana Solombavambahaoka Frantsay, Antananarivo (tel 20-22-235990; fax 20-22-235773; e-mail ariomad@ bow.dts.mg) is the general sales agent for Air Austral in Madagascar.

Réunion: 4 rue de Nice, St Denis, Réunion (tel 90-9090; fax 90-90910);

Air France:

Britain: 1st Floor, 10 Warwick Street, London W1R 5RA (tel 0845 084 51111);

France: 119 Avenue des Champs Elysées, F-75384 Paris Cedex (tel 1-42 99 23 640);

Madagascar: 29 Avenue de l'Indépendance, Analakely, Antananarivo (tel 20-22-22321; fax 20-22-229103);

USA: 120 West 56th Street, New York NY 10019 (tel 1-800-237 2747).

Air Mauritius:

Britain: 49 Conduit Street, London W1R 9FB (tel 020-7434 4375; fax 020-7439 4101);

France:	11 bis Rue Scribe, F-75009, Paris (tel 1-44 51 15 64; fax 1-44 51 15 55; e-mail air.Mauritius.paris@wanadoo.fr);
Madagascar:	Ario 77 Lalana Solombavambahaoka Frantsay, Antananarivo (tel 20-22-235990; fax 20-22-235773; e-mail ariomad@bow.dts.mg);
Mauritius:	Air Mauritius Centre, Rogers House, President John F Kennedy Street, Port Louis (tel 207-7070; fax 208-8331; e-mail resa@airmauritius.com);
USA:	560 Sylvan Avenue, Englewood Cliffs, New Jersey 07632 (tel 201-871 8382; fax 201-871 6983; e-mail airmkusa@concentric.net).

Interair:

Britain:	4th Floor, Buckingham Palace Road, London SW1W 9TA (tel 020 7707 4581; fax 020 7707 4165);
Madagascar:	Hilton Hotel, Galerie Marchande, Anasy, Antananarivo (tel 20-22-22406; fax 20-22-62421);
South Africa:	Private Bag 8, Johannesburg International Airport 1627, (tel 11-390 2555; fax 11-390 2778).

Virgin Airways:

Britain:	The Office, Crawley Business Quarter, Manor Royal, Crawley, West Sussex RH10 2NU (tel 1293-61 6161/56 2345; fax 1293-44 4085);
USA:	Belden Avenue, Norwalk CT 06850 (tel 1-800-862 8621; fax 1-203-750 6490).

Airport

Antananarivo International Airport, also known as Ivato Airport, is about 9 miles (15 km) from the city centre and is linked by a sporadic bus service. If you are booked into a hotel you might find they have a courtesy minibus waiting. If you take a taxi from the airport to Antananarivo it will cost anything from £5-£13 ($8-$20). Watch out for hustling porters at the airport, they expect a small fortune for their help. When leaving you must pay an international departure tax, which is not included in the price of your air ticket. You can pay in Malagasy francs, although the foreign currency equivalent is preferred. This is £16 ($24 or FF120) per person for flights to Europe. Children under two years are exempt.

BY SEA

Madagascar has six international ports for ocean-going vessels and 12 ports for coastal vessels, providing maritime links with the Indian Ocean countries and Europe. The principal ports are Toamasina (or Tamatave) on the east coast and Mahajanga (or Majunga) on the west. Coastal shipping is used around Madagascar to transport non-perishable products, linking the secondary harbours of Nosy Bé, Antsiranana, Manakara, and Taolagnaro to Toamasina, where cargo is loaded on to international carriers. A number of shipping lines, cruise ships, and freighters that carry passengers call at Madagascar. Contact them directly to find out more about their sailings, schedules and costs. The most widespread is the **Malagasy Shipping Company** (MSC), which has offices in Madagascar and many countries throughout the world.

MSC (Malagasy Shipping Company) Offices:

Madagascar: 72 Avenue 26 Juin 1960, Analakely, Antananarivo (tel 20-22-32130; fax 20-22-30188; e-mail mscmad@dts.mg);
9 rue la Fayette, Antsiranana (tel/fax 20-82-29395);
8 rue Carnot, Boite Postale Nr 18, Mahajanga (tel 20-62-23689);
Lot 1 K 122 Ambalasonjo, Manakara (tel 20-72-21013);
Societe Moyse et Fils, Nosy Bé (tel 20-86-61320); Immeuble Ny Havana, Boulevard de l'Oua, Toamasina (tel 20-53-32196; fax 20-53-33847; e-mail msctmmsec@dts.mg);
Societe de Representation du Sud Sarl, BP 383, Toliara (tel 20-94-42403).

Australia: MSC (Aust) Pty Ltd, Level 8, 155 George Street, Sydney, New South Wales 2000 (tel 2-9252 1111; fax 2-9252 1258).

France: MSC France SA, 23 Avenue de Neuilly, 75116 Paris (tel 1-53 64 63 00; fax 1-53 64 63 10).

South Africa: MSC Holdings, MSC House, 54 Winder Street, Durban 4001, PO Box 10687, Marine Parade 4056, (tel 31-360 7911; fax 31-332 9277).

USA: MSC (USA) Inc, 420 5th Avenue (at 37th Street), 8th Floor, New York, NY 10118-2702 (tel 212-764 4800; fax 212-764 8592).

The branch office of MSC Croisieres Sarl dealing with cruises is at 59 rue Beaubourg, 75003 Paris (tel 1-48 04 76 20; fax 1-48 04 51 65).

Cruise Ships

Fred. Olsen Cruise Lines Ltd: Fred. Olsen House, White House Road, Ipswich IP1 5LL (tel 01473-292222; fax 01473-292201; www.fredolsen.co.uk), runs ships which call at Madagascar periodically.

Royal Viking Lines: 750 Battery Street, San Francisco, CA 94111, USA (tel 415-398 8000).

Salen-Lindblad Cruising: 133 East 55th St, New York, NY 10022, USA (tel 800-223 5688).

Freighters with passenger accommodation:

American President Lines: 1800 Harrison Street, Oakland, CA 94612, USA (tel 415-272 8148).

Lykes Lines: 300 Poydras Street, New Orleans LA 70130, USA (tel 1-800-535 1861).

For more information about freighter travel write to *Freighter World Cruises:* 180 South Lake Ave, Suite 335, Pasadena CA 91101, USA.

Shipping lines in Madagascar

Besta Line (represented by SCTT): PO Box 171, Rue Nationale, Toamasina (tel 20-53-32401/33147).

Compagnie Malgache de Navigation (CMN): PO Box 1621, Antananarivo (tel 20-22-25546; fax 2-22-30358).

Compagnie Generale Maritime (CGM): PO Box 12042, Antananarivo (tel 20-22-

20113; fax 20-22-26530; e-mail cgmtana@dts.mg).
Ilderim Shipping Ocean Indien (ISOI): PO Box 1182, Antananarivo (tel 20-22-27144; fax 20-22-34853).
Jules Roy: PO Box 3958, Antananarivo (tel 20-22-31340; fax 20-22-32493).
Société Commercial d'Affretement et de Combustible (SCAC): PO Box 514, Antananarivo (tel 20-22-20631; fax 20-22-33730).
Scandinavian East Africa Line (SEAL): PO Box 679, Antananarivo (tel 20-22-29478/22356; fax 20-22-339112; e-mail sealtana@dts.mg).
Agence pour la Sécurité de la Navigation en Afrique et à Madagascar (ASCENA): Ivato (tel 20-22-44098).
Société Nationale Malgache de Transport Maritime (SMTM): PO Box 4077, Antananarivo (tel 20-22-27342/27454; fax 20-22-33327).
In South Africa contact SMTM, in Durban, c/o Seaclad (tel 31-332 5736; fax 31-337-2986).

To get there by sea from South Africa your best bet is to contact the various yacht clubs during the southern hemisphere cruising season (April-November) to see whether any skipper will give you a berth as a paying passenger or as an unpaid hand. As it's the closest jumping off point, Durban is the first place you should try. Royal Natal Yacht Club, Durban (tel 31-301 5425); Point Yacht Club, Durban (tel 31-301 4787; fax 31-305 1234); and Royal Cape Yacht Club, Cape Town (tel 21-421 1354/5; fax 21-421 6028). The SA Cruising Association in Durban (tel 31-305 2125) is another good place to check.

TOUR OPERATORS

More and more **British** tour operators are featuring Madagascar as a holiday destination. Most of them recommend combining a guided adventure tour with a more relaxing stay of three or four days at the beach.
Africa Extraordinaire: Cottney Meadow, Old Park, Bradley, Ashbourne, Derbyshire DE6 1PL (tel 01335-372170; fax 01335-327171).
Art of Travel: 21 The Bakehouse, Bakery Place, 119 Altenburg Gardens, London SW11 1JQ (tel 0207-738 2038; fax 0207-738 1893).
David Halford Travel: 102 Stanley Road, Cambridge CB5 8LB (tel 01223-779200; fax 01223-779090; e-mail ArcJourney@aol.com).
Discover the World: 29 Nork Way, Banstead, Surrey SM7 1PB (tel 01737-218800; fax 01737-362341).
Exodus Travels: 9 Weir Road, London SW12 0LT (tel 0208-657 5500; fax 0208-673 0779).
Explore Worldwide: 1 Frederick Street, Aldershot, Hampshire GU11 1LQ (tel 01252-319448; fax 01252-343170).
Grenadia Safaris: 11-12 West Stockwell Street, Colchester, Essex CO1 1HN (tel 01206-549585; fax 01206-561337).
Ornith Holidays: 1-3 Victoria Drive, Bognor Regis, West Sussex, PO21 2PW (tel 01243-821230; fax 01243-829574).
Partners in Travel: Greenleaf House, Darkes Lane, Potters Bar, Hertfordshire EN6 1AE (tel 01707-222444; fax 01707-661072).
Rainbow Holidays: Stanford House, York, North Yorkshire YO1 9PF (tel 0845-601 0500; fax 01904-654830).
Reef and Rainforest Tours: Prospect House, Jubilee Road, Totnes, Devon TQ9 5BP (tel 01803-866965; fax 01803-865916).
Worldwide Journeys and Expeditions: 8 Comeragh Road, London W14 9HP (tel

0207-381 8638; fax 0207-381 0836).

France
Terres Malgache et Mascarines: 17 rue de la Bucherie, Paris 75005 (tel 1-44 32
    12 87; fax 1-44 32 12 89; e-mail demanche@worldnet.fr).

Germany
Madagaskar Adventures: Knesebeckstrasse 30, 10623 Berlin (tel 49 30-881 1190;
    fax 49 30-881-1630).

South Africa
Tropical Adventures: 109 Eccelston Crescent, Bryanston, Johannesburg (tel 11-
    706 5987; fax 11-706 6205; e-mail tropicladv@icon.co.za).
Unusual Destinations: Johannesburg (tel 11-805 4833/4; fax 11-805 4835; e-mail
    unusdest@global.co.za).

United States
Betchart Expeditions: 21601 Stevens Creek Boulevard, Cupertino, CA 95014 (tel
    408-252 4910; fax 408-252 1444).
Blue Chameleon Ventures (tel 941-728 2390; fax 941-728 3276; e-mail
    blove@cyberstreet.com).
Cortez Travel & Expeditions: 124 Lomas Santa Fe Drive, Solana Beach, CA
    92075 (tel 619-755 5136; fax 619-481 7474; e-mail Cortez-
    USA@mcimail.com).
Field Guides: PO Box 160723, Austin, TX 78746 (tel 512-327 4953).
Forum Travel International: 2437 Durant Avenue, #208, Berkeley, CA 94704 (tel
    415-843 8294).
International Expeditions: 1776 Independent Ct, Birmingham, AL 35216 (tel 205-
    870 5550; fax 205-870 5554).
Lemur Tours: 2562 Noriega St #203, San Francisco, CA 94122 (tel 415-681
    8222).
Questers Tours & Travel: 257 Park Avenue South, New York, NY 10010-7369 (tel
    212-673 3120).
Wilderness Travel: 801 Allston Way, Berkeley, CA 94710 (tel 415-548 0420).

TRAVEL SAFELY

Both the UK Foreign Office and the US State Department have travel
information offices which provide regularly updated free advice on countries
around the world (see also *Health and Hygiene* p.52 for information on the health
situation).

Travel Advice Unit: Consular Division, Foreign & Commonwealth Office, 1
    Palace Street, London, SW1E 5HE (tel 020-7238 4503/4504 Website
    www.fco.gov.uk/travel).

US State Department: 2201 C Street, Washington DC 20520, USA (tel 202-647
    4000 Website http://travel.state.gov).

Red Tape

ENTRY REQUIREMENTS

PASSPORTS AND VISAS

To enter Madagascar you must have a passport
valid for at least a further six months and an entry visa, unless you are a transit
passenger continuing your journey within 24 hours. If you are not a resident of

Madagascar you must also have a return ticket. You can get a visa at any Madagascar embassy or office of its foreign representatives. All you need is to complete an application form and attach three identity photographs. The cost for a 30-day visa is about £17 ($26) for a single entry. Multiple entry and three-month visas cost a few pounds more. If required, you can apply for these in Madagascar but you should do this in Antananarivo as soon as possible after arrival. Normal visas are available on the spot at customer services at the airport in Antananarivo, although problems are not unknown. Savvy travellers will tell you that officials issuing them often strangely have no change for, say, a £20 note or other large denomination foreign currency banknote. Faced with the alternatives of either getting back on the plane or forfeiting the change it's easy to guess what visitors usually decide to do. Visitors are recommended to register with their embassy or consular representative in Antananarivo on arrival, and if you plan to visit remote areas you should always leave a rough itinerary of your proposed trip with officials and try to avoid travelling alone. It is also a good idea to keep photocopies of your passport, health and insurance documents, and any other important papers you are carrying.

HEALTH DOCUMENTS

A certificate of immunisation against cholera (children less than six months are exempt) is required and, if you are coming from an infected area, you'll need a similar certificate for yellow fever (children under 12 months are exempt). The cholera certificate is valid for a period of six months beginning either six days after the vaccination date or the same day in the case of revaccination during the initial six-month period; the yellow fever certificate is valid for a period of 10 years, beginning either 10 days after the vaccination date or the same day in the case of revaccination during the initial 10-year period. Health requirements change, so check with your doctor or Health Department for the latest information.

CUSTOMS REGULATIONS

You are allowed to take in the following duty-free if you are over the age of 18: 500 cigarettes, or 50 cigars, or 17¹/2 oz (500 g) of tobacco; 1 litre of alcoholic beverage; and perfume for personal use. Cameras should be declared on arrival, or you might have trouble taking them out again. You are allowed a reasonable amount of film for your own use, and a reasonable amount of gifts, although what customs regard as reasonable is difficult to guess, so take as much film as possible and hope for the best. You might never come back. If asked, you should be scrupulous in declaring what currency you are bringing into the country as undeclared currency might be confiscated.

When leaving you face severe penalties if you are found with any protected plant or animal species and cannot produce an officially authorised export licence. This restriction has been extended to cover crystals, gemstones and the like, the souvenirs you can buy virtually anywhere on the street, although these are more likely simply to be confiscated. Buy from shops rather than street traders, and make sure you get a sales certificate (*certificat de vente*).

MALAGASY EMBASSIES AND CONSULATES ABROAD

Australia: 92 FIH Street, Sydney NSW 2000 (tel 2-9221 3007).

Austria: Potzleindorferstrasse 94-96 A, A-1184 Vienna (tel 1-47 41 92)

Belgium: 276 Avenue de Tervueren, B-1150 Brussels (tel 2-770 1726; fax 2-772 3731).

Britain: 69-7C Mark Lane, London EC3 R75A (tel 020-7481 3899); and 16 Lanark Mansions, Pennard Road, London W12 8DT (tel 020-8746 0133; fax 020-8746 0134).

Canada: 649 Blair Road, Gloucester, Ontario K1J 7M4 (tel 613-744 7995; fax 613-744 3520).

France: 4 Avenue Raphaël, F-75016 Paris (tel 1-45 04 62 11; fax 1-45 03 34 54).

Germany: Rolandstrasse 48, D-5300 Bonn (tel 228-95 3590).

Italy: Via Riccardo Zandonai 84/A, Rome (tel 6-36 30 77 97; fax 6-36 29 43 06).

Mauritius: Avenue Queen Mary, Port Louis (tel 65015).

Réunion: 73 rue Juliette Dodu, St Denis (tel 21 0521).

South Africa: 13 6th Street, Houghton Estate, Johannesburg 2001 (tel 11-442 3322; fax 11-442 6660).

Switzerland: 32 Avenue Riant Parc, CH-1209 Geneva (tel 22-602 5411; fax 22-740 1616).

United States: 2374 Massachusetts Avenue NW, Washington DC 20008 (tel 202-265 5525; fax 202-483 7603).

What Money To Take

French francs, US dollars, and pounds sterling are the best currencies to take and can be exchanged for Malagasy francs either at banks or the larger hotels. Other currencies are not so popular, although most can be changed at banks in Antananarivo.

MONEY IN MADAGASCAR

The national currency is the Malagasy franc (MGF), made up of 100 centimes. Banknotes come in denominations of MGF 25,000, 10,000, 5,000, 2,500, 1,000, and 500. Coins come in denominations of MGF 1, 2, 5, 10, 20, 50, 100 and 250, as well as 5, 10 and 20 ariary coins (20 ariary = MGF 100). There are two denominations printed on most notes, with the franc value always the higher one. Be wary of the ariary as the MGF 25,000 note, for instance, also has the figure 5,000 on it, its equivalent in ariary, and some vendors, taxi drivers and the like are always on the lookout for naive visitors who are not familiar with the difference between francs and ariary. Everything you need to pay for will be quoted in MGF so it's best always to ignore the ariary denomination. Malagasy francs cannot be converted back into hard currency at the airport when you leave, so don't wind up with a wad of Malagasy notes; change money carefully as you go along. You are not allowed to take more than MGF 25,000 (about £2.50/$3.75) out of the country. You'll be relieved of anything over this in local currency by an obliging official, who will in many cases pocket it. This seems to be one of the perks that go with the job at the airport.

Exchange Rates

When you arrive in Madagascar you might be asked to fill in a form saying how much foreign money you are carrying. If you are, you'll be given a stamped copy of this form and each time you change money for Malagasy francs the amount will be noted on the form. When you leave the country, you return the form for possible checking at the emigration desk. In the past currency was subject to a strict check but as there's a government drive to make entry and exit easier for tourists this is not so much of a hassle as it used to be. Still, there's no reason not to comply with whatever are the latest rules and regulations; there's no currency black market in Madagascar. The main thing is not to buy more local currency than you plan to spend. The currency exchange window at Ivato International Airport is always open when international flights arrive or leave and it is advisable to change your foreign currency on arrival as it is quicker and you'll get a better rate at the airport than anywhere else. You can also change money in banks (travellers cheques or bank notes) as well as in some hotels (notes only). Exchange rates, although subject to fluctuation, have been fairly constant for some time at around MGF 10,000 to the pound sterling, 6,500 to the US dollar, and 1,000 to the French franc. Other approximate conversions are:

Europe	Euro 1	=	MGF 6,000
Germany	DM	=	MGF 3,000
Canada	Can$	=	MGF 4,300
South Africa	R	=	MGF 900
Australia	A$	=	MGF 3,700

BANKS AND BANKING

Any international banking transactions you might need to make will be less of a hassle if you use one of the banks in the capital. All the following commercial banks are in Antananarivo and most of them have branches in the major towns. The bank most used by travellers is the *Banque Malgache de l'Océan Indien (BMOI):* Place de l'Indépendance, Antananarivo (tel 20-22-34609; fax 20-22-34610).
Others are:
Banque Centrale de Madagascar (BCM): Antaninarenina, PO Box 550, Antananarivo (tel 20-22-21751/2).
Banky Fampandrosoana'ny Varotra (BFV): 14 rue Jeneraly Rabehevitra, Antaninarenina, PO Box 196, Antananarivo (tel 20-22-20691; fax 20-22-33645).
Bankin'ny Tantsaha Mpamokatra (BTM): 2 Place de 'l Indépendance, Antaninarenina, PO Box 183, Antananarivo (tel 20-22-20251; fax 20-22-29408).
Union Commercial Bank (UCB): 77 rue Solombavambahoaka Antsahavola, PO Box 197, Antananarivo (tel 20-22-27262).
Bankin'ny Indostria-Credit Lyonnais (BNI-CL): 74 rue du 26 Juine 1960, PO Box 174, Antananarivo (tel 20-22-22800; fax 20-22-33749).

Hours. Banks are usually open from 8am to 11am and 2pm to 4pm Monday to Friday, with the exception of public holidays.

Credit Cards and ATMS

This is Third World territory so be prepared for the worst and you'll never be disappointed is the rule if you intend to use plastic cash during your stay. Credit cards are only slowly becoming familiar to the Malagasy, but they are still not widely accepted and should be kept as an emergency back-stop or used to pay air fares or bills in up-market hotels and restaurants. Where credit cards are accepted they will be Visa (Carte Bleue), American Express, MasterCard, Eurocard, Diners Club, and Carte Blanche. Bankin'ny Tantsaha Mpamokatra (BTM) will advance cash on American Express and MasterCard.

Tipping

Tipping is not a Malagasy custom, although open-handed tourists have led waiters, taxi drivers, porters and others involved in the tourist industry to expect at least 10% on top of the bill. Use your discretion and remember that most of the people working outside the towns and cities have an income of far less than £40/$59 a month.

EMERGENCY CASH

The myth persists among people travelling in foreign countries that all you need to do if you are in a fix and need some money is to knock on the door of your embassy or consulate and they will oblige. Not so, although there is a complicated procedure of last resort to get you home if you are truly desperate or destitute. Far better to get family or friends at home to send you cash if you find yourself financially pinched. A quick, if not *the* quickest, way for them to send you funds is via the Western Union Money Transfer service, which has agencies in more than 170 countries – 29 in Madagascar and nine of them in Antananarivo. For the addresses of these and Western Union branches in other towns telephone Western Union in Antananarivo on 20-22-31307. You can literally receive money within minutes if it is sent to you via the Internet (www.westernunion.com) and all you need to collect your funds is some form of identification, such as a passport.

Health and Hygiene

BEFORE YOU LEAVE

The best advice is difficult to heed: it's don't fall ill in Madagascar, at least not outside of Antananarivo. Medical facilities are limited and generally not up to Western health standards. The next best advice is to make sure that you organise a comprehensive health travel insurance policy before you leave your home country. In particular, ascertain if payments can be made to overseas hospitals or doctors, or whether you will be have to pay and claim reimbursement later. Also make sure there's provision for your medical evacuation in an emergency. The higher premium for this is well worth it compared to the cost of a medical evacuation. See your doctor about vaccinations, anti-malarial treatment and ways of avoiding food and waterborne infections. Vaccinations for tetanus, typhoid, rabies, and hepatitis should be considered. Take copies of any accident insurance documents, and important medical records. Make sure you take an adequate supply of all prescriptions and any other medications you use. Take a letter from your doctor on his/her letterhead stationery (signed and dated) certifying your need for any medications you might be carrying. Keep all medications in their original wrapping and pack them in your cabin bag so they don't get lost en route.

You should also know what blood group you are, just in case you should ever need emergency treatment while travelling. The Blood Care Foundation is a UK charity dedicated to the provision of fully screened and tested blood through a worldwide network. You can enrol with them through any British Airways Travel Clinic or through MASTA (see below).

Medical advice

In the UK the Medical Advisory Services for Travellers Abroad (MASTA) is a good source of information and advice in the UK. It was set up in 1984 at the London School of Hygiene and Tropical Medicine to raise the awareness of health issues associated with travel. Services range from the supply of vaccines and travel medicines, to research on important travel issues, as well as the development of products for travellers. As part of their brief MASTA operates a Travellers Health Line (0906-822 4100, calls charged at £0.60 per minute) and a very informative website on the illnesses travellers face and precautions that can be taken. By telephoning them you can obtain a briefing tailored to your journey that covers up to six countries, which is then posted to you (to any country except the USA and Canada).

If your home base is the UK or South Africa, a visit to a British Airways Travel Clinic (BATC) should be on your must-do list. BATC has 28 clinics in the UK and 3 in South Africa and services include personal consultations, with advice tailored to your specific trip. With instant access to an on-line database BATC can call up the very latest information on 84 different health hazards in more than 250 countries worldwide. All information provided by MASTA or BATC is approved by the London School of Hygiene and Tropical Medicine, so you can rest assured you'll benefit from accurate advice on all appropriate vaccinations and any other recommended precautions. Such reliable advice is invaluable.

A range of healthcare products is available from MASTA or BATC, from simple but effective single and double-bed mosquito nets to a comprehensive sterile medical equipment pack, including sun protection lotion in both adult and child formulations; Trekker Travel Well pump-action purifier, which removes bacteria, viruses and parasitic cysts from water; an emergency dental pack to provide temporary replacement for dislodged crowns, bridges, fillings and the like; and a malaria wheel, which is a simple device for ensuring that you take anti-malaria tablets at the right time.

Travel Clinic Helpline is a 24-hour service run from the Hospital for Tropical Diseases on 0839-337733 (calls charged at £0.50 per minute). You can also get a Travellers Guide to Health by calling the Department of Health's 'Health Literature Line' on 0800-555777.

The British Consumers' Association has published the results of an investigation into medication obtained while away from home for such common ailments as upset stomach, earache, and a cold. Nearly a third of the foreign pharmacies consulted offered medication that was either considered inappropriate, contrary to accepted practice, or downright dangerous. The association recommends that if you have any misgivings about any medicine you have bought, don't take it, and find another pharmacist you think more clearly understands your symptoms. If you decide that the symptoms are so severe or persistent that you need to see a doctor, find an English-speaking pharmacist or doctor through your tour operator's representative or your medical assistance company, some of which offer help and advice on a 24-hour helpline. Keep this number handy at all times. In a pharmacy, try to speak to the pharmacist, not a counter assistant. If the pharmacist can't speak English, see if someone in the shop can interpret. If you know what you want, ask for medicine by its generic name and tell the pharmacist about any allergies you have or if you have ever experienced adverse reactions.

Jet-lag

Getting into physical trim for a week or two before you travel helps to increase your stamina and reduces the fatigue known as jet-lag. Drink plenty of water before, during, and after the flight as dehydration is a distinct problem due to the dry air in pressurised cabins. Drink water even if you don't feel thirsty. Don't drink large amounts of alcohol; do try to sleep during long flights. On-board exercise – stretching and walking around – is a good idea. Limit activities on the day after your arrival until you feel rested and acclimatised and you'll enjoy your holiday that much more.

Useful Adresses

British Airways Travel Clinics: (Head Office) 29 Harley St, London, W1 (tel 020-7323 5862; www.british-airways.com/travelqa/fyi/health/health.shtml). For contact details of all 31 clinics telephone 01276-685040.
MASTA: Keppel Street, London, WC1E 7HT (www.masta.org).

WHEN YOU RETURN

Plan not just for your holiday but for what to do when you get home. A disease or ailment picked up on holiday can sometimes take weeks or even months to become evident after returning home and the connection between the problem and your holiday can easily be missed. You should keep this in mind, especially if you suffer an intestinal ailment; if it does not clear up within three of four days, see your doctor and tell him/her where you were, what you did, how long you were there, what you ate and drank, and whether you can remember being bitten by any insects or animals, and whether you have been exposed to any sexually transmitted diseases. If you had any medical treatment while away for which you had to pay claim on your insurance as soon as possible. If you received any medicines while away it may not be legal to bring them back. If in doubt, declare them at customs on your return.

MEDICAL SERVICES

The government has committed itself to the principle that good health is a right of each Malagasy citizen, and has made significant strides in the area of health care, but such advances are largely from a zero base. About two-thirds of all Malagasy live far from a medical centre or clinic and more than a third lack access to any form of health service. For those unable to obtain medical treatment, traditional medicine – the use of herbs or the exorcism of malicious spirits – remains popular. Medical services have been deteriorating since the late 1980s because of the country's economic decline. Figures are difficult to come by or to verify, but by 1993, for example, Madagascar had only one doctor for every 17,000 people. In some provinces the ratio was as low as one doctor for 35,000 people, and on the entire island it was down from one for every 9,850 inhabitants in 1982, 234 medical centres were under the supervision of one doctor, with the remaining 1,728 were under the direction of paramedics, midwives, nurses, and health aides.

Malnutrition, malaria, respiratory infections, and diarrhoeal diseases are major causes of death, especially among children. There are several expatriate medical practitioners in Antananarivo. A Seventh Day Adventist Dental Clinic offers emergency procedures and is up to US standards in normal procedures and in cleanliness. There are also competent laboratory and X-ray facilities. Medications available locally are mainly of French origin. Doctors and hospitals often expect immediate cash payment for services rendered.

Medical Centres

Ambulances Municipales: Route de l'Université, Isotry (tel 20-22-23555).
Centre Medical Ambatomena: 28 rue Jean Jaurès, PO Box 3213, Antananarivo (tel 20-22-21170).
Clinique Maternité Saint Francois d'Assise: rue Dr Rajoanah Ankadifosty, PO Box 748, Antananarivo (tel 20-22-23554; fax 20-22-23095).
Hospital Militaire d'Antananarivo: tel 20-22-40341.
Espace Médical: tel 20-22-62566.
Institut Pasteur: (for medical testing) PO Box 1274, Antananarivo (tel 20-22-26492; fax 20-22-28407).
Centre de Diagnostic de Tananarive: (for X-rays) Lot IV 176 Anosivavaka Ambohimanarina, PO Box 111, Antananarivo (tel 20-22-30760; fax 20-22-21930).

Pharmacies

Pharmacie Ankodifotsy: 50 Arabe Lenine Ankadifotsy, Antananarivo (tel 20-22-22007; fax 20-22-30673).
Pharmacie de l'Océan Indien: Analakely, Antananarivo (tel 20-22-22470).
Pharmacie Croix du Sud: 9 Avenue de l'Indépendance Analakely, Antananarivo (tel 20-22-22059).
Pharmacie Pergola: Antaninarenina, PO Box 756, Antananarivo (tel 20-22-23717).

EVERYDAY HEALTH

A change of climate, water, food, and lifestyle generally tends to lead to stomach upsets of one form or another, but these usually settle down of their own accord after a day or two or are alleviated by simple medication. You can avoid or at least reduce the risk of contracting anything debilitating by observing strict food hygiene precautions throughout the island. Avoid raw fruit and vegetables; eat only thoroughly cooked meats, even if this means well-done steak and you like yours rare. Be particularly careful about food bought from street vendors. Dairy products generally are not pasteurised and should be avoided. Boil all milk before use. Avoid tapwater or purify it by boiling or using purification tablets. There are lots of ways to treat water to make it safe to drink. You can use iodine, boil it, chlorinate it – easy, effective and cheap – flocculate it, or filter it. Best of all is to chlorinate it to kill the bugs, flocculate it to settle and clear the water, and then filter it. You can rely on iodine (2% aqueous solution) as an emergency stop-gap to purify water, or at least to render it safe for drinking. Filter the water before adding three teaspoons (15ml/0.5fl oz) iodine to a litre of water and let it stand for 30 minutes before using it. More up-market and reliable systems are available at outdoor supply shops and should be considered before you leave home. Drink bottled beverages without ice.

AIDS

Travel in Third World countries can increase your chances of contracting a sexually transmitted disease (STD) or having an accident and requiring medical treatment which might put you at risk from HIV (Human Immuno-deficiency Virus), which is the virus that causes AIDS (Acquired Immune Deficiency Syndrome), known in French as *syndrome-déficitaire acquis* (*Sida*). Some of the ways this can be passed on are through unprotected sex with an HIV-infected person, by sharing needles and other equipment with an infected person, through infected medical and dental instruments, and by blood transfusion with infected blood. HIV doesn't affect only gays and drug users, it is most commonly transmitted through heterosexual relations. Condoms are the most effective protection against HIV and other sexually transmitted diseases. Take condoms with you on holiday but make sure they carry the British Standard Kitemark or the European Standard mark. You should know how to use condoms properly and if buying them abroad buy only good quality ones. Always use a condom with a new partner, each time you have sex.

Madagascar does not have the same standards of medical and dental care as the UK and other countries of the West. For instance, needles and other equipment may not be adequately sterilised, and blood for transfusion is not always screened for the presence of HIV or Hepatitis B. This means there may be an increased risk of your contracting one of these or some other infection. The sterility of medical equipment used can be difficult to check and medical and nursing staff may not be able to understand your concerns, or they may not understand English. Make sure any medical equipment used is freshly sterilised or is taken from a sealed pack. It is sensible to carry a first-aid kit with you, but you may also want to take a medical kit containing basic sterile medical equipment for use in an emergency. These kits are available from chemists and independent suppliers. Ask your doctor, pharmacist or travel agent for information. Have medical treatment only if it is absolutely necessary. Some doctors may give blood transfusions when they are not really needed, so make sure any recommended transfusion is absolutely essential. If you need a blood transfusion, ask for screened blood. Other HIV risks to avoid include anything involving puncturing the skin as this carries the risk that the equipment may not be sterile, so don't have a tattoo, acupuncture or your ears pierced. Sharing needles and syringes is a major cause of the spread of HIV infection. Don't inject unprescribed drugs, don't share equipment, but if you do, always clean everything properly.

HIV cannot be spread through everyday social contact. It can't be passed on through kissing, dirty crockery or food, swimming pools, insect bites, toilet seats, coughing, or sneezing. If you haven't had a recent check-up go and see your dentist before you go to avoid treatment abroad that could put you at risk from HIV. The incidence of sexually transmitted diseases (STDs), known in French as *maladie sexuellement transmissible* (MST), has shown a marked increase in Madagascar in the decade since the early 1990s when the World Health Organisation (WHO) noted that only a handful of AIDS cases had been reported. AIDS is also on the increase in the islands of the neighbouring Comoros archipelago, where health authorities blame it on their menfolk's trips to Madagascar to enjoy freer sexual liaisons.

AIDS Hospital. Service de Lutte Contre les MST et le Sida, Antananarivo, tel 20-22-29861.

AIDS and HIV Advice. In the UK, the Terrence Higgins Trust Helpline (noon to 10pm), tel 0207-242 1010, provides advice and counselling on HIV/AIDS issues. This number can be reached from abroad. Calls to the National AIDS Helpline on 0800-567123 are free and confidential. Lines are open 24 hours a day but the Helpline cannot be reached from outside the UK. Leaflets on HIV and AIDS are published by the Department of Health and the Health Education Authority and can be obtained free of charge by calling the National Drugs Helpline on 0800-776600. Lines are open 24 hours a day and all calls are free and confidential.

HEALTH HAZARDS
Bilharzia

This parasitic ailment (schistosomiasis) is spread mainly through the passing of human waste into ponds, irrigation canals, slow-moving streams and stagnant water and is widespread due to the lack of adequate sewage systems, especially in rural areas. The disease is found largely in those areas also affected by malaria. It is caused by a microscopic organism found in rivers, streams, dams, and lakes. There is no practical way of distinguishing infested from safe water, so all contact with open water should be avoided. This means no drinking, washing, paddling or swimming in such water, no matter how inviting it looks. Bilharzia is caused by a worm that penetrates your skin and can cause damage to your intestines, liver and urinary tract. Symptoms begin with a slight itch where the skin was penetrated, followed a few days later by a rash. The onset of fever and muscle pain occurs after a month and is soon followed by abdominal pain and diarrhoea, or the appearance of blood in the urine, together with a burning sensation when urinating. If not diagnosed and treated, serious and irreversible damage may be done to the bladder, liver and kidneys. If you are accidentally contaminated by suspect water you can reduce the risk of infection by towelling off vigorously. There is no vaccine against bilharzia.

Cholera

An outbreak of cholera killed more than 1,000 people all over the island between April 1999 and March 2000 and an estimated 15,500 cases were treated, although many more are believed to have gone unreported. The rainy season poses the greatest risk if there is cholera around as its spread is assisted by human excrement being washed into surface waters. Travellers should be scrupulously disciplined about food and water hygiene. British Airways Travel Clinics (BATC) warn that immunisation against cholera with the older injected vaccine is not very effective, and is not generally recommended. Check this out with your doctor. The newer oral cholera vaccine *orochol* may be indicated for some travellers and is available from BATC.

Malaria

Malaria remains the most serious tropical disease, although the eradication campaigns against carrying mosquitoes that started in 1948 initially resulted in spectacular declines in incidence and a dramatic decrease in the island's mortality rate over 21 years. Prevention practices faltered during the late 1970s and throughout the 1980s, and the mosquito staged a comeback to the point where malaria now exists throughout the year in all regions, including urban areas, and is particularly bad in coastal areas. Malaria is caused by the bite of the female anopheles mosquito, which transmits a microscopic protozoan parasite called *Plasmodium*, of which four species affect humans. The most dangerous is *P. falciparum*, which causes cerebral or malignant malaria. The female mosquito lays eggs in open, stagnant water and warm weather aids the breeding process. Mosquitoes bite mainly once dusk has fallen and then throughout the night. To avoid being bitten sleep under a mosquito net, and liberally spray it with an insecticide. Make sure the net has no holes and keep it tucked in. Spray the room with a knock-down repellent before you climb under the net. Sleeping or awake, rub your face, arms and legs and any other exposed skin with a repellent containing diethyltoluamide (DEET). Always wear light-coloured clothing – long sleeves, long trousers – from dusk onwards. Dark clothing, perfume and after-shave attract mosquitoes. Symptoms of all forms of malaria appear seven to 30 days after infection and usually start with vague pains and a general feeling of weariness, most noticeable in the morning. Next come severe headaches, aching joints and muscles, and a feeling of coldness, with shivering in spite of an elevated temperature, which may exceed 104°F (40°C). There is something of a controversy about malarial medication. Mefloquine (Larium) is an effective anti-malarial medication, but it can have some adverse side-effects. Your doctor or pharmacist can tell you about these and recommend what you should take. Pregnant women and small children should not visit malarial areas at all.

Tetanus

This is a dangerous disease, causing severe and painful muscle spasms. It is caught from bacterial spores getting into your body through even the slightest wound. These spores are found mainly in soil and manure. Tetanus is particularly dangerous where medical facilities are not available for immediate treatment. You should be protected by immunisation, especially if you plan to travel to remote areas. If you were immunised as a child, see your doctor about a booster; if you were not, you will need a course of three injections.

Typhoid

Typhoid fever results from contaminated food or water. Immunisation against the disease is recommended if you are travelling to places where sanitation is primitive – which means most places outside the tourist centres.

Viral Hepatitis

This is an infection of the liver than can cause jaundice. There are two forms: Hepatitis A, sometimes called infectious hepatitis, and Hepatitis B. Health authorities recommend immunisation against Hepatitis A, which is usually caused by contaminated food or water. This disease can also be spread from person to person, since the virus is present in faeces, and travellers to places where sanitation is primitive need to be especially aware of this risk. An injection of normal immunoglobulin (Gamma Globulin) shortly before travelling will reduce risk. Hepatitis A is the most common vaccine-preventable infection suffered by travellers. While Hepatitis A infection is common, the risk for visitors is low, unless you are exposed to unhygienic conditions. A course of vaccine is recommended for non-immune individuals. Hepatitis B occurs throughout the world and is spread in the same ways as the virus that causes AIDS. There is a vaccine that gives good protection against the disease, but it can take months to become effective. The best way to prevent infection is to avoid high-risk activities and take a travel kit for use in medical emergencies.

SENSIBLE PRECAUTIONS

Many infections and parasitic diseases are contracted by consuming unhygienic food and water. If you are off the beaten track remember always to wash your hands after using the toilet, and certainly before handling food or eating. If you have any doubts about water for drinking, washing food or cleaning your teeth, boil it, sterilise it with disinfectant tablets or use bottled water – preferably carbonated – from sealed containers. Eat fresh, well cooked food while it is still hot; avoid uncooked food, food that has been kept warm, or food that is likely to have been exposed to flies. Eat only fruit you have peeled or shelled yourself. A variety of diseases is spread by insects. Use insect repellent and cover your arms and legs with appropriate clothing when walking, especially in wooded or grassy areas.

Rabies. Animal bites can start infections that can be serious and sometimes fatal. Be wary of approaching or touching animals, even when they seem tame.

NATURAL HAZARDS

Do not swim in fresh water or the sea without first getting advice from locals – you risk bilharzia in fresh water and there's a danger of **sharks** in coastal waters. **Stonefish** and **scorpionfish** as well as **sea urchins** are potential hazards on the reef as they can all give you varying degrees of stinging punctures. Stings from any form of sea life can be extremely painful, but rarely result in permanent harm or death. Keep the stung part immobile and lower than your heart. Do not squeeze any sting. Wash well. If there is any sign of shock or you have difficulty breathing, get medical attention. For other stings soak the area in water that is as hot as you can bear without scalding yourself. Continue this for 30 minutes to an hour if you can while on your way to the doctor. All cuts, grazes and bites should be thoroughly washed and disinfected as soon as possible. Merthiolate is effective for minor cuts, stings and punctures from marine organisms. General cuts and scratches from barnacles, rocks, coral and the like should never be left untreated. Wash well with hot water and disinfectant, dry and paint with mercurochrome. Don't walk barefoot over sand in the full heat of the afternoon if you want to avoid painful blisters.

There are no dangerous snakes in Madagascar, but annoyingly persistent **leeches** are common in the rainforests and are virtually impossible to avoid, as they can even get through the eyelets of shoes and boots to attach themselves to your flesh. Never attempt to forcibly dislodge leeches, known as *dinta*, use salt or the tip of a burning cigarette. They will, of course, drop off of their own accord once they have filled up on your blood.

Sun

Avoid over-exposure to the sun for the first few days of your holiday. The Madagascar sun can be scorching, so wear a hat and sunglasses when out during the day. You should stay out of the sun between 11am and 3pm and regularly apply sunscreen while tanning or swimming. Protect your eyes from ultra-violet radiation by wearing sunglasses which block more than 90% of visible light and have protective side-shields. Cream to protect your lips from exposure is also recommended. Protect your skin by using a sunscreen that filters out damaging UV rays. SPF stands for Sun Protection Factor, and the number indicates the degree of protection a product offers. The higher the number, the better the protection. A factor of at least 10 is recommended for Madagascar. Children and those with sensitive skins or pale complexions need higher protection than adults with darker or less sensitive skins. Apply the stuff regularly, especially after you have been swimming or exercising. The back of your neck, upper arms and upper legs need special attention. Protection is necessary even on cloudy or hazy days, and especially at altitude.

Apart from burning, you can also get **sunstroke (heatstroke)** or suffer from **heat exhaustion** from over-exposure to the sun. Symptoms of sunstroke are chills, fever, nausea and delirium. Itching and peeling may follow any degree of sunburn and normally begin four to seven days after exposure. Severe sunburn or sunstroke should always be treated by a doctor. Heatstroke and heat exhaustion are different conditions and are treated differently. The first is a medical emergency. If in doubt, treat for heatstroke, which occurs when high temperatures overwhelm the body's heat-control system. Immediate medical help is necessary. Heat exhaustion is caused by loss of salts and fluid during heavy sweating and can be rectified by drinking fresh fruit juice, which contains the right combination of water and electrolytes to fix you up. Avoid strenuous activity during the hottest hours and make sure you drink plenty of non-alcoholic, caffeine-free liquids to make up for the loss of body fluid through sweating.

Humidity

Constant high humidity may affect you if you have an arthritic condition. Among those with a predisposition to respiratory problems the climate in the interior highlands tends to cause colds and bronchitis.

FIRST AID HINTS

Carry a first aid kit. A minimum would be a packet of adhesive dressings, some insect repellent, a tube of antiseptic cream and a packet of water sterilisation tablets. More ambitiously, you can buy an emergency medical travel kit from a pharmacy or travel clinic containing a variety of sterilised and sealed items, such as syringes, needles and suture materials. This kit should normally be handed to a doctor or nurse for use in a medical emergency, especially in remote areas where there might be a shortage of equipment. A typical kit contains two syringes, five needles, a dental needle, an intravenous cannula, a skin suture with needle, a packet of skin closure strips, alcohol swabs for skin cleaning, a variety of non-stick dressings, and a roll of surgical tape. These kits should be easy to identify by customs officials so that the contents are not exposed until needed. It is also a no-no to carry loose syringes or needles without a letter from a doctor verifying your need for them. You might, for example, be a diabetic, but to the customs man you might be a drug addict.

Tips

Take plenty of toiletries as well as a first-aid kit if you intend to go off the beaten track. Take along bug repellent, sun-block, a reliable torch with extra bulbs and plenty of replacement batteries, a notepad, pen and pencil. Throughout the Indian Ocean islands we found a small hand-held battery-operated fan a boon in humid conditions.

CLOTHING

What to Wear and When

The Malagasy must have invented the word casual and dress by day and night is generally informal, so take cotton clothing that will keep you cool and comfortable in the heat. Men and women should pack at least one set of long trousers for walking in rainforests or thorny terrain and for wear on cool evenings in the highlands. In the winter months normal-weight clothing is suitable, except for wear on the coast, where tropical clothing is a must throughout the year. Take swimwear and rainproofs for the inevitable shower or storm. Comfortable walking shoes or boots are a must. Take two pairs so that you always have one pair dry and ready to change into. Pack extra socks and a broadbrimmed hat. A good quality pair of sunglasses (and a spare set) are essential for protection from the ultra-violet rays.

Mail

There are post offices in all the main towns. They are generally open Monday to Friday from 8am to noon and 2pm to 6pm, and Saturday morning until noon. Don't include anything of value in your letters.

TELEPHONES

Madagascar had fewer telephones in the 1990s than in 1975. There are only 60,000 terrestrial telephone lines, covering a bare 10% of the country, including Antananarivo and some of the bigger towns. Although you'd expect the shortage of private telephones to result in flimsy telephone directories they are bulked out by the fact that Madagascar is a land of extremely long names. The phone book contains surnames such as Ratsifandrihamanana, Randrianomenjanahary, and

Razakaratitrimo, and back in history the name of one famous king was 53 characters long. Most telephones (60%) are naturally located in the capital. Two satellite ground stations near the capital provide excellent international links via the International Telecommunications Satellite Corporation's (Intelsat) Indian Ocean satellite and the Symphonie ground station, working with a European telecommunications satellite.

Charges

A local (urban) call costs MFG 500 for 3 minutes and MFG 400 a minute from a public telephone. Interzone calls (*interurbaines*) cost MFG 5,375 a minute; a call to Europe costs MFG 12,500 (£1.25/$1.87) a minute; to France and Italy MFG 8,750 a minute; to the USA and Canada MFG 13,125 (£1.31/$1.96) a minute; to Asia (Singapore) MFG 16,667 a minute; and to the Indian Ocean sub-region (Réunion/Mauritius) MFG 10,000 a minute.

Access code

To call Madagascar dial the international access code +261-20, followed by the area code and the number you want. For any call within the country dial seven digits – the first two digits are the geographical area code, the other five are for the subscriber number.

Area Codes

22=Antananarivo
42=Ambatolampy
44=Antsirabe
47=Ambositra
48=Mid-West
53=Toamasina (Tamatave)
54=Ambatondrazaka
56=Moramanga
57=Maroantsetra – Nosy Boraha (Ile St Marie)
62=Mahajanga (Majunga)
67=Antsohihy
69=Maintirano
72=Manakara – Mananjary
73=Farafangana
75=Fianarantsoa
82=Antsiranana (Diego Suarez)
86=Nosy Bé
88=Sambava
92=Taolagnaro (Fort Dauphin)
94=Toliara (Tuléar)
95=Morondava

It is customary in Madagascar to express seven-digit telephone numbers in groups of two, three and two, as in 22-345-39. This numbering scheme was introduced late in October 1997.

In Madagascar: For access to automatic international, dial 00 (followed by international country code)
For access to international line via operator, dial 10
For inquiries, dial 12
For access to intercities, dial 15
Time, dial 211-22

Cell (Mobile) Telephones

There are four cellular (mobile telephone) networks, but they operate mainly in Antananarivo and the larger urban areas. You can rent a mobile telephone from *Telecel* (Lot IA 68 rue Ramelina, Ambohijatovo; tel 20-22-33041; fax 20-22-

32621), or contact mobile telephone service provider *Madacom* (tel 261-0- 33-11-00789).

Call Boxes

In Antananarivo you can buy telephone cards (*telecarte*) in units of 25, 50, and 100 from just about any hotel or post office and there are lots of public telephones (*Publiphone*) around.

MEDIA

Broadcast stations are scattered around the island. The entire country has only 17 medium wave amplitude modulation (AM) radio stations – a powerful transmitter in the capital and 16 low-power repeaters in other towns and cities. A government-owned AM shortwave station broadcasting in French and Malagasy on five frequencies reaches listeners in remote locations and in neighbouring countries. Antananarivo and two other cities each have a single frequency modulation (FM) station. Radio and TV are diffused by Radiotélévision Malagasy and Radio Madagasikara, two public enterprises. Low-power TV transmitters broadcast daily in urban areas. If you pine for BBC and Voice of America take your own shortwave radio.

Television

The classier hotels usually have satellite TV for guests, otherwise it's offerings in Malagasy and French from local channels.
MA-TV Maeva 7 Television: PO Box 1414, Antananarivo (tel 20-22-34416).
Television Malagasy (TVM): Immeuble Solima, Antaninarenina, Antananarivo (tel 20-22-25648).
TVF-Televiziona Fialamboly: 41a rue Andriba, Mahamasina Sud (tel 20-22-20730; fax 20-22-20302).

Radio

Alliance FM92: tel 20-22-32861; fax 20-22-22504.
Alliance RLI FM 106: tel 20-22-29016.
Malagasy National Radio (RNM): tel 20-22-21745; fax 20-22-31719.
Radio Lazan'iarivo: tel 20-22-29016.
Radio Tsiokavao: tel 20-22-21749.
Radio Korail: tel 20-22-24494.

Newspapers and Magazines

Daily newspapers include:
Express Madagascar: Enceinte Stedic (tel 20-22-20310; fax 20-22-21383; e-mail lexpress@bow.dts.mg), French.
Gazety Maresaka: 12 rue Ratsimba Rajoan, Isotry (tel 20-22-40372), French.
Midi Madagasikara: Ankorondrano (tel 20-22-62122; fax 20-22-27351; e-mail midi@dts.mg), French and Malagasy.
Madagascar Tribune: rue Ravoninahitriniarivo, Ankorondrano (tel 20-22-32994; fax 20-22-22254; e-mail tribune@bow.dts.mg), French.
Weeklies include:
Dans le Média Demain: 58 rue Tsiombikibo Ambatovinaky (tel 20-22-63615; fax

20-22-35979; e-mail dmd@dts.mg).
Journal Océan Indien Actuel: tel 20-22-25634.
Imongo Vaovao: Lot II 4a Andravoanhangy (tel 20-22-32879).
The weekly *Tana 7 Jours* carries local TV and radio programmes.
La Revue de l'Océan Indien Madagascar (Immeuble Madprint, rue H Rabesahala, Antsakarivo; tel 20-22-22536; fax 20-22-34534; e-mail roi@dts.mg), is published monthly.

Maps and Guides

In Antananarivo excellent tourist and topographic maps can be bought at Foiben-Taosarintanin'i Madagasikara (FTM), rue Dama-Ntsoha RJB, Ambanidia (tel 20-22-22935). This is the Malagasy name for the *Institut National de Géodésie et Cartographie*. Scales available include 1:1,000,000 road and relief maps (4 sheets cover the country); 1:500,00 road and relief maps (12 sheets cover the country); 1:100,000 and 1:50,000 topographic maps; and 1:10,000 street maps of important towns. A useful scale for hikers is the 1:50,000, which is roughly 1¼ inches to the mile (2 cm to 1 km). A bookshop with a good selection of maps and street plans is the *Tout pour l'Ecole*, across from the *Hotel Mellis* on rue Indira Gandhi, Antananarivo.

BY AIR

Air travel is the preferred mode of transport on the island for all who can afford it, since the generally poor state of the roads makes land transport difficult, if not impossible. Domestic air links are fairly good, although you quickly learn that with any form of transport in Madagascar scheduled or published times mean very little. The country actually has 136 airfields, but only 50% are usable, and only 30 maintain permanent-surface runways. Air Madagascar flights serve towns all over the island, with the exception of a few places in the central highlands. The domestic fleet consists mostly of Boeing 767, 747 and 737s, HS 748s, De Havilland Twin Otters, and ATR-42s. The airline has an excellent safety record. Fares can be paid in foreign currency (cash or credit card) and in local currency. All flights are non-smoking. There is no seat assignment, flights are almost always full, and over-booking is common. Be sure to reconfirm in advance every flight you've booked, as failure to do so will almost automatically result in cancellation of your reservation. Check in well on time, and stay within the baggage allowance as some of the aircraft are small. Short flights are cheap and can save you a lot of discomfort and delay. An air tourist pass is available and allows unlimited travel for certain periods.

DOMESTIC FLIGHTS

You can fly from Antananarivo to:

Toliara, Mahajanga, Toamasina, Ile St-Marie, Morondava	Every day of the week.
Nosy Bé, Antsiranana, Tolagnaro	Every day except Wednesday.
Antsalova	Monday.
Tsiroanomandidy	Monday and Tuesday.
Maroantsetra, Mananara, Maintirano	Monday and Thursday.

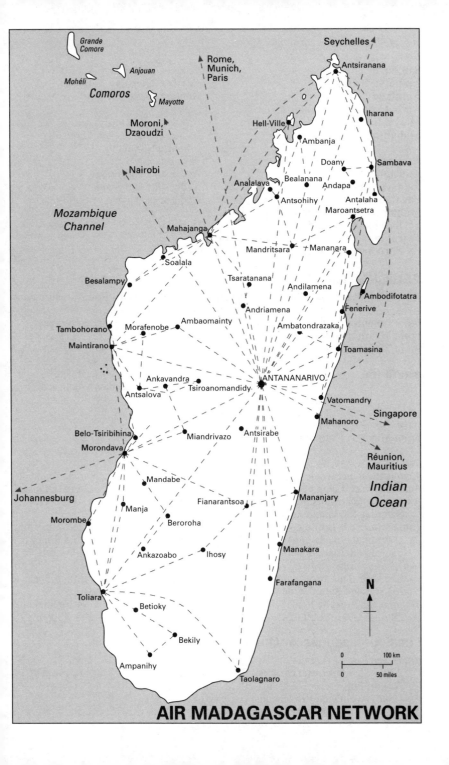

Grande
Comore

Anjouan

Mohéli

Comoros

Mayotte

Rome,
Munich,
Paris

Seychelles

Antsiranana

Iharana

Moroni,
Dzaoudzi

Hell-Ville

Ambanja

Doany

Sambava

Nairobi

Analalava

Bealanana

Andapa

Mozambique
Channel

Antsohihy

Antalaha

Mahajanga

Maroantsetra

Mandritsara

Mananara

Soalala

Tsaratanana

Besalampy

Andilamena

Ambodifotatra

Andriamena

Fenerive

Tambohorano

Morafenobe

Ambaomainty

Ambatondrazaka

Maintirano

Toamasina

Ankavandra

ANTANANARIVO

Antsalova

Tsiroanomandidy

Vatomandry

Singapore

Belo-Tsiribihina

Miandrivazo

Antsirabe

Mahanoro

Morondava

Réunion,
Mauritius

Mandabe

Indian
Ocean

Manja

Fianarantsoa

Mananjary

Johannesburg

Beroroha

Morombe

Manakara

Ankazoabo

Ihosy

Farafangana

Toliara

N

Betioky

Bekily

0   100 km

Ampanihy

0   50 miles

Taolagnaro

AIR MADAGASCAR NETWORK

Sambava	Monday, Wednesday, Saturday.
Ambatondrazaka	Monday, Thursday, Saturday.
Antalaha	Monday, Wednesday, Friday, Saturday.
Ambatomainty, Manakara	Tuesday.
Morombe	Tuesday and Saturday.
Mananjary	Tuesday, Wednesday, Thursday, Saturday, Sunday.
Ambanja	Wednesday.
Antsohihy	Wednesday and Friday.
Fianarantsoa	Wednesday and Sunday.
Farafangana	Wednesday, Thursday, Saturday.
Mahanoro, Vatomandry, Morafenobe, Besalampy, Mandritsara	Thursday.
Tsaratanana, Belo, Manja, Mampikony, Port-Berger, Soalala	Friday.

REGIONAL LINKS

Air Madagascar flies Réunion to Antananarivo on Thursday, Friday, Saturday and Sunday; and to Toamasina on Wednesday.

From Comoros   to Antananarivo on Tuesday; and to Mahajanga on Sunday.
From Mauritius   to Antananarivo on Tuesday, Friday, Sunday.
From Mayotte   to Mahajanga on Saturday.

Air Austral   flies (from Roland Garros International Airport, St Denis) Réunion to Antananarivo on Monday, Tuesday, Wednesday, Thursday.
to Toamasina on a Friday.
to Nosy Bé on Saturday.
From Mayotte   to Mahajanga on Tuesday and Thursday.
to Nosy Bé on a Wednesday.

Ario is the general sales agent for Air Austral in Madagascar and can be found at:

Antananarivo: Làlana Solombavambahaoka Frantsay 77 (tel 20-22-25990; e-mail ariomad@bow.dts.mg). Open Monday to Friday from 8.30am to 5.30pm and Saturday 8.30am to noon.

Toamasina: 81 Boulevard Joffre (tel 20-53-31243; fax 20-53-31244; e-mail ariotmm@bow.dts.mg). Open Monday to Friday from 8.30am to 5.30pm and Saturday 8.30am to noon.

Hell-Ville: Villa Malibu, rue Passot La Batterie (tel 20-86-61240; fax 20-86-61237; e-mail arionos@bow.dts.mg). Open Monday to Friday from 8.30am to 5.30pm and Saturday 8am to 11am.

Mahajanga: Hotel de France Building, cnr. Georges V and Maréchal Joffre Street (tel 20-62-22391; fax 20-62-22417). Open Mon.day to Friday 8.30am to 5.30pm.

Local Air Madagascar Offices

Antananarivo: 31 Avenue de l'Indépendance, Analakely (tel 20-22-33254; fax 20-22-25728) for reservations; flight schedules, tel 20-22-28865; and Ivato Airport (tel 20-22-22222; fax 20-22-44674).

Antalaha: Avenue de l'Indépendance (tel 20-88-81322).

Antsiranana (Diego Suarez): 5 rue de Surcouf (tel 20-82-21475; fax 20-82-29375).

Mahajanga (Majunga): Avenue Gillot (tel 20-62-22421; fax 20-62-29375).
Morondava: Avenue Philibert-Tsiranana (tel 20-95-52101).
Nosy Bé: Route de Dzamandzar-Ambonara (tel 20-86-61357).
Sambava: tel 20-88-92037
Ile St Marie: Igossa-Ambodifotatra (tel 20-57-40046).
Taolagnaro (Fort Dauphin): Avenue du Maréchal-Foch (tel 20-92-21122).
Toamasina (Tamatave): Avenue de l'Indépendance (tel 20-53-32698).
Toliara (Tuléar): rue Henri-Martin (tel 20-94-41585; fax 20-94-42233).

Charter Flights

Fraise et Cie SA: PO Box 28 Antananarivo (tel 20-22-22721; fax 20-22-29123).
Madagascar Air Services: tel 20-22-27957; fax 20-22-23179.
Madagascar Flying Service: tel 20-22-313627; fax 20-22-35206.
Malagasy Airlines: Villa la Roseraie, Ivato (tel 20-22-44137; fax 20-22-44330).
Travaux Aériens de Madagascar (TAM): 31 Avenue de l'Indépendance, PO Box 876, Antananarivo (tel 20-22-29691; fax 20-22-30540).

BY SEA

There are six international ports for ocean-going vessels and 12 ports for coastal vessels. Toamasina (Tamatave) on the east coast is the main port for commerce and for visiting cargo ships. Other important ones are Mahajanga and Antsiranana. A variety of cargo boats and other craft make journeys to, from, and around the island and the best way to find out whether you can take advantage of these sailings is to contact the local shipping agents in one or other of the ports (see *Getting There*).

BY RAIL

The state-controlled railroad consists of about 680 miles (1,095 km) of track in two limited and separate railroad systems. The railway network is the responsibility of a state-owned company, *Réseau National des Chemins de Fer Malagasy* (RNCFM). There are four main connecting lines:
Fianarantsoa-Manakara: linking the southern highlands to the south-east coast.
Antananarivo-Antsirabe: linking the two cities in the highlands.
Antananarivo-Moramanga-Toamasina: linking the capital in the highlands to the main commercial harbour in the country on the east coast.
Moramanga-Ambatondrazaka: linking Ambatondrazaka, the major rice-producing region of the country, to Moramanga, Antananarivo and Toamasina.

Criss-crossing the island are the remains of a once magnificent rail infrastructure and buildings such as stations, platforms, storehouses, and offices, but like so much else on this entrancing island, this network is decrepit and disused, with buildings and abandoned rolling stock alike taken over by the homeless.
One thing that has survived is the Michelin train, apparently one of only two of its type left in the world. This is a rail-car built like a 1930's bus, with a long bonnet and inflatable tyres. This hybrid was born around 1930 after tyre manufacturing tycoon André Michelin spent a sleepless night on a train, kept awake by the noise of the wheels. He adapted the tyred train from a previously derided idea first patented in 1859. The amazing result seats 40-50 people on wicker chairs, next to a small bar, and trundles them on sight-seeing tours between Antananarivo and Toamasina. This weird vehicle can be rented by groups for

about £132 ($200) one-way, and £200 ($300) for a round-trip. Book at Antananarivo railway station.

For a similar trip between Fianarantsoa and Manakara, a *draisine* can be rented. This can carry up to 17 passengers. Book at the Fianarantsoa railroad station. For more rail information contact RNCFM, 1 Avenue de l'Indépendance, PO Box 259, Antananarivo (tel 20-22-20521; fax 20-22-22288).

BY ROAD

Some parts of the country can be covered by train, bus, taxi, or hired car, but the road network has deteriorated considerably and many areas are inaccessible.

Buses

Buses are seen almost everywhere, chock-a-block with passengers and baggage irrespective of the number of seats, manufacturer's recommendations or safety regulations. They are the best way to meet local people and travel cheaply, so long as you are not overly concerned about safety and have all the time in the world. Services can be unreliable. A flat fare is usually charged irrespective of the distance travelled.

Taxis

In spite of their usually dilapidated condition, taxis are reputedly quite safe. There are two types of taxis which run around between the major towns, the *taxi-bé*, which is quick and comfortable, and the *taxi-brousse* (bush taxi) which is smaller, cheaper, slower, makes more stops or has more breakdowns, and generally operates on cross-country routes. There are no set rates and the fare should be agreed in advance. Since it is sometimes difficult to find a taxi for the return trip, you should ask the driver to wait for you or come back and pick you up. Taxis can be hired on a daily basis, and this is a good idea if you want to make a number of stops as the taxi drivers are familiar with the routes. To rent a taxi costs about £20 ($30) a day but it is advisable to discuss the rate prior to departure. From one destination in town to another will cost you about £1 ($1.50).Tipping is unnecessary.

Another, more leisurely, way to get around is by *pousse-pousse*, or two-wheeled rickshaw, if you are not averse to being pulled around by an undernourished human 'horse.' You'll find these clamouring for your custom in every town and you should experience a *pousse-pousse* ride at least once. Bargaining is expected and you should always make sure you receive the correct change. You can also get around by bicycle, although this calls for a high level of physical fitness, a strong sense of adventure, and a large degree of self-sufficiency. Mountain bikes are available for hire in most of the larger tourist centres.

DRIVING

Licences

All you need to drive a car or a motorbike is an international driving licence. Traffic 'officially' drives on the **right-hand** side of the road.

ROADS

Nobody seems to know for sure the size of Madagascar's road network, although official and other educated guesstimates put it at 15,845 miles (25,500 km) of which nearly 3,418 miles (5,500 km) are surfaced. The remainder are, at best, earth tracks. The most serious national problem remains the state of the roads, which don't seem to have been maintained or repaired for decades. The principal towns of Toamasina, Mahajanga, Antsirabe, Fianarantsoa, Toliara, and Taolagnaro are said to be accessible by road at all times of the year. Tarred roads also link the main towns to the central highlands although many roads are impassable in the rainy season.

VEHICLES

It is estimated that there are around 40,000 vehicles on the road, about 70% of them in Antananarivo. Most are poorly maintained. A lot of old cars are imported from France and Réunion and veteran car enthusiasts will love Madagascar as 99% of the vehicles on the roads are ancient, mostly Renaults and Citroens, with some of 1940's vintage. Road transport is used to move some 40% of all merchandise and goods around the island. Distances are considerable and roads are often deplorable and although the main route from Antananarivo to Toamasina (Tamatave), built with Western and old Eastern Bloc aid, is good, roads and streets within the two cities themselves are in a bad state of repair. The problem in Antananarivo is compounded by the mass of people living in the capital and the increasing number of vehicles on hilly, winding streets that were never designed to handle such heavy traffic.

Fuel

Petrol costs around MGF 2,300 a litre, which is the equivalent of £0.23/$0.35 a litre and around MGF 1,800 (£0.18/$0.27) a litre for diesel.

VEHICLE RENTAL

You can rent small cars, four-wheel-drive (4x4) vehicles and even 11-passenger minibuses with or without a chauffeur in Antananarivo. Bearing in mind the vast distances involved and the uncertain state of many roads, this can be an expensive way to get around the island and the reason why most time-constrained visitors opt for hops on Air Madagascar's domestic flights. On roads outside the towns, motorbikes are for daredevils or bionic riders, and a 4x4 vehicle is really the only way to travel.

Car Rental Agencies:

Hertz are located at Ivato International Airport, and at Horizon Madagascar, Galerie De L'Immeuble, Antananarivo (tel 20-22 22961; fax 20-22 33673). Open Monday to Friday from 8am to 6pm, Saturday from 8am to noon and 2pm to 6pm.

Aventour: Nouvel Immeuble Aro Ampefilohoa, Antananarivo (tel 20-22-21778/31761; fax 20-22-27299).

Avis: 3 rue Patrice Lumumba Tsaralalana, Antananarivo (tel 20-22-20435; fax 20-22-21657).

Budget: tel 20-22-31708.

Clovis Arthur: Tsaralalana (tel 20-22-31537).
Espace 4x4: Isoraka (tel 20-22-26297; fax 20-22-27296).
Europcar has two offices in Antananarivo: at Ivato airport, and at Route des
    Hydrocarbures, Ankorondrano (tel 20-22-33647; fax 20-22-31165).
Euro Rent: Ambatonakanga (tel 20-22-29766; fax 20-22-29749).
Gasy Cars: Ivandry (tel 20-22-43223; fax 20-22-43260).
Locauto: Analakely (tel 20-22-21981; fax 20-22-24801).
Madagascar Airtours: (in the Hilton Hotel lobby) PO Box 3874, Antananarivo (tel
    20-22-24192; fax 20-22-34370).
Procar: tel 20-22-45004.
Suntour: 4x4 Toyota (tel 20-22-25770; fax 20-22-22447).
Tropicar: tel 20-22-20803.
Check that any vehicle or motorbike you hire is in good condition as roadside
breakdown service is non-existent. Remember that road conditions and driving
standards are different and always wear a seatbelt or a crash helmet, and place
children in a child restraint. Don't drink and drive as this is even more dangerous
on unfamiliar roads and in an unfamiliar vehicle.

HAZARDS

You should be able to dine out forever on your stories if you are bold enough
to tackle Madagascar's roads by car or motorbike. The sight of cars speeding
towards you, doors wide open, to shut as they pass, then re-open, can be
nerve-racking. You'll be told that this is simply 'air-conditioning Malagasy-
style.' Road signs can vary from the confusing to the explicit, such as a sign
bearing a red skull and crossbones and the warning *'Danger de Mort!'*. Few
traffic lights or signals are in working order. Roads are the arteries for a
constant stream of people, chickens, donkey carts, pigs, cattle, and other
animals – all with the right of way – and are everywhere gouged by the
mummies and daddies of all potholes. Avoid travelling out of towns at night if
you can. Don't become irate when things don't happen on time, or when there
are numerous delays; this is the worst possible reaction. Madagascar is a place
where you must learn the art of being patient, summed up in the popular
Malagasy saying *mora, mora* ('easy, easy') meaning 'it can wait' or 'tomorrow
is another day.'

Accommodation

Madagascar cannot compare with other Indian
Ocean islands such as Mauritius and Seychelles
when it comes to hotels, resorts and general
tourism infrastructure, but there is a range of
accommodation that's quite adequate if you are on
the island for its unique biodiversity and not for the
luxury you might be accustomed to. Stars awarded to Malagasy hotels tend to be
a reflection of the currency exchange rate – you get more of them for their
European or American equivalent. Accommodation generally is relatively cheap
because it's unsophisticated and basic. This doesn't mean there are no good
hotels, simply that there are varying degrees of comfort from air-conditioned
rooms for the comfort-minded to bare-bones accommodation that might give
pause to all but the hardiest backpacker. Hotels range from up-market, expensive
establishments such as the *Hilton, Colbert* and *Gregoire* in Antananarivo; the
Miramar in Taolagnaro (Fort Dauphin) and the *Manda Beach* near Toamasina

(Tamatave), down to basic but comfortable establishments such as the well-known *Hotel Buffet de la Gare* at Périnet Special Reserve and *Chez Chabaud* in Mahajanga. Outside Antananarivo, accommodation can generally be described as modest country guest-house style, basically furnished and often with primitive plumbing facilities. In some areas of the country there is electricity only for a few hours at night, there may be no power after 10 pm, or the power might go off while something is being repaired. This means that hot water is not always available, although in Madagascar's climate you'll probably prefer cold showers. Bliss in Madagascar is an air-conditioned room and a shower that works. Breakfasts are French continental in style with bread rolls, butter, jam and fruit, unless otherwise requested. Hotel rooms are more expensive for foreign visitors than for residents. You'll usually be quoted prices in French francs with an exchange rate that works out to an MFG figure at least twice that paid by local guests. Tariffs vary between the capital and the provincial towns, but up-market means about £20-25/$30-37 a night and basic means around £3-5/$4-7. On top of this, you'll pay a tourist bed tax (*vignette touristique*) of around £0.40/$0.59 a night which is meant to help fund the government's campaign to improve tourist facilities. The government is promoting the upgrading of existing hotels and resorts and is active in trying to attract foreign investment to build more. Its aim is a rapid 50% increase in the 6,600 rooms presently available in the island's hotels, lodges, and resorts.

The following organisations could help you to choose the right hotel for your requirements and budget:

Syndicate des Industries Hotelieres de Madagascar: (Hotels Association) 34 rue Marguerite Barbier, BP 3389, Antananarivo (tel 20-22-29120).

National Institute for Tourism and Hotel Business (INTH): PO Box 8043, Antananarivo (tel 20-22-34479).

Syndicate of Hotel Industry of Madagascar (SIHM): c/o Hintsy Hotel de l'Ikopa, PO Box 8421, Antananarivo (tel 20-22-26379; fax 20-22-26414).

Camping

Camping is unrestricted throughout the island, although you should always ask for permission from the nearest likely looking landowner or village head. There are campsites at all reserves, which have the advantage of giving you access to knowledgeable resident guides. You should without fail take your own mosquito net if you plan to camp. It's also a good thing to pack if you intend to stay at middle to low bracket hotels and resorts.

Eating and Drinking

CUISINE

Rice has an almost mystical role in Malagasy life. It's eaten three times a day and it's grown everywhere there's soil and water – and there's even a special way of growing it 'dry' without using normal paddy fields. Statistically, every Malagasy eats at least a pound (450 g) of rice, or *vary*, a day and it's not only a food, it's also a measure of time and space. 'The time it takes to cook rice' (*indray mahamasa-vary*) means 'about half an hour' to a Malagasy. Distance may be expressed as 'twice the time it takes to cook rice,' meaning that it is about an hour away. Instead of mentioning a specific month a Malagasy can refer to seasons at which rice is at different heights and different stages of its growth. *Mena vary*, 'when the rice is gold' is a common time reference. Measures of volume and weight use rice as a standard measure, with the basic unit being called *vary iray*, or 'a rice.' Rice was the common currency in Madagascar before the people came into contact with Europeans. When the Malagasy first got coins they simply chopped them up and made the value of the pieces equivalent to their weight in rice. You don't order a meal with a side order of rice; this revered grain *is* the meal and the rest is regarded as a bonus of appetising titbits. This bonus can be any kind of meat, fish, seafood, vegetables, or fruit. You won't get much of a helping with your rice in a *hotely*, which is not a hotel but a cheap wayside eaterie, but in a *hotely fisakafoanana*, or restaurant, you can expect any number of things ranging from the unusual to the delectable. The same goes for a meal in the home of a Malagasy, although the variety will depend on their social status and finances.

A normal meal in a private home will start with *lasopy*, which is a hearty veal and vegetable concoction more a thick puree than a soup. Next might come *varenga*, roasted shredded beef, accompanied by *vary amin anana*, rice and steaming hot green vegetables, and a tomato and spring onion salad known as *lasary voatiba*. Mountains of fluffy white rice will be the centrepiece of the spread. The traditional drink with this would be *ranon'apango*, which is made by letting an inch or two of leftover rice scorch in the pan and then pouring boiling water on it. Once this cools it is strained, chilled and served. The meal will be rounded off with vanilla-flavoured fresh fruit (*voankazo*), and *ravinboafoby*, Malagasy tea. One thing to remember if you are a guest in a Malagasy home is that each family member is expected to eat in turn according to age and the youngest is served last. Children can be punished if they start to eat before their elders and it would be a serious breach of etiquette if you were to start eating before your host. Not all Malagasy follow this tradition, but it's still widespread enough for you not to risk offending anyone. A favourite Malagasy breakfast food is *kitoza*, which is made by drying strips of beef in the sun for a few hours before crisping them well over hot coals. This is an improvement on normal jerked beef and makes a good lightweight snack for travellers. Another popular snack or dessert you'll be urged to try is *koba*, a rich and aromatic kind of cake made with rice flour, brown sugar, and crushed peanuts, which is wrapped in banana leaves and poached in a bain-marie. You can buy slices of this in the marketplace, as well as its near relative, which is a less fussy plate of rice, bananas and peanuts. Other, more familiar, delights are rice pudding, noodle soup, crispy French-style baguettes, cheese, and yoghurt. While yoghurt is said to be safe to eat anywhere the same thing doesn't apply to ice-cream, which can be a fertile breeding ground for stomach bugs. In the coastal towns fish and seafood dishes are naturally your best bet and you can enjoy wild oysters, clams, prawns, squid, octopus and fresh line fish at bargain prices. Try ginger and lime-flavoured crab and lobster meat on a bed of fresh green salad, or *Foza sy hena-kisoa*, a mountainous serving of stir-fried crab, pork and rice.

If you are eating in restaurants you'll usually have a choice between French cuisine, or the local version of it, and Malagasy dishes. Fresh ginger, chillies, vanilla and other spices are common ingredients of local food and add zip and flavour to everything from meat and veg to fish and sauces. Malagasy cooks are subtle in the use of spices and prefer the understated flavours of Malaysian cuisine. Their curries are not overpowering and in dishes which call for hot chillies these are often served separately so that you can control your intake. *Romazava*, is the national dish of Madagascar, a savoury beef, ginger, and green vegetable stew, but the quality can vary enormously depending on the age and previous lifestyle of the zebu ox used to make it. The hump of the zebu is the choice part of the animal and in prime condition is more like venison than beef. Pork and chicken are cooked in a variety of ways with garlic, ginger, tomatoes and greens called *brèdes*, a kind of spinach. Then there are festival favourites of pork and eel stew, and a duck and ginger stew. The Malagasy enjoy fatty meat dishes, but to cut through the fat they serve it up with a relish, rather like an Indian sambal, called *sakay*, which is a mixture of minced ginger, garlic, and red chilli. Another accompaniment is *rougaille*, a salad of chopped red onion, spring onion, chillies, and tomatoes, mixed together with a little salt. A raw chopped vegetable salad (often more like a pickle) known as *achard* appears in many forms and with many different spellings according to region and individual whim. The best-known is *Achard de Legumes*. This is found all over Madagascar and can be served on its own, as an hors d'oeuvre, or as an accompaniment to stew, and other fatty food. At the markets, stallholders chop the ingredients with a mandoline, and you can buy it ready-made. If you want to try it before you get to Madagascar (or when you return) this is how to make it:

Achard de Legumes~

Ingredients
Half a white cabbage, shredded
6 carrots, grated
3 onions, halved and finely sliced
4 oz (100 g) sliced French or runner beans
Handful of crushed fresh peanuts
Salt to taste
Dressing
2 chopped small red chillies
1 oz (25 g) chopped fresh root ginger
3 crushed garlic cloves
4 fl oz (100 ml) groundnut oil
1½ fl oz (40 ml) white wine vinegar
1 teaspoon curry powder
1 teaspoon crushed mustard seeds
½ teaspoon ground turmeric
Method
Mix all the dressing ingredients together. Toss the vegetables in the dressing, sprinkle with the peanuts and season with salt to taste. This should be enough for 6-8 people. *Mazotoa homana!* – which means 'Bon appétit!'

One word of warning if you are an adventurous eater: If you take a boat trip with locals in Madagascar be very circumspect if you are offered a helping of food prepared by the crew. Marijuana (cannabis) is liberally used by boatmen as an ingredient in their cooking.

Some Useful Words

I'm hungry	*Noana aho*
I'm thirsty	*Mangetaheta aho*
Food	*Sakafo*
Water	*rano*
Soup	*Lasopy*
Bread	*Mofo*
Ox/beef	*Omby*
Pork	*Kisoa*
Chicken	*Akoho*
Fish	*Trondro/drano*
Eggs	*Atody*
Sugar	*Siramamy*
Orange	*Voasary*
Banana	*Akondro*
Milk	*Ronono*
Wine	*Divay*

DRINKING

Drinking habits have moderated on Madagascar since the days when pirate crews washed down the decks of their ships with rum and 500 of them drank themselves to death on stolen whisky in 1704 during a mammoth beach party carousal. There's still plenty of rum (*toaka gasy*) around, but it's largely given way in popular affection to Three Horses Beer – better known as THB – and soft drinks such as Coca-Cola, Bon-Bon Anglais, Fanta Orange, Sprite, and a variety of other bubblegum-coloured and flavoured refreshments. Rum of the illegal moonshine variety comes into its own at the ritual exhumation ceremony of *famadihana* when it goes down the hatch among the merrymakers in astounding quantities as they parade the corpses of deceased relatives around the family tomb before reburial. Other local drinks and cocktails you'll undoubtedly come across include the north's fermented coconut milk *trembo* and the fermented sugarcane brew of the east coast called *betsabetsa*. The coast also offers a cocktail-type tipple based on coconut milk called *punch au coco*. Another cottage industry concoction is *litchel*, a potent alcoholic drink based on litchi fruit, and the raffia palm unique to Madagascar is ingeniously tapped to produce a potent toddy. Some of the best commercially produced rum comes from the sugarcane island of Nosy Bé and is sold under a variety of labels and in a range of strengths. The most explosive is *Dzama, pur Rhum Nosy Bé* (52%), next comes *Cuvée Noire Dzama* (43%), and then *Cuvée Spéciale, Rhum Ambré de Nosy Bé* (42%). There's also a *Dzama Rhum* (42%), and a *Dzama Coco Punch* (18%). If you want to say 'Cheers,' or 'Good Health' when proposing a toast the local Malagasy equivalent is *Ho ela velona!*

You'll pay through the nose for imported French and South African wines, and if you must have wine with your meal it's much more sensible to drink a cheaper local variety. The knowledgeable recommend the *blanc* and the *gris* of L'Azani Betsileo from the Fianarantsoa upland region where the vine was introduced some 40 years ago by Swiss winegrowers. If you like Swiss-type wines you should like these light, fruity offerings. Avoid the paint-stripper reds from all growers. Prices tend to yo-yo, but a bottle of local wine in a restaurant usually costs five to six times the price of a bottle of beer, and the price of a bottle of beer can vary from about £0.30/$0.44 in a supermarket to £1.50/$2.22 in an upmarket hotel. A recommended end-of-meal digestif with the excellent local coffee is *Eau de Vie Orange* (or Mandarin).

Tea lovers might enjoy a cup of *ravinboafoby*, the locally grown tea, or *citronelle*, a fragrant and refreshing tea made from lemon grass.

Caveat

Tap water is said to be safe to drink in Antananarivo and most of the other main towns, but our advice is buy bottled water such as Eau Vive, La Source or Olympiko, which comes in one-litre bottles. Make sure the cap seal on the bottle is unbroken before you pay for it; it's really not worth risking an unpleasant gastric experience for the sake of saving a bit of cash every day.

SONG AND DANCE

Madagascar is the home of vibrant music and dance, and you cannot travel far on the island without being entertained by one or the other, and mostly they go hand in hand. Dances often illustrate important occasions, such as the coffee dance which celebrates one of the riches of the coastal villages, and they can last for hours during major celebrations. Tradition is alive and well throughout the country and popular culture needs no help from electricity, stages or professional artists. The performers are peasants and fishermen, and their shows are held in slack times, when the sea is too rough, or on the occasion of large family or religious gatherings. The *hira gasy* are open-air shows performed by peasant groups during winter on the central highlands. Lots of them are staged all around Antananarivo. The *hira gasy* ('Malagasy Art') is the realm of the *mpilalao*, peasant-troubadours, who hand down their inspiration from one generation to another. They have a distinctive song and dance routine, which they combine with a string of witticisms derived from *hainteny*, proverbs and metaphors used in the elusive traditional poetry of Madagascar. During dictatorial periods in the country's history this acrobatic use of words was a clever way for the disenchanted to circumvent censorship.

The *mpilalao* leave their fields during June to September for engagements which might be at important family celebrations, exhumation ceremonies or political meetings. This rural theatre, in which they perform bare-footed but dressed in rich costumes, was established just over a century ago, at the end of the era of the three Queens. In the 19th century, Queen Ranavalona used to assess the mood of her people by listening to songs from the country, especially those inspired by traditional and often impertinent *hainteny*. The structure of a *hira gasy* performance is precise and generally made up of three parts of equal length, corresponding to three themes chosen by the company. Each part invariably begins with music to signal the entrance of the male players. They warm up the audience before the entry of the women, following an introductory speech given by the main orator. The theme is then taken up in various songs and orations more or less improvised. Then come the dances, individual, in pairs or in groups, before the final scene, in which the youngest members display their acrobatic talents. Often, two companies compete with each other within the same show, each performing in turn. Each company vies for the audience's favour and the winner is chosen by the volume of the applause and the amount of cash collected. The *hira gasy* can go on for several hours. It owes part of its success to the artists' striking and colourful stage costumes: red frock-coats and beribboned straw hats for the men, flowing long dresses and parasols for the women. It's not always easy to find a *hira gasy* performance but well worth the effort.

For information try La Maison du Tourisme de Madagascar, in the Place de L'Indépendance, Antaninarenina, tel 20-22-35178; fax 20-22-69522; e-mail mtm@simicro.mg). They're open from 9.30am to 11.30am and 3.30pm to 5.30pm every day except Sunday.

MUSIC

Music has become a successful Malagasy export and it has already made a strong impact in musical circles worldwide. The best-known Malagasy musical group is **Tarika**, which in Malagasy simply means 'the group.' They have evolved a unique, modern blend from the musical roots of the different regions of Madagascar, playing traditional music with the energy of punk rock. The group's albums have topped music charts from Japan to the US. The band plays up-dates of traditional Malagasy instruments, including the *marovany* (box zither), *valiha* (bamboo zither), *kabosy* (the small Malagasy guitar), and the *jejy voatavo* (gourd dulcimer). The 21-string *valiha* is the most common of Madagascar's musical instruments. It is often made from an oblong wooden box and bicycle-brake cable, although traditionally it is made from a length of thick, hollow bamboo. The instrument, usually played at a variety of religious ceremonies, is one of the mainstay sounds of both traditional and pop versions of Malagasy music. Other popular Malagasy recording artists and groups are the **Justin Vali Trio**, **Rossy**, **Jaojoby**, **Njava**, **Mahaleo**, and **Dama**.

Supermarkets in Antananarivo such as *Champion*, *Magri*, and *Conquette* are good places to pick up Malagasy music CDs and cassettes. You can check out a list of solo artists and groups on the Internet at www.froots. demon.co.uk/madagcd.html and if you want to listen to some of them before you go, *Stern's African Record Shop* (293 Euston Road, London W1P 5PA) should be able to help.

SPORT AND RECREATION

Madagascar is first and foremost a destination for nature lovers and outdoor enthusiasts, scuba-divers and snorkellers, hikers, cavers, and those into aquasport – although there are even three golf courses on the island, two in Antananarivo and one in Toamasina. The main attraction for nature lovers is that this is lemur land, and these and other creatures unique to this gigantic island have always been a major draw for visitors (see *Flora and Fauna* p.87). Many of the more common lemur species have become so used to tourists that you don't even need to use a long-distance telephoto lens to capture them.

DIVING

Scuba-diving pioneer Jacques-Yves Cousteau once described Madagascar as having the most beautiful underwater sites he'd ever dived, with a vast array of numerous unexplored dive sites among the hundreds of tiny islands off its endless coastline and accessible only by boat. Many other experienced European scuba-divers agree that the vast, pristine reef areas off Madagascar provide some of the best diving spots in the southern hemisphere. The **most popular dive sites** are among the islands off the Nosy Bé archipelago in the north-west, Toliara and Nosy Vé on the west coast, Ile St Marie off the east coast, where you can often see whales, and the scores of bays and tiny islets around the northern tip of Madagascar, in the Antsiranana region. If you plan to take part in scuba activities you should have at least an Open Water One certificate or its equivalent from a recognised institution, such as the National Association of Underwater Instructors (NAUI) or the Professional Association of Diving Instructors (PADI).

HIKING

Hiking in the rainforests and among the mountainous country of the central highlands calls for a high degree of physical fitness and experience and unless you are a solo addict such treks are best undertaken in a group or at least with a local guide. If you are not into high-level activities less demanding tours and rambles are available that will enable you to see more of the island people, and learn something of their history, traditions and culture.

OTHER ACTIVITIES

Other adventurous activities that might be of interest include sea kayak safaris around the Masoala Peninsula, sailing among the countless isles, canoeing or white-water rafting down the Canal des Pangalanes, caving in the labyrinths of the Ankarana Massif, and deep-sea angling for some of the finest fighting fish in the tropics. (See *Exploring Madagascar* for regional Sport and Recreation)

Opening Hours. Shops are generally from 8am to noon and 2pm to 6pm Monday to Saturday, although some street markets can open well before dawn and be gone by daylight and others never seem to close at all.

GIFTS AND SOUVENIRS

Every town has covered or street markets which are good places to hunt for bargain price souvenirs and gifts. Throughout the island, you'll find a wide range of hand-made articles in wood, leather, horn, metal, stone, clay, cloth, feathers, silk, everything, in fact, that can be transformed into a useful or eye-catching object. You should always bargain when shopping, it is common and usually expected, and it's part of the fun. You will invariably be quoted a price that is twice what the vendor expects you to pay. Since there are not many tourists, it is a buyer's market. Good buys among the handicrafts are beautifully hand-embroidered cottons (clothes, table-cloths), Malagasy musical instruments, such as the multi-stringed *valiha*, woven mohair carpets, silk *lambas*, the traditional squares of cloth used as wraps or shawls, woven basketwork, and the delicate, almost papyrus-like hand-made Antaimoro paper, which is decorated with pressed, dried, and embedded wild flowers. You'll also find crocodile-skin bags and other leather products, marquetry furniture, chessboards and boxes, tiny dolls, silver crosses and bracelets, and jewellery made from semi-precious stones. An amazing variety of precious and semi-precious gemstones are found in Madagascar, including tourmaline, amethyst, citrine, rhodonite, celestine, amazonite, moonstone, rose quartz, milky quartz, garnets, and a rare dark blue variety of aquamarine. The largest crystal ever found came from Madagascar and weighed more than 380 tons (see *Exploring Madagascar*).

An unusual gift or memento is the traditional Malagasy board game going by the modern name of Solitaire. This consists of a carved wooden base with shallow hollows which cradle 37 hand-polished semi-precious stones. The centre stone is removed from the board to start the game. You then attempt to capture each of the other stones, using a manoeuvre similar to the jump in draughts or checkers. The game is over when no more jumps can be made, and you win if you are left with only one stone at the end of the game.

HANDICRAFTS

Carvings of an extremely high standard find their way to outlets all over the island from Ambositra, the capital of Malagasy woodcarving in the south-eastern part of the central highlands. This is the main centre for the **Zafimaniry** sculptors and carvers who live and work in the nearby forest. This artistic ethnic Malagasy community is noted for its delicate pieces carved in rosewood, ebony, and other rare woods. The Zafimaniry are the main producers of this traditional woodcraft and sale of their works enables them to maintain their traditional lifestyle. They are born sculptors and much of their art, while sober and simple, seems to be imbued with a deep religious feeling.

Another success story involves **raffia work**, which is growing from cottage industry to big business for local artisans. Raffia comes from the *Raphia* palm, which is unique to Madagascar. It produces a natural fibre of exceptional quality. It is used in many woven handicrafts and has now entered the world of high fashion both in Antananarivo and in Paris. In the fashion shops of the capital you will find numerous creations made from raffia and all over the country, at markets and in boutiques, items made of raffia abound. Here are a few addresses where you'll find examples in Antananarivo:

Markets:

Marché du Camp Pochard behind the railway station.
Marché du COUM in the 67 hectares zone.
Marché Artisanal on the road from the town to the airport (this is ideal for a final shop before flying out).

Boutiques and Designers:

Herylala Ramiandrisoa: tel 032 070 1477.
Service Mad at Ankadifotsy.
La Boutique de Madagascar, Immeuble Kobama at Soanierana.
Compagnie d'Orient (showroom near CITE) at Ambatonakanga.
Terre des Arts at Ambanidia (on the Route Circulaire).
Alize at Ambatonakanga.

Before buying it is a good idea to familiarise yourself with a few definitions. The word 'raffia' describes the fibre an item is made of. It is not necessarily woven; it may be crocheted, plaited, or tied. The term *rabane* is a term for the different quality plaited raffias. What is called *langara* is a *rabane* with a coarser filling. The *emyrne* is halfway between the two, whereas the *bestsy* describes the finest of braided raffia. The *jabo* (pronounced 'dzab') combines raffia with cotton or silk for a finished feel that is very close to that of cloth. This was the preferred fabric of Malagasy aristocrats in the pre-colonial days.

Specialist and upmarket shops in and around Antananarivo:

Art Deco: 1a rue Rahamefy Ambohijatovo (tel 20-22-34108).

Centre National de l'Artisanat Malgache (Cenam): rue Aghostino Neto 67 Ha Sud (tel/fax 20-22-23945).

Maison de L'Artisanat: Route de l'Aerogors, Lot 2000 G-a Ambohiboa (tel/fax 20-22-44435).

Ferronnerie d'Art: Route d'Abohimanga, Amboditsiry (tel 20-22-40728).

Atelier Dera: Lot II B49 Amboditsiry (tel 20-22-40016).

Denis Export SA: IVA 16a Ambodivonkely (tel 20-22-33273; fax 20-22-22000).

RED TAPE

Whenever you buy anything worth more than £3 ($5), ask the merchant to give you a signed *certificat de vente* (sales certificate) describing the article and giving its value. You may be asked to show this at Customs when you leave the country. The reason is to prevent antiques and prohibited exports leaving the country.

Exportation of handicrafts in commercial quantities and certain categories of objects require authorisation by the appropriate ministry:

Commercial exports: Ministère du Commerce, Direction des Exportations, Ambohidahy.

Semi-precious and precious stones: Ministère de l'Industrie, des Mines et de l'Energie, Direction du Contrôum; le Economique, Ambohidahy, Antananarivo.

Fauna (birds, butterflies): Direction des Eaux et Forêts, Nanisana.

Plants, medicinal herbs: Ministère de la Recherche Scientifique, Tsimbazaza.

CRIME

Even the island known as the land at the end of the earth is not immune to the increasing levels of crime noticeable in tourist destinations everywhere. The criminal threat level in Antananarivo, for instance, has gone from a medium to a high threat. This change is associated with Madagascar's deteriorating economy. Muggers and bag snatchers generally operate in or near public mass transit systems, and often tackle people walking at night in the city centre, where they will try to snatch your jewellery or handbag. Thieves have been known to use razor blades to cut open handbags. Don't expect local police to respond to an emergency call in less than 30 minutes; Madagascar's poor telephone service sometimes makes it difficult to contact them, and when you do they often lack the transport to get to you. In the market place a thief who steals from a fellow

Malagasy runs the risk of being beaten by an angry mob, but a tourist relieved of his expensive watch or her designer handbag is unlikely to cause much concern. Pickpockets of old have now added mugging to their activities in the capital and other urban areas. Take sensible precautions in crowded areas, such as markets. Do not carry excessive amounts of money or wear jewellery, such as wrist-watches, bracelets and necklaces, while on foot or when using public transport. Although crimes, such as burglary, do happen in areas outside the capital, the threat of violent crime is less common in rural areas. Avoid travelling at night in private or public vehicles outside Antananarivo, where there is poor lighting and bad road conditions. Carry a photocopy of your passport and keep the original document somewhere safe, such as a hotel deposit box, which is also a good place for your valuables. Antananarivo is the worst place for street crime, as well as theft from residences and vehicles. Valuable items should never be left in an unattended vehicle. Do not walk alone or in a group at night in urban areas, especially in the vicinity of Western-type hotels. Hire only an authorised guide and be cautious when visiting beaches and other isolated areas.

Photography

Every now and then the generally easygoing people of Madagascar take to the streets to voice their dissatisfaction with one thing or another and these demonstrations often deteriorate into violent protest. If you stay around to watch demonstrations or photograph political gatherings, especially in towns outside Antananarivo, you could put yourself at risk. You may also risk arrest or a serious grilling if you are noticed taking photographs of any airports or military and police establishments.

Tips

Find out on arrival how you can contact the police, fire and ambulance services and make a note of the telephone numbers for emergencies. Also make a list of the following:
Passport number and date issued.
Credit card numbers and emergency number to report theft.
International driver's licence number.
Serial number of air or sea tickets, and of your travellers cheques.
Any serial numbers on valuables, such as cameras, tape recorders and radios.
Serial number of travel insurance policy, and note any emergency contact
    number.
Make copies of any prescriptions for spectacles and contact lenses.
   Make two copies of the above list. Leave one copy with someone you can reach in an emergency and carry the other copy with you, keeping it separate from your luggage and valuables. List-making is a bore, but if the worst comes to the worst the above list will be invaluable.
   The British Foreign Office and US State Department recommend that visitors register with their respective embassy on arrival. Travellers to remote areas are also advised to leave a rough itinerary with their embassy before travelling.

DRINK, DRUGS AND THE LAW

Drugs

Penalties for possession, use, or trafficking in illegal drugs in Madagascar are strict and convicted offenders can expect jail sentences and heavy fines. Anyone who has ever seen the inside of a Malagasy prison will tell you it's not worth the risk. There's plenty of marijuana (cannabis) around; it grows wild as well as being cultivated for the local market. The island is raising international concern that it is increasingly becoming used as a transhipment point for heroin and other addictive drugs.

Hookers

Nightclubs all have their share of prostitutes (*makarely*). When they arrive it is customary for the management to take their identity cards, which are returned only when the guest entertaining them telephones to say that nothing has been stolen from him and that the room is still intact. Malagasy are ambivalent on the subject of prostitution, saying it is a concept foreign to Malagasy morality. They believe you should pay for everything, even sex, and women readily accept this easygoing approach. Mistresses are engagingly known in Malagasy as *bodofotsy*, which literally means 'blanket' or 'bedcover,' and their local colloquial French name is the *deuxième bureau* (the 'second office').

THE POLICE

There are numerous state security services in Madagascar, but the main ones are the Civil Police and the National Gendarmerie. Civil Police force members serve in the island's cities, where the head of each prefecture has a contingent under his control. The National Gendarmerie maintains public order, preserves security at rural village level, protects government facilities, prevents cattle rustling, and chases criminal elements. Units are stationed throughout the island. Although all arms of state security have been trying to brush up their public images for the past few years it's wise policy to stay away from them and their installations.

Help and Information *i*

TOUR OPERATORS IN MADAGASCAR

AKL Travel International: Ambatoroka VB 72a V, Antananarivo (tel 20-22-26205; fax 20-22-35505; e-mail akltana@malagasy.com).
        Aventour: Nouvel Immeuble Aro Analekely, Antananarivo (tel 20-22-31761; fax 20-22-27299).
Boogie Pilgrim: 40 Avenue de l'Indépendance, Analakely, Antananarivo (tel 20-22-25878; fax 20-22-25117; e-mail bopi@bow.dts.mg).
Cortez Expeditions: 25 rue Zafindriandiky, Antanimena, Antananarivo (tel 20-22-21974; fax 20-22-21340; e-mail Cortez-MAD@mcimail.com).
Island Tours & Services: Immeuble Anjarasoa, Ivandry (tel 20-22-42289; fax 20-22-42246).
Madagascar Airtours: Hilton Hotel, 33 Avenue de l'Indépendance, Antananarivo (tel 20-22-24192; fax 20-22-64190; e-mail airouts@

dts.mg/airtours).

Madagascar Discovery Agency: Route de l'Universite (tel 20-22-35165; fax 20-22-35167).

Mad'Caméléon: Lot IIK6, Ankadivato, Antananarivo (tel 20-22-63086; fax 20-22-34420).

Mercure: 17 rue Rabafiraisana Analakely, Antananarivo (tel 20-22-22961; fax 20-22-33673).

Rova Travel Tours: 35 rue Refotaka, Antananarivo (tel 20-22-27676; fax 20-22-27689).

Setam: 56 Avenue du Juin 1960, Analakely (tel 20-22-27249; fax 20-22-34702).

Silverwings: 78 rue Ranavalona III, Ambatonakanga (tel 20-22-20092; fax 20-22-20179).

Tropic Tours: 30 rue de Russie, Antananarivo (tel 20-22-29548; fax 20-22-25893).

Voyages Bourdon: 15 rue Patrice Lumumba, Tsaralalana, Antananarivo (tel 20-22-29696; fax 20-22-28564).

TOURIST INFORMATION CENTRES

La Maison du Tourisme de Madagascar: Place de l'Indépendance, Antaninarenina, PO Box 3224, Antananarivo (tel 20-22-35178; fax 20-22-69522; e-mail mtm@simicro.mg).

Ministry of Commerce and Tourism: rue Fernand Kassanga, BP 610, Tsimbazaza, Antananarivo (tel 20-22-26298; fax 20-22-26710).

FOREIGN EMBASSIES AND CONSULATES

Austria: Rue Ravonihitriniarivo (tel 20-22-22721; fax 20-22-29123).

Belgium: 19 rue Rèv Père Callet Behoririka (tel 20-22-22368).

Britain: Lot 11, 1, 164 Ter, Alarobia Amboniloha, 101 Anatananarivo (tel 20-22-449378; fax 20-22-49381; e-mail ukembant@simicro.mg).

Canada: Villa Paule II M62 Androhibe, BP 4003, Antananarivo (tel 20-22-42559; fax 20-22-42506).

France: 3 rue Jean Jaurès, Ambatomena, BP 204, Antananarivo (tel 20-22-20008; fax 20-22-25000).

Germany: 101 rue Pasteur Rabeony Hans, Ambodirotra, BP 516, Antananarivo (tel 20-22-23802; fax 20-22-26627).

Mauritius: Route Circulaire Anjahana, BP 6040, Antananarivo (tel 20-22-32157; fax 20-22-21939).

South Africa: Lot IIJ Ivandry, BP 4417 (tel 20-22-42494).

United States: 14-16 rue Rainitovo, Antsahavola, BP 620, Antananarivo (tel 20-22-21257; fax 20-22-34539).

GAY TRAVELLERS

Same gender relationships are not illegal in Madagascar unless one or other of the parties is under the age of 21. Nonetheless, open displays of homosexual behaviour will create problems for those involved. There are no recognised gay resorts or venues.

DISABLED TRAVELLERS

Madagascar can be tough territory for the traveller, and for the disabled visitor it is off-putting for all but the most dogged. This does not place it totally out of bounds, but for the foreseeable future the disabled should consider an as up-market as possible package tour, and preferably one that offers more time at the beach than one tackling the rigours of the interior.

USEFUL INFORMATION

Time Zone

Madagascar is three hours ahead of GMT, eight time zones ahead of US Eastern Standard Time, one hour ahead of Europe in summer (April to end September) and two hours in winter (October to end March), and one hour behind South African time. There is no summer/winter time change in Madagascar as the length of the day varies little throughout the tropics.

Electrical Appliances

There is no national power grid and only 10% of the country has access to electricity generated by isolated power stations, which are either hydro-powered or oil-fuelled. Where there is electricity it is 220 volts/50 cycles. Two-pin European plugs are required.

Weights and Measures

Madagascar uses the metric system, but just to spice it up even more for visitors from imperial measure countries there's also a variety of obscure Malagasy weights and measures based on ancient rice weights and modern condensed milk can volumes.

USEFUL ADDRESSES AND TELEPHONE NUMBERS

Emergency Calls:
Police Aid: tel 17.
Police Patrol: tel 20-23-80137.
Police Central: tel 20-23-22736.
Ambulances: tel 20-22-23555.
Fire Brigade: tel 18.
Centre Hospitalier de Soavinandriana: tel 20-22-40341.
Polyclinique Ilafy: (24 hours) tel 20-22-42566.
Clinique MM: (24 hours) tel 20-22-23555.
Clinique des Soeurs Franciscaines: tel 20-22-23554.
Clinique Saint-Paul: tel 20-22-27147.
Cabinet Médical & Dentaire: tel 20-22-23166.
Institut Pasteur: tel 20-22-40164.

Others
Air Madagascar: flight reconfirmation, tel 20-22-35880.
Breakdowns: Jirama, tel 20-22-23030.
Co-ordination Cell for Tourism Development (CCDT): PO Box 51, Antananarivo

(tel 20-22-22327).

Grouping of Tourism Association and Syndicates (GAST): c/o Sofitrans, 2 rue Andianampoinimerina, Antanimena, PO Box 8310, Antananarivo (tel 20-22-22330; fax 20-22-20390).

Immigration and Emigration Department: tel 20-22-26662.

Madagascar's Travel Agencies Association (AAVM): c/o Transcontinents, 10 Avenue de l'Indépendance, PO Box 541, Antananarivo (tel 20-22-22398; fax 20-22-28365).

Ministry of Foreign Affairs: tel 20-22-21198; fax 20-22-34484.

Services des Musées et Monuments Historiques (Museums and Historical Monuments Department): tel 20-22-20091.

Société pour l'Exploitation du Tourisme a Madagascar (SETAM): tel 20-22-35914/32431; fax 20-22-32435/34702.

Tourist Institutions and Associations (Professional Tour Operator Association of Madagascar): c/o Madagascar Airtours, Hilton Hotel, Anosy, Antananarivo (tel 20-22-24192; fax 20-22-25270).

World Wildlife Fund: IIM 85b, Antsakarivo, tel 20-22-34638; fax 20-22-34888.

Public Holidays

Set Dates

New Year's Day	1 January
Insurrection of 1947, or Memorial Day, or Martyr's Day	29 March
Labour Day	1 May
Independence Day	26 June
St Vincent de Paul's Day	27 September
All Saints' Day	1 November
Christmas Day	25 December
Anniversary of the Republic of Madagascar	30 December

Variable Holidays

Easter	March/April
Alahamady-Bé (Malagasy New Year)	March
Taralila (music festival)	May
Donia (traditional music festival)	June
Celebration of the Exhumation of the Dead (*Famadihana*)	July-September
Malagasy Fashion Fair	October
Gasytsara (contemporary music festival)	November/December.

SOLAR ECLIPSE 2001

If you happen to be in south-west Madagascar in the **Morombe** to **Isalo National Park** region at the end of the day on **21 June 2001** you will be ideally placed to see the first total eclipse of the sun in the new millennium, as this is the part of the island that will lie in the path of totality. The centre of the eclipse comes ashore north of the small and dusty coastal town of Morombe, 190 miles (306 km) north of Toliara. The park is a 4-5 hour drive from Toliara on the west coast. Climatological records and satellite images mark this western coastal region of Madagascar as the second best eclipse site along the track. At this time of the year rain is virtually unknown in the area and you can expect cloudless blue skies for the event, which is one of nature's most awesome phenomena. The sky will darken, the air will cool, unusual colours will bathe the dry scrub landscape and birds and animals will fall quiet. Maximum expected duration of the total eclipse is four seconds short of five minutes but people travel thousands of miles from all over the world for even such a brief experience. In Madagascar it will be of even shorter duration – around $2^1/_2$ minutes – but no less spectacular. The sun will be only 12 degrees above the horizon at totality and actually sets moments before the eclipse ends. You'll be treated to the sight of a fiery red orb with a tiny bite taken out of it, setting on the horizon in the west. A green flash might provide extra pyrotechnics. Less than 1% of the Earth's surface is usually bathed by the shadow, which most often passes over sea or uninhabited land, and only observers within this narrow band of totality will have this stunning experience. Outside the band of totality, a partial eclipse will be visible. The eclipse begins over the Atlantic Ocean, off the coast of Brazil, and its track will reach the African continent just north of Lobito Bay in Angola, before traversing Angola, Zambia, Zimbabwe, Mozambique, and Madagascar.

Total eclipses of the sun occur when the moon passes in front of it, blocking out its light for a few minutes. Although the entire eclipse can last for a couple of hours, the spectacular total phase lasts only for a few minutes. In England, for instance, the last solar eclipse was in August 1999 and the next will be in 2090. For the Earth as a whole, total solar eclipses occur roughly seven or eight times every 10 years. The path of totality is a long narrow strip, usually less than 124 miles (200 km) wide, snaking a third of the way around the globe.

Safety

It is important to remember that the sun can be viewed safely with the naked eye only during the few brief seconds or minutes of total solar eclipse (but the beginning and end of the eclispe require filtering if the sun's rays are not to damage the viewer's eyesight). The sun can be viewed directly only when using filters specifically designed for this purpose. One of the most widely available and useful filters for safe solar viewing is a number 14 welder's glass, available at welding supply outlets.

Unsafe filters include colour film, some non-silver black and white film, medical x-ray films with images on them, smoked glass, photographic neutral density filters and polarising filters.

A safe and inexpensive alternative is projection, in which a pinhole or small opening is used to cast the image of the sun on a screen placed a half-metre or more beyond the opening. Projected images of the sun may even be seen on the ground in the small openings created by interlacing fingers, or in the dappled sunlight beneath a leafy tree. Binoculars can also be used to project a magnified image of the sun on to a white card, but you must avoid the temptation of using these for direct viewing. In spite of these precautions, the total phase of an eclipse can and should be viewed without any filters whatsoever as the naked eye view of totality is completely safe and is overwhelmingly awe-inspiring.

Information excerpted from *Total Solar Eclipse of 2001 June 21* by Fred Espenak and Jay Anderson, NASA. You can browse more detailed information on website www.sunearth.gsfc.nasa.gov/eclipse/eclipse.html.

FLORA AND FAUNA

Introduction

Madagascar's fame as a Lost World of amazing birds, animals, plants and trees has been growing ever since the 13th century, when Marco Polo correctly described it as 'a large and beautiful island,' but mistakenly reported that it held more elephants than anywhere else in the world. He stretched his readers' credulity even further when he wrote that Madagascar was the home of the Griffin, or Roc, adding that 'it is not, as related, half-bird and half-lion, but rather a gigantic eagle, which covers with its wings a space of thirty paces and carries off elephants in its talons; these it drops down from a height and then feeds on the crushed flesh.'

Six centuries later people were still reading of the weird and frightful things to be found on this mysterious island continent and one that grabbed the imagination was a traveller's story of a man-eating tree, which gobbled up human sacrifices, preferably girls, offered by local tribesmen. The alleged eye-witness account which appeared in the *South Australian Register* in 1881 contained this graphic description of one sacrificial victim's last moments:

The slender delicate palpi, with the fury of starved serpents, quivered a moment over her head, than as if instinct with demoniac intelligence fastened upon her in sudden coils round and round her neck and arms; then while her awful screams and yet more awful laughter rose wildly to be instantly strangled down again into a gurgling moan, the tendrils one after another, like great green serpents, with brutal energy and infernal rapidity, rose, retracted themselves, and wrapped her about fold after fold, ever tightening with cruel swiftness and the savage tenacity of anacondas fastening upon their prey.

Even in the 20th century readers were still thrilling to pseudo-scientific studies such as the 1924 book *Madagascar, Land of the Man-Eating Tree*. Even without elephant-eating giant eagles and carnivorous trees with a preference for young girls, the flora and fauna of Madagascar is full of wonders to be found nowhere else on earth. Scale down the exaggeration and there once was a giant bird, but this, the *Aepyornis*, or flightless elephant bird, was only 10 ft (3 m) tall, and weighed less than half a ton (450 kg). It has been extinct for at least 300 years, but folk tales about it live on among the rural Malagasy, who call it *vorombe*. There is even a carnivorous plant, the pitcher plant (*Nepenthes madagascariensis*), but this is a large enough only to digest insects which venture into its inviting urn-shaped greenish-yellow flower, which is equipped with a trapdoor.

Still, for its size, the micro-continent can chalk up enough attractions to leave everywhere else on earth in the shade. The bald statistics would pall were they not a reflection of a biodiversity that, where it is not unique, is still truly exceptional. Madagascar literally teems with life forms that have changed little in hundreds of thousands, even millions of years. In many ways Madagascar is literally a land that time forgot. Think Madagascar and you think lemurs. More than 30 species are found here and nowhere else. Nearly half its nesting birds are endemic to the island, as are 95% of its 260 reptiles (compared to only six native species for the whole of the British Isles), all but two of its 150 amphibians, 59 of the world's 135 species of chameleon, from the smallest to largest, four of the five land tortoises, and somewhere between 7,300-12,000 varieties of plants, of which 80% are unique to Madagascar. By comparison the UK has about 1,750 plant species. The island also has many more species of palms (175), orchids (1,000), baobabs (7), and succulents (9), than the entire continent of Africa.

Add to all this 20,000 species of beetles, 21 species of hedgehog lookalikes known as tenrecs, the most primitive of all mammals, 3,000 species of moths and butterflies, 2,900 native to the island, 10 endemic aloes, 63 species of geckos, and four species of sea turtles and you'll have a rough idea of why Frenchman Dr Joseph Philibert Commerson wrote in 1771, 'May I announce to you that Madagascar is truly the naturalist's promised land' and why visiting scientists still get feverish with excitement. Gilding the natural lily is the fact that even in this day and age new specimens of flora and fauna are still being discovered on a regular basis. The 'fossil-fish' coelacanth is only one recent spectacular addition. In this Indian Ocean Eden the only dangerous creatures are the increasingly rare, endangered wild crocodile and a black spider with a venomous sting. Not one of the 65 known species of snakes is dangerous to humans, although the same cannot be said for the various species of sharks (*antsantsa* in Malagasy) in the offshore waters. There are only eight species of carnivores, but the largest, and most powerful predator, the *fossa*, is a cat-like animal which at most weighs 27 lb (12 kg) and is timid and harmless to humans.

The **best time** to visit Madagascar to see wildlife is from September to December, when lemurs are carrying their young, and birds are sporting their most brilliant plumage for the breeding season. The hot, rainy season from December to March is best for frogs, and orchids are in bloom throughout the island in February.

FLORA

In many ways Madagascar rivals the Amazon in its biodiversity, except that the island's unique plants and animals are concentrated in a much smaller area than those of the famed South American rainforest. Its wide range of plant species makes it one of the richest in flora in the world. The island has 191 families of plants, of which eight families are endemic. About 240 of the island's 1,300 plant genera are endemic and 26 genera are found only in Madagascar and South America, and not even in intervening Africa. Their density is such that even some individual mountain tops have 150-200 endemic plants found nowhere else on earth. About a quarter of the African continent's flowering seed-bearing plant species are endemic to Madagascar, even though its surface area covers only half that of South Africa. One reason advanced for this staggering plant diversity is the continental drift which permitted isolated Madagascar to take some strange twists and turns in its floral evolution, the other is the island's range of microclimates, each of which gives rise to a type of vegetation providing a habitat for specific families of plants and animals. There's a remarkable variety of vegetation types, ranging from humid tropical forests, where average annual rainfall is around 138 inches (3,500 mm), to arid semi-deserts that receive less than 14 inches (350 mm) a year. The high mountain range that runs down the east-centre of the island, descending sharply to the Indian Ocean, leaves only a narrow eastern coastal plain that is wet and humid. The western plain is wider and experiences mostly dry weather. The interior highlands are cold and dramatic and covered in a prairie-like carpet of green; the southern reaches of the island are characterised by semi-desert and amazing rock formations; the north-east, with its tropical climate, is covered in rainforests that lead into magnificent coral reefs.

CENTRAL MADAGASCAR

On the central plateau of the interior highlands forests have completely disappeared and where they stood there are now vast empty areas, burned to provide new pasture every year for cattle, a destructive process known in Malagasy as *tavy*, which means 'fatness.' Over the last century eucalyptus trees have been introduced in the area and these are now the primary cover of the central plateau, along with a plant originally from Mexico which the Malagasy call 'Madagascar' (*Pointsettia pulcherruna*), and which has become the island's floral emblem. Areas where it flourishes look as though they have been painted red when this plant is in full bloom. In areas around Ambatolampy and Antsirabe a species of mimosa from Australia (*Acacia dealbata*) has been planted as it is resistant to fire and a good source of fuel for heating and for making charcoal. In the Merina and Betsileo regions around the capital flowers are rare, but some ornamental succulents which do grow here, such as aloes, euphorbias, and kalanchoe, resist the annual torchings tucked in the protected recesses of the inselbergs which dot the region.

THE NORTH

The northern region, home of the Antankarana people, has seven months a year of dry weather, 90% of its rain falling between December and April. These changes in climate stimulate many varieties of flora and splendid rainforest covers the highest mountains in the area. Madagascar is famous for its unique evergreen rainforests and most of these are found on the east coast.

THE EAST

Humid tropical rainforest stretches along the lowlands and coast of the eastern region, its last stronghold. The rainforest is not the jungle of South America or South-East Asia; the trees are smaller, with a lower canopy than that of rainforests elsewhere, but it is the world's densest. The forest is shrinking rapidly because of the felling and burning off to clear for the cultivation of rice. The most typical native tree of the secondary forest which often springs up in clearance areas is the Travellers tree (*Ravenala madagascariensis*), a member of the banana family, whose distinctive fan-shaped crown of leaves is the inspiration for Madagascar's national seal and for the emblem used by Air Madagascar. The tree is not only a source of drinkable water, which can be tapped from the base of its leaf stalks, but its buds can also be made into a type of crude flour. In the north-east, on the Masoala Peninsula, two of the most biologically rich eco-systems in the world can be found, lying side by side – one of the largest remaining tracts of virgin lowland rainforest plunges almost vertically into the sea to meet a pristine coral reef.

THE WEST

The western region is characterised by wide plains, empty beaches, rolling hills and deciduous forests which harbour a wealth of rare and unusual flora. The region is largely covered by grassy savannah scattered with small trees and shrubs. Forest trees in the drier parts of the west are essentially deciduous and in the dry season of seven to eight months they tend to present a depressing shrivelled appearance. These areas are also regularly burned to clear patches for cultivation. Near Morondava are some fine examples of western dry deciduous forest, dominated by thousands of enormous baobabs (*Adansonia grandidieri*). Just north of Morondava, in the Tsingy de Bemaraha Reserve, is an area of riverine forests, towering calcareous cliffs and a great variety of succulents uniquely adapted to live in their nooks and crannies.

THE SOUTH

The southern region is the most exotic part of Madagascar. Rain seldom falls on the spiny forests and towering baobab trees which typify this area. These forests are home to thorny, water-retaining trees, plants, and shrubs, many of which are unique to Madagascar. This semi-arid region is usually referred to as spiny desert or forest because it is full of thorn bush known to the Mahafaly, Masikoro, Veso and Antandroy people who live there as *androy*. This area is a mass of twisted thorny scrub full of such drought-resistant trees as the baobab, the octopus tree (*Didiera madagascariensis*) with its writhing thorny branches, huge bloated pachypodiums, or 'elephant foot', and harpoon plants, with delicate yellow blooms, and seed capsules studded with such diabolical barbs that the desert tribes tie them to the ends of poles and use them to hook and pull down sleeping flying fox bats for the pot. Other desert plants have gone to great evolutionary lengths to protect themselves in this hostile environment, some with thorns like bodkins, while others produce a milky goo that can cause blindness if it gets in your eyes.

NOTABLE FLORA

A **baobab** specimen growing in the centre of Mahajanga, on the west coast, is believed to be 700 years old, but this is an infant with regard to the *Andansonia* species as they are known to grow to a prodigious size and survive for more than 1,000 years. Seven of the world's nine baobab species are unique to Madagascar, and the Malagasy refer to this weirdly shaped tree, which has fascinated travellers from the earliest times, as *Reniala* (mother or father of the forest). Others call them the upside down trees, and that is exactly what they appear to be, with their writhing limbs looking more like roots than branches. The pleasantly astringent fruit in their large pods is known in the West as cream-of-tartar and weight for weight the pulp has four times more vitamin C than oranges. The tart pulp can be used in several ways, but it is generally made into a porridge, mixed with milk or honey or some type of cereal. The shiny dark seeds can also be ground into meal to make porridge or used as a coffee substitute. The pulp can also be stirred into water to make a refreshing drink, not unlike sherbet, and this is a sure-fire thirst quencher for parched hikers. The young leaves are like wild spinach when cooked. Baobabs grow to an immense size and the tree is central to a lot of Malagasy activities, as its huge bulging hollow trunk makes it a good place to find and store water, to use as a handy shelter, perform tribal rituals and to bury and conduct ceremonies in memory of dead ancestors.

Mangrove trees are well represented, with nine species in three families, largely along the estuaries of the west coast where seven defined tracts cover more than 50,000 acres (20,000 ha). In all there are around 815,000 acres (330,000 ha) of mangrove swamps around the island, the largest area in all the islands of the western Indian Ocean.

For lovers of **orchids** there's a riot of more than 1,000 species to admire. You can always distinguish by their size and their colour *Cymbidiella rhodochila*, which have grouped clusters of yellow-greenish flowers marked with large green spots; *Aeranthes* have hanging inflorescences with large white flowers; but the most famous orchid is the comet orchid (*Angraecum sesquipedale*), whose creamy-white, star-like flowers are unmistakable. When Charles Darwin first saw this orchid in 1862 he postulated that somewhere on Madagascar there had to be a giant moth with an amazingly long proboscis capable of reaching the nectar at the bottom of the 14-inch (35 cm) deep flower. His prediction came true 41 years later, when a hawk moth with a nine-inch (22 cm) long proboscis was discovered feeding on the orchid. Orchid flowers are fertilised by birds or insects which sip the nectar, get dusted with pollen while enjoying it and carry the pollen spores to other flowers. In some cases only one insect species can do the task. This is the case with the vanilla orchid, except that the insect necessary for its fertilisation does not live in Madagascar, but in Mexico, from where the original plants were imported. Commercial vanilla, therefore, has to be tediously pollinated by hand.

There are 60 endemic **aloes**, with the *vaombe* one of the tallest, growing to a height of 10 ft (3 m) or more. It is found throughout the dry south, where its flowers provide a conspicuous red splash of colour in June and July what would otherwise be a monotonously arid and unrelieved landscape.

FAUNA

Many mammals familiar in other parts of the world are not found in Madagascar, because their ancestors were not on the island when it broke away from Africa millennia ago. There are, for instance, no dogs, cats, rabbits, antelope, horses, squirrels, moles, shrews, hedgehogs, monkeys, and apes, but their very absence has led to an intriguingly diverse number of species unique in every way.

LEMURS

More than any other natural attraction lemurs draw visitors from all over the world. They survive only on the island of Madagascar and on the neighbouring islands of the Comoros archipelago. Although it was once thought that lemurs were on Madagascar when the island separated from Africa, recent advances in geological science have shown that Madagascar had separated from Africa by hundreds of miles before primates evolved. This means the ancestors of Madagascar's lemurs must have rafted across from Africa on floating trees and other vegetation. Once on Madagascar, the lemur evolved into about 55 different species and sub-species. The absence of monkeys and apes gave them free range to flourish without competition. This freedom was curtailed primarily by the humans who arrived on the island less than 2,000 years ago and helped to drive an estimated 17 species of lemurs, many of them gigantic, into extinction with a variety of other animals and birds.

The species living today are small to medium-sized mammals ranging from the tiny **pygmy mouse lemur** (*Microcebus myoxinus*) which weighs about an ounce (30 g), to the largest lemurs, the baboon-sized **indri** (*Indri indri*) and the **diademed sifaka** (*Propithecus diadema diadema*) which can weigh more than 15 lb (7 kg). Lemurs spend most of their time in trees or large bushes, although the **ring-tail**, the most terrestrial of the lemurs, spends up to half of the day on the ground. Various species of lemurs can be found in habitats as different as the lush, wet, rainforest of eastern Madagascar and the arid spiny desert of the south-west. Smaller species tend to be nocturnal, while most of the larger species are active during the day. Lemurs feed primarily on leaves and fruits in the forest canopy. Insects form a large part of the diet for some nocturnal lemurs. One species of **bamboo lemur** thrives on a diet of bamboo that contains enough cyanide to kill a human being. With the exception of the tailless indri, lemurs have long furry tails, which they use for balance when leaping from tree to tree, but unlike monkeys with prehensile tails lemurs cannot hang from theirs. Generally, the behaviour of lemurs, all known as prosimians (before monkeys), is quite different from that of monkeys and apes. Lemurs tend to have longer fox-like, wet noses, whereas monkeys have flatter faces and dry noses, a difference suggesting that smell plays a greater role in prosimian behaviour than it does in the activities of monkeys, which tend to rely more on sight.

As well as being awed by the spectacular leaps lemurs make through the tree-tops, one of the most captivating sights you might be privileged to see while lemur-watching is the amazing dance of the sifakas. These beautiful animals cannot walk on all-fours and when on the ground they stand upright and prance across clearings like a perfectly timed corps de ballet. Apart from humans, lemurs have few enemies. The most dangerous natural threats come from the vicious weasel-like predator fossa and raptors such as the Madagascar harrier hawk, both of which prey on the younger and smaller lemurs. Some of the most popular places to see lemurs are the parks and reserves of Berenty, Ranomafana, Mananara, and the islands of Nosy Bé and Aye-Aye.

LEMUR SPECIES AND GENERA

AYE-AYE

(Family: Daubentoniidae. *Daubentonia madagascariensis* – Malagasy names *Hay-Hay, Ahay, Aiay*)
The aye-aye was discovered in 1774 by the visiting naturalist Sonnerat. It is

the only member of its family and for a century or more scientists argued as to whether it was even a lemur. One uncharitable description says the aye-aye seems to be made up from the spare parts of other animals, with the ears of a bat, the face of a rodent, and a long, thin, bony middle finger which it uses like a probe to find and fish out grubs hidden inside trees. The aye-aye is regarded as the most bizarre of all primates. It is also the largest nocturnal primate in the world, with a head and body 15.75 inches (40 cm), tail 16 inches (42 cm), and weighing 6.5 lb (3 kg). It has mixed short white hairs and long white-tipped black hairs also huge black ears and a pale face. It is a solitary, nocturnal forager eating insect larvae, the interior of the ramy nut, nectar and fungi, spending up to 80% of the night travelling and feeding. They spend most of their time in the trees although travelling on the ground is not uncommon. Aye-aye sleep in nests in trees during the day and spend most of their lives alone. The only social interactions occur during courtship, breeding can occur at any time of the year, and when an infant is dependent on its mother. During these interactions, females are considered to be dominant over males, giving them preferential access to food. Female dominance in primates is unique to prosimians.

A large percentage of the aye-aye's diet consists of insect larvae found inside dead wood. The animals find the larvae by tapping on branches and listening to the reverberations through the wood. When they find a gap or crack in the wood they bite through the outer layers of bark with their razor-sharp teeth and stick their long, bony finger inside the hole to pull out juicy grubs and other prey.

Aye-aye are very sparsely distributed along the east coast and in the north-western forests. The main threats to their survival are loss of habitat and hunting. Unlike many lemur species that are hunted for food, aye-aye are killed as a pest on farms or because their strange appearance makes many Malagasy believe they are an omen of evil (or *fady* in Malagasy). They are found in at least 16 protected areas, and several of these locations appear to have healthy populations.

SIFAKAS

(Family: Indriidae. *Propithecus*)
The sifakas of Madagascar are distinguished from all other lemurs by their mode of locomotion: they maintain a distinctly vertical posture and leap through the trees using the strength of their back legs. They are all relatively large-bodied, with short faces and extremely long legs which enable some species to clear as much as 33 ft (10 m) in one leap. There are three recognised species, as well as several subspecies.

Golden-crowned sifaka

(*Propithecus tattersalli* – Malagasy names *Ankomba Malandy, Simpona*) Coat is mostly white, with a cap of golden fur between the ears. The face is black with some whitish hairs, and the ears are prominent and tufted. Body is 20 inches (50 cm) long, tail 16 inches (40 cm), and it weighs 8 lb (3.5 kg). Their habitat is dry deciduous and semi-evergreen forest. They eat seeds, unripe fruit, young and mature leaves and flowers. Golden-crowned sifaka have a very restricted distribution. This species is limited to forest patches between the

Loky and Manambato rivers in north-eastern Madagascar. The golden-crowned sifaka is probably one of the most endangered lemurs in Madagascar. It has one of the smallest ranges and documented population sizes of any lemur. It is not found in any protected area, and its unprotected habitat is rapidly being cleared for agriculture. Gold has recently been discovered within their small habitat range and the influx of miners threatens the species even more by destroying the remaining habitat; the hunting of the animals of the region for food is another growing danger.

The four sub-species of *Propithecus verreauxi* are: Coquerel's sifaka (*Propithecus verreauxi coquereli*), Verreaux's sifaka (*Propithecus verreauxi verreauxi*), the crowned sifaka (*Propithecus verreauxi coronatus*), and Decken's sifaka (*Propithecus verreauxi deckeni*).

Coquerel's sifaka

(Malagasy names *Tsibahaka, Sifaka, Ankomba Malandy*) Coat is mostly white to off-white, with large maroon patches on the chest and fronts of thighs and forelimbs. Ears are hairless and small, but quite visible. There are no distinct colour differences between males and females. Body 16.5-18 inches (42-45 cm), tail 22-24 inches (55-60 cm), weight 8-8.5 lb (3.75 kg). Their habitat is mixed deciduous and evergreen forests and their diet combines young leaves, flowers, fruit, bark and dead wood in the wet season, mature leaves and buds in the dry. Coquerel's sifaka is found throughout the forested areas of north-western Madagascar to the north and east of the Betsiboka River.

Verreaux's sifaka

Verreaux's sifaka is seriously endangered. Their habitat is in the rain and dry forests and diet consists of leaves, buds, blooms, fruit. They do not drink. The main threat to their survival is habitat destruction. The sub-species is found in only two protected areas in Madagascar and these have been damaged by tree-cutting for charcoal and by the fires set every year to encourage the growth of new grass for livestock.

Diademed sifaka

One member of the four sub-species of *Propithecus diadema* is the Diademed sifaka (Malagasy names *Ankomba Malandy, Simpona*). Coat is primarily long white fur, but the back of the neck and top of the head are black. The hindquarters and limbs are light golden, and the hands and feet are black. Body 21 inches (52 cm), tail 18 inches (46.5 cm), weight 13-16 lb (6-7.25 kg). Their habitat is rainforest and their diet is principally leaves, flowers and fruit. This sifaka can be found in the eastern rainforest, north from the Mangoro River to below the Antainambalana River. They are threatened by the destruction of their habitat through agricultural clearance and timber felling, and are hunted for food throughout much of their range. This sub-species can be found in several protected areas in Madagascar. Others in the sub-species are the silky sifaka (*Propithecus diadema candidus*), Milne-Edward's sifaka (*Propithecus diadema edwardsi*), and Perrier's sifaka (*Propithecus diadema perrieri*).

Indri

Also a member of the family is the Indri (*Indri indri*) species (Malagasy name *Babakoto*). They are like the sifakas in form, but are larger and have only a stump of a tail. They are found in the northern half of eastern Madagascar, from Masora River in south to Vohemar in north in mountains to 5,906 ft (1,800 m) and upwards. They eat leaves, shoots, and fruit. On the ground and when climbing they usually stay upright.

Avahi

Of the Avahi genus in this same family are the sub-species eastern avahi (*Avahi laniger*), which live in eastern Madagascar from Vohemar in the north to Taolagnaro in the south, as well as north-west Madagascar from Bombetopa Bay northwards to the region of the Ambre mountains. Their habitat is mountain rainforest and their diet consists of leaves, buds, bark, and fruit. The other is the western avahi (*Avahi occidentalis*).

MOUSE LEMURS

(Family: Cheirogaleidae. *Microcebus*)
There are four species – grey mouse lemur (*Microcebus murinus*), brown mouse lemur (*Microcebus rufus*), pygmy mouse lemur (*Microcebus myoxinus*), and golden-brown mouse lemur (*Microcebus rufus*). Grey mouse lemurs live in the rainforest, dry forest, and bushy woodlands (also in small isolated patches of forest) in the coastal regions. They eat small, sweet fruits, leaves, flowers and insects. In this family is the hairy-eared dwarf lemur (*Allocebus trichotis*), which is found in eastern Madagascar. Up to now only four of these animals have been seen. Also found in eastern Madagascar and of the same family is the greater dwarf lemur (*Cheirogaleus major*), which lives in the rainforest, eating fruit, flowers, insects, small vertebrates, and perhaps young nestling birds. The endangered fat-tailed dwarf lemur (*Cheirogaleus medius*) is found in the coastal areas of western Madagascar but is uncommon, and Coquerel's dwarf lemur (*Mirza coquereli)* can be seen in the Sambirano region, Kirindy forest, and near Ambanja in the north-west. Another species of this family is the forkmarked lemur *(Phaner furcifer)*, which is found in western Madagascar north of Onihaly and Fiherenana Rivers, up to the northern tip, Ambre Mountain, as well as the north-east, and the Masoala Peninsula north of Antongil Bay. Their habitat is moist, dry, secondary or gallery forests and their diet consists of fruit, leaves, and flowers. The nectar, sap of trees, and the juicy secretions of plant aphids, as well as other insects are especially favoured. The four sub-species are the eastern fork-marked lemur (*Phaner furcifer furcifer*), the pale fork-marked lemur (*Phaner furcifer pallescens*), Pariente's fork-marked lemur (*Phaner furcifer parienti*), and the Amber mountain fork-marked lemur (*Phaner furcifer electromontis*).

BAMBOO LEMURS

(Family: Lemuridae. Malagasy names *Bokombolo, Kotrika*)
There are three recognised species of bamboo lemurs: the grey bamboo lemurs (*Hapalemur griseus*), the greater bamboo lemur (*Hapalemur simus*), and the golden bamboo lemur (*Hapalemur aureus*). Grey bamboo lemurs come in three

sub-species: eastern grey bamboo lemur (*Hapalemur griseus griseus*), western grey bamboo lemur (*Hapalemur occidentalis*), and the Lac Alaotra bamboo lemur (*Hapalemur alaotrensis*). They are all about the same size, with a body 11 inches (28 cm) long, a tail of 14.5 inches (37 cm), and weigh 1.5-2.2 lb (700g-1 kg). Both sexes have a grey coat with a reddish head. The muzzle of these lemurs is noticeably shorter than that of other lemurs. They live in sociable group densities of 2-6 animals. Within the group females are dominant, which gives them preferential access to food and the choice of mates. Most prosimians have six lower teeth that stick straight out from the lower jaw, forming a dental comb the animals use to groom themselves and the fur of other members of their social group and social bonds within the group are established and reinforced by such grooming. Habitat is various types of eastern forest, usually in association with bamboo and bamboo vines. They eat mostly bamboo, primarily new shoots and leaf bases. Supplemental food sources are fig leaves, grass stems, young leaves and small fruit. In the wild, female eastern lesser bamboo lemurs give birth to one offspring in the late autumn to early winter. Infants are carried on their mother's back soon after birth and may be 'parked' for short periods of time. Females also transport very young animals in their mouths and males in captivity have also been seen carrying infants. Eastern lesser bamboo lemurs are found throughout all remaining eastern forests from the Tsaratanana Massif in the north to Taolagnaro in the south.

Lake Alaotra Bamboo Lemurs

(Malagasy name *Bandro*) This sub-species is restricted to the reedbeds of Lake Alaotra, where it eats leaves and shoots of the reed *Phragmites communis* (a type of Malagasy bamboo). Locomotion is vertical clinging and leaping, and it is possible that this sub-species is capable of swimming. Body 15 inches (40 cm), tail 15 inches (40 cm), weight 2.2 lb (1 kg). Both sexes have a dark grey coat. The snout of these animals is noticeably shorter than that of most other lemurs. Lake Alaotra bamboo lemurs are restricted to the reedbeds of Alaotra, the largest lake in Madagascar, and its extremely restricted range makes it vulnerable to any habitat disturbance. Unfortunately, this region is the largest area in Madagascar devoted to rice cultivation and much of the lake margin has been converted to rice paddies. The reedbeds crucial to the survival of these animals are frequently harvested for the manufacture of mats, fish traps, screens, barriers and fencing. Additionally, Lake Alaotra bamboo lemurs are under considerable pressure from hunting for both food and the pet trade. None of the area surrounding Lake Alaotra is protected.

RING-TAILED LEMURS

(*Lemur catta* – Malagasy names *Maki, Hira*) Ring-tailed lemurs are classified in their own genus, but there is considerable debate about their relationship to the members of the *Eulemur* and *Hapalemur* genera. Head and body 17 inches (42.5 cm), tail 24 inches (60 cm), weighs 6.5-7.75 lb (3-3.5 kg). Ring-tailed lemur backs are grey to rosy brown, limbs and haunches are grey, and their heads and neck are dark grey. Their undersides are white, and their faces are white with dark triangular eye patches and black noses. Tails are ringed with 13 alternating black and white bands, which give this lemur its common name.

Habitat is arid, open areas and forests. They spend a lot of time on the ground. They eat fruit, leaves, flowers, herbs, and other plant parts, occasional insects and small vertebrates. Ring-tailed lemurs are found in south and south-western Madagascar, from Taolagnaro west and as far north as Morondava on the west coast. A small additional population lives near the mountains of Andringitra on the south-western plateau. The gallery forests that ring-tailed lemurs prefer are rapidly being converted to farmland overgrazed by livestock and felled to make charcoal. Ring-tailed lemurs are also hunted for food in certain areas and are frequently kept as pets. Fortunately, ring-tails are found in several protected areas in southern Madagascar, but the level of protection varies widely in these areas, offering only some populations protection from hunting and habitat loss.

BLACK LEMURS

(*Eulemur macaco* – Malagasy names *Ankomba, Komba*) These lemurs come in two sub-species which are very similar in shape, size and behaviour, but occupy different habitats and have different coloured coats and eyes. They are the black lemur (*Eulemur macaco macaco*) and the blue-eyed black lemur (*Eulemur macaco flavifrons*). Body length in both lemurs is 16 inches (41 cm), tail 22 inches (55 cm), weight 5 lb (2.4 kg). Although the males are also black, female blue-eyed lemurs are markedly different in colour from female black lemurs. Male black lemurs are completely black; females have brownish-grey backs, off-white stomachs, and black faces. Both sexes have long ear tufts that are black in males and white in females. Habitat is undisturbed forest, secondary forest, timber plantations and disturbed forests, intermingled with coffee and cashew trees. They eat ripe fruit, leaves, flowers and, occasionally, insects. Black lemurs have not been studied extensively in the wild. Females are dominant, giving them preferential access to food and the choice of mates. Black lemur groups maintain separate home ranges during the day, but several groups may congregate at night. Black lemurs are found in the north-west corner of Madagascar, including the islands of Nosy Bé and Nosy Komba.

Blue-eyed Black Lemurs

(Malagasy names *Ankomba, Ankomba Joby, Ankomba Mena*) All blue-eyed lemurs have blue eyes, something not seen in any other primate except humans, and live in dry western forests and coffee and citrus plantantions with adjacent dry forest patches. They eat ripe fruit, leaves, flowers, and occasionally, insects. Blue-eyed lemurs are found south of the Sambirano in north-west Madagascar, south of the Andranomalaza River near Moromandia, and south to the Sandrakota River near Befotaka. Blue-eyed lemurs are not found in any protected areas in Madagascar, and they are severely threatened by hunting, trapping and forest destruction across their entire range.

BROWN LEMURS

(*Eulemur fulvus*) There are currently six sub-species of brown lemur: the common brown lemur (*Eulemur fulvus fulvus*), the white-fronted lemur (*Eulemur fulvus albifrons)*, the collared brown lemur *(Eulemur fulvus collaris)*, the red-fronted lemur *(Eulemur fulvus rufus)*, Sanford's lemur *(Eulemur fulvus sanfordi*), and the white-collared brown lemur (*Eulemur fulvus albocollaris*). All sub-species of brown lemur can interbreed, but geographical isolation of sub-species in the wild prevents this. All brown lemurs are similar in body size and life history but have different coat markings and coloration, especially the males.

Common Brown Lemurs

(Malagasy names *Varika, Varikosy, Dredrika*) Both males and females are brown to dark-grey with light beards and dark faces. Body 20 inches (50 cm), tail 20 inches (50 cm), weight 5.75 lb (2.6 kg). Their habitat is in stands of scattered forest in the high plateaux. They eat mostly fruit, young leaves and flowers. Social groups will often break into sub-groups throughout the day and come back together at night. Unlike many prosimians, brown lemurs do not show marked female dominance. Common brown lemurs are found in western Madagascar north of the Betsiboka River. Forest destruction is the primary threat to their survival, and they are also hunted throughout much of their range. This sub-species is found in several protected areas in Madagascar.

White-fronted lemurs

(Malagasy name *Varika*) In colour they are generally dark brown with a lighter underside. Males have a white or cream-coloured head, ears and beard. Body is 15.5 inches (40 cm), tail over 20 inches (50 cm), weight 5.5 lb (2.3 kg). Their habitat is rainforest patches. They eat mostly fruit, young leaves and flowers. White-fronted lemurs are found throughout most of the remaining north-eastern rainforest. The main threat to their survival is the destruction of Madagascar's eastern rainforest for slash-and-burn agriculture. It is also hunted for food throughout most of its range. It currently occurs in several protected areas in Madagascar, including the conservation centre at Ivoloina, near Toamasina.

Collared Lemurs

(Malagasy name *Varika*) Males are brownish-grey with a dark stripe down the back, a dark tail and tail tip, and a lighter underside. Females have a reddish to brown coat and grey face. Both sexes have a distinct beard that is reddish-brown in females and cream to reddish-brown in males. Body is inches (50 cm), tail 20 inches (50 cm), weight 5.75 lb (2.6 kg). Their habitat is scattered forest areas of the high plateaux. They eat mostly fruit, young leaves and flowers. Collared lemurs are found in south-eastern Madagascar from the Mananara River, near Vangaindrano, south to Taolagnaro. Forest destruction is the primary threat to their survival, but they are also hunted for food and are being trapped for the pet trade.

Red-fronted Lemurs

(Malagasy names *Varika, Varikamavo*) Males are grey to grey-brown, females are reddish-brown. Both sexes have pale patches over their eyes, and the males have a reddish crown. Body is 16 inches (40 cm), tail 22 inches (55 cm), weight 6 lb (2.7 kg). Their habitat is deciduous forests where they eat leaves, stems, flowers, bark and sap of the *kily* tree (*Tamarindus indica*).

Red-fronted lemurs are found in the wild in western and eastern Madagascar. There is also a small introduced population in the Berenty Reserve. Forest destruction is the primary threat to the survival of red-fronted lemurs. In the west, forests are being cleared for pasture, while in the east, they are destroyed for slash-and-burn agriculture and cut down for charcoal production. Red-fronted lemurs are found in several protected areas in Madagascar, and may be one of the better protected sub-species of brown lemur.

Sanford's Lemurs

(Malagasy names *Ankomba, Baharavoaka*) Both sexes are dark brown with a lighter underside. Males have white-reddish ear tufts and thick beards giving the animals a ragged mane around their faces. Noses, snouts and the area between the eyes are black, and the head is dominated by a dark T that connects the eyes and nose. Body is 16 inches (40 cm), tail about 20 inches (50 cm), weight 5 lb (2.3 kg). Their habitat is secondary forest. They primarily eat fruit, occasional plant parts and invertebrates. Sanford's lemurs have a very restricted range in northern Madagascar, ranging from the Ampasindava Peninsula south to the Mahavavy River in the west and the Manambato River in the east.

CROWNED LEMURS

(*Eulemur coronatus* – Malagasy names *Ankomba, Gidro*) Crowned lemurs have an orange V-shaped pattern on the top of their heads, giving the species its common name. Males are dark brown-grey with a dark tail, grey face and black nose. Females are distinctly lighter in colour with mostly grey hair fading to off-white on their bellies. Head and body is 13 inches (34 cm), tail 18 inches (45 cm), weight 4.5 lb (2 kg). Their habitat is dry to moist forest. They eat fruit, young leaves, flowers, pollen and, occasionally, insects. Larger groups will often split into smaller foraging groups of one to four animals. These sub-groups maintain contact with one another vocally. Crowned lemurs are found from the extreme north, on the Cap d'Ambre Peninsula, and south-west to Ambilobe. Crowned lemurs are under threat from poaching, brush fires and logging throughout most of their habitat. The species is found in several national parks and reserves in Madagascar, but they appear to offer little if any protection for these endangered animals.

RED-BELLIED LEMURS

(*Eulemur rubriventer* – Malagasy names *Tongona, Soamiera, Barimas*) Coats are a dark chestnut brown ending in a black tail. Male undersides are reddish-brown, while female undersides are cream-white. Males can be further distinguished by the dramatic white 'teardrops' under their eyes. These lemurs have a head and body 15 inches (40 cm), tail 20 inches (50 cm), and weigh 4.5 lb (2 kg). Their habitat is middle to high altitude rainforests and they eat fruit, flowers, and leaves of a wide variety of plant species. They occur at low densities throughout the forested eastern escarpment and suffer primarily from the destruction of the eastern rainforests. This species can be found in several protected areas in Madagascar, with the largest known population in Ranomafana National Park. The red-bellied lemur is one of the only monogamous lemur species.

MONGOOSE LEMURS

(*Eulemur mongoz* – Malagasy names *Ankomba, Gidro*) Although this species is protected, it is hunted extensively for food and the pet trade. Females have grey heads, forelimbs and shoulders, with a dark back and a white beard. Males are generally darker with a reddish-brown beard. Head and body is 13 inches (35 cm), tail 19 inches (48 cm), weight 4.5 lb (2 kg). Their habitat is dry deciduous forests. They eat flowers (especially pollen), fruit and leaves. Groups typically occupy small home ranges which often overlap with the those of neighbouring groups. Mongoose lemurs are found in the north-western part of Madagascar and are found in only one protected area, which is being cleared for crops, pasture, and charcoal production.

RUFFED LEMURS

(*Varecia variegata*) Ruffed lemurs come in two sub-species: black and white ruffed lemurs (*Varecia variegata variegata*) and red ruffed lemurs (*Varecia variegata rubra*). The two sub-species are very similar in shape, size and behaviour, but are different in colour and habitat. Black and white ruffed lemurs have a black tail, a black face and white patched body, and a white ruff around their faces; red ruffed lemurs have a black tail, face and hands, a reddish-brown body, and a white patch between their shoulders. Body is 22 inches (55 cm), tail 24 inches (60 cm), weight 8-10 lb (3.5-4.5 kg). Their habitat is rainforest. Diet is entirely vegetarian, mainly fruit, leaves, nectar and seeds. Ruffed lemurs have an elaborate system of alarm calls that alert group members to danger from predators. As many as 12 different calls have been recorded at the Duke University Primate Center, in North Carolina, and they seem to vary with the location of the source of danger: in the trees, in the air, or on the ground. Natural predators that can trigger alarms include boa constrictors, eagles and hawks, and the weasel-like predator fossa. Black and white ruffed lemurs live in the eastern rainforests of Madagascar and are found up to 3,900 ft (1,200 m) above sea level. Black and white ruffed lemur populations are rapidly disappearing with the loss of habitat. They are also heavily hunted and trapped for food. Black and white ruffed lemurs are currently found in several protected areas in Madagascar. Red ruffed lemurs are restricted to the forests of the Masoala Peninsula in the north-east. They have been seen east of the Antainambalana River, which divides their range from that of the black and white ruffed lemurs. Deforestation in this region is a major threat to the survival of red ruffed lemurs, and the hunting and trapping of these animals for food has dramatically reduced their numbers.

FAMILY: MEGALADAPIDAE

Seven species belong to this family. They are the grey-backed sportive lemur (*Lepilemur doralis*), red-tailed sportive lemur (*Lepilemur ruficaudatus*), Milne-Edward's sportive lemur (*Lepilemur edwardsi*), white-footed sportive lemur (*Lepilemur leucopus*), weasel sportive lemur (*Lepilemur mustelinus*), small-toothed sportive lemur (*Lepilemur microdon*), and the northern sportive lemur (*Lepilemur septentrionalis*). They are exclusively nocturnal lemurs and are found in the rain and dry forests of Madagascar. They eat mainly leaves and bark, flowers and fruit.

CHAMELEONS

After lemurs, most people find chameleons the most interesting of Madagascar's varied creatures and the island is home to 55 of the world's 135 species. Chameleons are lizards and in Madagascar range in size from the giant Oustalet's chameleon (*Chamaeleo oustaleti*), which can grow to 27 inches (68 cm) in length, and Parson's chameleon (*Chamaeleo parsonii*) which can reach 24 inches (60 cm), down to the diminutive stumptailed chameleon (*Brookesia minima*), which at around an inch (2.5 cm) is the world's smallest chameleon. Malagasy people of the north believe that if you inflict an injury on a tiny *Brookesia* chameleon the same fate will quickly overtake you. Aristotle has a lot to answer for, not least the fact that most people believe his theory that chameleons always match their colour to their background. Their colour changes, in fact, are not used as camouflage, but to make them more conspicuous so that they can communicate for species and gender recognition and to advertise feelings such as reptilian anger and sexuality. Madagascar's panther chameleon (*Chamaeleo pardalis*), for instance, can change in seconds from shades of green to lemon and lime daubed with bright scarlet. This is one of the most hostile and territorial of the island chameleons, which explains their common name. It is also the most common and conspicuous chameleon and is found in resort areas such as Nosy Bé and along the east and northern coasts. Most of Madagascar's chameleons belong to the genus *Chamaeleo*, but about one-fifth are *Brookesia* or *Rhampholeon*, which are also known as stumptailed or leaf chameleons. Chameleons have the poorest hearing of all reptiles and don't respond to tones much above middle C. One expert says that if they listened to music, they would probably favour works for the tuba. Unable to hear, smell or run down prey – they cover less than 20 feet (6 m) a minute – they depend on their miraculous eyes and tongue when looking for food. Each eye can swivel 180 degrees and operates independently. No other animal has this advantage of seeing to the side and behind at the same time. The tongue can extend with astonishing speed up to one and a half body lengths, and a tongue of 5 1/2 inch (14 cm) zaps out its full length in one-sixteenth of a second and can pull in about half its owner's body weight. Throughout Madagascar it is taboo to kill a chameleon and drivers will risk life and limb to avoid running over a chameleon dawdling across the road. If you want to know more about these fascinating creatures we can recommend *Chameleons: Nature's Masters of Disguise*, by James Martin (Blandford, London 1992).

BATS

There are about 28 species of **bats** on the island, some with a wing span of more than three feet (1 m). Nine of these bats are endemic, including the largest species, the fruit-eating flying fox (*Pteropus rufus*) group, and a poorly known species from an endemic family of sucker-footed bats, the *Myzopodidae*. Bats in their untold millions are found in the caves of the limestone pinnacle fortress of Ankarana.

SMALL MAMMALS

Tenrecs

The island is unusually rich in spiny tenrecs, small primitive insectivorous mammals that occupy the niches of the missing shrews and moles. The smallest tenrec (*Microgale cowani*) is just over 2 inches (5 cm) long and the biggest species is the common tenrec (*Tenrec ecaudatus*) which weighs in at around 3.3 lb (1.5 kg). This tenrec is found all over the island and is regarded as one of Madagascar's most successful indigenous mammals. It is also the one most favoured for the pot. There are about 30 species, all of which are endemic.

Rodents

Madagascar has only 11 species of **rodents**, all of them endemic. All members of this species are rare, with the most interesting being the highly endangered giant jumping rat (*Hypogeomys antimena*). This reaches 3 lb (1.2 kg) and looks more like a rabbit than a rat. It is found only in a small area of western deciduous forest north of Morondava. When chased, the jumping rat hops like a kangaroo, although it normally moves on all fours. The brown rat of Europe *(Rattus rattus)* has, unfortunately, also found a secure niche for itself since it was introduced by visiting ships.

Carnivores

All eight species of **carnivores** are endemic. These include the striped civet and six species of mongoose. One of the most interesting carnivores is the island's largest predator, the agile fossa (*Cryptoprocta ferox*), which looks like a giant weasel. It hunts on the ground and in the forest canopy and is the main natural enemy of the lemurs.

REPTILES

There are about 257 species of reptiles (only six species in the UK) and more than 90% of them are unique to the island. There are 48 species of **skinks**, 47 of which are endemic; and 12 species of girdle-tailed **lizards**, 11 of these are endemic.

Geckos

There are 63 species of **geckos**, 53 of which are endemic. One of these, the Madagascar leaf-tailed gecko (*Uroplatus spp*), is an outstanding expert at natural camouflage. It is often found in the reptile parks of zoos. The Madagascar ground gecko (*Paroedura pictus*) has unfortunately become popular in the pet trade.

Crocodiles

The **Nile crocodile** (*Crocodylus niloticus*) is Madagascar's largest reptile. It is under serious threat and is more likely to be seen as a handbag or a belt than in the wild.

Turtles

Four species of **marine turtles** nest on the island beaches. The declining green turtle (*Chelonia mydas*) suffers from making an agreeable meal for Malagasy villagers and the more common hawksbill turtle (*Eretmochelys imbricata*) is hunted for its beautiful amber-coloured carapace. Their numbers are reduced by several thousand every year, even though both turtles are officially protected. Small numbers of loggerheads (*Caretta caretta*) nest and the olive ridley turtle (*Lepidochelys olivacea*) is also believed to breed occasionally in the north-west. The luth or leatherback turtle (*Dermochelys coriacea*) is a vagrant in local waters. There are five species of land **tortoises**, four of which are endemic. Two species, the ploughshare tortoise (*Geochelone yniphora*) and the radiated tortoise (*Geochelone radiata)*, are being hauled back from the brink of extinction by captive breeding projects.

Snakes

Not one of Madagascar's 60 or more species of **snakes** is poisonous. With its closest relatives in South America, the elegant constrictor boa appears once again to demonstrate the link between these two land masses from the time they were both part of ancient Gondwanaland.

OTHERS

Amphibians

While there are no newts, salamanders, toads, or the blind, legless burrowing amphibians known as caecilians, there are at least 170 species of **frogs**, all but two of them endemics. These are found mainly in the eastern forests, and 40 have been discovered since 1970. New species are still regularly being found. At Périnet in the Andasibe National Park alone, 50 species of frogs have been identified. Madagascar has a mind-boggling host of invertebrate fauna.

Insects

Nobody really knows how many **beetle** species there are on Madagascar, although they are estimated at around 20,000. One of the most commonly seen insects is the giraffe-necked weevil, which can often be spotted sitting on leaves in clearings and at the roadside in the forests of the east. Only the males have the spectacularly long necks which give both sexes their common name. There are good descriptions and extraordinary photographs of these and many otherwise unimaginable **insects** and **spiders** in Ken Preston-Mafham's book *Madagascar, A Natural History*.

BIRD-WATCHING

There are many spectacular birds to draw twitchers to Madagascar, but one you'll never be able to tick off on your spotting list is the elephant bird. This was a gigantic flightless bird that at 1,000 lb (450 kg) was the heaviest bird the earth has ever known. It was also a lofty 10 ft (3 m) tall and one of its 27 lb (12 kg) eggs was the equivalent of 180 chicken eggs. It became extinct about 300 years ago. Really keen birders can see the only complete skeleton of this monster bird (*Aepyornis maximus*) and its egg in an Antananarivo museum, the Musée de l'Académie Malgache, in the grounds of the National Botanical Gardens at Parc Tsimbazaza. Still alive and relatively well are around 250 species of birds, of which 197 are resident breeders. This is quite a small number for a tropical country, but what they lack in numbers they more than make up for in colourful and rare species – and more are still being discovered. Between 1994 and 1998 field studies conducted on the island found that there were actually at least 10 more species unique to Madagascar than previously thought. A new vanga was identified in the south-west in 1996 at the Beza-Mahafaly Special Reserve. Three of the world's most endangered birds of prey exist on Madagascar – the Madagascar serpent eagle, Madagascar red owl and Madagascar fish eagle, now at around 80 breeding pairs – the first two only recently rediscovered by Peregrine Fund biologists after a hiatus of six decades. There are other rarities on Madagascar, including one which is regarded as among the rarest on earth, the white-breasted mesite (*Mesitornis variegata*). It was first spotted in 1834, though the twitcher who made the discovery didn't record the exact site and nearly a century passed before another one was identified in the forest at Ankarafantsika.

Five bird families are found only in Madagascar and in the nearby Comoros islands. These are the primitive mesites and beautiful ground-rollers which potter about on the forest floor, the cuckoo roller, the asity (false sunbird) and the 15-member species of vangas. The couas, relatives of the cuckoo and the African coucal, form a sub-family endemic to Madagascar. Some of the most colourful island birds are also among the most common, such as the red fody (*Foudia madagascariensis*) and the olive bee-eater (*Merops superciliosus*). Among the perching species (passerines) the Madagascar bulbul (*Hypsipetes madagascariensis*) is a bird you'll see virtually everywhere, as it's found in every kind of habitat. A surprising number of island birds are tame and thrushes of the family *Turdidae* are, headed by the bold Madagascar magpie robin (*Copsychus albospecularis*), among the tamest of all species on the island. The male red fody tops the designer list as the most flamboyantly plumaged of Madagascar's birds. The crested drongo (*Dicrurus forficatus*) is the most easily recognised bird in Madagascar and the subject of Malagasy folk tales. Woodpeckers (*Picidae*) and the barbets (*Capitonidae*) never made it from Africa across the Mozambique Channel to Madagascar. Their niches have been taken in the island's avifauna by birds such as the sicklebill vanga and the coral-billed nuthatch vanga. All three island species of parrot are endemic, and thrive more or less everywhere. The lesser vasa parrot (*Coracopsis vasa*) is so populous it's even on the government's pest list. Madagascar has only 16 species of birds of prey (raptors) but 11 of these are unique to the island. The Madagascar kestrel (*Falco newtoni*) is the most common raptor. The Madagascar fish eagle (*Haliaeetus vociferoides*) is still one of the rarest raptors in the world and the Madagascar serpent eagle (*Eutriorchis astur*) has only recently come back to life in birding terms. In 1988, a party of British ornithologists checking out the birds of the Marojejy massif spotted one of these large eagles after the species had not been detected for more than 50 years. There are six species of owls, four of which are endemic. The rarest is the Madagascar red owl *(Tyto soumangei)*. Common ones are the barn owl *(Tyto alba)* and the marsh owl *(Asio capensis)*. The much smaller Madagascar Scops owl *(Otus rutilus)* is widely distributed both in primary and in degraded forest areas. Game birds such as sandgrouse, ground partridges and quails are not well represented, with only nine species, but those that are present on the island are usually plentiful and easily seen. Five of them are endemics. Madagascar is relatively well off for ducks and wading birds, with 58 species of waterbirds.

The most popular birding spot is the reserve still commonly known as **Périnet** or Analamazoatra although it has been incorporated along with Mantadia into Andasibe National Park. This is a three-hour drive east of Antananarivo. It shelters more than 110 species, including many endemics such as the Madagascar crested ibis, blue coua, velvet asity, sunbird asity, wedge-tailed jery, nuthatch vanga, and tylas. North, within **Mantadia**, are rare endemics, such as the brown mesite, red-breasted coua, red owl, scaly ground-roller and helmet vanga. Madagascar little grebes breed here and can be seen all year round. Others are the Madagascar squacco (pond) heron, the cryptic warbler and short-legged and pitta-like ground-rollers, the dusky greenbul and the red-breasted coua. Some 109 bird species have been recorded at Périnet, including such rarities as the brown mesite *(Mesitornis unicolor)*, the slender-billed flufftail *(Sarothrurus watersi)* and the Madagascar red owl.

Ranomafana National Park is the place for ground-rollers. The pitta-like ground-roller is common and rufous-headed and short-legged ground-rollers are also possible sightings, the grey-headed greenbul, brown emutail, yellow-browed oxylabes, forest rock thrush and Pollen's vanga are easily spotted. There have also been sightings of the rare Madagascar serpent eagle and yellow-bellied sunbird-asity. Marsh areas of the forest shelter the elusive Madagascar snipe and the grey emutail. The bird species identified at Ranomafana have almost reached a hundred species and four species of ground-rollers, including the rare short-legged ground-roller *(Brachypteracias leptosomus)* and the rufous-headed ground-roller *(Atelornis crossleyi)*, can be seen. Pollen's vanga *(Xenopirostris polleni)* and the brown mesite are also resident. Inside the rainforest look for Henst's goshawk, brown mesite, Madagascar woodrail, blue coua, short-legged, pitta-like and rufous-headed ground-rollers, brown emutail, yellow-browed oxylabes and Pollen's and Tylas vangas. Privately owned **Berenty Reserve** two hours' drive west of Taolagnaro (Fort Dauphin) has some species restricted to sub-arid thorn scrub, among them running coua and sub-desert brush-warbler. You can also expect to see the Madagascar sparrow hawk, giant coua, white-browed owl and the Madagascar Scops owl. Humblot's heron is not unusual on the Mandrare River bordering the reserve. In all, about 100 bird species have been recorded here. At **Ifaty**, about 17 miles (28 km) north of Toliara, is an arid spiny forest area which is the only place where the sub-desert mesite and the long-tailed ground-roller are common. You can also probably tick off banded kestrel, running coua, Thamnornis warbler, Archbold's newtonia, sickle-billed vanga, and sub-desert brush warbler. Also in the Toliara region is Saint Augustine, where you might see such local endemics as Verreaux's coua and the sub-desert brush warbler in the thorn scrub of the hills, and the sub-desert rock thrush in the scrub of the coastal dunes. At the flat-topped hill, appropriately known as La Table, you might be lucky enough to see the recently discovered red-shouldered vanga.

A three-hour drive from the west coast city of Mahajanga is the Ampijoroa forest station area, next to the tightly controlled Ankarafantsika Strict Nature Reserve, which is a rewarding spot for Humblot's heron, Madagascar jacana, and Bernier's teal. In the most humid part of the forest you can see white-breasted mesite and Schlegel's asity. The drier sandy areas are home to white-breasted mesite and to the very localised Van Dam's vanga. Ampijoroa endemics include Coquerel's and red-capped couas, Madagascar pygmy kingfisher, and rufous vanga. Ampijoroa's birdlife is rich and varied, with 101 species recorded. The rainforest of **Montagne d'Ambre National Park**, 16 miles (25 km) south of Antsiranana (Diego Suarez), is good for Madagascar crested ibis, pitta-like ground-roller, dark newtonia, and white-throated oxylabes, but its outstanding attraction is the local endemic, the Amber Mountain rock thrush. In the north-east, **Masoala National Park** is a sanctuary for the most bizarre of the vanga species, the helmet vanga, along with red-breasted coua, scaly ground-roller, Bernier's vanga and the recently, but regularly, sighted Madagascar serpent eagle and Madagascar red owl, two rare endemics. Forty miles (65 km) south of Diego Suarez, **Ankarana Special Reserve** offers 85 recorded species, including the local banded kestrel (*Falco zoniventris*), white-breasted mesite, common in some areas here but rare elsewhere, and the Madagascar fish eagle. The crested wood ibis (*Lophotibis cristata*) is common and the Madagascar paradise flycatcher (*Terpsiphone mutata*) can often be seen or heard, along with the crested coua (*Coua cristata*) and the orange and white forest kingfisher (*Ipsidina madagascariensis*). **Manjakatompo Forestry Station** is close enough to Antananarivo for a day's outing. The most important of the 38 species there are the Madagascar cuckoo falcon, the grey emutail and a local sub-species of the forest rock thrush. Probably the only place where you can hope to see Benson's rock thrush is in **Isalo National Park**, in the south-west, near Toliara. The fascinating little forest of **Zombitse**, an hour's drive from Isalo in the direction of Toliara, is the only locality in which you can hope to see **Appert's Greenbul**, a bird discovered by a priest 25 years ago. Another resident here, the olive-capped coua, was discovered only in 1997.

To visit the most rewarding areas birders should ideally plan to spend two to three weeks in Madagascar and itineraries should be tailored to include the eastern rainforest: Andasibe (Périnet) and Ranomafana, with the option of a trip to Masoala; the western tropical dry forests: Ampijoroa; and the south-western spiny bush around Ifaty, north of Toliara. Other good birding areas are the Zombitse and Isalo national parks, Mantadia (Andasibe) National Park, and Kirindy, north of Morondava. The island of Nosy Ve, 37 miles (60 km) south of Toliara, has a nesting colony or red-tailed tropic birds, and white-tailed tropic birds breed on Nosy Tanikely, near Nosy Bé. The best time for birding in Madagascar is from late August to December. This is the time most birds breed and tend to be easiest to spot. Birds of the rainforest, especially ground-rollers, are not very active during the dry, cold season (May-August); bird-watching during these months in the deciduous dry forest and the sub-arid thorn scrub, however, is generally much better. The best way to get around these extensive birding areas is by air, as few sites are easily accessible by road from Antananarivo. Apart from your binoculars and other necessary birding accessories you shouldn't be without either Olivier Langrand's *Field Guide to the Birds of Madagascar* or *Birds of the Indian Ocean Islands* by Ian Sinclair and Olivier Langrand to identify everything

from the rarest species down to what are commonly known to birders as LBJs
– little brown jobs.

Worth contacting for information are BirdLife International, Wellbrook
Court, Girton Road, Cambridge CB3 0NA, UK (tel 01223-277318; fax 01223-
277200; e-mail birdlife@birdlife.org.uk), and partner organisation BirdLife
South Africa, The Lewis House, 89 Republic Road, Randburg, Johannesburg,
PO Box 515, Randburg 2125, South Africa (tel 11-789 1122; fax 11-789 5188;
e-mail info@birdlife.org.za). Their websites are www.ao.com.br/birdlife.htm
and www.birdlife.org.za. Specifically for birding in Madagascar browse
www.southern-africa.com and check out specialist tour organisers Unusual
Destinations, or contact them in Johannesburg (tel 11-805 4833/4; fax 11-805
4835; e-mail unusdest@global.co.za). American birders might try birdwatching
tour company Wings, 1643 N Alvernon Way, Suite 105, Tucson, Arizona
85712, USA (tel 520-320 9868; fax 520-320 9373; e-mail
wings@wingsbirds.com) or contact Field Guides Incorporated, 9433 Bee Cave
Road, Building 1, Suite 150, Austin TX 78733, USA (tel 512-263 7295; fax
512-263 0117; e-mail fgileader@aol.com).

NATIONAL PARKS AND RESERVES

The tragedy of Madagascar is the devastation of its environment and wildlife
caused by a rapidly growing and desperately poor population which slashes
and burns the indigenous forested land in order the plant rice and other crops.
The encouraging thing is that both government and people are becoming
increasingly aware of their island home's unique assets, and assisted
financially by international organisations are proclaiming national parks and a
variety of reserves to protect this priceless and irreplaceable heritage. There
are now some 30-odd proclaimed parks, reserves and protected areas –
beacons in a sea of environmental degradation. Biologists estimate that 2%-
3% of the island's surface is nominally given over to one form of conservation
area or another; the government claims that the figure is closer to 6%. Both
are far from the 10% advocated as the ideal conservation targets for all
countries by the International Union for the Conservation of Nature (IUCN).
When you visit any of these nature reserves, you should realise that the money
you pay for the permit to enter one and the fee you are obliged to pay for a
compulsory local guide is helping to protect what the World Wildlife Fund
regards as the world's prime biodiversity spot. Entrance fees visitors pay, for
example, are shared by the protected areas authority (ANGAP) and local
communities. The government has proclaimed six different categories of
protected areas: National Parks (*Parcs Nationaux*), Special Reserves (*Réserves
Spéciales*), Strict Nature Reserves (*Réserves Naturelles Intégrales*), Classified
Forests (*Forêts Classées*), Reafforestation Zones (*Périmètres de Reboisement
et de Restauration*), and Hunting Reserves (*Réserves de Chasse*). The national
parks and the special and strict reserves are the ones most involved in the
protection and conservation of important ecological areas and threatened or
endangered wildlife species. They are not fenced, and generally not patrolled
either. Access is usually on foot.

National Parks

There are 10 of these, although the drive is on to proclaim more. They are:

Ranomafana. This 98,800-acre (40,000 ha) park is north-east of Fianarantsoa, on the road to the east coast town of Mananjary. It is one of the most important sanctuaries for lemurs, with 14 species recorded.

Montagne d'Ambre. A rainforest reserve 24 miles (38 km) south of Diego Suarez, covering 44,954 acres (18,200 ha) and encompassing the highest mountains in the region. Noted for Sanford's lemur and the crowned lemur.

Isalo. This 203,900-acre (82,515 ha) park lies in the desolate central south-west, near Toliara, and is regarded as Madagascar's answer to the Grand Canyon. Famed for its ancient burial caves guarded by bleached ancestral skulls and bones, and for puffed-up plants which look like a cross between the bagpipes and an elephant's foot.

Andasibe. This eastern rainforest area now includes the reserves of Analamazoatra (Périnet) and Mantadia National Park, and is Madagascar's most visited national park, being the closest to the capital. Species found here include the largest member of the lemur family, the threatened black and white mythical *indri*, as well as a wealth of amphibians.

Andohahela. This park in the southern part of the island, 25 miles (40 km) north of Taolagnaro (Fort Dauphin), was opened at the end of 1998 and is unusual in marking the transition of rainforest to the spiny forest of the arid south. The park is the last refuge of the triangulated palm (*Neodypsis decaryi*).

Mananara National Park. This eastern rainforest reserve is inland from the southern shore of the Bay of Antongil, in the north-east of the island. Good for botany buffs.

Masoala. Declared a national park in 1996, this 1,013,131-acre (410,000 ha) chunk of the Masoala Peninsula in the north-east is one of the most biologically rich eco-systems in the world and it is believed the largest number of unidentified species in Madagascar are yet to be found in its vast virgin rainforest.

Marojejy. This recently proclaimed national park (1998) is in one of the wettest places in Madagascar (118 inches/3,000 mm annually), north-west of Andapa in the province of Diego Suarez. It is one of the few places where you might spot the rare Madagascar serpent eagle. Another attraction is the silky sifaka.

Tsingy de Bemaraha. In one of the most inaccessible parts of Madagascar, their 375,600-acre (152,000 ha) park lies 37-40 miles (60-80 km) inland from the west coast northern Antsingy region, north of the Manambolo river. The *tsingy* here is a labyrinth of razor-sharp limestone needles stretching north as far as the eye can see.

Zombitse. A relatively small (53,128 acre/21,500 ha) trackless scrub forest area an hour's drive from Isalo towards Toliara, on the west coast. It is home to one of the rarest birds in the world, Appert's Greenbul.

Special Reserves

These reserves are scattered throughout the island but you can't visit many of them unless you are an accredited scientist with a special research permit. Several are, however, open to non-scientists. In order to visit one of the following you should obtain a permit from the Département des Eaux et

Forêts (the Department of Water and Forests) in Antananarivo or Mahajanga.

Analamera. The rare black sifaka is found only on the remote plateau covered by this 85,745-acre (34,700 ha) reserve to the south-east of Diego Suarez. There are also populations of crowned and Sanford's lemurs.

Ankarana. This 45,035-acre (18,225 ha) reserve is 40 miles (64 km) south of Diego Suarez and its most striking feature is the spectacularly eroded limestone massif, which is a maze of gorges, caverns and fluted karst pinnacles known as *tsingy*.

Beza-Mahafaly. This is a lemur sanctuary and species include the beautiful black-faced, snow-white Verreaux's sifaka. The reserve is in the south about 22 miles (35 km) north-east of Betioky, west of the Sakamena river.

Nosy Mangabe. This little (1,285-acre/520 ha) granite island in the Bay of Antongil on the east coast is a 45-minute launch trip from the little town of Maroantsetra. It's famous for its population of aye-ayes, relocated here in 1966 when they appeared to be on the brink of extinction on the main island.

Strict Nature Reserves

Around a dozen of these have been demarcated but, like the majority of the special reserves, they are out of bounds to all but research scientists. If you qualify for the appropriate permit you should be able to visit:

Andringitra. This is in the southern highlands 22 miles (35 km) south of Ambalavo. It offers ring-tailed and bamboo lemurs, as well as the island's second highest summit, Pic Boby at 8,720 ft (2,658 m).

Ankarafantsika. A 149,548-acre (60,520 ha) area protecting dry western deciduous forest and the watershed for the areas around the bays of Bombetoka and Mahajamba. To the south of the reserve is the forest reserve of Ampijoroa.

Betampona. Situated 25 miles (40 km) north-west of Toamasina, this is a lowland rainforest reserve in a region of great biodiversity. A group of international organisations are improving its conservation status by releasing captive-bred species there to reinforce the depleted population of black and white-ruffed lemurs.

Lokobe. This 1,830 acre (740 ha) reserve protects the last tract of original rainforest on the south-eastern tip of the island of Nosy Bé, off the north-west corner of Madagascar.

Tsaratanana. This reserve south-east of Ambanja in the province of Diego Suarez is a haven for birdlife and includes Madagascar's highest peak, Mt Maromokotra, at 9,422 ft (2,877 m).

Tsimanampetsotsa. Located 4¹/₂ miles (7 km) from the west coast and 62 miles (100 km) south of Toliara this is a large soda lake that is home to a variety of waterbirds.

Tsingy de Namoroka. South of the seaside town of Soalala, on the Baie de Baly in the province of Mahajanga, this reserve lies between the Kapiloza and Namahota rivers.

Zahamena. This is in the Toamasina province, to the east of Ambatondrazaka, and is the haunt of such noteworthy birds as the scaly ground-roller and the red-breasted coua.

Private Reserves

There are also a few private reserves which are open to the public, the best known of which is the 655-acre (265 ha) **Berenty**, which is 53 miles (85 km) south of Taolagnaro and on the Mandrare river, straddling the ecological frontier between the rainy east coast and the dry south. This is probably the most visited reserve in Madagascar. Nearby is **Amboasary Sud**, also known as **Kaleta Park**, which is frowned on by pukka wildlife enthusiasts for its near-tame lemurs, which seem to rely on visitors to feed them fruit.

For more information on all these categories of reserves offering wildlife and ecological protection see under each region in **Exploring Madagascar**.

CONSERVATION

'When the last individual of a race of living things breathes no more, another heaven and another earth must pass away before such a one can be again,' wrote naturalist William Beebe. Since the first people settled on Madagascar around 1,500-2,000 years ago vast tracks of deciduous and tropical rainforest have vanished along with all of the island's megafauna, with the exception of the Nile crocodile. Those that disappeared were the large endemic animals, birds and reptiles, which were the offspring from an isolated evolutionary nursery left when Madagascar broke off from mainland Africa 165-million years ago. For instance, by the time the Europeans who had any interest at all in the natural history of the island reached Madagascar in the mid-1600s, 17 species of lemurs, forming eight entire genera, had become extinct. All 17 species were larger than any of those still around today. The largest of the vanished lemurs was *Archaeoindris*, which is estimated to have weighed as much as an adult gorilla. Another group, the 'sloth lemurs' including *Babakotia* and *Paleopropithecus*, weighed 44 lb (20kg) and 88 lb (40kg) respectively, and probably travelled by swinging upside down from branches. Another unusual extinct lemur, *Megaladapis*, appears to have hung on to trees like an Australian koala bear, even though it was about the size of a great dane. Also doomed to extinction were gigantic flightless birds and predatory raptors, enormous land tortoises and dwarf hippotamuses.

There is widespread international concern about the fate and future of Madagascar's biodiversity and, as in Africa, efforts to involve the people are principally directed at education, with an economic spur that hopefully illustrates to impoverished rural communities how they can benefit from the animals they have traditionally killed and the forest and vegetation they have always unthinkingly destroyed. The rationale is that if the rural farmers whose practices contribute to the ecological havoc come to understand that the money paid by one tourist for a permit to enter a national park or reserve is roughly equivalent to what an average family earns from the fields in a month, then farmers will naturally want to increase their income by helping and not hindering conservation efforts. Eco-tourism is part of Madagascar's overall conservation strategy campaign, which is detailed in the government's National Conservation Strategy and Environmental Action Plan, drafted in the 1980s to arrest environmental destruction, reduce poverty, develop sustainable management plans for natural resources, and protect biological diversity in parks and reserves. The baseline of its integrated conservation and development approach is that people living near parks and reserves must benefit from them and must be part of the conservation effort. To achieve long-term conservation goals three key factors are the drivers. The government is committed to developing a sense of pride among the Malagasy in their country's unique wildlife heritage; training a cadre of Malagasy conservation professionals to promote and implement biodiversity conservation into the future; and most important of all, demonstrating the concrete economic value of the environment and its wildlife to rural people and the nation as a whole. Since the National Environmental Action Plan was formulated Madagascar has established new protected areas enclosing close to 3,861 sq miles (10,000 sq km), and the National Association for the Management of Protected Areas (Association Nationale pour le Gestion des Aires Protégées – ANGAP) has taken over the management of several of the key national parks earmarked for increased tourism. One result has been the creation of the country's largest reserve, the Masoala National Park, on the Masoala Peninsula, in north-eastern Madagascar. The government and a consortium of international organisations (including the Wildlife Conservation Society, CARE International Madagascar, and the Peregrine Fund) planned the parks so that it takes into account the needs of both the region's wildlife and the 45,000 people who live in the area. The consortium found that the most important areas for biological diversity were those that were also least accessible and these have become integrated in the park; accessible areas were ignored, encouraging sustainable development by allowing communities around the park to collect timber and other forest products within its confines. The Wildlife Conservation Society and CARE International have continued to work in the area since the creation of the park in 1997, improving the infrastructure for tourism and working with local communities. All these efforts are already bearing fruit in one form or another. For example, at Masoala there's a community-based venture to breed rainforest butterflies and sell them to zoos around the world. At Périnet, which is part of the Andasibe National Park and home to a small number of indris, a group of about 30 young guides have organised themselves to provide a high-quality tour service to visitors. Their organisation, known as the *Association des Guides d'Andasibe*, is a true grassroots effort, and it is hoped tourists will encourage such local initiatives by supporting them wherever they are found.

Madagascar was once almost completely covered by forests, but the practice of burning the woods to clear the land for rice cultivation has denuded most of the landscape, especially in the central highlands, and it is estimated that less than 10% of the original forest cover remains intact. What remains of this once vast forest is confined to the upper ridges of the mountain ranges which run around the perimeter of the island and this slender band of forest is now the last stronghold for many of the island's unique forest-dwelling species. Photographs taken from the space shuttle *Endeavour* at the end of 1993 show the remnants of the original forest cover as a dark green ribbon running around the island just inland from the coast. Rainforests are concentrated on the steep hillsides along a slender north-south axis bordering the east coast, from the Tsaratanana Massif in the north to Taolagnaro in the south, and contain a great number of unique plant species. Secondary growth, which has replaced the original forest and consists to a large extent of Travellers trees, raffia, and baobabs, is found in many places along the east coast and in the north. The island's interior has little in the way of vegetation to retain topsoil, and washaway gullies known as *lavaka* scar the landscape and are spreading. The vegetation of the central highlands and the west coast is for the most part savanna or steppe, and coarse grass predominates where erosion has not exposed the red lateritic soil. In the south-west, the vegetation has adapted in weird and ingenious ways to desert conditions. Torching of forests for agriculture and pasture continues, and as a consequence Madagascar is regarded as the world's most eroded country and is now as often referred to as an appalling ecological disaster as it is as an island of unparalleled biological diversity. Madagascar's environmental crisis has resulted in the country becoming one of the world's foremost conservation priorities, and various international agencies are working in collaboration with the Malagasy government to save what still remains of the natural heritage. In many regions, resources have been depleted to such an extent that people are moving to hitherto relatively untouched areas to continue the cycle of destruction in what are the last sanctuaries for many seriously endangered species of flora and fauna. Wood and charcoal from the forests are used to meet 80% of domestic fuel needs and, as a result, wood has become extremely scarce. Charcoal is considered a cash crop; farmers will burn a rare tree to make a bag or two for their own use or to sell in the nearest town or city. The World Bank has backed an environmental programme to build up plantings of pine and eucalyptus trees to meet the demand for fuel and stands of the alien eucalyptus tree, imported from Australia, are widespread. Madagascar is a signatory of the Convention on International Trade in Endangered Species (CITES) treaty, the international agreement regulating the traffic in threatened and endangered flora and fauna, and while among other things the treaty limits damage to wild populations from the pet trade, unscrupulous Malagasy traders in wildlife often ignore it, and smuggle out consignments of animals and reptiles from Madagascar by greasing a few palms. Madagascar forbids the export of wild chameleons, for instance, but so-called farms, ostensibly raising captive-bred specimens, are often nothing more than thinly disguised transit stations for reptiles captured in the wild.

Deeply involved in all key areas of biodiversity conservation is the World Wildlife Fund (WWF), which has a Madagascar Programme Office to oversee and co-ordinate the Fund's efforts there. WWF says the long-term success of Madagascar's National Conservation Strategy and Environmental Action Plan depends on creating the skills necessary to implement its initiatives. Conservation projects now underway do provide opportunities for technical and managerial training, but relatively few academic openings exist, and high-quality academic training is vital. The demand by conservation organisations for well-trained Malagasy graduates exceeds supply and this situation is unlikely to improve unless urgent action is taken. An adequate investment now in Malagasy researchers and students is vital to ensure that a cadre of highly trained, competent conservation professionals is available to play a lead role in Madagascar's current and future conservation initiatives. WWF believes that the conservation of all of Madagascar's current biodiversity and ecosystems without further loss is, in reality, likely to be an impossible task, but practical activities and objectives must be developed to safeguard those biological communities most at risk, while longer term sustainable strategies are developed. There is no quick fix for the sort of problems threatening Madagascar's biodiversity, and WWF's approach is to test the effectiveness of alternative types of intervention and to develop responses appropriate to local conditions. You can help by supporting organisations involved in conservation and by observing a few simple rules.

To fully enjoy the country and its wildlife you should:

Find out what you can about Madagascar before you leave home. What are the social and environmental problems facing the country and its communities?

Show respect for the country's cultural history, beliefs and social conventions. Find out more about them.

Check out your tour operator. Does your tour operator promote awareness of the need for the sustainable use of natural resources, and how is this demonstrated?

Be aware of your impact and what effect it could have on local eco-systems.

Know where your money goes. Find out how much of the money you spend will benefit the places you visit. What does your tour operator, lodge or resort do to support local environmental and community-based projects?

Help to employ. Do the places you will be staying in employ local people, and are any of them managers or business partners, or do they merely fill menial roles with little opportunity for advancement?

Be prepared to lobby politicians, the media, environmental and conservation groups to draw attention to issues you believe to be of importance.

Help indigenous communities by buying local products and services. Do not buy curios and mementoes without checking the source of the materials used and whether they have been legally obtained.

Question your lifestyle. Does your lifestyle at home have any negative affect on the area you are visiting? If so, what can you do to change it?

Help in the wise use and management of the environment by joining or supporting a caring conservation organisation.

Like many other animal species, wild populations of prosimian primates in Madagascar are declining rapidly due to increasing loss of their forest habitat. Lemurs depend on forested environments for some, if not all, of their primary habitat and cannot survive in deforested areas. Additionally, lemurs are hunted for food by many rural Malagasy. These two factors combine to threaten many of these prosimians with extinction. The following are among the organisations with programmes and projects designed to safeguard lemurs – and other species – from these threats.

The **Duke University Primate Center (DUPC)** is the world's leading facility dedicated to prosimian primates. The mission of the DUPC is to promote research and understanding of prosimians and their natural habitat as a means of advancing the frontiers of knowledge, to contribute to the educational development of future leaders in international scholarship and conservation and to enhance the human condition by stimulating intellectual growth and sustaining global biodiversity. To achieve these goals the Center furthers undergraduate, graduate and professional education in primatology, palaeontology, and tropical conservation; conducts and facilitates innovative research on prosimian behaviour, physiology, and captive management; encourages efforts to preserve prosimians and tropical biodiversity through international collaboration; and serves as a national and international centre for the dissemination of information on prosimians and their natural habitat. The Center has a resident primate colony consisting entirely of prosimians, the majority of which are lemurs from Madagascar. DUPC is also involved in a conservation centre and primate rehabilitation programme at the Ivoloina Zoological Park near Toamasina in eastern Madagascar, in co-operation with the Department of Water and Forests (DEF), and the Madagascar Fauna Group (MFG). The Ivoloina Zoo was closed in 1986 when nearly all the cages and infrastructure were destroyed by a major cyclone. It was re-opened to the public in 1990 after MFG/DUPC technical advisors had worked for three years on staff training and the rehabilitation and development of grounds, animal enclosures and other facilities. Enclosures have been built for priority lemur species, including the aye-aye, the ruffed lemur, the blue-eyed lemur, and the diademed sifaka, as well as for radiated tortoises, native boas and endemic tomato frogs. A large lake created near the zoo entrance provides a five-acre (2 ha) peninsula for free-ranging lemurs. A botanical tour of endemic and exotic plant species provides visitors with information about the island's unique flora. The Ivoloina Environmental Education Centre opened in March 1997. Development at Ivoloina has been undertaken with an emphasis on the training of Malagasy staff. Financial contributions to support special projects and activities at Ivoloina are needed and always greatly appreciated, and similarly for a black and white ruffed lemur restocking project at Betampona Nature Reserve, 25 miles (40 km) north-west of Toamasina, which is being undertaken in conjunction with the breeding and conservation education programmes at Ivoloina. For more information or to make a donation, contact Andrea Katz, technical adviser for Parc Ivoloina, at DUPC. Director of the Duke University Primate Center is Dr Kenneth E Glander. Scientific Director is Dr Elwyn L Simons, who is in charge of the Center's collaborative programmes with Madagascar. You can contact the Duke University Primate Center at 3705 Erwin Road, Durham, North Carolina 27705, United States (tel 919-489 3364; fax 919-490 5394; e-mail primate@acpub.duk.edu; website www.duke.edu/web/primate/home.html).

Other organisations involved with lemurs and conservation in Madagascar:

Primate Conservation Inc (PCI) is an all-volunteer not for profit foundation dedicated to studying, preserving and maintaining the habitats of the least known and most endangered primates in the world. Noel Rowe, author of *The Pictorial Guide to the Living Primates*, founded PCI in 1992 after witnessing the destruction of a lowland forest in Madagascar. Contact PCI, 1411 Shannock Road, Charlestown, Rhode Island, United States (tel 401-364 7140; fax 401-364 6785; e-mail nrowe@primate.org).

The **Madagascar Fauna Group (MFG)** of the American Zoological and Aquarium Association (AZA) is an international consortium of zoological institutions concerned with the conservation of all classes of Malagasy fauna, particularly those with populations falling below viable minimums. MFG member institutions are committed to preserving endangered lemurs and other wildlife, and other habitats, through breeding and field research programmes, and by providing technical advice and training to Malagasy institutions and biologists. The MFG has its headquarters at the San Francisco Zoo, 1 Zoo Road, San Francisco CA 94132-1098, United States, (tel 415-753 7080; website www.sfzoo.org/).

The **Durrell Wildlife Conservation Trust (DWCT)**, originally known as the Jersey Wildlife Preservation Trust, was founded in 1963 by the noted naturalist and author Gerald Durrell, who was responsible for many of the early captive breeding and other conservation initiatives in Madagascar. Training in endangered species management is offered to Malagasy students at DWCT's International

Training Centre at Jersey Zoo. It welcomes donations to support its work. Contact DWCT at Les Augrès Manor, Trinity, Jersey JE3 5BP, Channel Islands, UK (tel 01534-860000; fax 01534-860001; e-mail jerseyzoo@ durrell.org).

Wildlife Preservation Trust International (WPTI) is the American branch of the Durrell Wildlife Conservation Trust. The WPTI is active in funding conservation projects in Madagascar. Contact them at Lamont-Doherty Earth Observatory, Palisades, NY 10964 (tel 845-365 8337; fax 845-365 8177; e-mail homeoffice@wpti.org) or 1200 Lincoln Avenue, Suite 2A, Prospect Park, PA 19076 (tel 610-461 2744; fax 610-461 2745; website www.wpti.org/).

Conservation International (CI) is a field-based, non-profit organisation that protects the earth's biologically richest areas and helps to improve the quality of life for people who live there. It is actively involved in many aspects of conservation in Madagascar. They publish the excellent *Lemurs of Madagascar* field guide. Contact Conservation International, 2501 M Street, NW, Suite 200, Washington, DC 20037, United States (tel 202-429 5660; toll-free 1-800-429-5660; fax 202-887 0193).

The **Wildlife Conservation Society (WCS)**, with headquarters at the Bronx Zoo in New York has several research and conservation projects in Madagascar. Since it was founded in 1895 WCS has helped to establish more than 110 wildlife parks and reserves around the world, and now conducts about 270 conservation field projects in 51 countries. Contact WCS at 2300 Southern Boulevard, Bronx, NY 10460, United States (tel 718-220 5141; e-mail feedback@wwc.org).

The Peregrine Fund (PF) has major projects in Madagascar. In 1995, its biologists re-discovered the Madagascar serpent eagle and the Madagascar red owl after they had not been seen for 60 and 30 years respectively. Contact PF at 566 West Flying Hawk Lane, Boise, Idaho 83709, United States (tel 208-362 3716; fax 208-362 2376; e-mail tpf@peregrinefund.org).

World Wildlife Fund (WWF) was set up in 1961 by a small but eminent group of people, including the naturalist and wildlife painter, Sir Peter Scott, with the aim of saving threatened wildlife species and their habitats. WWF works closely with local and indigenous people to find long-term practical solutions to the over-exploitation of natural resources. Madagascar is a key conservation priority for WWF because of its unique species and habitats. Contact WWF International at Avenue du Mont-Blanc, CH-1196, Gland, Switzerland (tel 22-364 9111; fax 22-264 5358); or WWF-UK at Panda House, Weyside Park, Godalming, Surrey GU7 1XR (tel 01483-426444; e-mail wwf-uk@wwf-uk.org; website www.wwf-uk.org/).

The **International Union for the Conservation of Nature (IUCN)** is the principal international conservation organisation with headquarters in Switzerland. It has both nations and conservation groups as members. It is particularly relevant to lemur conservation. You can contact them through the World Conservation Monitoring Centre (WCMC), 219 Huntingdon Road, Cambridge CB3 0DL (tel 01223-277722/7314; fax 01223-277136; e-mail info@wcmc.org.uk). WCMC maintains an animal database which helps to generate the IUCN's Red List of Threatened Animals. You can access this at www.wcmc.org.uk/data/database/rl_anml_combo.html.

The **Royal Botanic Gardens** (RBG) at Kew, which was the repository of a number of the first botanical specimens collected in Madagascar, maintains its links with the island through a number of conservation initiatives. Contact Dr Aaron Davis at the RBG, Kew, Richmond, Surrey TW9 3AE, UK (tel 020-8332

5239; fax 020-8332 5278; e-mail A.Davis@rbgkew.org.uk).

PROOF FROM THE PAST

Recent palaeological and archaeological discoveries in Madagascar have not only reaffirmed the existence of now extinct megafauna, they have provided another supportive link for the theory that the island was once, with Africa, part of a super-continent until tectonic plate movement and continental drift nudged it out into the Indian Ocean. In December 1997, the journal *Nature* reported that a group of fossil mammals, until then known only in South America, had been found on Madagascar and in India. The 65-70 million-year-old mammals, dating from the Late Cretaceous period, are unrelated to any group living today and have been called *gondwanatheres*, after the super-continent of Gondwanaland, which once included all the southern hemisphere's land masses. Their discovery in such diverse locations suggests that the three now widely separated land masses were connected in the Late Cretaceous period, with India and Madagascar attached to eastern Antarctica and South America to the western end. More reports in mid-2000 highlighted the discovery of the exquisitely preserved fossilised remains of an early type of crocodile whose pug nose and dental structure suggested that it could have been a vegetarian. This was found in north-west Madagascar and also dates from the Late Cretaceous era, between 65 million and 97 million years ago. This prehistoric find has been named *Simosuchus clarki* from the Greek for pug-nosed and after the Egyptian crocodile-headed god. In 1998, one of a series of ongoing palaeontological expeditions funded by independent US federal agency National Science Foundation (NSF) unearthed a raven-sized fossil bird which revealed clear evidence of a close relationship between birds and the theropod dinosaurs which many scientists believe were the ancestors of all modern birdlife. The journal *Science* reported the fossil bird to be 65-70 million years old. Scientists named the bird *Rahona ostromi*, meaning 'Ostrom's menace from the clouds,' as not only was it a capable flyer but, unlike most birds, it had a long, bony tail and a large sickle-shaped killing claw at the end of a thick second toe. This toe and claw are identical to those characterising ancient theropod dinosaurs.

Reports in October 1999 announced the discovery of a treasure trove of fossils, including the bones of two calf-sized animals found in an ancient river bed that may be the oldest dinosaur fossils yet found. The fossils are from the Middle to Late Triassic period, 225-230 million years ago. With the remains of eight other types of reptiles found, they could shed fresh light on this period, which was a misty time when dinosaurs and the first mammals began to appear on earth. Sites excavated in the Ankarana mountains and in south-western Madagascar have yielded up bones too recent to have become fossilised from animals that lived on the island before the arrival of the first human settlers. Excavations at some of these sub-fossil sites by a team from Duke University of North Carolina and other US and Malagasy scientists have turned up the bones of elephant birds, pygmy hippopotamuses, giant tortoises, and at least 17 species of extinct lemurs. Radiocarbon dating of extinct lemur bones places the oldest of them at about 12,000-26,000 years and the most recent at only 1,000-500 years old. This indicates that giant lemurs must have survived the pressures and dangers of human occupation by at least 1,500 years, and there is also evidence that pygmy hippos, thought long extinct, may still have been roaming the island as recently as 100 years ago, both highly controversial suggestions. The Duke University Primate Center in North Carolina has a collection of more than 15,000 fossils representing prosimians, monkeys, apes, and other mammals ranging in age from less than 1,000 years to more than 60-million years old.

For more information about prehistoric and archaeological digs contact the Primate Center or the Musée d'Art et Archéologie/Institut de Civilisations de l'Université d'Antananarivo, 17 rue Docteur Vilette Isoraka, Antananarivo (tel 20-22-21047; fax 20-22-28218).

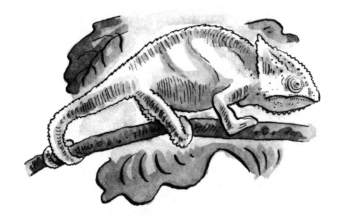

EXPLORING MADAGASCAR

TOURIST ATTRACTIONS

Andasibe National Park in the eastern rainforest known for the ape-like indri lemur and numerous other interesting animals. Scenic hiking trails and a staggering variety of plant life. Adjoining Périnet rainforest area holds even rarer species.

Ampijoroa Forest Station, easily Madagascar's top spot for nocturnal wildlife species, with pleasant trails into dry deciduous forest that are accessible all year round.

Ankarana Reserve known as a 'Lost World within a Lost World' a bizarre lunar landscape featuring a formidable fortress-like karst plateau fretted with needlepointed limestone pinnacles. Forested gorges, and abundant wildlife, and awesome caves with resident bat colonies and even occasional crocodiles in the underground rivers.

Ifaty and **Toliara** seaside hotels offer scuba-diving and snorkelling on vast coral reefs. Inland, the spiny desert never fails to fascinate. Boat trips from Ifaty to Nosy Ve, remote St Augustine's Bay and Anakao.

Île Ste Marie (Pirate's Island), coral reefs, palm trees, secluded coves, hospitable locals and laid-back Indian Ocean ambience contribute to the magical island that could be the site of Captain Kidd's lost treasure. Humpback whale-watching between July and September.

Isalo National Park in the rugged Isalo mountains, this is southern Madagascar's premier hiking destination. An hour's drive away is **Zombitse Forest**, one of the island's top destinations for all bird-watchers.

Mahajanga, Morondava and the **Tsingy de Bemaraha**. Three wild west coast towns with wide beaches, safe swimming, access to mysterious caves, forests, wildlife sanctuaries, and to a region of truly amazing landscapes.

Masoala Peninsula and **Nosy Mangabe**. The **Masoala National Park** is the biggest sanctuary on the island. The lowland rainforest is a dream place for wildlife, trekkers and photographers. Nosy Mangabe island is a delightful lemur reserve in nearby Antongil Bay.

Nosy Bé Archipelago, palm-fringed beaches and exquisite coral reefs around a scattering of such tropical islands as Nosy Sakatia, Nosy Komba and Nosy Tanikely.

Ranomafana National Park, slashed by the whitewater Namorona river, a wild mountainous rainforest sheltering 12 species of lemur, and numerous endemic birds.

INTRODUCTION

You could spend your life exploring Madagascar and still not see everything there is to see. One reason is that many places are inaccessible, another is that they have not yet all been discovered and placed on the tourist map. What we have selected in the five main regions is obviously not exhaustive, but they are the attractions,

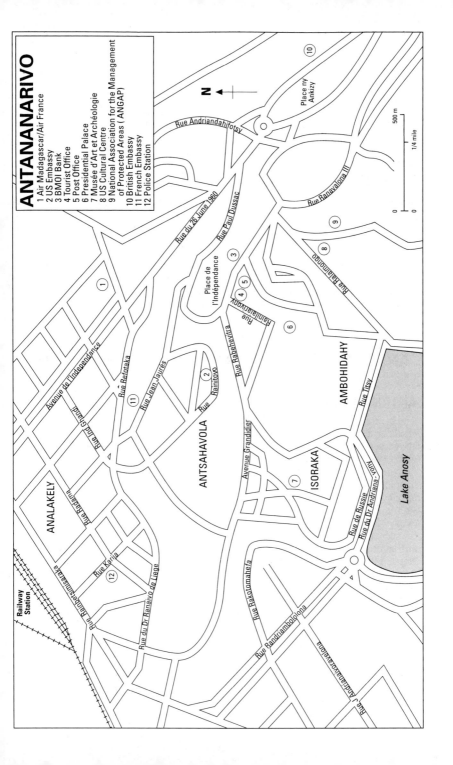

ANTANANARIVO

1 Air Madagascar/Air France
2 US Embassy
3 BMOI Bank
4 Tourist Office
5 Post Office
6 Presidential Palace
7 Musée d'Art et Archéologie
8 US Cultural Centre
9 National Association for the Management
  of Protected Areas (ANGAP)
10 British Embassy
11 French Embassy
12 Police Station

N

Railway
Station

ANALAKELY

ANTSAHAVOLA

ISORAKA

AMBOHIDAHY

Lake Anosy

Place ny
Ankizy

Place de
l'Indépendance

0   500 m
0   1/4 mile

Rue Andriandahifotsy
Rue Ranavalona II
Rue Ratsimilaho
Rue Ratomanga
Rue du 26 June 1960
Rue Paul Dussac
Rue Retotaka
Avenue de l'Indépendance
Rue du Gd Grand
Rue Jean Jaurès
Rue Rainitovo
Rue Rabehevitra
Rue Hamilalainavony
Avenue Grandidier
Rue de Russie
Rue du Dr Andriana
Rue Tsy
Rue Karija
Rue du Dr Ranaivo de Liege
Rue Rabehangitsara
Rue Rakotomaheta
Rue Randriambolojona
Rue Andriamaheramanana

natural and man-made, that we believe are representative of this unique and wonderful island. If it's light on night-clubs, discos, bars and cinemas that's because there aren't all that many, and anyway if you're reading this you'll probably be more interested in wildlife than in a wild life.

National parks and the various reserves around the country are all governed by strict rules and regulations and one of the most important is that you have a permit to enter them. While this can sometimes be obtained at the gate it's better to check out the latest information at the Department of Water and Forests, the National Association for the Management of Protected Areas (ANGAP), or the World Wide Fund for Nature (WWF) offices in Antananarivo, Mahajanga or any other large centre. At almost all parks and reserves a local guide is compulsory. To avoid hassles over fees check these out as well when you get your permits.

The island is a photographer's dream, whether you are a happy snapper or a professional, so pack your camera (take two if possible) and take plenty of film, flash batteries and other photographic supplies, as they may not always be easy to find. Protect your cameras, film and other stuff with a waterproof backpack. There are many people, especially older men and women in rural areas, who do not like having their pictures taken, so be polite and ask their permission first.

ANTANANARIVO AND THE CENTRAL HIGHLANDS

ANTANANARIVO

The capital Antananarivo is well situated virtually in the middle of the island on the Hauts Plateaux, or central highlands, at an invigorating altitude of 4,816 ft (1,468 m) above sea level. Ranged around it peaks alternate with valleys, plateaus and hills where vast gullies have been carved out of the red earth by erosion. Commonly known to locals and visitors alike as Tana, the city is packed with around 2-million people who live in medieval-looking balconied, narrow, red-brick houses spread out higgledy-piggledy on the 12 sacred hills over which the city stretches. These double-storey, faded ochre, pink clay and wood houses with terracotta tiled roofs sprawl everywhere. The lower town is called Analakely, bisected by its own Champs Elysees, the broad thoroughfare of the Avenue de l'Indépendance. which is lined by airline offices and some grand hotels. Analakely is connected to the upper town, or Haute Ville, by a succession of stairways. No other Indian Ocean town has so many steps. One particularly taxing climb, through a maze of buildings, is known in Malagasy as *Tsiafakantitra* ('Old people can't make it'). Winking in the midst of it all is Lake Anosy, once a royal pleasure resort, and now the site of the World War I **Monument aux Morts** ('Monument to the Dead'). This stands on an island in the middle of the lake and is connected to the shore by a causeway. Close by is the capital's only truly high-rise building, the Hilton Hotel. Isoraka is the quarter housing administrative buildings, night-clubs, some smart restaurants, galleries and boutiques. Analamanga, the highest (575 ft/175 m) hilltop above the lower town, is crowned by the ruined *Rova*, or palace and attendant buildings, of the first Queen Ranavalona, dating back to the era of the Merina aristocrats who made Antananarivo their royal capital, naming it 'Citadel of a Thousand Warriors.' Until 1995, when arsonists torched it, the Rova, or royal enclosure, was the focal point of the Imerina kingdom. Although restoration work has started on the Rova it's still a sorry sight, but it's not difficult to imagine how it must have been when it was the heart of the island empire. In his monumental *History of Madagascar*, written in the late 1800s, Alfred Grandidier recalls it at the height of its glory...

'At Antananarivo were palaces which provided the city with an architectural crown which would have been thought remarkable even in Europe. From whichever angle the city was viewed, this cluster of palaces could be seen grouped together in a large Rova, or courtyard, situated on what was, before its levelling, the highest point on the ridge. The level platform of the Rova surmounted a surrounding wall of stones. Its chief entrance faced north and consisted of a triumphal arch approached by a massive stone flight of stairs. The arch was elaborately decorated. Over it stood the national falcon emblem, the *voromahery*, with its outstretched wings made of copper. Facing this archway was the great place, the Manjakamiadana, or Reigning Prosperously. It was an enormous structure, 70 ft high, with a pitched roof adding another 50 ft to make a total of 120 ft from the ground to the peak of the wood-shingled roof. Originally this palace was built entirely of wood by Jean Laborde. Cameron surrounded the original structure with a massive stone facade with a square turret at each corner, and two great verandas. The internal wood structure, 100 ft by 60 ft in extent, remained. It has beams of enormous size, cut and dragged by slaves all the way from the eastern forests. The great central posts, made of single spars, projected above the ridge and ended in lightning conductors. The roof was surmounted by another *voromahery* bird. The ground floor inside was divided into two impressive state rooms, in which great receptions and affairs of state were held. East of this palace stood the smaller Tranovola, or Silver House, while a number of less important structures were also grouped around the Rova: the Besakana, or Great Breadth, on the west, where the Lapa, or throne, was kept; the Masoandro, or Sun, on the east; and the Mahitsy, or Upright, on the north, where the idols were originally kept. On the east side stood the royal tombs, while north of the Tranovola stood the fascinatingly ornate Elizabethan period residence of the Queen. This was known as Manampisoa, or Adding What is Pleasant. It was built by the indefatigable Mr Cameron in 1865-1867. It was 62 ft by 30 ft in extent and 50 ft high... Behind the palaces stood the stone church with its 112 ft-high tower, built by (British architect) William Pool for Ranavalona II. East of it, was a new private residence for the Queen. This was of brick, and two storeys high. An attractive garden filled the rest of the Rova, and from it there was a superb view, with the whole of Antananarivo spread out. Outside, around the precincts of the Rova, stood the official buildings, with the imposing palace of the prime minister as the principal structure. All these places, with the palaces, were notable for their lofty, pitched roofs, finished at the gables with crossing timbers forming horns, the extremities of which projected beyond the ridge of the roofs to various heights, indicating by their length the rank of the occupant. In the case of the royal houses, these horns reached a length of 12 to 14 ft beyond the roofs.'

You can still see the royal tombs and you can look out on a vista that once entranced royalty and nobles. Reports of the time also bring to life some of the old barbaric splendour. In July 1828 when Radama I died 12,000 Spanish silver dollars were beaten together to make his coffin and in a receptacle in the tomb a further 10,000 were packed for the king's body to rest on. All his most treasured possessions were also placed in the tomb, including 80 costly British uniforms, hats, feathers, a golden helmet, swords, spurs, a whole sideboard of superb silver plate, gold cups, silks, satins, and the finest cloth. Twelve of his most beautiful horses were killed and their bodies were buried around the tomb. 20,000 oxen were slaughtered to feed the mourners. Forty years later the body of the last pagan queen, Rasoherina, was encased in a similar coffin, but this time made of 22,000 silver dollars. Does all this wealth still lie in the hilltop tombs of the Rova, one wonders?

Stretching away on the plateau into the distance all round the capital there were, as there still are, the vast fields of rice that were the city's natural pantry. The rice is of superlative quality and no matter how fine their other crops might be rice alone is considered *Mahavoky* ('Able to Appease Hunger') by the Malagasy. This crop still tolls the seasons for the farmers. Towards the end of the dry season (*Ririnina*, or 'Time of Bareness'), the first seed is sown in well-watered beds, to sprout ready for the spring plantings, known as *Lohataona*, or the 'Head of the Year.' When the young rice plants are 6 inches (15 cm) high they are transplanted. This is done towards the end of October, at the beginning of the season known as *Fahavaratra*, or 'Thunder Time.' It is harvested when the season of *Fararano*, or 'Last Rains', starts in March.

Local Attractions

Antananarivo is not overloaded with officially designated tourist attractions – the city itself is the main one, a wonderland of colours, smells, textures and faces – but there are a few places you should not miss after you've visited the ruined Rova. The first is nearby, the **Musée d'Andafiavaratra**, housed in the restored **Prime Minister's Palace** down rue Ramboatiana from the Rova. This museum displays a few things salvaged from the fire that destroyed the Queen's Palace. The **Musée d'Art et Archéologie** – also known as the Musée d'Isoraka – is also an interesting museum to visit. It's on rue du Dr Villette, in the Isoraka quarter and you'll recognise the entrance by the bronze tree decked out with pots. It has some nice craftwork displays. About two miles (4 km) from the city centre is **Parc Botanique et Zoologique de Tsimbazaza** (it's Malagasy name means 'They are not children'). It's not the finest zoo or botanical garden you'll ever see but it has a wonderful variety of lemurs, some caged, but mostly inhabiting small islands surrounded by a lake which means you are able to see up-close these remarkable primates before you visit them in the wild, from the tiny fat-tailed dwarf lemur to the ring-tailed lemur, the crowned lemur, and the aye-aye. In the grounds is the **Musée d'Académie Malgache** which is quite primitive, with dusty exhibits not exactly well displayed, but what you can see here is the huge skeleton of the extinct 'elephant bird' standing 10 ft (3 m) over its egg, which is more than six times the size of an ostrich egg. At the other end of the extinction scale is a pygmy hippopotamus.

Excursions

One of the most popular day excursions is to another Rova, this time the original home of the Merina royal family at **Ambohimanga** ('Blue Hill'), which is regarded as a sacred site. This is situated 13 miles (21 km) north-east of Antananarivo. The surrounding landscape is spectacular, and entry to the village is through one of seven gateways. To one side of the hill is an immense flat stone that was rolled into place by slaves at any hint of a danger to the community. The Rova itself is situated a few hundred yards uphill from the village. It doesn't compare in size to the Rova in Antananarivo, but the surroundings are lovelier, with restful gardens and astonishing views. The Rova contains an historical museum where you can see with such items as the monarch's bed and royal eating utensils, portraits of, among others, Ranavalona I, the queen who outlawed Christianity on the island and martyred its adherents. She ordered them bound hand and foot and tossed from the cliffs overlooking the capital, which are still referred to as the 'Place of Hurling.' In the royal compound you can also see royal baths, tombs and a sacrificial stone which, if the stains are anything to go by, is still used. There's also a sacred hill at **Ilafy**, 8 miles (12 km) from the capital, where the Merina royal family had a country residence. There's a wonderful collection of relics and artefacts, including hairstyles and wigs worn by the family, which make this a worthwhile visit.

MANTASOA

About 50 miles (80 km) east of Antananarivo is Mantasoa, a town that was once the home of Jean Laborde, a Frenchman shipwrecked in 1831 who became the architect-engineer (and lover) of pagan Queen Ranavalona I. He settled in Mantasoa in 1833 and you can still visit his house, which has been cleverly restored and turned into a museum. Laborde turned the little town into a hive of industry, using 2,000 pressed men to make guns, powder, brass, steel, swords, glass, silk, lime, paint, ink, soap, sugar, candy, potash, bricks, tiles, and lightning conductors. As well as this he introduced merino sheep, draught oxen, antelope, apples, and grapes to Madagascar. He also made roads, and found time to build palaces for the Queen. While Laborde is often credited with starting up industry (see *History*), a report by a French slave trader called Mayeur who visited Madagascar in 1777 noted: 'The Europeans who visit the coast of Madagascar will find it difficult to believe that in the centre of the island, but 30 miles from the sea, is a country hitherto unknown, in which, although it is surrounded by brutish and savage persons, there is more light, more industry, more active policy, and where the arts are more advanced than at the coast.' He was in part referring to such Malagasy skills as the distilling of rum by passing the steam of fermented sugar-cane juice through bamboo pipes immersed in cold water, the mining of iron, and the improvisation of furnaces, with bellows made from hollowed-out tree trunks. Each trunk had a piston which was pumped up and down by slaves. With this the Hova made a variety of excellent metal tools and weapons. Stone masonry was another ancient skill, and some marvellous old tombs and village gateways are still a credit to forgotten craftsmen. Mantasoa is a nice place for a picnic, with its artificial lake and beach surrounded by pine trees. Laborde is buried in the cemetery outside the village. *Les Amis de Jean Laborde* will be happy to tell you more about the Frenchman and Mantasoa and its environs. E-mail them at topoi@dts.mg.

Manjakatompo Forestry Station

East of the RN7 between Antananarivo and Antsirabe, 10^{1}/2 miles (17 km) east of Ambatolampy, is the **Manjakatompo Forestry Station**, which offers a wonderful selection of hiking and rambling trails. The area comprises part of the rocky Ankaratra Massif at an altitude of 5,085-8,530 ft (1,550-2,600 m). There are numerous clear, cold streams running among the 5,680 acres (2,300 ha) of mainly pine plantations, and 1,600 acres (650 ha) of natural indigenous forest split up into a number of smaller areas. Birders in particular will enjoy the forest as it holds 38 species of birds, of which the most important are the Madagascar cuckoo-falcon, the grey emutail and a local sub-species of the forest rock thrush. With its close proximity to the capital, Manjakatompo Forestry Station is an ideal spot for a day visit using transport hired in Antananarivo.

ANTSIRABE

Antsirabe lies on the slopes of the island's third highest peak, **Tsiafajavona** ('Mountain of Mist') at 8,671 ft (2,643 m), in the volcanic Ankaratra mountains, which cover an area of about 2,000 sq miles (5,200 sq km) in central Madagascar. It's the principal town of the region and it is the terminus of a railway line running from Antananarivo, 70 miles (110 km) away to the north-east. The town was once known by the French who used to come here from Réunion to enjoy this spa as 'the Malagasy Vichy' because of its hot springs and their reputed healing powers. The thermal baths have changed little since they were built early last century, but nowadays the town relies more on industry – textiles, brewing, tobacco, and food processing – than on gouty French, although the springs still flow and the climate at 4,921 ft (1,500 m) remains bracing. This elegant, attractive city is famous for its gemstones, such as tourmaline, beryl, aquamarine, amethyst, rose quartz, and other indigenous stones, and you can watch skilled craftsmen cutting and polishing the beautiful stones in the *bijouterie* shops. It is also the *pousse-pousse* (rickshaw) capital of Madagascar, a mode of transport that is an unusual way to see the town.

FURTHER AFIELD

An excursion to the spectacular 262 ft (80 m) deep crater lake of **Tritriva** is a pleasant outing. This odd volcanic lake epitomises all that is weird on the island. When the water level of other lakes drops in the dry season Tritriva's levels rise and when normal lakes' water levels rise in the rainy season Tritriva's water level drops. This is probably explained by subterranean lava tube activity. **Andraikiba** is another lake in an extinct volcano where you can swim or go boating. You will find horsemen willing to take you on horseback for a canter around Antsirabe and the surrounding area. There is a golf course nearby. The Saturday market is a crowd puller, with an impressive assortment of goods for sale.

Ambositra

About 55 miles (89 km) south of Antsirabe, through some spectacular highland scenery, is Ambositra, commonly known as the town or roses and the centre of Madagascar's wood-carving industry. Even the houses have ornately carved wooden shutters and balconies. The finest and most intricate statues and furniture come from the remote villages in the nearby forests and the town of Analamarina. You'll find the Arts Co-operative Centre in a monastery, where you can view a collection of wood carvings mainly from the famed Zafimaniry region, south-east of Ambositra. You can buy any carving that takes your fancy. A visit to the cluster of villages situated in the forests outside of Ambositra makes an enjoyable day's outing. The main village is Antoetra. Here you'll find master woodcarvers nonchalantly turning out veritable works of art. You should be sensitive to the villagers' customs and taboos, and it's best to hire a guide for your visit, who will also show you some odd-looking Zafimaniry tombs.

Ranomafana

The village of Ranomafana ('Hot Water'), is a thermal bath centre near the Ranomafana National Park, a 2-hour drive from Fianarantsoa and 10 hours from Antananarivo. The baths are open daily, except Friday and are reportedly a better bet than those at Antsirabe. The Station Thermale offers a steamy outdoor swimming pool of mineral-rich water surrounded by smart chalets which each has a private bath supervised by white-coated attendants. **Ranomafana National Park** is located in the rainforests, hills and deep valleys west of the hot-water village. This rainforest reserve is one of Madagascar's most beautiful protected areas. The park is home to 29 different species of mammal, as well as 14 different lemur species, including the aye-aye. Golden bamboo lemurs were discovered here in 1986 and these magnificent primates were the reason the park was established in 1991. It is also an exceptional area for bird-watching. There are also 96 species of birds, reptiles, butterflies and other insects. Well-built trails allow you to see plenty of variety in the scenery and vegetation, but the sheer majesty of the forest itself is what makes the visit so memorable. The park encloses 102,796 acres (41,600 ha). It lies at an elevation of 3,937 ft (1,200 m) and consists mainly of rainforest-covered hills traced by numerous small streams which run down to the beautiful whitewater river of Namorona. A popular excursion is a night walk through the park. Watch out for leeches – they are everywhere. The best time to visit is during the dry season, from July to October. There's a network of trails which can take up to a week to cover thoroughly. There are camp sites, as well as excellent forest guides.

FIANARANTSOA

Fianarantsoa ('Place of Good Learning') is the second largest city in Madagascar and is renowned as a town of intellectuals. The colleges, schools and universities are crowded with students and academics. The town was founded in 1830 and lies on the eastern fringe of a forested escarpment at an average altitude of 4,000 ft (1,200 m). This lovely, cool town is situated in the middle of the island's richest wine and tea-producing area. The town is an interesting maze of cobbled lanes, steep alleys and medieval architecture and it is one of the main gemstone centres of Madagascar. It is connected by rail with the port of Manakara, about 70 miles (110 km) to the south-east. Air Madagascar flies here from Antananarivo twice a week, or you can take a bush taxi from anywhere.

Ambalavao

Thirty-six miles (54 km) south of Fianarantsoa is the quaint town of Ambalavao. The region is home to the Betsileo people and this is where the famous Antaimoro papyrus paper embedded with dried wild flowers is made by hand to be sold throughout the island in scrolls, as lampshades and wall hangings. The open-air factory is worth visiting to view the fascinating step-by-step process by which this lovely paper is made. The wine estate of **Soavita** lies nearly two miles (3 km) north of Ambalavao. Here you can watch the fermentation and production processes and enjoy a tasting session. Tour operators in Fianarantsoa offer day trips to Ambalavao or you can take a bush taxi.

About 22 miles (35 km) south of Ambalavao is the 76,998-acre (31,160 ha) **Andringitra Strict Nature Reserve**, which is on its way to achieving national park status, once ways have been worked out to fully involve local communities in sustainable eco-tourism. The reserve lies on a massif dominated by the island's second highest mountain, **Pic Boby** at 8,270 ft (2,658 m), and contains seven species of lemur, which include all three species of bamboo lemur, and ring-tails which have adapted to living at such chilly heights. There are also 22 species of amphibians, as well as a wide variety of endemic flora. Visits are out of the question in the wet season and a four-wheel-drive vehicle (or a mountain bike) is necessary even when it's dry. As with all other parks and reserves, check first with the authorities in Antananarivo if you want to visit Andringitra.

ACCOMMODATION

Antananarivo

Superior

Hilton Hotel: rue Pierre Stibbe-Anosy (tel 20-22-22260; fax 20-22-26051). 10 miles (6 km) from the airport, on the western side of Lake Anosy, 165 air-conditioned rooms, TV with CNN, private bathrooms. *L'Oliveraie* serves Mediterranean cuisine, *La Serre des Orchidées* overlooking the pool serves lunch and themed evening buffets, the restaurant at the pool serves snacks, sandwiches, pizzas, and cocktails, and there's a pastry shop called *L'Éclair*. The Bistro Bar is typically French, with daily piano bar entertainment and cybernet café, tennis courts, health club, facilities for disabled, casino, transfers to and from airport.

Hotel Colbert: rue Prince Ratsimamanga, Antaninarenina (tel 20-22-20202; fax 20-22-34012, e-mail colbert@bow.dts.mg). In the heart of Haute Ville ('Upper Town'), views of the Queen's Palace, 120 climate-controlled rooms with satellite TV, video, full bath, and mini-bar, two restaurants, two bars, a casino, a tea room, several quality gift shops, regarded by expats and visitors alike as the grandest hotel of them all.

Hotel de France: (Groupe Siceh) 34 Avenue de l'Indépendance (tel 20-22-21304; fax 20-22-20108). 37 air-conditioned rooms with private bathroom, *La Brasserie* restaurant, snack bar and bureau de change .

Hotel Gregoire: rue du 12th Bataillon Malagasy Besarety (tel 20-22-22266; fax 20-22-29271; e-mail gregoir@bow.dst.mg). 2½ miles (4km) from downtown, 27 rooms with TV, private bathroom, *L'Aquarium* restaurant specialises in seafood, and *Le Traiteur* restaurant, bureau de change.

Ibis Hotel: tel 20-22-62929; fax 20-22-64040.

Palace Hotel: (Groupe Siceh) 8 Avenue de l'Indépendance (tel 20-22-25663; fax 20-22-33943). Has 25 air-conditioned rooms, self-catering studios and apartments, equipped with kitchenettes, for rent by the week of month, TV.

Radama Hotel: 22 Avenue Grandidier, Isoraka (tel 20-22-31927; fax 20-22-35323). Malagasy-style hotel equipped with modern amenities, 19 rooms with TV, live Malagasy music every Friday and Saturday evening.

Le Royal Palissandre: (Apavou Group), 13 rue Andriandahifotsy, Faravohitra (tel 20-22-60560; fax 20-22-32624; e-mail HotelPalissandre@simicro.mg). In the centre of the city on the hillside facing the setting sun where there is a fine view of the city and the famous Avenue de l'Indépendance. The building material – pink bricks, Mantasoa granites, marbles and rosewood – makes it one of the most elegant and welcoming hotels in the capital. The 46 bedrooms have been decorated by Benjah, a famous Malagasy artist. Overlooking the main city, the *La Table des Hautes Terres* restaurant serves local specialities and French cuisine, while the *Amphore* bar mixes delicious cocktails.

Tana Plaza: Groupe Siceh (tel 20-22-25663; fax 20-22-33943), on the wide square at 2 Avenue de l'Indépendance opposite the ornate Victorian main station. The 83 rooms are modest rooms, but with efficient air-conditioning, *La Veranda* restaurant.

Tourist
Auberge du Cheval Blanc: tel 20-22-44646. At Ivato International airport, old-style Malagasy architecture, 22 rooms, handicraft store, bureau de change, and restaurant.
Hotel Mellis: rue Indira Gandhi (tel 20-22-234250). 48 standard rooms, 29 with private bathroom.

Budget
Aina Hotel: 17 rue Ratsimilaho, Antaninarenina (tel 20-82-22262).
Club Double M: a private club, three miles (5 km) from downtown, three bedrooms, swimming pool, tennis courts, horse riding, motor cycles.
Hasina Chinese Hotel: Grandidier Avenue.
Le Hintsy: 4 route Digue (tel 20-22-26379; fax 20-22-26414).
Hotel Panorama: about 2 miles (3 km) from downtown area, 86 single rooms, 69 double rooms and seven suites, coffee shop, restaurant, bar, swimming pool
Muraille de Chine: Avenue d'Indépendance, 23 rooms with private bathroom, Chinese restaurant.
Le Rendezvous des Pêcheurs: in Ambatolampy, 47 miles (75 km) from the city on the road to Antsirabe, 12 rooms, common toilets, popular for its freshwater fish dishes.
Le Rubis: tel 20-22-63045.
Solimotel: about 2 miles (3km) from downtown area, 32 rooms with private bathroom, restaurant, pizzeria, swimming pool.
Sunny Hotel: Ambohidahy (tel 20-22-26304; fax 20-22-29078).

Backpacker-friendly hotels:
Le Relais des Pistards: Tsimbazaza (tel 20-22-29134; fax 20-22-33986).
Sakamanga: rue A Ratianarivo (tel 20-22-35809). 10 rooms.

Mantasoa

Hotel Ermitage: 37 miles (60 km) from Antananarivo, surrounded by a forest bordering the lake, 31 rooms with private bathroom, restaurant and bar, horse-riding, tennis courts, mini golf, ping pong, discothèque.

Motel le Chalet: PO Box 12, Mantasoa (tel 20-42-66005), five bungalows.

Antsirabe

Recommended is the grand old but newly renovated colonial-style *Hotel des Thermes:* PO Box 72, Antsirabe (tel 20-44-48761; fax 20-44-49202).
Arotel: rue Ralaimongo (tel 20-44-48573).
Cercle Mess Antsirabe: opposite SA Ranomanoro on Boulevard Maréchal Foch (tel 20-44-48366).
Diamant Hotel: Route d'Andranobe, PO Box 42, Antsirabe (tel 20-44-48840).
Hotel Baobab: Avenue de l'Indépendance (tel 20-44-48393).
Hotel Rubis: PO Box 336, Antsirabe (no telephone).
Villa Nirina: private home, Route d'Andranobe, PO Box 245, Antsirabe (tel 20-44-48597/48669).

Ambositra

Grand Hotel: Lot VIII F16 (tel 20-47-71262).
Hotel Violette: rue du Commerce (tel 20-47-71175).

Fianarantsoa

Hotel du Betsileo: PO Box 1161, Fianarantsoa (tel 20-75-50003). Adjunct to *Chez Papillon* restaurant.
Hotel Plazza Inn: PO Box 1161, Fianarantsoa (tel 20-75-51572; fax 20-75-51086).
Hotel Soafia: PO Box 1479, Fianarantsoa (tel/fax 20-75-50353). Situated in the downtown area, 4 miles (7 km) from the airport, 52 rooms, restaurant, tennis court, swimming pool, sauna.
Hotel Tombontsoa: PO Box 1150, Fianarantsoa (tel 20-75-51405).
Tsara Camp: at Andringitra, luxury tents, tastefully furnished with exotic wood, private facilities with solar shower, hand basin and chemical toilet. Guests are welcome all day long under a spacious mess tent where they have at their disposal purified water, hot tea and coffee, as well as a fruit basket. Cuisine is simple but tasty, with Malagasy accents. Book through Boogie Pilgrim in Antananarivo (tel 20-22-25868; fax 20-22-62556; e-mail bopi@dts.mg).
Tsara Guesthouse: PO Box 1373, Fianarantsoa (tel 20-75-50206). Comfortable rooms, some with en-suite bathrooms, trekking excursions organised.

Ranomafana

Hotel Domaine Nature: c/o 32 rue Andrinary, Ratia Nairivo Ampasamadinika (tel 20-44-31072; fax 20-44-31067), six bungalows.

EATING OUT

Antananarivo

The view from one of Antananarivo's 12 hills across the city makes the terrace of the *Grille du Rova* (tel 20-22-62724; fax 20-22-62213) a pleasant dining venue. It's regarded as one of the city's best restaurants. Traditional music every Sunday. A few minutes from the ruins of the Queen's Palace.

The Hotel Colbert has an internationally famous restaurant, *Le Taverne*.

O!Poivre Vert (tel 20-22-21304), is in the Hotel de France, off the capital's main street, l'Avenue de l'Indépendance, which reportedly serves the best pizza in the southern hemisphere. You can watch the chef cook them in the wood-fired oven.

La Veranda restaurant at *Tana Plaza* hotel is a small, elegant restaurant where the food is sublime, French influenced but cooked with Malagasy flair, such as fresh seafood starters, roasted quail, superb lobster, and wonderful desserts.

Villa Vanille (tel 20-22-20515), is an extraordinary place patronised by rich Malagasy and foreign diplomats. It is an old French colonial house staffed by deferential waiters and prim hostesses. Traditional Malagasy music most nights.

Other restaurants of note are the *Darafify*, French/Creole, with excellent seafood, and the *Fortuna* and *Jade*, both Chinese.

Others to try:

Acapulco: 14 rue Ratsimilaoho Antaninarenina (tel 20-22-23225; fax 20-22-22824), Malagasy food.

Auberge du Cheval Blanc: Mamory Ivato, Ambohidratrimo (tel 20-22-44646). Excellent for weekends.

Chez Maxime: tel 20-22-43151.

Grand Orient: PO Box 1572, Antananarivo (tel 20-22-23225; fax 20-22-22824), Chinese food.

La Boussole: tel 20-22-35810.

Le Chapiteau: tel 20-22-21624.

Le Jasmin: tel 20-22-34296.

Le Jean Laborde: 3 rue de Russe, Isoraka (tel 20-22-33045; fax 20-22-32794). Also a dubious hotel, serves French cuisine, open every day from 6.30 am to midnight.

Le Relais d'Ambohibao: tel 20-22-44060. Panoramic restaurant on Lake Ambohibao, 5 minutes from Ivato airport, specialises in fish and seafood.

Le Restaurant: 65 Avenue Foch, Behoririka (tel 20-22-28267; fax 20-22-35625), French cuisine.

Le Regency: 15 rue Ramelina, Ambatonakanga (tel 20-22-21012; fax 20-22-28729).

Le Relais Normand: 21 rue Rainibetsimisaraka, Tsaralalana (tel 20-22-20788).

La Rotonde: at the *Gregoire Hotel*, rue 12 eme Bataillon Malagasy, Besarety (tel 20-22-22266; fax 20-22-29271).

Saka manga: rue Ratainarivo Lot IBK 7a Ampasamadinika (tel 20-22-35809).

Samara: tel 20-22-41715.

Solimotel: Anosy (tel 20-22-25040; fax 220-22-35820).

Try dinner at *Chez Papillon* in Fianarantsoa – it's reputed to be one of the best restaurants in Madagascar.

ENTERTAINMENT

Antananarivo has a few cinemas, discos and night-clubs. The US Cultural Centre screens free films (in English or French) on Tuesday, Wednesday and Thursday nights. The Centre Culturel Albert Camus is the city's cultural venue, hosting regular theatre performances and exhibitions. A trendy discotheque/night-club in Antananarivo is **The Bus** which opens at 10.30pm (tel 20-22-69100). The **Les**

Sons Bleus at the Hilton Hotel is supposed to be the trendiest nightclub in town with live music. A good late-night bar/restaurant/disco is **Le Beau Rivage**, 29 Printsy Ratsimamanga (tel 20-22-20202; fax 20-22-34012). There is also the **Le Caveau/Kaleidoscope**, rue de Général Rabehevitra Antaninarenina (tel 20-22-34393).

Theatre performances can be seen at the following cultural centres:

Alliance Francaise: rue Seimad, Andavamamba-Ampefiloha (tel 20-22-21107/20856; fax 20-22-22504).

Centre Culturel Albert Camus: 14 Avenue de l'Indépendance, Analakely (tel 20-22-23647; fax 20-22-21338).

Centre Culturel Américain: 4 rue Razafindratandra, Ambohidahy (tel 20-22-20238; fax 20-22-21338).

Centre Culturel Arabe Lybien: IVF 10 A Behoririka (tel 20-22-28830).

Centre Culturel Indonésien: 15-19 rue Patrice Lumumba, Tsaralalana (tel 20-22-29189).

For some outdoor activity, two of Madagascar's three **golf courses** are in the region: Ivohitra Antsirabe, 106 miles (170 km) from Antananarivo; and Golf Club du Rova (Pk 20 Andakana Ambohidratrimo; tel 20-22-22961), 8 miles (13 km) from Antananarivo.

NORTHERN REGION

There are hundreds of fascinating natural attractions in Madagascar's northern region, but unfortunately you'd have to parachute in to get to most of them as the terrain makes this one of the most untouched of provinces in what is anyway a generally underdeveloped country. Most of the people in the northern region live in the lowlands of the east and west coasts, and a road of sorts runs along each littoral. What is accessible with a bit of gumption, however, makes this part of Madagascar a must on any adventurous traveller's itinerary – awesome gorges and dramatic peaks, immaculate beaches on quiet inlets, national parks and nature reserves with species found nowhere else on the island, and a pattern of tiny picture-postcard islands to the west offering superlative snorkelling, scuba-diving, sailing and big-game fishing, not to mention sunbathing and swimming. One of these, Nosy Bé ('Big Island'), is a tourist magnet and this has, unfortunately, made it virtually the only island in the archipelago showing signs of wear from the more coarsening effects of increased tourism. It's still the best base though for excursions to satellite islands in the group, which are without doubt the equal of any in the Caribbean, South America or the South Pacific.

ANTSIRANANA (Diego Suarez)

Way up near the northernmost point of the island, on the east coast, is Antsiranana (Diego Suarez), which has sprung up over 200 years on a promontory at the southern end of the picturesque bay of the same name. The bay was allegedly once the site of a pirate colony called Libertalia, run by the maritime equivalents of England's Robin Hood and his Merry Men. Much as the tourist brochures like to dwell on this story there seems to be no historical foundation for the legend of a pirate band dedicated to good works at a time their brothers under the Jolly Roger were butchering and enslaving locals to the south. This magnificent natural harbour encircled by hills is one of the finest in the western Indian Ocean and it was regarded by the French colonial power as one of the plums of conquest which led to Madagascar's becoming a French protectorate towards the end of the 19th century. Its isolation behind the mountainous barrier of the Tsaratanana Massif meant that it never really developed its full commercial potential and its only other appearance on the world stage was during World War 2 when, on 5 May 1942, British troops defeated the pro-German Vichy French defenders of what was then a vital naval base and occupied Diego Suarez, a sharp action which had the effect of denying a strategic naval base to Japanese warships and submarines. The British then established a military administration on Madagascar which functioned until mid-1943 when the island was handed over to the Free French forces of General de Gaulle. Close to town (about 4 miles/7 km) is **Montagne des Francais**, named in memory of the French and Malagasy Allied forces killed in the 1942 confrontation. After a toughish climb you'll find a cave, the ruins of a fort, and great views across the bay. In the bay is a mini Sugar Loaf mountain, a little conical island called **Nosy Lonja**, but visitors are not encouraged as it is the place where sacred ancestral rituals are performed by local people. Lovely palm-fringed **Ramena beach** is about 11 miles (18 km) east of the port, and is an ideal day trip, which you can combine with a visit to the lighthouse that guards the harbour entrance at **Cap Miné**, the **Baie des Dunes,** or the **Baie des Sakalava** south of the headland. On the west coast, about 25 miles (40 km) from Diego Suarez, is a 1,283 ft (391 m) high table-top rock with the improbable name of **Windsor Castle**. This name must have been bestowed on this towering lump by the British troops who used it as a lookout point after defeating the Vichy French. From the top, up the old stone stairway, you'll get a tremendous view of the **Baie des Courriers**, looking out to the islands.

How to Get There

The port is connected to Antananarivo by a single, unreliable road, which is unusable during the rainy season, so flying is the best way to get there. Air Madagascar flies from Antananarivo every day of the week except Wednesday, and the airport of Anamakia served by internal air services is 6½ miles (10½ km) to the south-west.

NATIONAL PARKS AND RESERVES

Montagne d'Ambre

Within easy reach of Diego Suarez, about 15 miles (24 km) to the south, is Montagne d'Ambre ('Amber Mountain') National Park, a splendid rainforest area of 44,954 acres (18,200 ha) that covers the highest mountains in the region, on a road that is tarred and in generally good condition as far as Joffreville, around four miles (7 km) from the park entrance. There are lots of rivers, several attractive crater lakes, some spectacular waterfalls, and giant trees rising 130 ft (40 m) into the canopy and festooned with creepers and bird's-nest fern. Many of Madagascar's endemic animals are found only here, and these include the two which draw most visitors, the crowned lemur and Sanford's lemur. Both are quite abundant in the park but being the target of poachers are quite wary. Insect life is particularly rich, and this is one of the best places to see some wonderful, giant butterflies such as the superb swallowtail (*Papilio delalandeo*) which like to flutter around the waterfalls. The park has an excellent trail network and you won't need a guide. There's a broad trail to **La Grande Cascade**, an impressive waterfall at the top of a gorge. The Amber Mountain rock thrush can be found both on the path to the cascade and along the **Botanical Garden Trail**. Small lakes in the forest are the haunt of the Madagascar little grebe and the Madagascar squacco heron. The park is worth a one or two-day visit. Watch out for leeches if it rains; smear your ankles and calves with a strong insect repellent.

Analamera Special Reserve

If you want to see Perrier's black sifaka the only place to do so is the Analamera Special Reserve, an 85,745-acre (34,700 ha) sanctuary which lies to the east of the Diego Suarez-Ambilobe road and is the last refuge on the island of this extremely rare lemur. It's believed there are now fewer than 2,000 of them on this remote plateau. Most of the other animals and birds are much the same as in the Ankarana Special Reserve. Be warned that the approach roads to the reserve can be almost impossible to use during the wet season. You can find guides in the villages of Menagisy and Irodo.

Ankarana Special Reserve

The 45,035-acre (18,225 ha) Ankarana Special Reserve is about 62 miles (100 km) south of Diego Suarez. Ankarana is not an easy reserve to reach – it's strictly four-wheel-drive country – but it's such an extraordinary place that it is worth making every effort to get there. It's on a remarkable plateau holding some of the best known of the island's *tsingy* formations, a chaotic stone forest of friable razor-sharp limestone pinnacles in a science fiction landscape, beneath which lies a bewildering network of bat-filled caves, passages and fast-flowing underground rivers. These are home to some fascinating subterranean fauna, including the Nile crocodile and several rare varieties of freshwater shrimp. The only time to visit is during the dry season, which is when this nearly impenetrable natural citadel is accessible through certain caves. In the gorges between precipitous cliffs where large caves have collapsed in on themselves deciduous forests rich in wildlife have sprung up. This is the best place to see the rare crowned lemur and Sanford's lemur, and it's also one of the best areas to see a nocturnal fossa on the prowl. Tenrecs are also often seen after dusk. An experienced guide is essential if you decide to visit this area as it is a dangerous place in which to get lost. You need a guide not only to avoid getting lost, but to help you respect the numerous *fady*, or taboos, relating to places in and around the caves, some of which are guarded by the bones of ancient ancestors. The **Grotte d'Andrafiabe** cave system in the park is nearly seven miles (11 km) long and, to date, more than 62 miles (100 km) of passages have been discovered.

Tsaratanana Strict Nature Reserve

Further south the region is dominated by the forested Tsaratanana Massif, which includes the highest mountain in the country, **Mt Maromokotra** at 9,442 ft (2,877 m). This peak rises from the middle of the Tsaratanana Strict Nature Reserve, south-east of Ambanja, which also encompasses other massive crystalline rock formations. This is not open to visitors, so don't make any plans to climb Madagascar's highest peak.

Marojejy National Park

The Marojejy National Park lies in a remote north-eastern enclave, inland from the island spice capital of Sambava and north of Andapa. If you really want to get away from the crowds this is the place, but it's for toughies. Few tourists venture into the dense green rainforest that clothes the mountainsides in this 148,263-acre (60,000 ha) reserve, but those that do and challenge the virtually trackless thickets are rewarded with sightings of usually difficult-to-see fluffy white silky sifakas and the extremely rare Madagascar serpent eagle. There's also the chance of spotting the rare helmet vanga and more than a hundred other bird species. Tourist-hungry leeches are one of the penalties you'll pay for all this in what is one of the island's wettest patches – 118 inches (3,000 mm) of rain a year.

Anjanaharibe Sud Reserve

Not too far away, about 12 miles (20 km) west of Andapa, is a smaller reserve which is not so demanding. This is Anjanaharibe Sud Reserve where you might also see silky sifakas, as well as white-fronted brown lemurs and the occasional indri. A clearly defined trail will take you to some hot springs in the forest.

NOSY BÉ

It's amazing that while the authorities have renamed virtually every city, town and island in the Malagasy language the main town on their foremost tourism island is still known by its French name Hell-Ville, although French Admiral de Hell left his name on Nosy Bé long before the island off the north-west coast became a top tourist destination. In September 1839, the French brig *Colibri*, under Captain Passot, anchored off the island while exploring the coast. Local Sakalava queen Tsioméko took advantage of this to ask the French for protection against the conquering Merina, and some of the chiefs on the islands around her did the same. Passot took their requests off to Bourbon (Réunion) where Admiral de Hell was governor. He was interested enough for the French to take possession of Nosy Bé and Nosy Komba from which the French could easily dominate the Bay of Ampasindava. They were officially annexed by France in 1841. With this unlooked for gift of islands, the French also inherited Nosy Mitsio, the 'High Pointed Island,' lying to the north-east, as well as Nosy Fàly, or 'Sacred Island,' to the east. On Nosy Bé the French developed a naval base and founded a town, which they named Hell-Ville, in honour of the governor, and not because of its mosquitoes or climate, which in 1649 had helped to kill off a British settlement there. The Russian Imperial Navy also left its mark on Nosy Bé's history, Between December 1904 and March 1905, 45 ships and more than 14,000 men were stationed in the harbour of Hell-Ville during Russia's disastrous war with Japan. An inscribed pillar commemorates their visit and in the local cemetery are a number of Russian graves. Nosy Bé is now one of Madagascar's most expensive, up-market tourist attractions, and second only to Zanzibar in the Indian Ocean as an exotic tropical island destination. From the airport at Fascène, on the eastern side of the island, sugarcane fields give way to ylang-ylang plantations along the 8 mile (12 km) road to Hell-Ville, which changes from clusters of straw huts on the outskirts to decaying but still flamboyant colonial architecture. Along the route and throughout the island is a pleasant pervasive aroma from the crops of vanilla, ylang-ylang flowers and coffee. The islanders are mainly Sakalavas, although from two branches of the tribe, the Zafimena and the Zafifotsy, meaning the 'Sons of Gold' and the 'Sons of Silver.' On the whole, they are cheerful and pleasant. They still have a king, although his power is now symbolic and his main responsibility is to ensure that Sakalava traditions are upheld. The island also has a large Comorian community and to the east of Hell-Ville the 10th century ruins of Marodokano mosque recall the time when Arabs were early inhabitants of the islands. Few islanders today remember Father Clement Raimbault, although a street is named after him. He was a French missionary whose passion for botany led him from 1903 to collect plants and establish the vanilla plantations, coffee, cacao, pepper, and ylang-ylang trees whose crops still make a contribution to Nosy Bé's economy. In 1927, Fr Raimbault was instrumental in creating the Société des Plantes a Parfum de Madagascar (SPPM), which still exists. Nosy Bé means 'Big Island' in Malagasy, although as it is only 14 miles (24 km) long and 11 miles (18 km) wide, it is big only in relation to the other 20 or so islands dotting this stretch of the Mozambique Channel. It is eight miles (13 km) from the north-west coast of Madagascar, and can be reached by ferry from the mainland port of Ankify or by plane from Antananarivo, a flight which takes about an hour. The terrain is mountainous, with lush tropical vegetation and a small rainforest area in the south-east in the **Lokobe Reserve**, which has the last tract of original rainforest on Nosy Bé. You can get to the reserve by road from Hell-Ville or you can take a motorised pirogue from the port. There are four species of lemurs here, including virtually tame populations of the local black lemur (*Lemur macaco*), about 35 species of reptiles – seven of them chameleons – and around 42 species of birds.

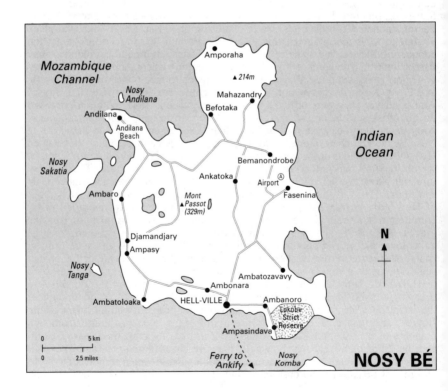

HELL-VILLE

The island's capital Hell-Ville is a large and vibrant coastal town with a small harbour, bustling markets, boutiques, shops and noisy night-clubs. Some visitors are now finding it all a little too 'touristy,' but others relieved to find more structured and reliable facilities. Most of the hotels are situated along the west coast, easily accessible from the airport and the capital. Hell-Ville must have been attractive in the French colonial days, if the remains of once-grand villas along the sea front are anything to go by. When Madagascar achieved independence from France and began its disastrous dalliance with Marxism, the town went into decline and it has been revived only by increasing injections of tourist cash. It rains for 220 days a year on Nosy Bé, but only during the night. The daytime weather is beautiful for 340 days and it only rains day and night for about 25 days. In winter, from June to September, the temperature varies between 66°F (19°C) and 75°F (24° C). In summer, from October to May, the average temperature is 84°F (29° C) during the day and 75°F (24° C) at night.

Places of Interest

The town **market** is a colourful, bustling hub of activity, where good buys include island rum and forest honey. Stallholders are always happy to bargain with you over prices. The **cemetery** is north of town and is unusual in that graves have been allotted according to the origin or nationality of the deceased. The history of the island seems to be written in the epitaphs. You'll find the **Marine Museum** at the Centre National de Recherche Océanographique (CNRO), on the road to Ambanoro. It features an assortment of poorly preserved exhibits, although there's a good collection of local seashells. The island has some wonderful beaches. The best is at **Ambataloaka**, which caters for budget to middle-range travellers, while **Ambondro** is nicknamed Palm Beach because it appeals to the more up-market tourist. All the **best beaches** are along the western side of the island, where tourist facilities and resorts are the most developed.

DJAMANDJARY

On the west coast, north of Ambondrona, is Djamandjary, the island's second largest town. There's an interesting sugar refinery and rum distilling plant here, and there are two 1903 steam locomotives which should draw train buffs to the sugar mill east of the town. They are still in working order but the sugar refinery with the capability to handle 20,000 tons barely produces half of its capacity. From Djamandjary it's a 5-mile (8 km) walk to the summit of **Mt Passot**, the highest point on the island at 1,079 ft (329 m), and its surrounding string of sacred blue crater lakes. The summit is popular as a sundowner spot and a place to watch Hollywood-type sunsets. On the far north-western corner of the island is **Andilana Beach**. There are lots of day excursions by pirogue and a great day out is to sail in one of these to one of the many other islands: Nosy Komba, Nosy Tanikely, Nosy Tanga, Nosy Tsarabanjina, Nosy Sakatia and the virtually uninhabited archipelago of the Mitsio islands.

SMALLER ISLANDS

Between Nosy Bé and the mainland is the island of **Nosy Komba**, which is Malagasy for the 'Island of Lemurs.' It has a flourishing population of virtually tame black lemurs, which happily take fruit from visitors. Nosy Komba has beautiful beaches and safe swimming. You can buy souvenirs, such as wooden outrigger canoe models, embroidery and vanilla pods here. **Nosy Tanikely** is a tiny island and marine reserve inhabited only by a lighthouse keeper. It is a mecca for snorkelling and scuba-diving and a full day excursion by speedboat or catamaran is easily arranged from Nosy Bé. Most trips to the island include lunch at a picnic spot directly opposite an excellent snorkelling beach. **Nosy Tsarabanjina** is a remote jewel, 40 miles (64 km) from Nosy Bé. This island is for the serious escapist. It is ringed by pristine coral reefs offering incredible diving, and it has some glorious white beaches. Transfers there are by powerboat or small aircraft. The **Nosy Mitsio** archipelago lies 37 miles (60 km) north-east of Nosy Bé and its 14 islands are prime scuba-diving and snorkelling destinations. Only **Grande Mitsio** is inhabited and here the waters offer a profusion of fish and other marine life. The waters around many of the other islands in this little galaxy have seldom been explored and are among the region's more pristine dive sites.

SPORT AND RECREATION

DIVING

Best months for diving are **April-July** and **September-November**. There are three main dive centres, which conduct courses for certification in CMAS, PADI, NAUI and ETDS. They are the *Madagascar Dive Club* based at Madirokely (tel 20-86-61418); *Oceane's Dream* at Ambatoloaka (tel 20-86-61426); and *Sakatia Dive Inn* on Nosy Sakatia (tel 20-86-25878). Marine life around Nosy Bé and the other islands varies according to the impact of tourism, but underwater exploration is likely to bring within mask range an array of boxfish, surgeonfish, triggerfish, damselfish, clownfish, yellowfin tuna, barracuda, sharks, eagle rays, manta rays, whale sharks, and the odd whale, not to mention sea urchins, starfish, eels, anemones and other reef life. There's good introductory diving around Ambatoloaka and the island of Nosy Sakatia.

Scuba-diving, sailing, game-fishing, and flyfishing enthusiasts are catered for by *Island Quest Adventures*, which specialises in tailormade packages for these pursuits aboard the 40 ft (12 m) luxury catamaran *Bossi*, based at Ambatoloaka. The yacht has a spacious outdoor living area as well as a comfortable saloon equipped with TV, VCR, music system and hi-tech navigational equipment, and the modern galley has ample refrigeration for never-ending cold drinks. You will be accommodated in one of four luxury double cabins or one of two single bunks. There's fully catered accommodation for two to eight people, with hot showers. Island Quest Adventures (direct bookings to yacht, tel/fax 20-86-61552; e-mail strauss@dts.mg) can also arrange hotel accommodation and island trips.

Dive Sites

Nosy Tanikely ('Island of the Small Hill'), 6 miles (10 km) west of Nosy Komba, is reputed to have the best average underwater visibility and 100 ft (30 m) is everyday stuff. Past the shallow coral reefs there's a drop-off of 56 ft (17 m) where spectacular fan, brain, and knob-horned corals abound; batfish hover and Moorish idols and long-nosed butterflyfish dart around. You can also expect to see bird wrasse, white-tailed dascyllus, clownfish, giant moray eels and turtles.

Far-off island dive sites include **Quatre Freres** ('Four Brothers'), a group of four rocks 875 yards (800 m) apart which rise up 197 ft (60 m) from the sea. Look out for giant manta, emperor angelfish, schools of bannerfish, groupers, unicorns, yellowback fusiliers, blueband snappers, oriental sweetlips, potato bass, snappers, wrasse, spotted sandsmelt, and bluefin kingfish. Divers who have been here say the Garden of Eden still exists, it's in Madagascar, but below, not above the water.

For a mid-ocean dive there's a ridge known as **Castors Shore** with a wall over a 190 ft (58 m) drop-off. *Tropical Adventures* will take you there, and to other spots on *Star Cat*, a 14.5 x 8m catamaran with six double berths, four bathrooms with showers, a Bauer diving compressor, six complete diving rigs, deep-sea fishing equipment, and a vast saloon with an eight-seater dining area and kitchen. The catamaran is based at Ambataloaka. You can contact them in Madagascar (tel 20-86-61586), or in South Africa at 109 Eccelston Crescent, Bryanston, Johannesburg (tel 11-706 5987; fax 11-706 6205; e-mail tropicaladv@icon.co.za).

FISHING

On Nosy Bé's virtually unpopulated west coast is **Terre Rouge** ('Red Earth') beach camp. This is a laid-back base for both diving expeditions and deep-sea angling, fishing for turbo-charged bonito, yellowfin tuna in the 110 lb (50 kg) class and sailfish. Swim out from the beach and you are on the edge of a reef where the seabed drops suddenly and you are in a world of fabulous corals and tropical fish. Reservations can be made through Charles Norman Safaris in Johannesburg (tel 11-888 3591; e-mail fishafrica@intekom.co.za).

SAILING

The Nosy Bé region is a treat for yachtsmen, especially during the cruising season between August and November. There are around 20 islands and islets offering ideal sailing conditions. Tidal range is 15 ft (4.5 m) during the equinoctial tide and 8 ft (2.5 m) the rest of the time. Ampasindava Bay benefits from a micro-climate with a Force 2-3 wind in the afternoon. This is the only area in Madagascar where the south-south-east trade winds known as the *varatrazo* don't blow.

CAVING

Most of the island caves of interest to serious speleologists are to be found in the limestone of the Ankarana Massif in the north. Since 1980, they have been explored on a number of occasions by British and French cavers. Four of the caves have a length of more than 6 miles (10 km), and the longest one, **Ambatoharanana**, is about 11 miles (8.1 km) long. Only one cave of any length has been surveyed outside the Ankarana area, and that's in the Narinda area, north-east of Mahajanga (see *Exploring: Western Region* p.142).

ACCOMMODATION

Antsiranana (Diego Suarez)

Hotel Fiantsilaka: PO Box 36, Antsiranana (tel 20-82-22348). In the town centre, 12 air-conditioned or ventilated rooms, Chinese restaurant.

Hotel de la Poste: rue Joffre, PO Box 121, Antsiranana (tel 20-82-22044). 6 miles (9km) from airport, near harbour in downtown area, 28 air-conditioned rooms, private bathroom, restaurant, bar.

Hotel La Racasse: rue Surcouf (tel 20-82-22364). In the downtown area near the Air Madagascar office, 24 air-conditioned or ventilated rooms, restaurant and bar.

Le Paradis du Nord: rue Villaret Joyeuse (tel 20-82-21405). Also in the downtown area, six air-conditioned rooms, one studio, bar, excursions, fishing.

Maymoune Hotel: 7 rue Bougainville (tel 20-82-21287).

Nouvel Hotel: 75 rue Colbert (tel 20-82-22262), 15 rooms.

Valiha Hotel: 41 rue Colbert, PO Box 270, Antsiranana (tel 20-82-21531).

At **Ramena beach:** 11 miles (18 km) from Diego Suarez is:

Fihary Hotel: PO Box 584, Ramena (tel 20-82-22862; fax 20-82-29413). 16 ventilated bungalows, restaurant, bar, *bureau de change:* amenities for water-skiing, diving, board sailing, and parasailing.

Ambanja

Hotel Palma Rosa: tel 20-82-30929. 56 miles (90 km) south-west of Diego-Suarez, 10 air-conditioned or ventilated rooms, a la carte restaurant, bar.

Sambava

Hotel Carrefour: PO Box 53, Sambava (tel 20-88-92060). On the north-east coast in the self-proclaimed world capital of the vanilla bean, 25 air-conditioned or ventilated rooms, restaurant, bar, trekking, diving.

Hotel Calypso: PO Box 40, Sambava (tel 20-88-92008). Budget-type accommodation.

Hotel le Club Plage: PO Box 33, Sambava (tel/fax 20-88-92064). Up-market hotel, swimming pool.

Las Palmas: PO Box 120, Sambava (tel 20-88-92087). On the north-east coast seafront, eight air-conditioned rooms, restaurant, bar, excursions.

Nouvel Hotel: PO Box 66, Sambava, medium-priced hotel.

NOSY BÉ

In **Hell-Ville** there is:

Blue Fish Hotel: PO Box 3409, Antananarivo (tel 20-86-61394) 2^1/2 miles (4 km) from the centre of town, facing the harbour, six air-conditioned rooms with TV and private bathroom, restaurant, bar, fishing, boutique.

Hotel de la Mer: Boulevard du Docteur Manceau, PO Box 159, Nosy Bé (tel 20-86-61353), with 24 rooms.

Beach hotels include:

Chez Louisette: (tel 20-86-61085; fax 20-86-61285) northern Nosy Bé, four basic bungalows, communal ablutions, suitable for budget travellers, on a lovely beach, restaurant.

Belle Vue:

Hotel Les Cocotiers Villages: PO Box 191, Nosy Bé (tel 20-86-61314; e-mail cocotier@dts.mg). 14 miles (23 km) from the airport, on the beach facing Nosy Tanga, which at low tide you can visit on foot, 26 air-conditioned bungalows, restaurant, bar, marine excursions.

Hotel Village Andilana Beach: (Club Med) Plage d'Andilana, (tel 20-86-61523). 25 miles (40km) from the airport and 17 miles (27 km) from Hell-Ville, air-conditioned rooms with TV, private bathroom, three restaurants, two bars, swimming pool, sea-front casino.

L'Ampasy Village: PO Box 19, Djamandjary (tel 20-86-61477; fax 20-86-61158). 16 miles (26km) from the airport, near the town of Djamandjary, 16 air-conditioned bungalows with veranda, restaurant, swimming pool, nautical club, motor-cycles.

Le Baobab: PO Box 45, Nosy Bé (tel 20-86-61437; fax 20-86-61293). Upmarket French-owned hotel, recommended for family groups with young children, seven air-conditioned beach bungalows, stunning beach, water-skiing. Pirogue excursions with leisure fishing, scenic hiking trails into the wooded surrounds. Regular boat transfer service to Nosy Sakatia island, pool, excellent a la carte menu.

Nosy Bé Hotel: tel 20-86-61430; fax 20-86-61406. 14 miles (23 km) from the airport facing Nosy Tanga, five bungalows, 22 rooms, restaurant, bar, shops, swimming pool. Fishing, kayaking, diving and hobie-cat excursions can be arranged.

Other areas of Nosy Bé:

Chez Gerard et Francine: PO Box 193, Hell-Ville (tel 20-86-61409). Villa with extra rooms at the end of Ambataloaka, no restaurant but several good ones a short walk away.

Eco-village Fihavanana: PO Box 203, Ambatozavavy (tel/fax 20-86-61475). Nine bungalows close to Lokobe forest reserve, no beach. Trips to surrounding islands. European-run, solar power, excellent restaurant.

Hotel Soleil et Découvertes: PO Box 3, Ambataloaka (tel 20-86-61424), four rooms, central.

Hotel Tropical: PO Box 198, Nosy Bé (tel 20-86-61416), seven bungalows.

Hotel Ylang Ylang: tel 20-86-61401; fax 20-86-61402. In the Ambataloaka area, basic accommodation, nine rooms, noted for its restaurant

Marlin Club: PO Box 205, Madirokely (tel 20-86-61418; e-mail marlin.club@simicro.mg). 10 miles (16 km) from airport at Madirokely beach (near Ambatoloaka village), 16 luxury rooms, Italian restaurant, bar, fishing, diving, aqua-sports centre. Day excursions to other islands.

Residence d'Ambatoloaka: PO Box 130, Ambataloaka (tel 20-86-61368). 11 miles (18 km) from the airport on the west coast, 12 air-conditioned rooms, restaurant and bar, shopping souvenirs, marine excursions.

Villa Blanche: PO Box 79, Ambondrona (tel 20-86-61085; fax 20-86-61285). 11 miles (18 km) from the airport, 32 air-conditioned bungalows, private bathroom, eight rooms, restaurant, marine excursions.

Nosy Komba

Hotel Lémuriens: PO Box 185, Nosy Bé. rustic but charming little hotel at a sunny beach. The new rooms are spacious with en-suite bathrooms, restaurant. Pre-book by fax 20-86-61371.

Les Floralies: PO Box 107, Nosy Bé (tel 20-86-61367). Seven bungalows, restaurant, bar.

Nosy Sakatia

Delphino Villa Bungalows: tel 20-86-61668. Budget Malagasy-style bungalows.
Sakatia Dive Inn: PO Box 186, Hell-Ville (tel 20-86-61514; fax 20-86-61367).
   Two types of bungalows: square bungalows with en-suite bathrooms, and
   basic tent-shaped bungalows with communal ablution facilities, good
   restaurant, geared up for divers, but not exclusively.

Nosy Mitsio

L'Hotel Tsarabanjina: Contact in Antananarivo (tel 20-22-28514; fax 20-22-
   28515, e-mail Groupe.Hotel@simicro.mg). Up-market venue for discerning
   travellers, 20 beach bungalows, tastefully designed and built out of wood,
   fans, en-suite bathrooms, very good restaurant with great sea view.

EATING OUT AND ENTERTAINMENT

For reasonable meals in **Diego Suarez** try *La Venilla* or *Halmah Resto* on rue Rois
Tsimiaro, which is where the locals like to eat. **Nosy Bé** has many excellent
restaurants, where you can savour spicy Malagasy, Creole, Continental and
seafood dishes. Try *Le Papillon* (tel 20-86-61582) in Hell-Ville for good three-
course dinners, or *Restaurant Classic* on Boulevard Poincaré (tel 20-86-61136) for
grills. There are also some lively night-clubs, such as *Vieux Port* at the old port;
and the French-run *Bar Nandipo*, in Hell-Ville, which is a popular place for expats
to gather.
   For motorbike hire, speak to La Caravane Malagasy in Madirokely (tel 20-86-
61635; fax 20-86-61411), they have a range of motorbikes available at excellent
rates.

WESTERN REGION

The west of Madagascar is the home of the Sakalava people, the largest and most
powerful tribe on the island in the 18th century until the highland Merina swooped
down from the interior to incorporate the region into their growing kingdom. The
racial characteristics and customs of the Sakalava show the distinctive influence
of African immigrants to this part of the island, the closest area to the African
continent. The western coastal belt is 60-125 miles (97-201 km) and much wider
than the east coastal plain, which has an average width of only 30 miles (48 km).
The west is a land of great rivers and wide stretches of savannah, which are the
grassland grazing grounds of the Sakalava's great herds of zebu cattle. The
tourism infrastructure is the least developed of any of the regions. Roads are poor
to non-existent, but this is one of the attractions for walkers and mountain-bikers
and makes the west a stamping ground for travellers in search of adventure.
Unless you have a lot of time to spare (months preferably) the best way to get
around is by air.

MAHAJANGA

Mahajanga (Majunga), is at the mouth of the Betsiboka River where the estuary
widens into Bombetoka Bay. It is Madagascar's second largest commercial
port. Its name is commonly translated as the 'Place of Flowers.' The town has a

large Indian population and is dotted with numerous temples and mosques, including a beautiful Vishnu temple. Comorians were almost as numerous in the town as locals until 1976-77, when there were a number of ugly racial riots and most of the immigrants were repatriated to Grande Comore. The Comorian community has slowly increased again since then. In the 18th century the town was a trading post for Arab slavers and Indian merchants whose descendants are still active in local business today, but these days they trade in commodities such as sugar, coffee, spices, cassava (manioc), vegetable oils, timber, and vanilla and are involved in industries such as meat processing, fishing, rice, palm fibre, saw-milling, and the manufacture of soap, cement, paper, tallow, bags and rum. Mahajanga is also the centre of a seafood and fishing industry, but none of the fish seems to be sold to locals except at high prices in the town's restaurants. The weather here can be oppressively hot, but the town gets fanned by cooling breezes from its seaward side. There are miles of deserted beaches, although the sea offshore here is stained blood-red by the soil which is carried down by the Bestsiboka River from the eroded highlands. It's an attractive if decrepit type of town, with potholes in the roads and many boarded-up, crumbling houses, with people living in shacks behind them. There's an ornamental garden in name only, the Jardin des Amours, which is derelict and unkempt; in the port ancient, mouldering twin-masted wooden boats rest in the mud at low tide, and other vessels lie rotting. More active sail-driven traders beat up and down the coast with cargoes of charcoal and raffia. It was once a stylish holiday resort, built on a grid system with wide boulevards and elegant buildings with wrought-iron New Orleans-style balconies and fine filigreed doors. There is still some interesting architecture, pleasant shady arcades and long, wide promenades with lots of gorgeous bougainvillea, the flowering plant identified and named by the renowned botanist Commerson in 1771, but the town gives the feeling of being caught in a time warp. The neo-brutal concrete cathedral near the post office on rue Batot seems oddly out of place amid the decadent air of the town. At dusk women make fires on the beach and their families gather round to dine on zebu beef kebabs. The town is proud of a natural attraction: still standing after 700 years is an enormous baobab nearly 50 ft (15 m) around dominating the seafront at the end of the Avenue de France, near its junction with Boulevard Poincaré. About 1^1/2 miles (2^1/2 km) uphill from the giant baobab, near the Plage Touristique, is the **Mozea Akiba** museum with displays that are relevant and worth seeing before you trek out of town to the Cirque Rouge, the caves at Anjohibe and the reserve at the Ampijoroa Forest Station. On the highest point in town is **Fort Rova**, built in 1824 by the conquering Radama and reached along rue du Maréchal Joffre. It's good for views over the town. Across the estuary from Mahajanga is the small fishing village of **Katsepy**, whose main claim to fame among travellers is Chez Chabaud, which serves wonderful French-style cuisine, local oysters and fresh seafood. A car ferry leaves twice a day for Katsepy from the quay not far from the bottom of rue du Col Barré.

FURTHER AFIELD

Mahajanga is a good base if you want to explore the interior. Seven miles (12 km) from the town, not far from Amborovy airport, is one of the island's great geological attractions – a large sandy canyon ending in the **Cirque Rouge**, a rosy amphitheatre studded with strange purple, red, and rust-coloured rock formations. Like the famous multi-hued Coloured Earth of Mauritius, the cirque and its rocks are best viewed either very early or late in the day when their rainbow colours come alive. This is a lovely secluded place to camp as you can draw fresh water from a little spring at the head of the cirque and the beach is quite close. Further afield are the caverns of **Anjohibe**, some 50 miles (80 km) north-east of town. A visit to these caves is a rare experience. Many of them hold huge colonies of bats, as well as glistening stalactites and stalagmites and fossilised remains. Anjohibe is the only cave of considerable length that has been surveyed outside the Ankarana Massif area. It is situated in the Narinda area, in the rough limestone known as karst. The caves are among the most interesting in the country and some are spectacular cathedral-like chambers with large natural swimming pools. The largest goes 5,800 yards (5,300 m) underground. These caves are accessible only between April and October and even then a four-wheel drive vehicle is necessary to get to the site; a professional guide is also recommended. About a mile (2 km) south-west of Anjohibe is **Anjohikely**, with only a mile (2.1 km) of passages so far explored. Anjohikely is a similar cave system to Anjohibe, and some crumbled passages seem to lead from its north-east end towards Anjohibe, but erosion appears to have made a viable connection between the two systems improbable.

Caving Madagascar's underground world remains one of the least explored in the southern hemisphere. Lots of limestone karst areas, such as Kelifely and Bemaraha, have never been investigated in depth due to problems of seasonal access, transportation of equipment, and lines of supply, especially food for visiting cavers. There are many excellent caving areas in the region, all offering serious speleologists the possibility of exciting exploration and the opportunity to go where no one has been before. Among them are the Narinda area around Anjohibe, the area around Mitsinjo, on the Mahavavy River, the Namoroka and Bemaraha *tsingy* regions between Mahajanga and Morondava, and around Toliara, in the south. Guides are a must in these areas, not necessarily for the underground bit, but to get you to the entrances in the first place.

Lying close to the shore in the landlocked bay of Mahajamba are two islets, **Nosy Manja** ('Handsome Island'), and **Nosy Lulangane** ('Island Where the Spirits are Raised'), which in the early 16th century formed the combined site of the largest Arab settlement on the west coast. This was looted and reduced to rubble by treasure-seeking Portuguese in 1506, but you can still see the ruins of the once-flourishing trading and fishing community and stumble over relics of those turbulent times. The 49,500-acre (20,000 ha) forestry station of **Ampijoroa** is the most accessible section of the 149,548-acre (60,520 ha) strict nature reserve of **Ankarafantsika**. It is about 75 miles (120 km) south of Mahajanga on the RN4 and contains a dry western deciduous forest with lots of trees carrying formidable arrays of spikes, known as *hazomvoay*. The reserve is also home to lemurs and is considered to be one of Madagascar's finest bird-watching areas, with more than 100 species flitting about. There are no hotels, so you'll either have to make do with a day visit or camp overnight. Local guides will help you to find your way around the excellent network of trails. As well as the deciduous dry forest, you'll see some very interesting wetland species at and near the Amboromalandy dam, about 19 miles (30 km) west of Ampijoroa, along the main road. Nearby **Lake Ravelobe** is home to a pair of Madagascar fish eagles. Ankarafantsika is one of the few areas established to protect western region vegetation. Extensive research is done here and the simple accommodation is reserved for scientists. There are, however, camping facilities. The reserve is famous for its abundant flora and fauna, including such rare birds as the Madagascar fish eagle, and many varieties of reptiles, flowers and plants. The forest paths are wide and well maintained. There are seven species of lemur. The easiest to see is Coquerel's sifaka (*Propithecus verreauxi coquereli*), one of the most beautiful of them all. Don't forget to get a permit from the Department of Water and Forests (*Direction des Eaux and Fôrets*) or ANGAP in Mahajanga or Antananarivo.

MORONDAVA

Morondava is a coastal town which lies in a prosperous rice-growing area and was once the centre of the Sakalava kingdom. It is still the site of many of their tombs. The magnificent Sakalava funerary art, their tombs and carvings can be seen to the north-east and south of the town, although most have been stripped of their more erotic decorations. This seaside resort has broad white beaches and excellent swimming spots. Morondava doesn't get many tourists groups but it is growing in popularity with the more adventurous independent traveller. It is the main centre for visits to the western deciduous forests. The quickest way to reach Morondava from Antananarivo is on one of the daily Air Madagascar flights. A major attraction, less than an hour's drive by car or bush taxi, is the splendid **Avenue of the Baobabs**, which is, in fact, the road connecting Morondava with Belo sur Tsiribihini. About 44 miles (70 km) to the north-east of Morondava is **Kirindy Forest**, widely known as Swiss Forest because of the company engaged in logging operations there. In spite of these commercial activities the 24,711-acre (10,000 ha) forest area is a top destination for anyone interested in nocturnal fauna such as fossas, tenrecs, mongoose, and giant jumping rats. You can see Madagascar's only freshwater turtle, the flat-tailed tortoise, the fat-tailed lemur and a variety of chameleons. Best time to visit Kirindy is between October and April. You can get more information on Kirindy from Swiss management company Centre de Formation Professionelle Forestière (CFPF) at their office in Morondava.

Also to the north of Morondava and south-east of the coastal town of Maintirano lies **Tsingy de Bemaraha**. This vast 375,590-acre (152,000 ha) national park, the biggest in the region, encompasses the magnificent canyon of the Manambolo River, and a spectacular area of needle-like limestone pinnacles known locally as *tsingy*. The landscape has been described as one of the most foreboding on earth, but its forests, lakes and mangrove swamps provide tranquil shelter for six species of lemur, including the rare Decken's sifaka, and a wide variety of birds. Towering calcareous cliffs and forests line the rivers and a great variety of succulents are uniquely adapted to thrive in the cliff crevices. Ancient ancestral tombs can be seen among the rocks in some areas and traditional rituals are still performed here. Most of the area is inaccessible to tourists and for a really memorable view you should club together with other visitors and pay for a flight over it. This area of the Tsingy Massif is a UN World Heritage site.

ACCOMMODATION

Mahajanga

Hotel les Roches Rouges: 58 Boulevard Marcoz, La Corniche (tel 20-62-23871).

22 rooms, 12 of which are air-conditioned, restaurant, swimming pool, tennis court.

Hotel le Tropicana: in Mangarivatra (tel 20-62-22069).

Kanto Hotel: Boulevard la Corniche (tel 20-62-22978). About a mile (2 km) north of town.

Le Ravinala: PO Box 645, Mahajanga (tel 20-62-22968). 11 air-conditioned or ventilated rooms, restaurant.

New Continental: PO Box 418, Mahajanga (tel 20-62-22570).

Nouvel Hotel: 13 rue Henri Paul (tel 20-62-22110), air-conditioned rooms.

If you are looking for budget-type accommodation try *Hotel Tropic:* PO Box 250, Mahajanga (tel 20-62-23610); or *Hotel Chez Chabaud* (tel 20-62-23327).

Katsepy

Chez Chabaud's has 10 basic bungalows, but it is better known for the food of Madame Chabaud, who trained as a cook in France. If you want to eat or sleep there you can book through her daughter's hotel of the same name on the Avenue du General Charles de Gaulle, not far from the Town Hall (*Hotel de Ville*) in Mahajanga (tel 20-62-23327).

Morondava

Le Royal Toera: (Apavou Group) PO Box 353, Morondava (tel 20-95-52027; fax 20-95-52443). Located on the west coast beach of Nosy Kely ('Little Island'), just off Morondava. It has 16 air-conditioned bungalows, mini-bar, private baths, *Le Voilier* restaurant on the beach serves seafood and other local specialities, and home-made cocktails at the *Ti Punch* bar. The beach gives access to a variety of watersports as well as big-game fishing and sunset cruises on the hotel's catamaran, swimming pool, tropical gardens.

Les Bougainvilliers: PO Box 50, Morondava (tel 20-95-52163). Facing the seashore, 3 miles (5 km) from the airport, 31 air-conditioned rooms or ventilated bungalows, restaurant.

Chez Cuccu Bungalows: PO Box 22, Morondava (tel 20-95-52319).

Chez Maggie: PO Box 73, Morondava (tel 20-95-52347). This beachfront hotel is 5 miles (7¹/₂ km) from the airport, five bungalows, restaurant and bar.

Renala au Sable d'Or: PO Box 163, Morondava (tel 20-95-52089).

For budget-style accommodation:

Hotel Continental: PO Box 141, Morondava (tel 20-95-52152). In the downtown area, 28 air-conditioned or ventilated rooms.

Hotel Li Oasis: PO Box 38, Morondava (tel 20-95-52222).

Hotel Menabe: PO Box 16, Morondava (tel 20-95-52065).

EATING OUT

In **Mahajanga** you can enjoy the *Kohinoor* restaurant's Indian food, a pizza on the Avenue de Mahabibo, or a French-style tuck-in at *Chez Chabaud* in **Katsepy**. *Chez Maggie* in **Morondava** has a restaurant open to non-residents which serves great seafood such as fresh crab steamed in coriander and spices, and very garlicky shrimps. The surroundings are as pleasant as the food.

SOUTHERN REGION

The Tropic of Capricorn cuts through the southern part of Madagascar, an invisible rule across the land which helps to demarcate the stark southern area that contrasts so vividly with the moist, tropical vegetation of the east coast. The southern region is the badlands by comparison, arid semi-desert covered in vast tangles of cactus-like plants, baobabs, writhing thorn trees, aloes, and bloated succulents. Down here among the sand and scrub gigantic *Aepyornis* 'elephant birds' laid their last clutches of huge eggs a thousand years ago before vanishing from the landscape forever. Fragments of their egg shells can still be found scattered among the dunes around Cape Faux and Cape St Marie Special Reserve on the island's southernmost tip. It's illegal to remove them, but you'll be pestered by local children selling bits of shell and carefully reconstructed two-gallon eggs. The region inland from the west coast town of Toliara at the end of the RN7 is Madagascar's most arid and is rightly known as the 'spiny desert.' The route inland to Isalo, a four-hour drive along the RN7, passes through the domain of a number of tribes. At the coast live the Vezo fisherfolk, a clan of the mighty lowland Sakalava tribe. The Vezo live off the sea, and many are semi-nomadic, paddling out their dug-out pirogues to small uninhabited offshore islets where they set up temporary fishing settlements, building crude shelters or using their sails as tents. This is also the land of the Antandroy ('People of the Thorns') and the Mahafaly ('Bringers of Joy'), who are best known for their ornamented burial tombs. These are often decorated with paintings and carvings depicting scenes from the lives of those interred. You'll also see zebu horns on some tombs, the cattle present at all important Malagasy rituals and ceremonies. These humped cattle are symbolic of wealth and function as a link with the ancestors, who are regarded as ever-present forces in the lives of their descendants. You'll find beautifully painted Mahafaly tombs at the village of **Andranovory**, about an hour's drive inland from Toliara along the main road. Some tombs in the south are topped by intricately carved *aloalo*, or wooden posts featuring figures and animals. At the village of **Sakaraha** on the way to Zombitse and Isalo you enter the land of the Bara people, who show the closest resemblance to African people of any Malagasy ethnic group. The capital of the Bara is the town of **Ihosy**, at the junction of the RN7 to Fianarantsoa and the RN13 going to the southern coast. It is a pleasant little market town where tall Bara men in dazzling *lambas* and straw homburg hats stalk through the streets, probably thinking about their next rustling raid, as a Bara is not held to be a man unless he has stolen a respectable number of cattle from a neighbouring herd. Bara dwellings, like those of other southern tribes, are simple and square-shaped. The Malagasy never build the round huts common throughout Africa and, ethnically speaking, you can often tell where you are in Madagascar just by looking at the style of the houses. In the south, overlapping upright wooden planks are used for the walls, in the eastern forest they are built of interlaced split bamboo and palm-thatched; on the inland plateau, rural houses are made of earthen bricks with thatched roofing, whereas urban houses usually have steeply tiled roofs and wide balconies balanced on brick columns. They are two or three-storeys high, with a kitchen at the top, living quarters in the middle, and storage below.

TOLIARA

Toliara is situated on St Augustine's Bay, on the Mozambique Channel above the mouth of the Onilahy River. The town is the major port of south-western Madagascar but its real interest to the visitor is that it's a convenient base from which to explore this incredible region. The town is on the verge of becoming a major west coast tourist destination as the jumping off point for trips along the Onilahy ('Grand River') and through Mahafaly country. Toliara has 60,000 inhabitants but no beaches to call its own, only mudflats, but it is the access point for some stunning areas north and south and is the centre of a vibrant cultural area. The forest of **Miary**, 4 miles (7 km) from Toliara, is sacred to local people, who will tell you that the forest grew from a single banyan tree when old branches fell and took root. Legend has it that the tree grew on the grave of a young girl who was sacrificed in order to divert the floodwaters of the neighbouring Fiherenana River, and also that a boa is coiled inside the root of the original tree. In the forest there's the royal **tomb of King Baba**, surrounded by some impressive octopus trees. Staff at Toliara's **University Museum** on the Boulevard Tsiranana will explain the region's burial customs. In the museum are masks – rare in Madagascar – and fetishes. One rather grisly fetish is known as a 'brain key,' and was used in sorcery. The hair on its head is real. If someone wants to place a curse on you, they obtain some of your hair and take it to a sorcerer, who uses it to make a 'brain key.' This spell then drives you insane. Another item on display is a frightening mask of the little-known Mikea people. The teeth in the mask are real and the Mikea wear the masks for protection when they have to leave their home territory. Other compelling exhibits are erotic sculptures from Sakalava tombs. The university also runs a **Marine Museum** on rue de la Porte, where you can see a preserved coelacanth. The 'road' north from Toliara to **Ifaty** village is a shocker, but the 14-mile (22 km) stretch and the time it takes to get to this area is well worth braving by bush taxi. The offshore reef here is gaining fame among the diving fraternity as a mini-Great Barrier Reef. At both full and new moon, there are dramatic tidal variations in the area, so you must time your diving, snorkelling and other aqua-sports to take account of this rise and fall. You can hire diving equipment in Ifaty but make sure you check it thoroughly before you use it. The coast here is a string of white sand beaches, sparsely dotted with the tiny ramshackle villages of Vezo fishing communities. Inland is an amazing landscape dominated by spiny octopus, finger and signature trees, as well as weird stands of baobabs, including the strange bottle baobab (*Adansonia fony*). Some of Madagascar's endemic birds are found only in this area and twitchers come from all over the world to glimpse the long-tailed ground-roller, running coua, sub-desert mesite and other endemic species.

Anakao

South of Toliara, below St Augustine's Bay, is the coastal village of Anakao, the largest Vezo settlement in the region, which can be reached by pirogue from Toliara in two hours. This is where you'll find a fisherman to take you across to the island of **Nosy Ve**, which also offers world-class diving sites around superb coral reefs, and to nearby **Nosy Satrana**. Anakao is an historical place: one of the first contacts between the southern Malagasy and visiting Europeans took place here at the end of the 16th century. **St Augustine** is 19 miles (30 km) south of Toliara and is the bayside site of ill-fated British attempts to establish a settlement on this coast in 1644. There's an easy 2¹/₂ mile (4 km) walk from here along a dirt track to the **Caves of Sarodrano**, which are fed both by a freshwater spring and by the sea. Take a mask and snorkel and you'll be able to swim here and watch some of the odd fish which seem to like the crystal clear but brackish water.

ISALO NATIONAL PARK

Isalo Massif lies between Toliara and Ihosy, an arid area of sandstone scored by ravines and gorges and speckled by weirdly shaped rock formations eroded over the centuries by wind and water. The altitude varies between 1,686 ft (514 m) and 4,160 ft (1,268 m). In the middle of this rugged, desolate area is a gem, the **Isalo National Park**, a 199,443-acre (82,515 ha) reserve which stretches the entire length of the massif and is one of Madagascar's most popular hiking areas. If you have time to visit only one wilderness trekking area this is the place to choose. Isalo has a haunting atmosphere and it's not surprising that local superstitions (*fady*) surround many of the places in the park. The Isalo area is the domain of the Bara tribe and many sites in the park are sacred to them. The rocks are full of hidden Bara tombs, which your guide will not want to point out to you or want you to visit. There are also much older, sacred sites of the Sakalava, who once lived here before moving to settle in the more fertile lowlands of the coast further north. You might come across caves where the Sakalava of old buried their dead, and then sealed them up. Many of these retaining walls have collapsed, leaving bleached skulls and bones open to view. Deciduous woodland covers about a fifth of the park, which has some interesting animals and birds, although poaching is reducing the wild populations. Most of the park's 55 species of birds can be spotted along the fast-flowing streams. One of them, Benson's rock thrush, is found only at Isalo. Mammals in the park include three species of lemur, of which the ring-tailed is the one you are most likely to see. The others are sifakas and brown lemurs. The high-walled **Canyon des Singes** ('Canyon of the Monkeys') probably gets its name from its resident white sifakas. Succulent enthusiasts visit to see the dumpy endemic 'elephant's foot' plant (*Pachypodium rosulatum*). A 5-6 day trek through Isalo will take you to the **Grotte des Portugais**, a deep cavern in the northern part of the park which some say was used by Portuguese sailors shipwrecked on the west coast in 1527. Bara legend, however, holds that the cave dwellers were *Vazimba*, aboriginal people they believe were the first inhabitants of Madagascar. There are other numerous trails and one pleasant hike is to the spring-fed **Piscine Naturelle** for a refreshing swim. The heat in the park can be fearsome. You can take a fully inclusive tour of the area or hire a guide and explore it on your own. Plan to spend at least three days in the park if you have the time. The town of Ranohira to the south of the park makes a good base for visits.

Sapphires

In mid-1999 something remarkable happened in the area of this peaceful wilderness. Near the village of **Ilakaka**, on the edge of the national park, a farmer unearthed an odd-looking rock in a river bed. It turned out to be a high-quality sapphire and the find has since turned the dusty little settlement into a mining boom-town reminiscent of the early Klondike, and with all its worst features. Sapphires of a quality and colour rarely seen on world jewellery markets are now being mined. People have flocked to the area, drawn by the dream of instant fortunes. Initial attempts by the authorities to regulate prospecting and mining ended embarrassingly when all the gendarmes sent to the area took off their uniforms and started digging themselves. With sapphire-crazed prospectors eyeing the national park area as a likely site for gemstones there are fears that one of the island's most magnificent stretches of unspoilt wilderness could be under serious threat. Madagascar's sapphires first made headlines back in 1995 when one the size of a football was found. The uncut blue rock was 89,950 carats, weighed about 38 lb (17 kg), and was nine times the size of the world's largest cut sapphire.

BEZA-MAHAFALY SPECIAL RESERVE

Directly to the south of Isalo, about 22 miles (35 km) north-east of Betioky-Sud and just west of the Sakamena river, is the Beza-Mahafaly Special Reserve. This reserve is split into two parts. The first (250 acres/100 ha) lies along the Sakamena River, the second parcel of 1,186 acres (480 ha) lies 3 miles (5 km) away from the first and it contains a rocky ridge among flat areas of spiny desert. There are five species of lemurs in the reserve. Sifakas are quite common and the Verraux's sifaka is particularly beautiful, with its snow-white fur, round black face, and a waving tail as long as its body. There are also sportive lemurs and ring-tailed lemurs, the most gregarious of the species, in the reserve. Among the 61 species of birds are a number characteristic of the southern spiny desert. A guide is essential if you plan to visit, as the tracks leading to the reserve from Betioky are a confusing maze. Trails in the reserve are overgrown, an indication of just how few tourists make the effort to visit. The best time to go is between June and October. Madagascar Airtours in Toliara specialise in this area and can set you up with a vehicle and a guide.

Zombitse National Park

Halfway between Toliara and Isalo, 16 miles (25 km) north-east of Sakaraha, is the 53,128-acre (21,500 ha) Zombitse National Park. This fascinating little forest straddles the RN7 and is one of the last remaining transitional forests, where the southern spiny bush meets the tropical deciduous forests of the island's western region. It has become so biologically significant that it is high on Madagascar's priority conservation list. The forest is home to what may be one of the world's rarest birds, Appert's Greenbul, first discovered in this dry, trackless, scrub forest, its only known habitat. The forest is also a good place to see butterflies.

On the southernmost point of Madagascar is the isolated **Cap St Marie** reserve atop high sandstone cliffs, accessible only by 4x4 vehicle (or on foot). Round the point heading north up the east coast is **Faux Cap**, a wild spot of shifting sand dunes and enormous breakers. This is where the now extinct elephant birds seem to have liked to nest and lay their monster yard-long eggs.

TAOLAGNARO

The coastal people of the south-east first came into contact with Europeans in 1504 when shipwrecked Portuguese sailors built a fort and spent 10 years on a small island close to the mouth of the Ambinanibe River and near to where Taolagnaro stands today. The first French toehold on Madagascar was the site on a peninsula at the south-eastern tip of Madagascar they claimed for their young Crown Prince, the future King Louis XIV, and named it Fort Dauphin in his honour. The French built their fort in 1643 on the site of an existing Malagasy village called *Taolankarana*, meaning 'grave site,' and it was here in 1661 that Etienne de Flacourt wrote his seminal *Histoire de la Grande Ile de Madagascar*. It was Flacourt who, when the French were forced to quit their settlement, recovered the old stone tablet left by the Portuguese at their island fort and added to it in Latin: 'You who pass by, read this and you will profit. Do not trust the natives. Farewell.' The old French settlement grew into the town now officially Taolagnaro, although it's still commonly referred to as Fort Dauphin. Some say this is the most beautiful town in Madagascar, sitting on a windy cape where the coastline is reminiscent of Cornwall or northern California, with its spectacular bays and beaches, overlooked in some areas by low sand cliffs and backed by high peaks. **Libanona** is one of the more attractive of the town's beaches. Taolagnaro combines the tropical humidity of the east coast with the dry heat of the southern interior and there are pleasantly refreshing breezes. The weather is warm but agreeable for eight months of the year, with a cool winter for the remaining four months. It gets very windy during September and October. The easiest way to get around Taolagnaro is either on foot or by pedal power, which can readily be hired. Mountain-bike excursions, mountain climbing, trekking, and river canoeing trips can all be organised locally. There are good views from **Pic St Louis**, the mountain that overlooks Taolagnaro, at 1,736 ft (529 m). It's a 1¹/₂-hour hike from the base to the summit.

Further Afield

The **Lokara Peninsula**, 7¹/₂ miles (12km) north-east of town has a chain of inland waterways which you can reach by pirogue from **Lake Lanirano**. A guided excursion is your best bet. If you take this watery route you'll negotiate rivers, lakes and humid mangrove swamps. You can get there along almost non-existent roads through spectacular land and seascapes. If you whistle to fishermen in their pirogues they will paddle inshore to give you a chance to buy some of their catch, oysters by the thousand, fish, mussels and crayfish. In the luxuriant forest along the way you'll find huge elephant ear plants with their white and yellow flowers, and an hibiscus which blooms yellow in the morning and changes to red at night. Access to the island of **Tranovato** ('House of Stone'), or Ilot des Portugais, is by pirogue. You can visit the ruins of the fort built by shipwrecked Portuguese sailors in 1504 and Madagascar's oldest monument. This little island is also noted for its lovely butterflies. Some 33 miles (53 km) north of Taolagnaro is **Manafiafy**, or Baie de Sainte-Luce, the place where the French first landed in 1642. There's a lovely beach and a small nature reserve established to preserve the humid coastal forest. On the way there, or back, the **Saiadi Botanical Park** is worth a halt to admire the orchids and palm trees. If you leave Taolagnaro at sunrise on a Monday morning you can reach **Ambovombe** 62 miles (100 km) to the south along the RN13 in time for the weekly cattle market. People walk up to 20 miles (30 km) in searing heat to buy and sell stock or just hang around this market, and the different tribes and castes can be recognised by their choice of headgear, hairstyles and weapons. On the way back to Taolagnaro a detour to the coast 9 miles (15 km) south of Amboasary will bring you to **Lac Anony**, a shallow 5,807-acre (2,350 ha) stretch of water, near the mouth of the Mandrare River, frequented by flamingos, waders and other water-loving birds.

NATIONAL PARKS AND RESERVES

Berenty Private Nature Reserve

The up-market Berenty Private Nature Reserve is 56 miles (90 km) west of Taolagnaro and offers comfortable if expensive accommodation if you feel like extending your visit. Forest trails, hordes of ring-tailed lemurs, white sifakas, fruit bats, radiated tortoises, 100 species of birds and 115 plant species, including endemic succulents, the rare triangular palm, euphorbias, baobab trees, and carnivorous pitcher plants, make this reserve one of Madagascar's top attractions for tourists. The reserve is a fascinating floral and faunal frontier between the moist east coast and the arid south and is one of the best protected and most studied forests in Madagascar. The highlight for most visitors to the reserve is the population of southern lemurs, the ring-tailed lemur and the Verreaux sifaka. Despite the reserve's small size (655 acres/265 ha) it has a well-planned network of broad trails. Night walks through the tamarind gallery forest along the Mandrare River and in sub-arid thorn scrub should reward you with sightings of white-browed and Madagascar Scops owls, as well as delightful grey mouse lemurs, fat-tailed dwarf lemurs and white-footed lemurs. Reserve excursions include visits to the spiny forest within the reserve boundary and to the vast nearby sisal plantation, said to be one of the world's largest. Berenty is a good place to watch birds. During the day you'll see or hear among others the crested drongo, banded kestrel, cuckoo shrike, kites, and lovebirds. Birds of prey are quite common, particularly the Madagascar buzzard. Giant couas are easily seen and are quite tame. Of particular interest is Berenty's **Museum of Antandroy Culture**, voted by visitors one of the best ethnological museums in Madagascar. The reserve is accessible throughout the year and can be reached after a two-hour drive by bush taxi or, more comfortably, by taking an organised tour from Taolagnaro.

Another private reserve nearby is **Kaleta Park**, or Amboasary Sud, which is regarded as a budget version of Berenty. Certainly its prices are lower, but visitors still enjoy a similar wildlife experience, which includes troops of semi-tame lemurs and sifakas taking any food on offer.

Andohahela National Park

Andohahela National Park, also known as the Manangotry rainforest, is 25 miles (40 km) north of Taolagnaro. It was established in late 1998 to preserve three distinctly different areas of forest – rainforest, spiny forest, and east-west transitional forest – and as it is still in a developmental stage you should check out the latest information at the **Andohahela Interpretation Centre** west of Taolagnaro. The centre issues permits and will give you directions to the three areas of the park. There are more than a dozen species of lemurs in the park.

ACCOMMODATION

Toliara

Chez Alain: PO Box 89, Toliara (tel 20-94-41527; fax 20-94-42379). Bungalows, popular place to stay.

Hotel le Capricorn: PO Box 158, Toliara (tel 20-94-42620; fax 20-94-41320). Downtown area, 26 air-conditioned or ventilated rooms, restaurant, bar.

Hotel Central: tel 20-94-42880. Budget accommodation, in the centre of town.

La Mangrove: tel 20-94-41527. 10 pleasant bungalows, near the Caves of Sarodrano, diving centre.

Hotel Plazza: PO Box 486, Toliara (tel 20-94-41900; fax 20-94-41903). Up-market, 32 air-conditioned or ventilated rooms, restaurant, bar.

Safari Vezo: PO Box 427, Toliara (tel 20-94-41381). In Anakao, popular beachfront bungalows, return trip by pirogue from Toliara included in price.

Ifaty

Bamboo Club: PO Box 47, Ifaty (tel 20-94-42717). 16 miles (26 km) from town on the Ifaty road, 16 standard bungalows and two family-size bungalows, restaurant.

Hotel Lakana Vezo: PO Box 158, Ifaty (tel 20-94-46220). 16 miles (26 km) north of Toliara, one of the oldest hotels along the coast, eight ventilated bungalows, restaurant, bar, water-skiing, and all the equipment you need for diving. You can hire a boat to reach the coral reef.

Mora Mora: PO Box 41, Ifaty (tel 20-94-41016). 16 miles (26 km) from town, 12 bungalows, restaurant, bar.

Isalo National Park

Hotel les Joyeux Lémuriens: popular backpacker hotel.

Isalo Ranch: basic accommodation.

Relais de la Reine: French-run up-market hotel, blended into the massif so you don't see it until you pull up in front, rustic-style with furni.ure and beams carved from local wood. Book through tour operators in Antananarivo.

Taolagnaro

Hotel Chez Gina: PO Box 107, Taolagnaro (tel/fax 20-92-21266). Downtown area, about a mile from the airport (2 km), 6 luxury bungalows, 14 standard bungalows, two studios, restaurant, bar.

Hotel le Dauphin: also up-market and about 2 miles (3¹/₂ km) from the airport, 32 comfortable rooms, restaurant and bar. *Hotel le Galion* is the annexe. Reservations for both can be made through PO Box 54, Taolagnaro (tel 20-92-21238).

Hotel Miramar: PO Box 54, Taolagnaro (tel 20-92-21238). Up-market hotel 2¹/₂ miles (4 km) from the airport, about a mile (1¹/₂ km) from town, 16 ventilated rooms equipped with private toilet and bathroom, restaurant serving Chinese specialities near the hotel, bar.

Kaleta Hotel: Galliéni Avenue, Taolagnaro (tel 20-92-21287; fax 20-92-21384). Government-owned, 32 rooms.

Budget

Baie des Singes is owned by a local Antandroy princess, picturesque wooden bungalows, meals include good local seafood.

Hotel Chez Jacqueline: tel 20-92-21126. Four rooms with bathroom.

Hotel Mahavoky: PO Box 137, Taolagnaro (tel 20-92-21332). Centrally located.

Berenty

Gite de Berenty: 12 ventilated bungalows with private toilet and shower, 10 ventilated rooms, restaurant, bar.

EATING OUT

In addition to the hotel restaurants in Toliara, you'll find the *Corail, L'Etoile de Mer* and the *Zaza Club* along Boulevard Lyautey and the seafront. The better menus offer Malagasy, Indian and French dishes. This area is famous for its seafood, especially lobsters. *La Mangrove* and its sister hotel, *Chez Alain*, are reputed to serve some of the best food around. The *Miramar Hotel* in Taolagnaro has a leading seafood restaurant where you can enjoy a memorable Chinese fondue and a choice of local wines. In the main street of Ambovombe you'll find real steak and chips in the *Relais Antandroy* at budget prices. The local mini-barbecue is known as the *fatapera*. The prickly pear, which thrives in this region, is an important food source to the local people and is a good thirst quencher. Also worth checking out is the inn at Ambohimahavelona.

ENTERTAINMENT

When it comes to night-clubbing in south-west Madagascar the best place is Toliara's **Zaza Club**. You have to get there by *pousse-pousse* (rickshaw) because taxis in Toliara don't operate after 10pm and the Zaza Club only opens at 11pm. You will find plenty of kamikaze rickshaw 'pilots' outside Toliara's hotels touting for business late at night.

EASTERN REGION

Madagascar is famous for its evergreen rainforests and most of these are found on the east coast. This area is a must for anyone interested in nature, with its great diversity of flora and fauna, magnificent rugged mountain scenery with rivers flowing down to the ocean, friendly people, abundant seafood and fruit, and the beautiful island gem of Nosy Boraha (Ile St Marie). The east coast is one of the island's richest agricultural regions, providing high quality produce for export. The main areas of the region are Toamasina, the Masoala Peninsula, Nosy Mangabe Reserve, the eastern rainforests of the Mananara National Park, and the Andasibe National Park (Périnet-Analamazoatra reserves). Getting around eastern Madagascar is easy; from flying to boating, hitchhiking, mountain biking and travelling by bus and bush taxi (*taxi brousse*). Although the beaches are beautiful, swimming is safe only in demarcated protected areas due to omnipresent sharks. December to March are the wettest months, although April to November can also be dampish.

TOAMASINA

Toamasina (Tamatave), the capital of the east coast, is said to have been named by a Portuguese navigator who baptised the then small fishing village with a name reminding him of St Thomas. Another version says that at the beginning of the 19th century the young Merina king Radama, continuing the island unification process his father initiated in the central highlands, is said to have exclaimed '*toa masina*' ('but it's salty') as he tasted the seawater here for the first time. Another, more unsavoury, explanation is that the name means 'filthy place.' From hereabout, two centuries ago, the Betsimisaraka started their long voyages along the northern part of the island in large outrigger pirogues loaded with warriors. They headed for the Comoros islands and the coast of Mozambique to pillage and capture slaves. In the 17th and 18th centuries, buccaneers made this part of the east coast their sanctuary. Northwards, Antongil Bay, protected from the winds, and delectable Ile St Marie (St Mary's Island), proved so seductive that many pirates settled for good in these havens, marrying daughters of local chiefs and kings, and giving rise to a mixed-blood generation that became famous as the Zana-malata. At the beginning of the 19th century, the Zana-malata were the masters of this coast. Now only a few place names remain to remind you of their heydey. The area was occupied repeatedly by the French in the 19th century, who used it as a base for their conquest of the interior in the latter part of the century.

Toamasina seems to have an everlasting holiday atmosphere, although it is a busy commercial hub. Cargo ships berth at the port, which is the gateway from Madagascar to the rest of the world. From here the main export products of the country are shipped: vanilla, coffee, cloves, graphite, chromite, and lychees. Like all big ports, Toamasina is a cosmopolitan town and has drawn people from all regions of the country. Though it is the old capital of the Betsimisaraka people, it is now populated by a great number of Antesaka and Antandroy who come from the south-east and the south. The city centre is characterised by colonial architecture, with wide avenues shaded by coconut palms, banyans and flame-trees. The impressive Avenue de l'Indépendance boasts a double line of royal palms. The town was rebuilt after a cyclone destroyed most of it in 1927 and the most modern part now radiates from tree-lined Avenue Poincaré. You can lose your sense of direction strolling in the outskirts because it is all so flat. Seamen on the spree might enjoy lively nights, but in the daytime the town has a sleepy atmosphere. Visitors are always struck by the wide deserted beach. The reason there are no people swimming is that sharks congregate offshore and have prevented Toamasina from becoming popular as a bathing resort. *Pousse-pousse* ('pull-pull') rickshaw men tout for passengers around the Town Hall and the terminus station of the railway from Antananarivo.

Bazary Bé (big market) and **Bazary Kely** (little market) are worth a visit and offer lots to see and buy, including fruits, spices, snacks, vegetables and handicrafts. The **Jardin d'Essai et Parc Zoologique d'Ivoloina**, 8 miles (13 km) north of the city, on the banks of the Ivoloina River, was created as a botanical garden in 1898. The gardens contain specimens of the region's flora and fauna. There is a small zoo on the site, which also acts as an education centre, and a captive breeding programme for endangered species, which uses the site as a halfway house for animals being reintroduced into the wild. It is sponsored by international research institutions. You can view various species of lemurs and turtles. It's open to visitors, as is the small regional museum at the university, not far from the seaside. **Foulpointe** is the gallicised name of the old landing place Hopeful Point (now officially Mahavelona), an hour's drive north from Toamasina. This is a popular bathing resort, thanks to its inviting shark-free lagoon. At the northern end of Foulpointe you can see the ruins of old fortifications. The thick walls of the circular enclosure are more than 20 ft (6 m) high. They are the remnants of a citadel built in the 1820s by order of King Radama I after he led an army of more than 10,000 men down to Toamasina in

May 1823 and subdued the whole coastal region. This was when the Betsimisaraka kingdom of the 'numerous inseparables' united the previous century by Ratsimilaho, a pirate's descendant, was absorbed into the Merina empire. A little further north along the coast is **Mahambo** which like Foulpointe, is a small village with cabins roofed with *falafa*, the fronds of the *ravinala*, the fan-shaped Travellers tree found everywhere in the region.

CANAL DES PANGALANES

Southwards, the harbour station at **Manangareza** is the end – or the starting point – of a world apart, the Canal des Pangalanes. For hundreds of miles this artificial canal created in colonial times joins lakes and lagoons inside offshore sand bars in one incredibly long protected navigable waterway which can be travelled in safety no matter how rough the waters are in the outer ocean. From Toamasina, the canal runs more or less parallel to the coast all the way down to Vangaindrano, some 435 miles (700 km) away. The name Pangalanes is derived from the Malagasy word *ampanaiana*, describing strips of sand separating lakes, but nowadays the name simply means the canals dug out between them. The rosary of linked lakes and lagoons is, in effect, an inland sea and the waterway is used by flotillas of pirogues travelling to deliver loads of wood, cargoes of bréde (spinach-like leaves), and bananas to Toamasina. It might not be the modern river highway originally planned by the French – only 261 miles (420 km) are at present navigable – but this small version of the Amazon is a very busy link in the east coast communications system, as well as rapidly developing into one of the island's tourist attractions. From Toamasina, there are various ways of exploring the Pangalanes, from long tours on the shallow draught *MV Mpanjakamena*, to day round-trips by speedboat. A cruise along the waterway passes through beautiful lush forest and small fishing villages and is a wonderful excursion. There are guesthouses and hotels at the tourist centre of **Lake Ampisabe**, a small resort in a lagoon known in Malagasy as *Ankanin'ny Nofy* ('House of Dreams'), and also in the surrounding forest. Bush House maintains a private reserve near the lagoon in which some of the rarer species of lemur can be seen, as well as chameleons and radiated tortoises. Further south the villages of **Mananjary** and **Manakara** are small coastal towns with lovely long beaches, but wide open to crashing surf. Swimming is not recommended at either place.

How to Get There

Air Madagascar has a round-trip daily flight between Antananarivo and Toamasina and also two weekly flights to and from Réunion. If you buy a round-trip regional ticket on an Air Madagascar flight you are offered 30% discount in off-season and 20% discount in high season on domestic flights. You can rent a car in Toamasina but with fairly reasonable fares taxis are the best way to get around. For short hops take a rickshaw. The railway to Antananarivo is not fully operational along its entire 135-mile (217 km) route, although there are passenger trains running on the 84-mile (130 km) line to Brickaville (Ampasimanolotra). These depart every two days. A bumpy but interesting way to reach Toamasina from Antananarivo is by road in a 4x4 vehicle. If you want to organise a 4x4 trip to the coast or a cruise down the Pangalanes contact Patrice de Comormond at TTM in Antananarivo (tel 20-22-25205).

FURTHER AFIELD

Some 19 miles (30 km) east of Moramanga, near the Antananarivo-Toamasina railway line, is the eastern rainforest **Andasibe National Park** (also known as Périnet-Analamazoatra), which also incorporates Mantadia National Park to create Madagascar's most visited wildlife sanctuary. Many species of lemur are found here, including the largest of the lemur family, the black and white indri, which is mentioned in Malagasy legends as a link with the origins of mankind. One tale is that long ago an indri gave birth to two boys, one of whom stayed in the trees while the other decided to walk on the ground, thus giving rise to the human race. Another tells of a father, Koto, who went into the forest with his son where they were transformed into lemurs. Locals say the name *babakoto* given to the indri means 'father Koto.' Most visitors come to the park to see the indri, whose eerie wailing cry can be heard like a siren early in the morning. Plenty of guides are available to lead you to their haunts and you will be very unlucky if you don't see one. Along with indris you can see grey bamboo lemurs and red-fronted lemurs, as well as 109 species of birds – at least 30 species of them warbling and chirping birds – seven species of chameleon, 10 tenrecs, three carnivores and five rodents. The forests are among the richest in Madagascar for amphibians, many of which breed in the small streams that meander through the park. The most striking for frog-watchers is the miniature golden mantella (*Mantella aurantiaca*). Also found here are beautiful and bizarre insects and spiders, many reptiles and a large variety of birds. Colourful orchids, creepers and ferns make this an Eden for those with an interest in botany. Guides are available for both day walks and night strolls and comfortable accommodation is available. The world-famous Périnet section itself is 2,002 acres (810 ha) in size, and lies in a region of low hills covered by degraded forests. It has some beautiful little lakes, including wishbone-shaped **Lac Vert**. The town of **Andasibe** is a three-hour drive to the west of Antananarivo. It was originally a lunch halt for passengers taking the train from the capital to the coast. Although trains still chug along the line the service is, to say the least, unreliable. Andasibe has a lively atmosphere and the Hotel Buffet de la Gare still serves meals in the old grand French colonial style. It's a toss up whether your main reason for visiting the town should be the national park or the slap-up meals. To the west and about 30 minutes' drive from Andasibe is the town of **Moramanga** whose few attractions include a market, a memorial to Chinese road workers, the *Chutes de la Mort* ('Waterfalls of the Dead'), and the **Musée de la Gendarmerie** at Camp Tristany, where you can view police memorabilia as well as more cultural exhibits.

To the north of Toamasina is the 56,834-acre (23,000 ha) **Mananara National Park** which includes a large inland rainforest and 2,471 acres (1,000 ha) of offshore islets and their surrounding reefs. The park is known for its dwarf lemurs. Other protected species include the indri, ruffed lemurs, aye-ayes, Nile crocodiles, and a range of colourful shore and reef life including the endangered dugong. Surrounding the park is a further area of 345,947 acres (140,000 ha), including 44 miles (70km) of coastline, which has been proclaimed an International Biosphere Reserve by UNESCO.

THE MASOALA PENINSULA

In the north-east, the Masoala Peninsula is an as yet untrammelled wilderness which probably harbours the largest number of unclassified species in

Madagascar. Little tourist infrastructure exists in this wilderness of trees and coral and, apart from local villagers, few people except unusually hardy adventurers visit this fascinating area. This is one of Madagascar's last great wildernesses, with some of the island's greatest treks. The trek route is a path connecting the numerous villages and settlements along the way. The trek from Maroantsetra to Antalaha takes about five days. For those with less time, the western side of the peninsula has shorter but fascinating day trails. Dense jungle and high mountainous terrain make many parts of the peninsula unapproachable by land, while coral reef barriers make access by sea difficult except by small craft such as sea kayaks. Kayak safaris start in Maroantsetra and sail 50 miles (80 km) along the peninsula's coastline to Nosy Bihento and other sites. Trips offer great snorkelling opportunities and lovely walks in the rainforests, as well as beach-hopping by kayak through the marine reserve area of the national park. For details about kayaking contact Island Retreats and Sea Kayak Safaris in South Africa (tel 21-689 8123; e-mail kayakafrica@earthleak.co.za). The **Masoala National Park**, best known for its unique and endangered terrestrial fauna, is also edged by extensive coral reefs, which are suffering increasingly from coral and sand mining. In October 1997, a conservation-minded government formally established this 1,013,131-acre (410,000 ha) national park, which also encompasses whale-breeding grounds among its other attractions. This is the country's largest national park and it contains many animal species unique to Madagascar, including the red-ruffed lemur, the Madagascar red owl, serpent eagle, and numerous species of rare butterflies. You should plan Masoala expeditions only from September to January, as the weather during the rest of the year can make walking an ordeal rather than a pleasure.

MAROANTSETRA

Maroantsetra, said to be the rainiest place in Madagascar, is the gateway to the Masoala Peninsula; it is also a popular destination for nature and wildlife enthusiasts because of its proximity to the nearby island of **Nosy Mangabe**. Transport to the island is easy to organise here. Any expedition to Masoala should begin or end with a visit to this extraordinarily beautiful tropical island, where there is a reserve protecting the aye-aye, as well as various other animals. Air Madagascar flies to Maroantsetra from Antananarivo twice a week. Lying 3 miles (5 km) offshore from Maroantsetra in the **Bay of Antongil** is the **Nosy Mangabe Special Reserve** where you can see the aye-ayes introduced in 1966, when they were thought to be in danger of extinction, and other species of lemurs, geckos, and frogs. There's even a harmless snake which is only found on this 1,285 acre (520 ha) island, which is composed of granite rocks rising steeply out of the sea and clothed in dense rainforest, full of huge jumbled boulders and tinkling, clear, freshwater streams. There are numerous tracks through the forest, and sandy coves, palm shelters and a waterfall add to the idyllic nature of the reserve. The island rises steeply in the middle to 1,086 ft (331 m). Birds are scarce, and only 39 species in low densities have been recorded here. Swimming is not advised because of the danger from sharks.

NOSY BORAHA (Ile St Marie, St Mary's Island)

Betsimisaraka legend says that when God finished creating Madagascar he had a morsel of material left over – nothing much, just a sprinkling of sand, soil, and rocks which He moulded, drawing it out to make a long (35 miles/57 km), narrow (4¹/2 miles/7 km) and low (200 ft/60 m) island. As a special boon he gave it more than the usual amount of fertility. He then placed it down in the sea just off the north-east coast of Madagascar, with a channel five to 10 miles (8-16 km) in width separating it from the mainland so that it was a tiny world of its own. From the seaward side, St Mary's does not look particularly enticing, just a sandy stretch covered in scrub. On the Madagascar side of the island is a placid channel. On this landward side, surrounded by the low and well-wooded hills, is a lagoon. The western side of St Mary's has plenty of coconut palms, breadfruit, pandanus, and lots of sturdy specimens of the Traveller's tree. Chameleons and lemurs survive in the protection of the luxuriant vegetation. Some islanders have grouped their huts in clearings, flimsy dwellings of bamboo standing on stilts because of rains that turn the ground into bogs and swell the brooks which cascade down from the low hills to lovely little creeks, each with a beach sloping gently to the sea.

Off the southern end of St Mary's is a smaller island, an islet known from the trees that grow there as **Ile aux Nattes**. It is separated from St Mary's by a narrow channel of water, surrounded entirely by coral reefs. On this islet flourishes one of the most magnificent orchids to be found anywhere in the world, the 6 ft (2 m) tall, rosy *Eulophiella roempleriana*, as well as the trees whose fronds are used to weave mats (*natte*) and other useful household things. The earliest European visitors to St Mary's were the cut-throat buccaneers of the 17th and 18th centuries, such as Captain Kidd and Thomas White. They made the island their resort and so notorious that ever since it has been known as *Forbans*, or Pirate's Island. Some pirates left their last earthly remains on the island; all contributed generously to the gene pool which produced the coast's Zana-malata community of half-breeds. There's an interesting modern footnote to the pirate era. For 300 years treasure hunters have searched the Indian Ocean for Captain William Kidd's buried booty. By the time he was hanged in London for piracy and murder in 1699 he was said to have amassed gold, silk and jewels worth more than £70-million in today's money. So far, no one has discovered the hiding place of this hoard. Now an American, Barry Clifford, says he has found the wreck of Kidd's ship the *Adventure* lying off St Mary's Island and he thinks it could hold clues that will lead him to the treasure. Burnt timber, ancient rum bottles and shards of porcelain dating from Kidd's era have already been brought to the surface from what Clifford believes to be the Scottish pirate's scuttled ship, lying close to the beach in less than four fathoms (8 m) of water. Kidd sailed the leaking *Adventure* to St Mary's Island and set fire to it before sailing off in a captured merchant ship to America, where he was arrested in Boston and sent in irons to London.

St Mary's is prettier and quieter than its opposite number on the west coast, Nosy Bé, and it is also less expensive. The best time to visit is in June and mid-August to late November, even though rain can, and does, fall throughout the year. December to March is the cyclone season, and the island has at times experienced some crackerjack blows. From July to September you might spot humpback whales (*baleines à bosse*) passing offshore on their way to their breeding grounds further up the east coast at Antongil Bay and indulging in such typical behaviour as breaching, lobtailing, flippering, spyhopping, and singing. Some local hotels offer whale-watching boat trips. Humpback whales (*Megaptera novaeangliae*) fast when they're in the warm waters of the tropics. Although they may have fed on the odd fish on their long swim north, they won't have enjoyed a satisfying meal of krill since leaving Antarctica, where they gorge themselves for nine months, gulping about 150 lb (68 kg) of krill, tiny shrimp-like crustaceans, in one mouthful and eating upwards of a ton of food every day. A few weeks after giving birth in the Bay of Antongil female humpbacks lead their nursing calves back to the feeding grounds they set out from, and the cycle begins all over again.

Ambodifotatra

The only town of any size on St Mary's is the capital, Ambodifotatra. The airport is situated 8 miles (13 km) away on the southern tip of the island and hotels do their own airport transfers. There are no telephones and few cars, but there are many trails and you can best explore it by hiring a bike or a moped. You can walk everywhere, even across the island from east to west, although you'll be pestered by children who want to 'guide' you. Diving enthusiasts and anglers are welcomed at the fully equipped activity centre on the island, which will fit you out for some marvellous snorkelling and fishing. St Mary's has the world's only **pirate cemetery** and it is one of the most visited attractions on the island. You'll find the cemetery overlooking the **Baie des Forbans**. The walk to the cemetery takes about 20 minutes, and the several tidal creeks have to be crossed along the way. It is accessible only at low water. The gravestones are weathered but some names and dates are still legible, as is the deeply engraved skull and crossbones on the stone slab over Joseph Pierre le Chatier, one of the last of his breed to die on St Mary's. A pirogue trip to the islet of Île Aux Nattes, with lunch at the Hotel Orchidee – *poulet an coco* – also makes a pleasant outing. There's a small aquarium on little **Ilot Madame**, south of town, housing sea turtles and varieties of tropical fish. It's connected by two causeways, one to Ambodifotatra in the north, and the other to Belle Vue in the south. Places of interest in and around Ambodifotatra include the island's oldest Catholic church (1857) which was a gift from the Empress Eugenie of France, and the 1753 **Granite Fort**. The fort is not open to the public, but it's still quite impressive from the outside. There's also a **market** which is open on Tuesday and Thursday, days when the islanders consider it taboo to work in their fields.

ACCOMMODATION

Accommodation ranges from the comfortably luxurious to the most basic.

Toamasina

As a centre for both tourists and businessmen, Toamasina has a wide range of quality hotels. The best ones – and most expensive – are the *Neptune, Miramar* and *Joffre*.

Hotel Joffre: 30 Boulevard Joffre (tel 20-53-32390; fax 20-53-23294). In the downtown area, restaurant, *bureau de change.*

Hotel Miramar: tel 20-53-32870. Is on Boulevard Ratsimilaho, at the seaside, close to town, 22 rooms and bungalows, swimming pool, two tennis courts, *bureau de change.*

Hotel Neptune: 53 Boulevard Ratsimilaho (tel 20-53-32226; fax 20-53-32426). On the seafront, 2¹/2 miles (4km) from the airport and close to the town centre, 47 air-conditioned rooms with TV, casino, *bureau de change*, and swimming pool.

Other up-market hotels are:
Les Flamboyants: downtown area, 15 rooms air-conditioned or simply ventilated.
Noor Hotel: Boulevard Oua (tel 20-53-33846). Downtown area, 55 rooms, 27 air-conditioned, shopping gallery, *bureau de change.*
At the beach resort of **Mahambo**, 53 miles (85 km) from Toamasina, is *Le Dola* (Avenue de la Liberation; tel/fax 20-53-32350), with 20 ventilated bungalows, restaurant and bar, marine excursions, plantation visit, diving, hunting during the season.

At the lagoon resort of **Foulpointe**, north of Toamasina:
Hotel le Gentil Pêcheur: 37 miles (60 km) from the airport, close to the beach, 25 bungalows, bar, the *Au Gentil Pêcheur* Chinese restaurant serves remarkably good food.
Manda Beach: (tel 20-53-32243; fax 20-53-27299) which claims to be one of the most comfortable hotels in the country, 37 miles (60 km) from the airport, on the beach, 16 rooms, eight suites, 18 bungalows, private bathroom, swimming pool.

Canal des Pangalanes

Bush House: located on Lake Ampisabe, 44 miles (71 km) from Toamasina, six double rooms and two bungalows, restaurant and bar, nautical club: surfing, canoes and kayaks. You can book through Antananarivo-based tour operator Boogie Pilgrim (tel 20-22-25878; fax 20-22-25117; e-mail bopi@ bow.dts.mg).

Andasibe

Most of these hotels do not have telephones so enquire at the tourist office in Antananarivo or organise your booking through a tour operator.
Buffet de la Gare Périnet: seven rooms with common bathrooms and five bungalows close to the forest. Memorable food in French colonial style.
Feon'ny Ala Périnet: 15 wooden bungalows facing rainforest-covered slopes, private bathroom, Chinese restaurant. Take a torch for a night walk with forest guides. You can also camp here.

Nosy Boraha

Accommodation here is in simple three-star beach hotels and rustic bungalows, rather than luxury resort properties, which add to the appeal of the island's unspoilt, natural charm. Most bookings are made through tour agents in Antananarivo and telephone numbers have been given where possible.
Hotel Boraba: tel 20-22-22398; fax 20-22-28365; e-mail transco@dts.mg. On the south-east coast, bungalows.
Le Bungalows de Vohilava: tel 20-22-63051; fax 20-22-21271. About 2 miles (3 km) from the airport, self-catering.
La Cocoteraie: on the north-west point, a hotel which must be seen and experienced to be believed, an amalgam of palm-frond huts, a little bar, outdoor restaurant, and pirogues lying on the beach complete the picture of a tropical island paradise. Fishing skin-diving, ping-pong, volley ball.
La Crique: a popular seaside hotel 19 miles (30 km) to the north-west of the island, eight bungalows, restaurant, mountain bikes for hire.

Orchidée Bungalows: tel 20-22-23762; fax 20-22-26986. 8 miles (12 km) from the airport, 10 bungalows and four air-conditioned or ventilated rooms, fishing, volley ball, surfing.

Lakana: 2¹/₂ miles (4 km) from the airport, 12 bungalows, restaurant, bar, mountain-bikes for hire.

Soanambo: tel 205740. Close to the airport at Vohilava, the most expensive hotel on the island, seafront, 21 bungalows, restaurant, bar, swimming pool, tennis court, surfing, bicycles for hire.

EATING OUT

Most of the hotels in **Toamasina** offer good, sustaining meals, but those of the *Neptune* and *Joffre* are especially notable. There are also many Chinese restaurants in town – if you enjoy Chinese cuisine the food at *Pacifique*, not far from Boulevard Joffre, is worth trying. At **Nosy Boraha** the *Hotel Antsara*, just north of La Crique, has a good set menu for dinner, otherwise scout the harbour area. Don't forget lunch at the *Hotel Orchidée*, on the Ile aux Nattes.

Mayotte

Swimming with turtles,
Ngouja, Mayotte

GEOGRAPHY

Mayotte is one of the four islands which geographically make up the Comoros archipelago, lying at the northern entrance to the Mozambique Channel between Africa and Madagascar and half-way between the Tropic of Capricorn and the Equator, but it is the only one of the quartet which is still a French possession. It is 44 miles (71 km) from the island of Anjouan, 149 miles (240 km) from the Comoros capital of Moroni, on Grande Comore, 186 miles (300 km) from Madagascar, 280 miles (450 km) from the African coast, 932 miles (1,500 km) from Réunion, and 5,592 miles (9,000 km) from Paris. It has an area of 145 sq miles (375 sq km), slightly more than twice the size of Washington DC, or just over half the size of the Isle of Man.

Mayotte – *Maoré* to the indigenous islanders – is made up of two main islands and about 20 islets, all inside an encircling coral reef which encloses one of the largest (463 sq miles/1,200 sq km) and most beautiful lagoons in the world. The main island is known as **Grande Terre** and its smaller (5 sq miles/12 sq km) neighbour across a mile (2 km) of water is known as **Petite Terre**, Big and Small Land respectively. Mamoudzou, the largest town, is on Grande Terre and the Pamandzi International Airport is on Petite Terre, which is linked by a single boulevard to a rocky islet called Dzaoudzi, which is both Mayotte's administrative centre and the base for a permanent contingent of the French Foreign Legion.

Topography
Mayotte is geologically the oldest of the islands in the archipelago, which means that it has had a few million years' head start on the other three, both in the erosion of most of its volcanic contours to make the terrain more gently undulating and in the creation of a superb coral reef, the only one of the islands in the Comoros virtually surrounded by such a barrier. There are only two major breaks in this 93-mile (150-km) coral girdle, and these passes permit the entry of ocean-going vessels to secure berths and protected anchorages within the lagoon. The encircling reef is up to a mile (2 km) wide in places and encircles a lagoon up to 2 miles (4 km) wide and 230 ft (70 m) deep. The 115 mile (185 km) coastline is heavily indented and if you look at a map of Mayotte you'll see that in shape the island looks like a sea-horse standing on its head. This fancied resemblance has led the island to adopt the sea-horse as its symbol and use it as supporters of the shield bearing its official coat of arms. Along the coastline there are numerous, usually deserted, beaches of golden or black sand, interspersed with belts of mangrove.

The highest point on the island is Mt Bénara in the south, which is a mere 2,165 ft (660 m), but a far more arresting peak is Mt Choungui, further south, which is 1,949 ft (594 m) high. In central Mayotte there is Mt Combani at 1,565 ft (477 m), and in the north-east is Mt Mtsapéré at 1,877 ft (572 m). On Petite Terre, the ancient volcanic activity that created Mayotte has left an unplumbed lake-filled crater in the north of the island called Dziani Dzaha, with a crater rim 338 ft (103 m) high. Erosion over the millenia gave Mayotte extremely fertile soil. At one time this mineral-rich mantle supported widespread tropical rainforest, but much of this was cleared for sugarcane plantations in the 19th century and now provides more depleted arable land for the food crops, grazing and coconut palms of subsistence farmers. Even so, more than a quarter of the island still has thick forest cover and abundant rains keep most of the island green all year round.

CLIMATE
The tropical climate in this part of the world produces only two recognisable seasons. There's a hot, humid, monsoon rainy season, from November to April, known as *kashkazi*, when you can expect the odd cyclone, and a more temperate dry season from May to October, known as *kusi*, which is the **best time** to visit the island. During the rainy season downpours are usual in the morning, followed by sun in the afternoon, a pattern which tends to create steam-bath weather, when humidity can

rise to 100%. The average annual temperature is 77°F (25°C), with the maximum from January to March of 82°F (28°C) and a minimum from July to September of 75°F (24°C). The coast basks in sunshine nearly 3,000 hours a year, about 8½ hours a day in the dry season, and six hours a day during the rainy season. The temperature of the water in the lagoon remains pleasantly warm throughout the year.

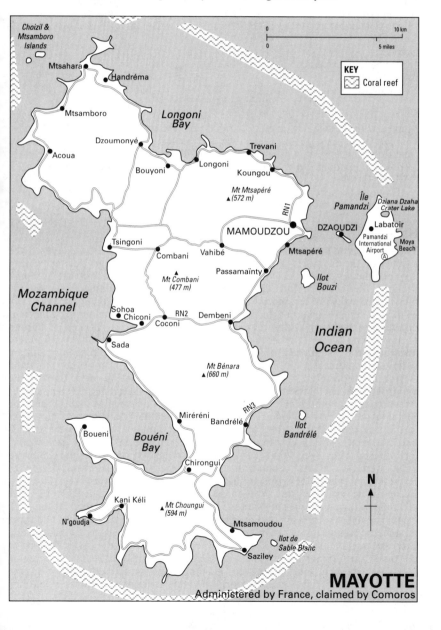

KEY

Coral reef

Choizil & Mtsamboro Islands

Mtsahara

Handréma

Mtsamboro

Longoni Bay

Dzoumonyé

Acoua

Bouyoni

Longoni

Trevani

Koungou

Mt Mtsapéré ▲ *(572 m)*

RN1

Île Pamandzi

Dziana Dzaha Crater Lake

Labatoir

DZAOUDZI

MAMOUDZOU

Tsingoni

Combani

Vahibé

Mtsapéré

Pamandzi International Airport

Moya Beach

Mozambique Channel

Mt Combani (477 m) ▲

Passamaïnty

Ilot Bouzi

Sohoa
Chiconi

RN2

Coconi

Dembeni

Indian Ocean

Sada

Mt Bénara ▲ *(660 m)*

RN3

Miréréni

Bandrélé

Ilot Bandrélé

Boueni

Bouéni Bay

Chirongui

N

Kani Kéli

▲ *Mt Choungui (594 m)*

N'goudja

Mtsamoudou

Ilot de Sable Blanc

Saziley

MAYOTTE

Administered by France, claimed by Comoros

Temperatures

Period	Maximum	Minimum
January to April	84°F (30°C	75°F (24°C).
May	82°F (28°C)	73°F (23°C)
June	81°F (27°C)	72°F (22°C)
July and August	79°F (26°C)	
July to September	70°F (21°C)	
September	82°F (28°C)	
October	84°F (29°C)	72°F (22°C)
November and December	88°F (31°C)	
November		73°F (23°C)
December		75°F (24°C)
	Average 84°F (28.8°C)	Average 73°F (22.7°C)

Months with the heaviest average rainfall are January with 10 inches (249 mm). February 8 inches (210 mm), and March 7 inches (183 mm). Driest months are June, July, and August, with an average rainfall of about 1/4 inch (6 mm). Hottest recorded temperature to date is 99°F (37°C) in December, and the coolest, 55°F (13°C) in October.

Daylight lasts from 5am to 7pm in the summer rainy season and from 6am to 6pm in the winter months May to October.

HISTORY

Tradition has it that ships of King Solomon's merchant fleet discovered the islands of the Comoros archipelago nearly 3,000 years ago during trading voyages down the east coast of Africa. There is even a legend that Solomon brought the Queen of Sheba, or Saba, down to these perfumed isles for the biblical equivalent of an amorous weekend. There is also speculation that as early as the 6th century seafaring Indonesian traders were already using the islands as convenient halts on their voyages around Madagascar. Traces of human occupation on Mayotte, however, are somewhat more modern. Shards of pottery unearthed in the south-east of Grande Terre date back to the 9th century and are believed to indicate the existence of permanent settlers from either mainland Africa or, more likely, Madagascar. The history of Mayotte, and of the archipelago, is one of successive waves of immigrants washing over the islands, Arabs from the shores of the Red Sea, Persians, Africans, Malagasy, and the Shirazi Arabs from the Persian Gulf who converted the hotchpotch communities to the true faith. During the course of these continuous invasions the islands became prime Indian Ocean entrepots for the trade in black slaves whose unwilling services were first monopolised by Malagasy, Arabs and the sultanates which were established to control the trade and the islands, and eventually by the French who took over from them (see *Comoros: History* p.216). The first Europeans to visit were the Portuguese navigators Diaz and Suarez in the 16th century, followed by passing Dutch, English, and even Germans. In the 17th century notorious English and French pirates appeared on the scene to add more pillage and rapine to the daily fare of the islands, men such as Captain 'Long Ben' Avery, Captain William Kidd, and Frenchman Olivier le Vasseur. Reports of the time said Captain Kidd and his buccaneers in particular roamed the region 'ravishing women, murdering men, burning houses, and behaving in a most villainous manner.' They paid the price for this villainy, of course, when they were eventually swung into eternity at Execution Dock in London. Captain Kidd's companion Darby Mullins is remembered in descriptions of the execution for his gallows humour. Spotting his wife among the sightseers he pulled off his sea-boots and hurled them at her. 'This will prove those wrong whoever said I'd die with my boots on,' were his last words.

The infamous Olivier le Vasseur known as 'The Buzzard' lost his ship *Indian Queen* on the reefs of Mayotte in 1720, but he and his crew built another there in order 'to proceed on their wicked Design.' Mayotte and the other Comoros islands also suffered from the fact that they lay close to the lair of marauding black Sakalava pirates and slavers from north-west Madagascar, who as a matter of course ransacked the towns and villages as they passed by. From 1785, they carried off thousands of islanders and sold them into slavery. As closest of the island group to Madagascar, Mayotte bore the brunt of these attacks and was at one stage virtually depopulated. In a strange twist of fate the Sakalava themselves were on the run 10 years later and helped to repopulate Mayotte by seeking refuge there from their enemies in Madagascar. Keeping the pot simmering were the island sultans, who when they were not trafficking in slaves were at war with each other. For Mayotte, a tenuous stability was achieved in April 1841 when the ruler of the island, the Sakalava sultan Andriantsouli, ceded the island to France in a treaty confirmed two years later by Louis Philippe. Part of the deal struck by the sultan was that the French had to pay him an annual rent of FF5,000 for Mayotte and finance the education of his children in France. At the time, France had high hopes for Mayotte's future value as a sort of local Gibraltar and replacement for the loss of Mauritius to the British, hopes bolstered by the island's position on the main trade routes to the east and its excellent roadstead and anchorage. By 1886, all the islands of the archipelago were French protectorates and by 1912, eight years after they had ended the slave trade, officially terminated in 1846, all were administered by the French as part of their colony of Madagascar, and remained so until 1947, when together they became a French overseas territory.

In 1961, a year after Madagascar gained its independence from France, the islands were granted a measure of autonomy. As more and more countries around the world, and particularly those in Africa, achieved independence from the major colonial powers pro-independence movements burgeoned and eventually, in 1974, the French were obliged to hold a referendum on the issue. Only Mayotte voted in favour (64%) of retaining its French ties. Less than a year later the other three Comoros islands made a unilateral declaration of independence and set up the Federal Islamic Republic of the Comoros, gaining immediate membership of the Organisation for African Unity (OAU) and the UN. Mahorais went to the polls in another referendum on the independence issue is February 1976 and once again voted overwhelmingly to remain French – Francophile if not exactly Francophone – with the election slogan 'Stay French to Stay Free.' In December of that year Mayotte was rewarded for its loyalty to the metropole by gaining the status of French Territorial Collectivity, a classification created especially for Mayotte and placing it somewhere between an overseas territory and a full French *département*. The Mahorais like to see this special recognition as a step on the road to the latter status, with all the increased benefits and privileges this confers.

POLITICS

In a world where colonisation has become a dirty word Mayotte is a political anachronism and something of a hot potato for France. Both the UN and the Organisation for African Unity (OAU) have consistently backed the claim of Comoros for the integration of the French Territorial Collectivity into the Federal Islamic Republic of the Comoros, but as the Mahorais themselves have set their faces against any such proposal the metropole cannot be seen to agree to such a radical step against the express wishes of the people. Many believe France would be happy to shuffle off Mayotte, as it no longer has the regional strategic importance it had when it first became a colony, on top of which it is a financial drain and presents complications with its hopes for a change in its French status from *collectivité territoriale* to *département*. Not the least of the obstacles to this are the Muslim practice of polygamy – a man can have up to four wives – and the fact that the Mahorais do not have first names and surnames, major headaches for the metropolitan legislators who would have to integrate the islanders into the French national social, political and legal framework.

As a territorial collectivity of 17 communes Mayotte is governed by a General Council elected by voters to advise the Prefect, representing the French president as head of state, on the administration of the island. Mayotte also returns a deputy to the French National Assembly in Paris, as well as a representative to the French Senate. Three major parties are active in the political arena: The *Mouvement Populaire Mahorais* (Mahorian Popular Movement, or MPM) which has traditionally supported full incorporation with France; the conservative *Rassemblement Mahorais pour la République* (Mahorian Union for the Republic, or RPR) and the *Parti pour le Rassemblement Démocratique des Mahorais* (Party for the Mahorian Democratic Union, or PRDM). There is also a *Parti Socialiste* (PS), which is the local branch of the French party, which commands minimal support.

The MPM has dominated the 19-seat General Council since its inception, and the fact that members are elected indicates the strength of island support for the retention of French ties. It was the MPM that originally organised Mayotte's opposition to independence. The party was founded in 1963 by Zeina M'Dere, a spokeswoman for the Mahorais shopkeepers, mostly women, who had been affected economically the previous year when the French colonial capital was moved from the Petite Terre town of Dzaoudzi to Ngazidja (Grande Comore). The women mobilised opinion against independence in the two referendums held on the issue and the people backed the MPM because they considered themselves culturally, religiously, and linguistically distinct from the people of the other three islands. Given Mayotte's smaller population, its greater natural resources, and higher standard of living, they also believed they would be economically viable within a French union and ought not to risk being reduced to the level of the other three poverty-stricken islands. Mayotte has generally enjoyed domestic peace and stability under its French administration, although there have been periodic tensions over social, rather than political, issues. When the Comoros government of the time rewrote the Constitution in 1978 it introduced a federalist concept in the hope that Mayotte would be tempted to join its Islamic republic and make a reality of the fourth star on its national flag. The Mahorais rebuffed the implicit invitation and have since seen Comorians in their thousands desert their home islands to seek a better, if illegal, life in Mayotte. The future for Mayotte seems to suggest the need for a resolution of the islanders' conflicting religious and ethnic ties with Comoros and their economic aspirations, best represented by France.

THE ECONOMY

Mayotte's economy is in a parlous state and without the continued massive support of France would totter from one crisis to another like the other three islands of the Comoros archipelago. France underpins an economy that is essentially agricultural, subsistence farming bolstered by fishing for the pot. Nearly 99% of everything required is imported, mainly from France, which takes more than 80% of Mayotte's exports and what exports there are include such precariously traded commodities as ylang-ylang floral oil, cinnamon and vanilla. As elsewhere in the region, the authorities are pinning their hopes on tourism to bring in foreign currency, create jobs and boost both industrial and commercial development. In the past, Mayotte's very remoteness has been an obstacle to the development of its tourist trade, but this has now become a plus factor as travellers the world over pore over their atlases looking for more untouched, pristine holiday destinations. Already plans are in place to put up more hotels and improve the infrastructure to cope with the confidently expected tourist influx. Annual export volumes have changed little over a decade, while imports have soared in the same period by more than 65% and are regularly at least a dozen times the value of exports.

Imports: in 1998, Mayotte imported about 121,000 tons of goods, principally foodstuffs, cement, fuel, vehicles, machinery and timber.

Exports

In the same year exports totalled 300 tons, of which ylang-ylang essence for perfumes accounted for more than 14 tons and 80% of the value, cinnamon (27 tons), and vanilla (2.5 tons). The rest was made up of copra and other agricultural produce, mattresses, and a variety of other fabricated oddments. The strain on the local exchequer will be obvious from the resultant deficit and this is compounded by a population growing at 6.9% a year – one of the highest growths in the world – and unemployment standing at 41.7% out of a total labour force of about 50,000. Between 4,000-5,000 new job seekers come into the market annually and although the French administration and the military presence are major providers of employment, only 1,000 new jobs are created every year, so the finances of the social security system are also taking a beating.

Tourism

This offers the best financial lifebelt for all the islands of the south-west Indian Ocean. In 1999, 21,000 tourists visited Mayotte, 44% of them from the other French Indian Ocean island of Réunion, 42% from metropolitan France, and 14% from other countries. The average stay was 11-14 days. Income derived was, at FF53-million, 25% more than total exports brought in for the year, hence the hopes Mayotte is pinning on improving its tourism.

THE PEOPLE

The indigenous islanders, known as Mahorais, are indistinguishable in appearance from other Comorians, although the young are much more western in their dress, speech and outlook. Although there is a strong French presence, principally members of the civil administration and soldiers of the French Foreign Legion, there is little, if any, inter-marriage between the two communities. This stems not from any racism, but from tradition buttressed by Muslim beliefs – loyal to France, faithful to Islam. The population of Mayotte is estimated at around 150,000, 125,000 on Grande Terre and the rest on Petite Terre. Population density is slightly over 1,000 inhabitants to the sq mile, or 400 to the sq km. Men and women are fairly evenly balanced in numbers, although not many (2%) make it to their 65th birthday. Life expectancy for the total population is under 60 years. Some 60% of the population is under 20. Most people live in small towns or rural villages, and they happily make contact with visitors and are always pleased to see them at their numerous ceremonies and festivities. One such traditional ceremony is the Islamic 'Grande Mariage,' a grandiose occasion that is one of the foundation stones of Mahorais society. Although the wedding ceremony differs from island to island, its social function remains the same throughout the archipelago. Only men who have fulfilled the obligations of the great wedding have the right to speak in public. This makes a dignitary out of a young bridegroom, a *notable*, and allows him to carry a staff to mark his status. This carries more weight on Grande Comore, where society remains more traditional than on Mayotte. On Grande Comore and Anjouan, however, the wedding may drain the savings of a lifetime. The status conferred by the 'Grande Mariage' guarantees the man a reserved space in the mosque and the privilege of entering through a door separate from the one used by the rest of the faithful. Young people in Mayotte and Comoros are growing increasingly vocal in their opposition to this staggeringly expensive traditional form of marriage, with festivities that can, and do, go on for nine days. They say it is a waste of money which in some cases condemns the man to a lifetime of debt. The elders' response is that the young want to spend the money on TVs, motor-bikes and cars instead.

Another interesting aspect of Mahorais cultural tradition is the *banga*, quaint and colourful little huts or cottages built and occupied by young single men when they move out of their parents' home. This solitary life is intended to make them mature and ready to find their feet, and a wife, without parental interference. When these *célibataires* (bachelors) marry, they move to their wife's house, which has already been built for her by her father. You'll see *bangas* in the countryside all over the island and the owners are always happy to show you around and let you take photographs of the colourful wall paintings and slogans decorating their home. A popular slogan says, in translation, that the bachelor's life is the only life.

The people of Mayotte enjoy a higher standard of living than other Comorians. There is free education, health benefits, social security and a minimum wage. The lowest salary in Mayotte for unskilled workers is FF2,600 a month. Employees with a degree – there are about 1,000 of them – get FF6,000 (£242/$338), and five years' experience in the workplace brings this up to FF10,000. Social welfare provides a monthly allowance of FF1,050 for a child, and FF4,500 for 3-10 children in a family. Welfare benefits are also paid to anyone over 65, and to the disabled. There are about 29,000 families on Mayotte, with average incomes of FF33,000-40,000 (£3,082-3,736/$4,314-5,230) a year. All this, plus free education up to the age of 16 and the chance of tertiary studies in France, makes Mayotte a vastly preferable place to be for increasing numbers of disillusioned and poverty-stricken islanders from

Comoros, and the authorities are constantly returning illegal immigrants who slip in by sea from Anjouan. It also helps to explain why Mahorais women were the driving force in keeping Mayotte French when the island voted in a referendum in 1975 on its future.

WOMEN

Although Mayotte is essentially an Islamic society, with women expected to stay discreetly in the background looking after the children, Mahorais women are the ones with their hands on the tiller, and they wield considerable influence in island politics and community affairs. In short, if women don't want something to happen, it doesn't happen. It is widely recognised that it was the women who kept Mayotte within the French family, when the other islands of the Comoros declared for independence and cut ties with the metropole. Most of the land belongs to women and if a man decides to divorce his wife, she keeps the land and the house built for her by her parents. Women have generally dispensed with the traditional Muslim veil. Instead, you might see them with their faces covered with what appear to be tiny golden grains of sand. This is a facial beauty mask which is made by rubbing a piece of sandalwood on a little wet coral to produce a perfumed powder. Mixed with water, and scented with the essential oils of mimosa, jasmine and other island flowers, this is applied to the face in dazzling patterns with a small shelled maize cob and is believed to be good for the skin. It is also used as a facial decoration, especially for celebrations and festivals. It takes only a few minutes to make the cosmetic, known as *dzindzano*. White sandalwood is used for making a light coloured mask, a deeper ochre tint is acquired by adding powdered turmeric. Special occasions call for red sandalwood facial masks embellished with intricate patterns drawn with a fine coconut-fibre brush. The art of preparing traditional cosmetics is handed down from mother to daughter and there is an association called *Au Royaume des Fleurs* ('The Realm of Flowers') on Petite Terre which has been established to preserve traditional know-how and develop the culture of ethno-cosmetics. The association manufactures and markets *dzindzano* and intends to start exporting its 'Made in Mayotte' cosmetics to an international market that seems more and more interested in natural and ethnic fashion products.

LANGUAGES

The two main languages in Mayotte are French and *Shimaoré*, and while the former is the official, administrative language the majority of the people cannot speak or understand it, although fluency in French is increasing as the younger generation completes its schooling in the language of the métropole. Shimaoré is a derivative of the Swahili of East Africa, the language in the dark old days of the Arab slave traders. The linguistic pot-pourri is further complicated by the fact that different languages or dialects are spoken in different parts of the island. Mayotte is a magnet for immigrants – legal and otherwise – from the other less prosperous and stable islands of the archipelago and from Madagascar. The Sakalava language of Madagascar has added significantly to the vocabulary of Shimaoré, and a Malagasy dialect called Kibushi is spoken in about 40% of the rural communities. Sakalava and this dialect are usually spoken in the southern region of the island, where Malagasy have tended to congregate. Most illegal immigrants who escape the dragnet and settle come from the neighbouring island of Anjouan, part of the Comoros, and speak Shindzwani. Added to this is the fact that children are taught the Koran in Arabic for several hours every day before they go to school for their free French education. However, even if you speak only English you'll get by without too many problems – unless you are trekking on your own in the rural areas. English is spoken or at least understood by most French expatriates, as it is in hotels and places such as airline offices. You'll even find young Mahorais in the middle of nowhere who'll come up to you to practise a few words of English and, surprisingly, you'll see *bangas*, young bachelors' huts, daubed with bright coloured slogans saying things like 'Eden, the Magic World' and 'Nice to Meet You.'

USEFUL WORDS AND PHRASES

English	French	Mahorais
Hello, good day	Bonjour	Kwezi
How are you?	Comment allez-vous?	Jéjé?
Goodbye	Au revoir	Kwaheri
Anyone here?	Y a t-il quelqu'un?	Hodi?
How many?	Combien (nombre)?	Ngavi?
How much (price)?	Combien (prix)?	Riali ngavi?
It's expensive	C'est cher	Lyo hali
It's good	C'est bon	Ndjema
It is not good	C'est pas bon	Tsi ndjema
It is pretty	C'est joli	Ndzuzuri
Whites	Blancs	Mzungu
Mr	Monsieur	Mouégné
Mrs	Madame	Bouéni
OK	ça va	Ndjema
Enter	Entrez	Karibou
Where is the beach	Où est la plage?	Mtsangani de havi?
Is it near?	Est-ce près	Oho caribou?
Is it far?	Est-ce loin?	Oho mbali?
Can I photograph you	Puis-je vous photographier?	Ntsaha nihu renge foto utso?
Cow	Vache	Nyombe
Goat	Chèvre	Mbuzi
Sea	Mer	Bahari
Fish	Poisson	Fi
Canoe	Pirogue	Laka
Fishing	Pêcher	Ulowa
Day	Jour	Asoubwihi
Noon	Midi	M'tsana
Today	Aujourd'hui	Léo
Yesterday	Hier	Vojana
Tomorrow	Demain	Mésgo
Sun	Soleil	Jua
Night	Nuit	Uku
Moon	Lune	Mwezi
Stars	Etoiles	Nyora
Wind	Vent	Pevo

One	Un	Moja
Two	Deux	M'bili
Three	Trois	Trarou
Four	Quatre	N'né
Five	Cinq	Tsano
Six	Six	Sita
Seven	Sept	Saba
Eight	Huit	Nané
Nine	Neuf	Shendra
Ten	Dix	Kumi
100	Cent	Miya

RELIGION

Muslims make up as much as 98% of the population of Mayotte, and differ little in their observance of the precepts of Islam from adherents in the rest of the Comoros archipelago. During the 19th century a large number of migrants from Madagascar settled on the island, and many of these embraced the Catholic faith after Mayotte became a French colony in 1841. They were followed by French and Creole Catholic settlers from Mauritius and Réunion. There's a Catholic church in Mamoudzou and a chapel in Dzaoudzi. In Tsingoni on the west coast is a mosque that is believed to date from 1450, built after Arabs from the Persian Gulf brought Islam to Mayotte and Comoros. Mayotte's Muslims are a tolerant community and rub along very well with Christians and other non-Muslims. Children spend hours every morning from 5am learning to recite in Arabic many of the 114 suras of the Koran before they go to public school for the rest of the day for lessons conducted in French. With the other Comoros islands, Mayotte celebrates the following major Islamic religious festivals which are based on the lunar year and are not, therefore, fixed dates.

Religious Festivals

Ramadan – This falls in the first quarter of the year. A month of daily fasting, during which Muslims are allowed to eat and drink only before sunrise and after sunset. As a mark of respect you should not eat, drink or smoke in public during this holy month.

Id-ul-Fitr – This is when the new moon appears to signal the end of the Ramadan fast. This is the biggest celebration in the Islamic calendar and a time for some epic feasts and parties.

Id-el-Kebir – End of the pilgrimage to Mecca, and honouring Abraham for his readiness to offer his son as a sacrifice.

Maoulida – Celebration commemorating the birth of the Prophet Mohammed.

Miradji – Marks the ascension of Mohammed to heaven.

Muharam – The Islamic New Year

Ashura – Day honouring martyr Imam Hussein.

One religious celebration which attracts visitors is the colourful dance known as the *déba*. This is a religious rite exclusively for women, an exhibition of song and dance inspired by prayer, and is a competition between rural villages. The girls wear richly embroidered lace-trimmed bodices, the *salouva*, with matching shawls in the colours of their village. Competing groups sit on benches, facing each other.

At the feet of the dancers sit the older women, who provide the music on their tambourines. Choirs from various villages chant in harmony while dancing to choreography miming invocations to Mohammed. Although the words of the sacred songs carry a message about morals and the rules of life, this religious occasion is also a recognised island marriage mart. The *déba* gives young people the opportunity to meet each other, and if a young man is attracted to one of the dancers he can express his admiration by sending her a gift, a gesture considered an official declaration of love and the first step towards marriage.

NATIONAL ANTHEM AND FLAG

The national anthem and flag used are those of metropolitan France. Mayotte's coat of arms is two sea-horses, emblematic of the shape of the island, supporting a shield bearing the crescent of Islam, two ylang-ylang flowers representing the islands of Grande Terre and Petite Terre, over the island's motto *Ra Hachiri* ('We are Vigilant').

FURTHER READING

You'll note from the annual tourist figures that remote Mayotte doesn't get many visitors, a fact which has kept it unspoilt, but which also means that not many books have been written about this French outpost in the Indian Ocean. The majority of the books that have been published are out of print, although you should be able to find *Last of the Pirates: the Search for Bob Dénard*, by Samantha Weinberg (1994, Jonathan Cape, London), and *The Comoros Islands: Struggle Against Dependency in the Indian Ocean*, by Malyn Newitt (1984, Gower Publications, London).

Reference books we found useful in our research were *The Rand McNally Atlas of the Oceans* (Rand McNally & Company, Chicago), *Where to Dive in Southern Africa and Off the Islands*, by Al J Venter (1991, Ashanti Publishing, Rivonia), *Whales and Dolphins*, compiled by Dr Anthony R Martin (1990, Salamander Books Ltd, London), *The Sea Fishes of Southern Africa*, by Professor JLB Smith (1965, Central News Agency, South Africa), *Islands in a Forgotten Sea*, by TV Bulpin (Howard Timmins, Cape Town), *Birds of the Indian Ocean Islands*, by Ian Sinclair and Olivier Langrand (1998, Struik Publishers, Cape Town), and *Mayotte en Poche*, by Mathilda Hory and Laurent Abad (1996, Les Editions Mahoraises, Réunion).

PRACTICAL INFORMATION

BY AIR

There are no direct flights to Mayotte from Europe. To get there you must island hop from Réunion, which has direct air links with France, or route through Kenya, South Africa, or Madagascar. The easiest route to take to Mayotte is by way of Réunion. Air France is the main airline with regular flights from Paris to Réunion. Some airlines offer flights from Europe to other islands in the Indian Ocean, such as Comoros, Mauritius, Madagascar, Seychelles, and from these islands you can fly to Mayotte. Dates, times and fares change according to the airline and the season, so check with your travel agent.

The **best way** to get to Mayotte from the UK is from London to Paris and then by Air France or one of the other airlines offering direct flights to Réunion, and then by Air Austral to Mayotte. Six airlines operate flights with varying frequencies to Réunion from France. They are Air France (9 weekly flights), AOM (daily flights), Air Liberté (4 weekly flights), Corsair (3-6 weekly flights), Aerolyon (1 weekly flight), and Jet Ocean Indien (6 weekly flights). The non-stop flight to Réunion takes 11 hours or up to 13 hours with stops en route. There are also flights from Lyons, Marseilles, and Toulouse on certain days and periods of the year. Prices depend on travelling dates, and there are often attractive promotional fares.

From Réunion, Air Austral flies to Mayotte every day, and sometimes twice a day. During French school holidays in December, January and August there are extra flights to cope with demand. The flight takes about two hours. Air Austral also has three flights a week from Madagascar (Saturday from Nosy Bé and on Tuesday and Thursday from Mahajanga); from Comoros on a Tuesday and Thursday; from Nairobi to Mayotte every Tuesday; and from Seychelles every Saturday. There are flights from Mayotte to Mahajanga, Madagascar, on Tuesday and Thursday, and Nosy Bé on Wednesday; to Comoros on Monday and Thursday; to Nairobi on Monday; and to Seychelles on Tuesday. Air Madagascar also has a flight to Mayotte once a week, on Saturday, from Mahajanga. From South Africa, Air Austral has two weekly flights to Réunion, on Thursday and Sunday, and usually increases its frequency during August, December and January. If you opt for a stop-over in Africa or another Indian Ocean island on your way to Mayotte you can complete your trip on an Air Austral connecting flight. For more information, contact your travel agent or get in touch with the airlines.

FLIGHTS FROM FRANCE TO RÉUNION:

Air France: Number of weekly flights: 9, of which 7 are non-stop flights Orly Ouest/Réunion, 2 non-stop Charles de Gaulle/Réunion on Friday and Saturday. Reservations (tel 08-02 80 28 02). Contact: 119 Avenue des Champs Elysées, F-

75384 Paris Cedex 08 (tel 01-42 99 23 64).

AOM (Air Outre Mer): Number of weekly flights: 7, of which 5 are non-stop Orly-Sud/Réunion, 2 with stop-overs in Lyons (Wednesday), and Marseilles (Sunday). Contact: Bàt 363 BP 854, 94551 Orly Aérogare Cedex (tel 08-03 00 12 34); Orly Airport (tel 1-49 75 24 95); Agence Opéra France, 45 Avenue de l'Opéra, 75002 Paris (tel 1-53 45 48 00).

Air Liberté (also agent for British Airways): Number of weekly flights: 4 flights direct from Orly Sud, on Mondays and Sundays, and 2 with stopover in Marseilles on Tuesdays, and in Toulouse on Fridays. Contact: Parc d' Affaires SILIC, 67 rue de Monthléry, Rungis (tel 1-49 79 23 00).

Corsair (Nouvelles Frontières): Number of weekly flights: 3-6 direct flights from Paris. Contact: 2 Avenue Charles Lindbergh, 94528 Rungis Cedex (tel 1-49 79 49 79; fax 1-49 79 49 68; Information 08-03 33 33 33).

Aerolyon: Number of weekly flights: one from Lyons on Sunday, one from Nantes and Toulouse. Contact: BP136, 69125 Lyon Satolas (tel 4-72 22 73 00; fax 4-72 22 73 10).

Jet Ocean Indien: Number of weekly flights: four Paris/Réunion, one from Marseilles and one from Toulouse. It also connects with flights in Nantes, Bordeaux, Toulouse, Perpignan, Montpellier, Marseilles, Toulon, Nice and Strasbourg. Contact: 4 rue Monge, 75005 Paris (tel 1-44 07 20 04/20 06; fax 1-43 25 69 94).

Air Austral. Since it was established in 1990 Réunion-based Air Austral has been the dominant air carrier in the south-west Indian Ocean, and is the only airline flying from Réunion to 11 destinations in the region. Its fleet of Boeing 737s has two classes: Comfort Class with 18 seats at the front of the aircraft, with five seats abreast instead of six; and Leisure Class, which is economy class with international standard comfort.

Paris office: 2 rue de l'Eglise, 92200, Neuilly (tel 1-92 01 33; fax 1-92 01 37).

Réunion offices: 4 rue de Nice, St Denis Cedex, (bookings tel 90 90 90; fax 90 90 91); Roland Garros International Airport (tel 48 80 20); St Pierre, 14 rue Archambaud (tel 96 26 96; fax 35 46 49; e-mail saint-pierre@air-austral.com); Pierrefonds Airport (tel 96 80 20; fax 96 80 19).

Mayotte offices: Air Austral (and Air France), Dzaoudzi, Petite Terre (tel 60-1052; fax 60-0387; e-mail agence.issoufali@wanadoo.fr); Air Austral (and Air France), Place du Marché, Mamoudzou, Grand Terre (tel 61-3636; fax 61-1053; e-mail mayotte@air-austral.com). Open Monday to Friday from 8.30am to 12.30pm and 1.30pm to 4.30pm, Saturday 8.30am to 11.30am.

Kenya office: Air France, International House, Mama Ngina Street, Nairobi (tel 33-3301; fax 33-5867);

South Africa office: Oxford Manor, 196 Oxford Road, Illovo, Johannesburg (tel 11-880-9039; fax 11-788-5440).

Mauritius office: Rogers House, 5 rue du President JF Kennedy (tel 212-2666; fax 212-8886; e-mail maurice@air-austral.com);

Madagascar offices: 77 Lalana Solombavambahoka Frantsay, Andsahavola, Antananarivo (tel 20-22-35990; fax 20-22-35773; e-mail tananarive@air-austral.com); 81 Boulevard Joffre, Toamasina (tel 20-53-31243; fax 20-53-31244; e-mail tamatave@air-austral.com); Immeuble Hotel de France, corner of rue Georges V and Maréchal Joffre, Mahajanga (tel 20-62-22391; fax 20-62-22417; e-mail majunga@air-austral.com); and Villa Malibu, rue Passot, Hell-Ville, Nosy Bé (tel 20-86-61240; fax 20-86-22417; e-mail majunga@air-austral.com);

Comoros office: rue Magoudjou, Moroni, Grande Comore (tel 73-3144; fax 73-0719).

Seychelles office: Pirates Arms Building, Victoria, Mahé (tel 32-3129; fax 32-1597).

Airport

Mayotte airport is in the Pamandzi area of Petite Terre and although it looks very Third Worldish it is quite efficient and it doesn't take long to complete passport and customs formalities and collect luggage. If, like most arrivals, you are headed for Mamoudzou, on the main island of Grand Terre, you have a choice of how to get to the ferry jetty, nearly 2 miles (3 km) away in Dzaoudzi. You can hire a car at the airport, or hire or share a taxi. If you wait until you get to Mamoudzou to hire a car you'll save the FF100 (£9.30/$13.90) it would have cost on the ferry. If you share a collective taxi you'll pay FF4 (£0.37/$0.55) fare, but make sure this is agreed with the driver before you get into the vehicle. If you need help or advice you'll find the Mayotte Comité du Tourisme has a small office outside the airport, to the left. This is open an hour before and after each arrival and departure. There's also a branch office to the left of the ferry terminal at Mamoudzou when you arrive. The Mamoudzou kiosk is open Monday to Friday, from 9am to 5pm, and on Saturday from 8am to noon. The airport is connected to Dzaoudzi, the main port and ferry terminal, by a long stretch of road which eventually becomes the Boulevard des Crabes.

INTER-ISLAND FERRY

Don't use any normal French words for the ferry, it's simply known as *la barge*. If you arrive in the normal tourist season, May to October, the ferry leaves for Mamoudzou from the eastern jetty, known as Issoufali; if you arrive in the rainy season, December to March, it leaves from the western jetty, or Ballou. The ferry service between Dzaoudzi on Petite Terre and Mamoudzou on Grande Terre is cheap and reliable. It is operated by the Collectivité Territoriale de Mayotte Service des Transports Maritimes, which uses the smart, fairly modern vessels *Salama Djema II* and *Salama Djema III* to ferry vehicles and passengers across the mile or so (2 km) neck of water between the two islands. The 10-minute trip to Grande Terre is free; you pay FF5 to get back if you are a pedestrian and FF100 for a light vehicle.

Tickets

You buy your ticket at the terminal office at Mamoudzou which is open from 5.45am to 00.30pm, from Monday to Friday, 6.15am to 2.30am on Saturdays and public holidays, and 7.15am to 00.30am on Sundays and public holidays.

Times

The first ferry leaves Dzaoudzi at 5.30am Monday to Saturday and then sails every half-hour until 7pm, then every hour until 2am. From Mamoudzou it starts at 6am and runs every half-hour until 7.30pm, then every hour until 2.30am. On Sundays and public holidays the sailings are 7am and 7.30am respectively until 7pm and 7.30pm, then every hour until midnight and 00.30am. This timetable has been constant for several years, but it could always change. For information contact the Service des Transports Maritimes in Dzaoudzi (tel 60-1069; fax 60-1613), or the ferry terminal in Mamoudzou (tel 61-0444).

TOUR OPERATORS

A to B Tours: 205 Winchester Road, Basingstoke, Hampshire G21 8YH (tel/fax 01256-351979).

Comet Travel: 21 Newman Street, London W1P 4DD (tel 020-7437 7878; fax 020-7636 3907).

Elite Vacations: Elite House, 98-100 Bessborough Road, Harrow, Middlesex HA1 3D7 (tel 020-8864 4431; fax 020-8426 9178).

Sunset Faraway Holidays: 4 Abbeville Manor, 88 Clapham Park Road, London SW4 7BX (tel 020-7498 9922; fax 020-7978 1337).

Tana Travel: 2 Ely Street, Stratford-Upon-Avon, Warwickshire CV37 (tel 01789-414200; fax 01789-414420).

Union Castle Travel: 86-87 Camden Street, Kensington, London W8 7EN (tel 020-7229 1411; fax 020-7229 1511).

Voyages Jules Verne: 10 Glentworth Street, London NW1 5P4 (tel 020-7616 1000; fax 020-7723 8629).

Wexas International: 45 Brompton Road, Knightsbridge, London SW3 1DE (tel 020-7589 3315; fax 020-7589 8418).

BY SEA

The chances of getting to Mayotte by sea are slender, but they do improve the closer to the island you are. For instance, it should be fairly easy to find a cargo ship from Mauritius, Réunion and Madagascar and a ferry from Comoros, but you must be prepared to kick your heels around the ports. The money you spend while waiting could buy you a seat on a plane. It's all a matter of luck.

The **Mediterranean Shipping Company** (MSC) of Geneva is a privately owned shipping line which is the fourth largest container carrier globally. MSC vessels call at 174 ports through 81 main direct and 55 combined weekly liner services and the company maintains agencies and offices all over the world. The company runs regular services to the Mascarene islands and it might be worth getting in touch with them.

Contact Details:

In Australia the head office of MSC (Aust) and the cruise office of Mediterranean Shipping Company Travel are at Level 8, 155 George Street, Sydney, New South Wales (tel 2-9252 1111; fax 2-9252 1258/1448).

In France MSC France SA, 23 Avenue de Neuilly, F-75116 Paris (tel 1-53 64 63 00; fax 1-53 64 63 10); and the cruise office MSC Croisieres Sarl, 59 rue Beaubourg, F-75003 Paris (tel 1-48 04 76 20; fax 1-48 04 51 65); and Centre Havrais de Commerce International, Quai George V, F-76600 Le Havre (tel 2-35 19 78 00; fax 2-35 18 78 10).

In Madagascar contact the head office of MSC Madagascar SA, 72 Avenue du 26 Juin 1960, Analakely, Antananarivo (tel 20-22-32130; fax 20-22-30188; e-mail mscmad@dts.mg).

In Mauritius MSC can be contacted at 5th Floor Rogers House, 5 President John F Kennedy Street, Port Louis (tel 202-6818; fax 208-5045; e-mail msc@rogers.intnet.mu).

In Réunion contact MSC France SA, 49 rue Evariste de Parny, Le Port Cedex (tel 42 78 00; fax 42 78 10).

In **South Africa** you can contact MSC Holdings at MSC House, 54 Winder Street, Durban 4001 (tel 31-360 7911; fax 31-332 9277); and MSC House, Duncan Road, Table Bay Harbour, Cape Town (tel 21-405 2000; fax 21-419 1546). The general sales agent for MSC cruises is Starlight Cruises at Starlight House, 1 Wessels Road, corner 5th Avenue, Rivonia 2128, Johannesburg (tel 11-807 5111; fax 11-807 5085; e-mail starlite@yebo.co.za).

In the US the head office of MSC (USA) is at 420 5th Avenue (at 37th Street), 8th Floor, New York, NY 10018-2702 (tel 212-764-4800; fax 212-764-8592).

TRAVEL SAFELY

Both the UK Foreign Office and the US State Department have travel information offices which provide regularly updated free advice on countries around the world (see p.48 for their contact details).

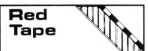

ENTRY REQUIREMENTS

PASSPORTS AND VISAS

All that United Kingdom and residents of other European Union (EU) countries need to enter Mayotte is a passport valid for at least three months from date of arrival. If you are a French national you need only your National Identity card. All other countries require a valid passport, with the mandatory consular visa. US citizens need onward transportation and a passport valid for 6 months beyond expected exit date, but no visa for a stay of up to one month. All non-residents must be in possession of a return ticket. Anyone needing a visa can get one from a French consulate or embassy (see Help and Information).

HEALTH DOCUMENTS

If you come from, or have been in, a country where yellow fever, cholera, malaria and smallpox are endemic you must have an International Certificate of Vaccination against these infections. The authorities recommend that a course of anti-malaria treatment is followed before, during and after your trip.

CUSTOMS REGULATIONS

Apart from personal goods, the following are duty-free:
200 cigarettes or 100 cigars.
2 litres of wine.
1 litre of alcohol or 2 bottles of whisky.
50cl of perfume or 100cl of eau de toilette.
Pets. People bringing in pets are required to produce a certificate of vaccination against rabies, with the last jab no earlier than one month prior to arrival; and a certificate of good health, signed by a vet five days or less before your departure.

FRENCH EMBASSIES ABROAD

Australia: Level 26, St Martins Tower, 31 Market Street, Sydney NSW 2000 (tel 2-9261 5779; fax 2-9283 1210).

Britain: The French Embassy is at 58 Knightsbridge, London SW1X 7JT (tel 020-7201 1000; fax 020-7201-1004; e-mail press@ambafrance.org.uk).

Canada: 42 Promenade Sussex, Ottawa, Ontario K1M 2C9 (tel 613-789 1795; fax 613-562 3704).

South Africa: 191 Jan Smuts Avenue, Parktown 2193, Johannesburg (tel 11-778 5600; fax 11-778 5601).

United States: 4101 Reservoir Road, NW 20007, Washington DC (tel 202-944-6000; fax 202-944-6072).

What Money To Take

The currency used in Mayotte is the French Franc (FF), which is divided into 100 centimes. Banknotes come in 500, 200, 100, 50, and 20 franc denominations; coins in 20, 10, 5, 2 and 1 francs and 50, 20, 10 and 5 centimes. For the past couple of years the exchange rate has fluctuated at around 10 francs to the pound sterling and 6 francs to the US dollar. Check the latest rates at the bank. It's recommended that you have a reasonable amount of French francs in currency with you when you arrive, especially small denomination notes and coins. Carry the rest of your funds in traveller's cheques.

BANKS AND BANKING

Banque Francaise Commerciale Océan Indien (BFCOI): has offices in Dzaoudzi (tel 61 10 91), and in Mamoudzou at Place du Marché (tel 61 10 91). ATM cash machines, some bank cards or the BFCOI's own bank card are accepted.

Banque de la Réunion: Place Mariage, Mamoudzou (tel 61 20 30; fax 62 20 28).

Crédit Agricole is in Mamoudzou (tel 61 12 00). ATM cash machines, some bank cards or Credit Agricole bank card accepted.

Hours. Banks are open on Monday to Thursday from 7.30am to 1pm and Friday 7.30am to 11am.

Credit Cards. Most major credit cards are accepted, but check if yours is before tendering it.

BEFORE YOU LEAVE

Mayotte's medical facilities and healthcare are way ahead of all the other islands in the Comoros archipelago, but it might be difficult to get hold of many of the things you take for granted at home. If you are on any sort of medication, take it along with you. It's also a good idea to take along a broad spectrum antibiotic, medicine for stomach upsets and pills or suppositories for nausea. Suppositories are a good idea because usually, when you get a stomach bug on holiday, whatever you swallow comes straight up again. Suntan lotion or cream with a protection factor of 15 is recommended, and so is sunblock. Take the stuff that doesn't wash off in the pool or the sea. A medical and dental check is a good idea before you leave. Take copies of any accident insurance documents, and important medical records. Make sure you take an adequate supply of all prescription and any other medications you use. Take a letter from your doctor on his/her letterhead stationery (signed and dated) certifying your need for any medications you might be carrying. Keep all medications in their original wrapping and pack them in your cabin bag so they don't get lost en route.

As Mayotte is nominally French territory any emergency treatment you might need should be free if you come from a European Union country. Travellers from the UK should obtain form E111 from the Post Office to show they have this right. It would be a wise precaution, however, to inquire about medical insurance with specific overseas and medical air evacuation coverage before leaving home, especially if you suffer from any chronic ailment. This insurance is often one of the last items on a checklist, yet it is one of the most important. Talk to your travel agent, insurance company or bank. Some credit and charge cards provide health insurance for travellers. Check that it is adequate for your needs, if not, take out extra cover.

MEDICAL SERVICES

There are about 10 private medical practitioners in Mayotte, and two hospitals, one in Mamoudzou, and one in Dzaoudzi. The hospitals also provide dental treatment. There are dispensaries in most large rural villages. There are three pharmacies in Mamoudzou, the *Pharmacie Mahoraise* (tel 61 12 39), the *Pharmacie du Centre* (tel 61 05 07), and the *Pharmacie Ylang-Ylang* in Kawéni (tel 61 37 68). On Petite Terre there is one, the *Pharmacie Kalfane*, in Dzaoudzi (tel 60 17 69). At Sada, on the west coast, there's the *Pharmacie de Sada* (tel 62 23 00).

Pharmacies are usually open Monday to Friday from 8am to 1pm and 2pm to 7pm, and on Sunday from 9am until noon.

EVERYDAY HEALTH

Food and water-borne diseases are the most common problems for travellers, so take precautions to avoid infection. Although tap water in the main centres in Mayotte is said to be safe to drink, it is best to stick to bottled water. Make sure bottled water is sealed when you buy it, and avoid ice cubes. Eat only piping hot, thoroughly cooked food; try to avoid cold foods, including salads (especially chicken or cold meat salad) and salad dressing; peel all fruit and vegetables; avoid food sold by street vendors, no matter how tasty it looks; wash any self-prepared food in decontaminated water; and avoid undercooked, or raw, fish and shellfish – boil it, cook it, peel it, or forget it is the motto.

AIDS

By the end of 1999 only 62 cases of HIV AIDS had been reported in Mayotte. Promiscuity is frowned on, to say the least, in Islamic societies and religious mores are no doubt a brake on the spread of the disease, known in French as *syndrome immuno-déficitaire acquis*, or SIDA. Local Muslim men usually go to

Madagascar for casual sex, and doctors believe this is where the cases reported contracted the disease. Try to avoid casual sexual encounters and activities where the skin may be damaged or there may be contact with bodily fluids. The risk of transmission of HIV, hepatitis B and other sexually transmitted diseases is reduced but not eliminated by the use of a condom. Condoms bought locally may not be as reliable as those bought before leaving home, so carry a supply with you if you think you may need them.

HEALTH HAZARDS

Malaria has not yet been eradicated in Mayotte, so anti-malarial precautions are necessary. Medication should be taken a week before arrival, continued throughout the time you are on the island and for a minimum of four weeks after you return home. Pregnant women and children should, of course, avoid travel to malaria areas. If you develop a flu-like illness within three months of leaving a malaria area, even if you took malaria medication and completed the course as recommended, you should see a doctor as soon as possible. *Moustiques* (mosquitoes) are especially active during the rainy season and in forest areas. Worst time is between 10pm and 5am, although you could be bitten from dusk onwards. It's advisable to wear light-coloured, long-sleeved clothing and to avoid outdoor activity from dusk to dawn; use mosquito repellent cream or spray; sleep under a mosquito net; keep doors and windows closed from dusk to dawn; and light a mosquito coil in your room at night before you go to sleep. Local expatriates will tell you there's no need to worry and that they never take prophylactic measures against mosquito. Ignore such advice.

NATURAL HAZARDS

Too much **sun** is usually the main hazard facing visitors, especially if you are pale-skinned and arriving from a northern hemisphere winter. Over-dosing on sunshine can result in sunburn, heat exhaustion, or heatstroke. A minor but irritating side-effect can be prickly heat, which usually develops as an under-arm rash. Over-exposure to the sun can result in anything from a mild burn to a more severe dose with swelling and blisters. Symptoms of sunstroke are chills, fever, nausea and delirium. Itching and peeling may follow any degree of sunburn and normally begin four to seven days after exposure. Severe sunburn or sunstroke should always be treated by a doctor. Avoid the sun between 11am and 3pm – the time the rays are at their strongest – and protect your skin by using a sunscreen that filters out damaging UV rays. Protect yourself from the sun by wearing clothing which reduces areas of exposed skin, wear good quality sunglasses and a floppy or wide-brimmed hat, and use sunscreen cream or lotion and lip protection whenever you are out in the sun.

Seasickness

Travel by boat between the islands of the Indian Ocean can sometimes by unpleasant if rough. Even the shortest voyage from Mayotte to Anjouan can take 8-10 hours. There are a number of things you can do to cope with seasickness. Try to move to a place where the motion is least noticeable. This will usually be near the middle of the ship on a low deck. Stabilise your head movement, by sitting with your head braced against a chair or wall. If you are in an enclosed space, such as a cabin, lie down and close your eyes. If you can see out, fix your gaze on the horizon or a fixed point. There are drugs that provide effective relief from motion sickness. Speak to a pharmacist if you think you might need some.

FIRST AID HINTS

Some **coral** can give you a nasty rash if you brush up against it and some reef dwelling fish such as **stonefish** and **scorpionfish** are very dangerous; sea-urchins and some shellfish can also be dangerous to touch or stand on. If stung the best thing to do until you can get proper treatment is to plunge the affected part into water as hot as you can bear. Another, possibly more practical, first-aid remedy is to douse the affected area in urine. This is also recommended by islanders for the painful bite of the *gros mille-pattes*, a large centipede you might come across in the forest. A basic first-aid kit is a good thing to carry. You can buy one from any outdoor equipment store or make up your own. See that it contains at least a disinfectant or anti-bacterial agent, anti-histamine cream, bandages, gauze and adhesive tape, a small pair of scissors, tweezers, a thermometer, aspirins, an anti-diarrhoea preparation, a bottle of medicinal alcohol, and a small bottle (30ml) of 2% mercurochrome solution.

CLOTHING

What To Wear and When

The average temperature throughout the year is around 77°F (25°C), so lightweight cotton clothes should be packed. For men, shorts and T-shirts are worn during the day with sandals or casual canvas shoes. The same applies to evening wear, although you might consider slacks for a visit to a restaurant or bar. Jackets and ties are rarely worn. For women, cotton tops and shorts for daytime wear, and cool cotton or linen dresses for the evening are ideal. A lightweight rain jacket is advisable if you are visiting between November and April, and a small umbrella won't go amiss. Sun-hats and good quality protective sunglasses are indispensable. A pair of rubber flippers for swimming and rubber-soled shoes you can wear in the sea for protection against coral, stonefish, and sea-urchins are also worth their space in your bag. Trainers or walking shoes are fine if you intend to explore, otherwise sandals or light shoes are adequate. Swimwear is worn only on the beaches or around the hotel pool. It is definitely not acceptable anywhere else, especially in the rural villages.

Women into topless sunbathing will find that it is tolerated on the main tourist beaches, although nowhere else. Mahorais women wear patterned brightly coloured lengths of cotton called *chirumanis* and women visitors might consider buying one or two at the outdoor market in Mamoudzou for casual wear. Muslim men often wear a *kanzu*, a flowing long white cotton shirt like an ankle-length nightie, and this is also an option for anyone who feels the urge to identify (and keep cool).

MAIL

Communications

The main post office is on rue de l'Hôpital, Mamoudzou, near the police station and about 200 yards (183 m) from the ferry terminal. It opens from 7am to 5pm during the week, and on Saturday from 7am to 11am (tel 61 11 11). There is also a post office in Kawéni (tel 61 11 18) and in Pamandzi, on Petite Terre (tel 60 10 03). Postal services are vastly superior to the other islands of Comoros and you can expect an airmail letter or postcard to the UK to take about six days and to France, four days. One unusual aspect of the mail is that, even though Mayotte has been French since 1841, you can't use French postage stamps there. Mayotte has been issuing its own stamps since 1997, when it renewed a practice abandoned in 1912. Along with the rest of Comoros, Mayotte was attached to and administered from Madagascar from 1912 and used the French colonial stamps printed for Madagascar. When Comoros broke away from France and declared independence in 1975 Mayotte retained its ties and became a French Territorial Collectivity and used the stamps of France. In 1997, Mayotte was once again permitted to issue its own postage stamps, promoting its culture and local flora and fauna. Since then its stamps have become prized acquisitions in the philatelic world, and proven a lucrative source of revenue. Various face values bear, among other things, Mayotte's armorial bearings, the ylang-ylang flower, an indigenous musical instrument, a *banga*, or young man's hut, and the endemic lemur, known as *maki*. It's worth buying a sheet or two of these stamps, or at least a selection, even if you are not a stamp collector. Who knows, they could pay for your holiday. Each new stamp issue is the occasion for a philatelic souvenir edition which can be obtained only from the Service Philatélic et de Cartophilie. For more information write to SMPC, BP 1000, F-97600, Mamoudzou, Mayotte.

TELEPHONES

There are only a few hundred telephones on the islands of Grande Terre and Petite Terre and public telephones outside of Mamoudzou are scarce. You can buy a *telecarte*, or phonecard, to use in any you find. Ideally, you should buy this at the kiosk at the ferry terminal when you arrive in Mamoudzou. Phonecards costs FF50 or FF100 (£4.65-9.30/$6.95-13.90). The island's relatively small telephone system is efficiently administered by the French Department of Posts and Telecommunications (France Télécom). To maintain its international links Mayotte uses a microwave radio relay and HF radio-telephone communications. You should be able to telephone anywhere in the world from Mayotte without any difficulty. Dialling code Réunion to Mayotte is 0269, and Mayotte to Réunion is 0262 + number. The international dialling code is 00, plus country code and town or city code, followed by the subscriber's number. Calls are charged at the full tariff rate between 8am and 7pm, Monday to Friday, but drop by up to 50% in off-peak hours. The island does not yet have a Global Systems for Mobile Communications (GSM) network, so there's no point in taking your mobile phone with you.

MEDIA

Radio and Television

Radio and TV broadcasts are provided by the French Société Nationale de Radio-Télévision Francaise d'Outre-Mer, which broadcasts to all the French overseas departments and territorial collectivities. Télé Mayotte RFO on Petite Terre (tel 60 10 17; fax 60 18 52), transmits from 6am to around midnight every night. In hotels with a satellite dish TV you can pick up Euronews, Eurosport, and Canal+. There are an estimated 5,000 TV sets on the island tuned into satellite programmes, and about 40,000 radios.

Newspapers and Magazines

If you are a newspaper junkie you'll suffer withdrawal symptoms in Mayotte. Only two newspapers are published locally, *Kwézi*, which comes out on Tuesday and targets the Mahorian reader, and *Mayotte Hebdo*, which comes out on a Friday. There's also a giveaway every Friday called *Le 97-6* which carries notices, classified smalls, and restaurant advertisements. It also publishes a useful tide table for the month of issue and the week's TV programmes.

Maps and Guides

As only three roads cross the island to link with the round-the-island coastal road on Grande Terre the free maps handed out by the tourist office in Mamoudzou are adequate to get you around by car or scooter without a problem. For greater detail you can get the contoured IGN tourist maps with scales of 1:50,000 and 1:25,000, but get them before you leave home. In London they cost £8.95 each at Stanford's, 12/14 Long Acre, Covent Garden, London WC2 9LP (tel 020-7836-1321). Stanford's also has a mailing service. If you plan to do a lot of walking you'll need the two 1:25,000 maps that cover the island. If you can find a copy, and if you can read French, the little glossy pocket guide *Mayotte en Poche* gives a brief overview of Petite Terre and Grande Terre. It's out of date (1996) but the colour illustrations are excellent. Try *La Maison des Livres Librairie* (bookshop), in the Place Mariage, Mamoudzou (tel 61 14 97), for this and for maps.

BY SEA

There are regular ferry services from Mayotte to the nearby Comoros island of Anjouan. A ferry also runs to the islands of Mohéli and Grande Comore en route to Madagascar, but this service is not so frequent and depends on demand. The *Frégate des Iles* is the vessel usually used on the Madagascar run and for information about the service tel 60 08 28, in Pamandzi. The single fare to Moroni, on Grande Comore, and Mahajanga, in Madagascar, is FF500 (£47/$69) and to Mohéli it is FF400. Two ferries make the Mayotte to Anjouan run. They are the *Tratringa* which departs from Mayotte on Monday, Tuesday, Thursday and Friday at 3pm. The *Ville de Sima* which departs from Mayotte on a Tuesday and Thursday at 10am and on Friday at 2.30pm. Both cost FF400 a person for a return ticket and FF250 a person for a one-way ticket. The trip can take 6-12 hours, depending on weather.

The **Mediterranean Shipping Company** (MSC) calls regularly at Mayotte and is worth a visit or a call if you are looking for a berth to another Indian Ocean island, or even to Europe, Australia, or the Americas. You'll find MSC in Mamoudzou at Centre Commercial Amatoula NR 8, Kawéni (tel 61 38 99; fax 61 37 99). Another possibility is a Transmart cargo container ship, contact Smart (Societé Mahoraise d'Acconage de Représentation et de Transit), Place de France, Dzaoudzi (tel 60 10 24; fax 60 19 57); or Port de Longoni (tel 62 11 67; fax 62 11 69; e-mail smartdza@wanadoo,fr).

Mayotte Croisieres offers cruises, and diving expeditions on its 57 ft (17.5 m) catamaran *Turquoise* for a maximum of 8 people. Departures from Mayotte for Madagascar, Comoros, and Seychelles. An 8-day, 7-night cruise costs FF8,350 per person (2 people/cabin). Contact Mayotte Vacances, Place du Marché, Mamoudzou (tel 61 25 50; fax 61 25 55).

Services for visiting yachts and catamarans are offered by the Association des Croiseurs Hauturiers de Mayotte (tel 60 20 09).

BY ROAD

There is no bus service around the island. The best way to get around is to hire a car or scooter (see *Driving*), join an organised tour, or take a taxi. *Taxi-brousse*, or shared bush taxis, are the only means of transport for most rural people. The standard price to travel around Mamoudzou or Dzaoudzi during the day is FF4.50 (£0.42/$0.63) and FF8 at night. On Sunday and public holidays it is FF7 day and night. Half price for children. You'll find bush taxis in Mamoudzou on either side of the ferry terminal, one for destinations in the north, the other for the south. Directions are usually indicated on the side of the taxis. Maximum fare to travel to any point on the island is FF35 (£3.25/$4.86), although you might have to share with a family and their livestock.

Taxis and larger vehicles are also available for tours. A half-day tour for 1-4 people costs FF300 (£28/$42); 5-8 people FF500; and from 9-15 and 26-30 people from FF850-1,600. A full-day tour for 1-4 people costs FF500; 5-8 people FF900; and from 9-15 and 26-30 people from FF1,500-2,550. Contact Comité du Tourisme (tel 61-0909; fax 61-0346).

Typical tours. Half-day car trip to the north or south of Grande Terre with a driver/guide or by 4x4 costs FF185 per person; full-day 4x4 excursion or tour of the island by car FF350, which includes a meal. These are average prices and should be confirmed by contacting one of the following:
Mayotte Aventures Tropicales: tel/fax 61 19 68.
Mayotte Vacances: tel/fax 61 25 50.
Siri za Maoré: tel/fax 62 30 87.

DRIVING

Licences

A French *permis de conduire* or an international driver's licence is necessary to hire and drive a vehicle in Mayotte. As in France, you drive on the right. The speed limit is 90 km/h on the open roads, but it's best to slow down to 30/40 km/h going through villages. Make sure your vehicle has a licence, insurance and a road tax disc.

ROADS

There are not many roads traversing the island, but the ones you'll use are fine if you drive carefully. All but 13 miles (21 km) of the 58-mile (93 km) coastal road round the island is paved. The surfaces are generally good, but there are plenty of snakelike bends. It takes about an hour to drive from the south of the island to Mamoudzou, less from the north, but you may be faced with 'rush-hour' traffic in the morning the closer you get to town. Seatbelts are not compulsory, but it's advisable to wear them.

Fuel

There is only one service station on Petite Terre, at Pamandzi, but there are five on Grande Terre, at Kawéni (Mamoudzou), Longoni, and Dzoumonye, on the RN1, Tsoundzou and, in the south at Chirongui, on the RN2. Service stations are generally open from 6am to 5pm, although they close at noon on public holidays (when you need them most). Petrol costs FF6.45 (£0.60/$0.90) a litre for Super, and diesel costs FF4.70 (£0.44/$0.65).

VEHICLE RENTAL

You must have had a full licence for at least two years in order to hire a car. You'll need an international driver's licence and must sign a credit card slip for a returnable FF2,000 (£186/$278) deposit. Cheapest cars are small Peugots, Mazdas and Renaults, starting at FF300 a day and going up in price through Citroën and Suzuki 4x4 at FF400 to 9-seater mini-buses at FF700 (£65/$97). A higher rate usually means an air-conditioned vehicle, but this is worth it whatever the cost. A two-seater scooter with insurance and helmets costs about FF160 a day. For FF80 a day you can hire a VVT (mountain-bike), Friday evening to 10am Monday morning costs FF100.

Petite Terre

You can hire a car at the airport but you will have to pay FF100 on the ferry when returning it from Mamoudzou. You will find *LMV* at Aéroport de Pamandzi, which charges FF300 a day for up to seven days to hire a car, FF520 at the weekend, FF260 (£24/$36)for 7-15 days, FF240 for 15-21 days, and FF220 for 30 days and over (tel 60 00 34; fax 60 25 71).

Grande Terre

Most hire companies charge FF300 a day for a no-frills Category A vehicle with unlimited mileage.

Fanny Loc: Place du Marché, Mamoudzou (tel 61 33 33; fax 61 34 34). FF300 a day for up to seven days, FF520 for the weekend, FF260 for 7-30 days, and FF200 for 30 days and more.

Maki Loc: 14 Place Mariage, Mamoudzou (tel 61 19 51; fax 61 19 52). Charge the same as Fanny Loc.

Multi-Autos: Garage Trophy in Mamoudzou (tel 61 36 89); Petite Terre: L'Eden Pres de la BFC, Labattoir (tel 60 23 02); and L'Ocean Pres du College,

Labattoir (tel 60 04 13). Prices range from FF220 a day for 1-10 days, FF500 for a weekend, or FF160 a day for 30 days.

SMA: Zone Industrielle de Kawéni, (tel 61 10 29; fax 61 16 36). FF300 a day, FF500 for a weekend, FF280 a day for 7-14 days, FF250 for 15-29 days, and FF220 for 30 days and more.

Tirard: 1 Route Nationale, Kawéni (tel/fax 61 13 58). For cars, 4x4, and scooters, FF300 a day or FF600 for the weekend (from Friday at 4.30pm, return Monday at 8am).

Scooters or *motos* are a cheaper alternative. You can expect to pay about FF160 a day, FF300 for the weekend, or FF900 for seven days.

You can hire them on Grande Terre from:

Loc'Utile: 6a Route Nationale 1, Kawéni (tel/fax 61 13 58). In Mamoudzou, open 7.30am to 12.30pm and 2.30pm to 6.30pm Monday to Friday, and 8am to noon on Saturday.

Multi-Autos: Kawéni branch (tel 61 36 89); Petite Terre branches in Labattoir (tel 60 23 02 and 60 04 13).

All three companies also hire out mountain-bikes, seven days for FF350, which is a big saving on the daily rate of FF80; otherwise you have a choice of taxis and tour companies offering sightseeing excursions (see *Getting Around*).

HAZARDS

There are about 16,000 vehicles on the roads and authorities estimate that 10%-20% of all drivers have no licence. This helps to explain why there are lots of erratic drivers, stopping or turning without signalling. Fairly regular pot-holes should ensure you travel at a sedate pace, which is just as well given the amount of animal and bird life on the roads. Main hazards here are *zébus* (cows), *cabri* (goats) and a variety of domestic fowls. Although it's officially illegal to leave cows and goats on the roads they seem to be everywhere, grazing along the luxuriant verges. They are not all tethered, so keep a sharp look-out when driving in the countryside.

Accommodation

Although Mayotte lacks the wide choice of hotels available in the more developed islands there are some good hotels, guest-houses and furnished apartments, and more are planned as Mayotte moves to expand its hospitality infrastructure to cope with an increasing influx of tourists. Camp sites are virtually non-existent on the island and there are only two *gîtes*, or inexpensive options for the budget conscious. Credit cards are accepted at most of the hotels, but check when you book. Most other places prefer cash.

HOTELS ON PETITE TERRE

Le Rocher: tel 60 10 10; fax 60 14 44. 25 air-conditioned rooms from FF450 (£42/$63), restaurant, bar and nightclub, swimming pool.

Le Royal: Boulevard des Crabes, Dzaoudzi (tel 60 12 45; fax 60 21 21) five minutes from the airport, 12 rooms with air-conditioning, restaurant.

Cottages/Guest-Houses/Furnished Apartments

L'Eden: 19 rue du Commerce (tel/fax 60 23 02). Three minutes from the centre of Labattoir, five rooms from FF200, TV.

Les Chambres du Coin: 87 rue des Amoureux, Labattoir (tel 60 33 74/04 97). 4 rooms from FF120.

Le Lagon Sud: Boulevard des Crabes, Dzaoudzi (tel 60 06 20; fax 60 17 27). Six rooms and three studios from FF220.

Les Jardins: 25 rue des Jardins, Pamandzi (tel/fax 60 02 67). One room at FF400.

Ocean'Hôte: 46 rue de Mouzdalifa, Labattoir (tel/fax 60 04 13). 5 rooms at FF200.

Villa Raha (gîte), 13 rue du Smiam, Pamandzi (tel/fax 62 03 64). 11 rooms from FF220, typical Mahorais cooking.

HOTELS ON GRANDE TERRE

Hotel Trevani: Accor Group (tel 60 13 83; fax 60 11 71; e-mail hotel-trevani@wanadoo.fr). About 15 minutes from Mamoudzou on the north-east coast, has 29 air-conditioned rooms in a tropical garden, from FF240 (£22/$34) per person, mini-bar, TV, notable restaurant, bar, swimming pool, daily shuttles, beach, diving club.

Jardin Maoré: tel 60 14 19; fax 60 15 19. This is the most beautifully situated resort hotel on Grande Terre. It's on the south-west tip of the island at N'goudja, 17 bungalows set in a lush tropical garden, from FF350 a person, gourmet seafood restaurant and bar. Turtles come up the beach fronting the hotel at night to lay eggs, and resident lemurs wait in the trees in the hope you'll bring them fruit for breakfast. Hotel can organise fishing, diving and sight-seeing excursions.

La Baie des Tortues: Bouéni (tel 62 62 53; fax 62 65 44). 5 bungalows, restaurant.

Le Caribou: Place Mariage (tel 61 14 18; fax 61 19 05; e-mail hotelcaribou.mayotte@wanadoo.fr). 42 air-conditioned rooms from FF440 in the heart of Mamoudzou, restaurant, bar, patisserie, swimming pool.

L'Oasis: in Mamoudzou (tel 61 12 35; fax 61 11 35). 15 air-conditioned rooms, restaurant-bar.

La Tortue Bigotu: 52 rue Marindrini, Mamoudzou (tel 61 11 32; fax 61 11 35). 12 air-conditioned rooms from FF370, TV, restaurant, bar, swimming pool.

Cottages/Guest-Houses/Furnished Apartments

L'Aventura: at Tsoundzou, south of Mamoudzou (tel 61 11 30; fax 61 48 13). 5 rooms with private bathrooms from FF260, TV.

Le Bacoco: at Kawéni (tel 61 25 90). 2 rooms from FF250, breakfast from FF20.

Les Flamboyants: tel/fax 61 41 90. 4 rooms from FF200 a person, TV .

L'Habitat Rose Doudou: 16 route de Majimbini, Quartier Convalescence, Mamoudzou (tel/fax 61 04 48). 4 rooms from FF200.

L'Hibiscus: Cavani Stade, Mamoudzou (tel/fax 61 46 61). 6 rooms from FF210, TV.

Le Jimaweni: near Mtsangachéhi on the west coast (tel 62 96 38 and 62 10 50). Has two *bangas* or small cottages, B&B from FF150. Mohammed and Halima will whip you up a Mahorais dinner for FF50-80.

Mont Combani: tel/fax 62 91 42. At Combani in the centre of Grande Terre, has two bungalows from FF150.

Residence Le Maoua: Mamoudzou (tel/fax 61 00 53/24 70). 12 rooms from FF220, *Soifa* restaurant serves Mahorais and French dishes.

SCI Alizées: 7 le Belvedere, at Pointe de Koungou on the north coast (tel/fax 61 05 52; e-mail patrick.rigole@wanadoo.fr). One apartment with one double room and two single rooms at FF2,200 a week.

Villa Florence: tel/fax 61 55 09. 3 rooms from FF150 a person.

Gîtes

Gîte Hagnoundrou: on the south-west coast at Bouéni Bay, (tel/fax 62 62 22). Has 13 rooms from FF100.

Gîte de Mliha: at Mliha on the north-west coast, (tel/fax 62 17 07). Has three double rooms with air-conditioning, 2 dormitories sleeping 8 each, from FF50 a person, breakfast FF10. Popular with young budget travellers and families. Organises fishing, diving, and trips to offshore islands.

Camping

As yet there are no official camp sites on Mayotte, and while bivouacing in the bush is not officially illegal, it is not advisable. However, you can find a camping spot at *Mont Combani*, in Combani, for about FF20 a person a night (tel/fax 62 91 42); and if *Gîte Mliha* is full they will let you camp (tel/fax 62 17 07). The owner of *La Jimaweni* near Mtsangachéhi, on the road south from Sada before Poroani, will let you bivouac in his garden (tel 62 96 38). The owner of *Villa Raha* on Petite Terre has plans for a camp site on Grande Terre at Milouan, near Bandrélé, on the east coast; telephone or fax 62 03 64 to see if it's up and running.

Eating and Drinking

CUISINE

Food on Mayotte is principally continental French, the choice of most expatriates and visitors, and Mahorais, the local food which differs from the rest of the Comoros islands only in the way the spices and other ingredients are combined. By no stretch of the imagination could you regard local food as haute cuisine but Mahorais cooking is made interesting by the freshness and quality of the ingredients used. Simple and practical, the base of all dishes is rice, manioc or bananas, or a combination of all three. The locals usually breakfast on maize, rice or manioc, and during the day they like to snack on spicy beef kebabs, known as *les mamas brochettes.* Try them in the market, near the ferry terminal in Mamoudzou. In Mayotte, *chahoula* (food) means anything that goes with *chiréou*, or *m'tsouzi*, which can be beef, goat, chicken or fish.

Under the heading of *chahoula* on the menu you could find:

Matsidza – boiled rice, with or without grated coconut.

Batabata – green banana, chopped into large pieces and boiled.

Trovi ya nadzi – a mixture of diced banana and manioc, cooked in coconut milk with meat or fish.

Trovi m'hogo – fried banana and manioc.

Pillawo – a rice pilau, or pilaff, cooked for festivals and special occasions.

Oubou – rice, maize, manioc, and pumpkin, boiled with sugar.

Tambi – vermicelli.

Mhogo piki – dried manioc, prepared like *trovi ya nadzi* with fish.

Brèdes – the main ingredient gives its name to the brède, or stew, and you can, for instance, have mushroom, pumpkin, sweet potato, aubergine, Chinese cabbage or manioc brède.

Dishes can be accompanied by a variety of local vegetables, and manioc leaves, which cooked in a broth or in coconut milk are like spinach and known as *mataba*. Cereals and green bananas are combined with beef and all kinds of root vegetables, such as manioc, taro, and sweet potato, in a stew known as *romazava*. For special occasions *embrevades* are cooked. These are a cross between dried haricot beans and lentils. Great stuff for vegetarians. No dish is regarded as complete without a dash of green or red chilli known as *piment* or *putu*, which is the signature of all Mahorian – and Indian Ocean – cuisine. *Mérou* (grouper, or stone bass) and *langouste* (crayfish) are often served with vanilla sauce, which is an unusual accompaniment but worth trying if only for the novelty, as are the *huitres de palétuviers*, delicious tiny oysters prised from the roots of tidal mangrove trees and regarded by the Mahorais as an oddity eaten only by *wazungu*, or Europeans.

There are other dishes attuned to the western palate, such as *ntouzi wankuhu*, (*poulet coco*, or chicken in coconut), which from the right kitchen can be a tasty dish. A similar dish is made with fish, and known as *ntouzi mfi wanazi* (*poisson au coco*). Anything that comes out of the sea or river needs little embellishment and fish, lobster, crabs and giant freshwater *camarons*, or prawns, are popular restaurant dishes with expatriates. The Mahorais do a nice line in finally sliced shark, grouper, and swordfish smoked over a wood fire, the tropical equivalent of smoked salmon. Excellent fruit includes mangoes, bananas, litchis, guavas, pineapple, cinnamon apples, and coconuts.

Local expatriate gourmets say the best table in Mayotte is spread by the *Le Couba* fish restaurant, a 10-minute drive north from the centre of Mamoudzou towards Koungou. Next they rate the restaurant at the *Caribou Hotel* in the centre of town, followed by the restaurant at the *Hotel Trevani* beyond Koungou. Other popular places for French cuisine in and around Mamoudzou are *Le Bar Fly*, the restaurant at the *Hotel La Tortue Bigotu*, and the *Bar Rond Point*.

VEGETARIAN AND SELF-CATERING

From all this you'll see that there are plenty of choices if you are a vegetarian, or a fruitarian, and dishes without *chiréou* are not so heavy on the pocket. The cheapest fruits are bananas and coconuts. As virtually everything is imported, self-catering is not all that cheap. You can buy whatever you need from one of the **three supermarkets** in and around Mamoudzou, *Score*, *Sodifram*, and *SNIE* (two new hypermarkets are scheduled to open sometime in 2001). If you are a budget traveller you'll probably need only something to sustain you through the day, in which case the bread baton known as a baguette with some fruit from market vendors should carry you through. This crispy, light bread is always sold fresh, no matter how remote the village might seem and you'll invariably see mounds for sale by the side of the road. If you are in Mamoudzou, try the baguettes at the Hotel Caribou's bakery or the **Boulangerie-Pâtisserie Ballou**, on rue du Commerce.

RESTAURANTS

Petite Terre

Le Faré: Boulevard des Crabes, Dzaoudzi (tel 60 13 31; fax 60 17 32). A restaurant, bar and pizzeria at Plage Mouriombeni, it's open every day except Tuesday. Expect to pay not less than FF100 (£9/$13) for a meal, but an excellent one of choice fish and seafood, with crayfish a speciality. Entertainment every Friday.

La Grillade: 7 rue de l'AJP, Pamandzi (tel 62 15 58). Open daily from 9am to 10.30pm, specialising in Senegalese and Mahorais food, FF30-40.

Le Royal Hotel: Boulevard des Crabes, Dzaoudzi (tel 60 12 45; fax 60 21 21). Five minutes from the airport, has a popular restaurant-bar serving French, Mahorais and Malagasy dishes, with meat and fish grills a speciality. Chicken, lamb, beef, and fish dishes FF60-70.

La Triskel: 12 rue du Four à Chaux, Labattoir (tel 60 12 26). A small restaurant and terrace bar in the commune with the unprepossessing name. You can play billiards while waiting for your hamburger and chips (FF50) and it's open from 10am to midnight.

Villa Raha: 13 rue du Smiam, Pamandzi (tel 62 03 64). Close to the airport, this restaurant is open every evening from 8pm, Mahorais cuisine, FF50 per person.

Grande Terre

L'Asiatica: tel 61 59 92. On the main road south, 15 minutes from Mamoudzou, specialises in Asian and Mahorais food, FF40-50. Open every day from 10am to 3pm except Sunday. Dishes FF30-40.

Le Bacoco: tel 61 25 90. On the outskirts of Mamoudzou, specialising in French, Réunionese and grills. Open every day from 11am. Plat du jour from FF50.

If you are a rugby fan you'll love *Le Bar Fly* on rue Mahabou, in Mamoudzou (tel 60 10 38). The owner used to play for France. There are good views of the harbour and the food is good, too. A Greek salad costs FF28, beef entrecôte or stroganoff is FF68, fish dishes FF63-68, and FF22-36 buys you an *Assiette Fly:* a sorbet with fruits in season, banana flambé, chocolate, and cream. Every Friday evening there's a party which usually lasts until the sun rises.

Bar Rond Point: 3a rue du Commerce (tel 61 04 61). It's air-conditioned, and specialises in French cuisine, charcoal grills, and seafood.

Les Choisils: tel 62 52 36. At Hamjago, on the beach on the north-west coast near Mtsamboro, open every day from 8am to 11pm. Traditional Mahorais lunch and supper dishes FF25-60 (£2-6/$3-8).

Le Couba: (tel 60 55 55) on the main road north 2 miles (4 km) from Mamoudzou. Open Tuesday to Sunday from 9am to 3pm and 6pm to 10.30pm. Specialises in fish and seafood, from FF35 .

Hotel and Restaurant Caribou: Place Mariage (tel 61 14 18; fax 61 19 05). Specialises in French, Réunionese and Malagasy food. It serves what is arguably the best coffee in Mayotte and has an inviting variety of cakes and pastries in its patisserie as you enter the hotel. This is the meeting and socialising centre of Mamoudzou.

The *Hotel Trevani* between Koungou and Kangan on the coast road north from

Mamoudzou has a popular restaurant and bar called *Le Maki Gourmand* (tel 60 13 83; fax 60 11 71) which, while not cheap (FF80-150), serves up excellent fish and seafood. Its heart of palm salad is also noteworthy. Sunday lunch attracts the Mamoudzou crowd for the poolside buffet.

Le Jimaweni: tel 62 96 68. On Bouéni Bay in the south-west, at Mtsangachéhi. Open every day from noon until 9pm, FF80 per person, or FF70 for parties of 10.

Le Massalé: 10 rue du Commerce (first floor), Mamoudzou (tel 61 07 03). Specialises in Creole and Indian food. You can get a *cari* (curry) for about FF50. There's couscous at lunchtime on Saturday.

La Reflet des Iles: Place du Marché, Mamoudzou (tel 60 10 30). A restaurant-pizzeria with a panoramic view of the area. Menu from around FF60.

La Soifa: tel 61 24 88. About 3 miles (5 km) south of Mamoudzou, at Passamaïnty. Open every day, except Sunday, from 7pm. Mahorais cuisine. Set menu from FF65, or a la carte dishes FF15-50.

Sud Restaurant: (tel 62 68 10; fax 62 68 39) at Chirongui, on Bouéni Bay. Open every day from 8am to 3pm and 6pm to 10pm. Specialises in Mahorais food and grills, especially *brochettes de poissons* (fish kebabs). Dishes FF30-45 (£2-4/$4-6).

Les Terrasses: 13 rue du Commerce, (tel 61 06 12). Near the post office in Mamoudzou, has a restaurant-bar where you can sit out on the terrace overlooking the lagoon while waiting for the French or Vietnamese meal, around FF100, in which the restaurant specialises.

Le Tortue Bigotu 52 rue Marindrini, Mamoudzou (tel 61 11 32). In a cul de sac at the end of rue du Commerce, this hotel has a highly regarded poolside restaurant with a terrace overlooking the town. The owner is a keen deep-sea angler and catches his own fish and you can be sure that if the fish served up were any fresher it would still be swimming. Whole baked fish *en papillote* is a speciality, as is fillet of grouper in vanilla sauce. Expect to spend about FF150 on a meal, although you can get a crêpe for FF15-45.

Yasmine: tel 62 05 05; fax 62 13 89. The only restaurant of note in the central part of the island. It's at Combani, about 6 miles (10 km) west of Mamoudzou. Its surroundings are unpretentious, but the food is good. The plat du jour, normally couscous, is FF100, salad of papaya costs FF20, prawns FF60, fish FF60, steak and chips FF50, tongue FF50, duck with Roquefort FF90, and ice-cream FF20.

DRINKING

As in the rest of the Indian Ocean region it's not advisable for visitors to drink local tap water. It is allegedly safe in Mamoudzou, but it tastes strange and it's better to stick to the still or carbonated bottled *Vital* water from Mauritius. Well known French designer waters are also available, but at twice the price. There's a factory in Mayotte producing such soft drinks as Coca-Cola, Fanta and Sprite. These usually cost the same as beer. Considering the amount of tropical fruit around there's a dearth of fresh fruit drinks on the island; the Mahorais seem to prefer something that comes out of a can or a bottle. Coconuts are the exception, and come in two categories: drinking coconuts (*shijavu*) and eating coconuts (*nadzi*).

The Mahorais live in an Islamic society and accordingly are subject to the dietary and drink laws prescribed by their religion. Ostensibly, this means they are forbidden to drink alcohol. However, by the amount of beer imported into Mayotte – far more than bottled water – and the phenomenal number of empty beer cans in the bush around rural villages it would seem that there must be some lapsed Muslims around, or lots of Frenchmen with cirrhosis of the liver. The beer of choice locally is *Castle* lager, which is imported from South Africa. It's not easy to find other beers, although you might find *Heineken* occasionally in a café. One place that's a magnet for beer drinkers is **Le Pub** on the Boulevard des Crabes on Petite Terre, a favourite watering hole for French expatriates, which boasts *un vaste choix de bières*. You can even get Guinness. The choice starts at around FF20 (£1.86/$2.78) a beer, which is expensive even by local standards, but the view from the terrace overlooking the beach is free and you can surf the Internet for 15 minutes for FF25. Wines and spirits are imported, usually from France, and are priced accordingly. If you like a drink as the sun goes down make the most of your duty-free allowance before you arrive.

Once out of Mamoudzou and Dzaoudzi your chance of finding any kind of western-style entertainment is virtually non-existent. You'll be able to watch traditional dances and ceremonies in the rural areas at various times of the year (see *The People* p.168 or *Religion* p.171) but if the drums and rattles don't get your feet tapping and you need a disco you'll have to go back to the two main towns.

Nightlife

Regarded as the classiest disco in Mamoudzou is *Le Mahaba Club*, a discothèque at the Place du Marché, near the ferry terminal. There's dancing Wednesday to Saturday. It opens at 9.30pm on these nights (tel 61-1689). Also near the ferry terminal and also open for dancing in the evening from Wednesday to Saturday is the disco at the *Bar 5/5*. Entrance is a high FF80, but you'll probably be allowed to take a partner in free. Also in Mamoudzou are *Le Golden Lagoon II* bar and disco, a local hot-spot catering to young Mahorais, with dancing on Fridays and Saturdays, and *La Gêole*, which is regarded as somewhat dangerous by local expats and maybe best avoided.

On Petite Terre, is *Le Ningha Club* in Dzaoudzi, where you can dance in more elegant surroundings (tel 60 13 48), and *L'Awak*, on the road to the airport at Pamandzi. This is a friendly laid-back discothèque where you don't have to pay an entrance fee, but you must buy drinks. The only other proviso is 'No shorts' (referring to clothes, not drinks).

Cinema and Theatre

This is all very hit and miss and the best way to find out what's happening in the local arts and cultural world is to contact the *Centre Mahorais d'Animation Culturelle* (CMAC), in rue l'Hôpital, Mamoudzou, which organises film shows and theatrical events and usually knows what is happening elsewhere on the island. On the west coast at Mtsangachéhi, near Poroani, is a surprising little association called *L'Art M'Attend*, which arranges film shows and other forms of entertainment (tel 62 26 93). As you travel around the countryside you might stumble on local un-advertised village film shows which might be projected in anything from a social centre to an open-air venue where the screen is a length of cloth stretched between two palm trees.

FLORA AND FAUNA

FLORA

The diversity of Mayotte's indigenous flora is related to rainfall: humid forests in the north and centre of the island and forests and vegetation typical of dry regions on Petite Terre and in the south of Grande Terre, where bulbous baobabs known locally as *la mère des arbres* ('the mother of trees') appear in the landscape. Trees, plants and flowers producing exotic oils, fruits and spices – palms, guavas, breadfruit, vanilla, cinnamon, ylang-ylang, mango, papaya, coffee, litchis, pepper, cocoa, and nutmeg – mingle with a riot of roses, bougainvillaea, hibiscus, frangipani, orchids, and other flowers, justifying the description of Mayotte as the 'Perfumed Isle.' Almost every variety of palm tree grows on the island, and you'll see the royal palm, wild date palms, the coconut palm, and the vacoa or dragon tree in profusion. Of the nine known genera of mangroves, known generally in French as *palétuvier*, seven have established themselves along Mayotte's shoreline, at Mamoudzou, Koungou, Longoni Bay, Soulou Bay, Dembeni Bay, Bandrélé, Kani-Keli, and Boueni Bay. They are the white mangrove (*Avicennia marina*), Mozambique mangrove (*Heritiera littoralis*), the spring-tide mangrove (*Lumnitzera racemosa*), the Indian mangrove (*Ceriops tagal*), black mangrove (*Bruguiera gymnorrhiza*), *Sonneratia alba*, and the red mangrove (*Rhizophora mucronata*), a remarkable tree whose stilt-like roots are equal in length to the difference in height between local tides – a useful bit of information for visiting divers.

FAUNA

Birdlife

While there are only three birds endemic to Mayotte – the **Mayotte drongo**, **white-eye** and **sunbird** – twtichers should enjoy ticking off a variety of other birds, including herons, budgerigars, cardinals, **white-tailed tropic birds** (*paille-en-queue*) egrets, plovers, curlews, greenshanks, and the **Indian Ocean harrier** known as the *papangue*. To spot the three endemics you should head for the Mont Combani forest reserve, the nearest area of mountain forest to Mamoudzou. All three endemic birds are easily seen along the track to the peak at 1,565 ft (477 m) and in the adjoining woodland. For seabirds, watch the sea from the headlands and from the inter-island ferry and you'll probably see wedge-tailed and Audubon's **shearwaters**, white-tailed and red-tailed **tropicbirds**, greater and lesser frigatebirds, brown, red-footed and masked boobies, the lesser noddy, and bridled, sooty, greater crested, common, and black-naped terns.

Wildlife

On the trails in the northern forest between Combani and Bouyouni you might startle **wild boar** (or they might startle you), otherwise there's not a great variety of animals on the island. The star of the fauna is the *maki*, the local name for an endemic species of **lemur** (*Lemur fulvus mayottensis*) which is a charming little animal with a penchant for hikers' bananas. This endearing furry lemur also has the peculiar habit of burying its dead. You'll find lots of them on l'Ilot Bouzi, a 10-minute boat trip from Mamoudzou, and in the south around the *Jardin Maoré* resort hotel at N'goudja. If you are lucky, or sharp-sighted, you might spot a rare **chameleon**. You'll have no difficulty in spotting the **giant bats** known as *la roussette* or *la Fanny*, especially at dusk when they circle like prehistoric pterodactyls.

Watch out in the forest for giant millipedes (*Diplopoda*), known locally as *gros mille-pattes*, which can grow up to six inches (15 cm) in length and can give you a painful bite. Interestingly, the fangs they use to bite you are not teeth at all, but modified front legs connected to their venom sacs. A swift douche of urine helps to neutralise the poison if you are bitten.

SEALIFE

The real profusion of island wildlife, however, is not on the land or in the air, but in the sea and the vast lagoon created by a huge encircling barrier reef of coral. Thousands of years ago, the sea level dropped and the lagoon emptied, allowing rivers to chisel their way through the dying reef. When the ocean level rose again the corals revived and resumed their building of the barrier. The channels left by the ancient rivers are now navigable passages. This turbulent geological history set the scene for the emergence of some extraordinary tropical underwater flora and fauna and a wide variety of eco-systems are found at depths down to 230 ft (70 m) in this 463 sq mile (1,200 sq km) lagoon, one of the largest in the world.

Turtles

Of the seven species of turtle in the world five are found in the south-west Indian Ocean and two, the **green turtle** (*Chelonia mydas*) and the **hawksbill** (*Eretmochelys imbricata*) are found in the lagoon. Green turtles grow up to 5 ft (1.5 m) and can weigh more than 551 lb (250 kg), while the hawksbill weighs in at 287 lb-397 lb (130 kg-180 kg). The hawksbill is the turtle which provides true tortoiseshell, and as a consequence is the most endangered species in the south-west Indian Ocean.

The green turtle – the one once famed as a soup served at aldermanic dinners in London – is much more common than the hawksbill and accounts for an estimated 90% of Mayotte's total turtle population. Research undertaken by the French Institute for Marine Exploration Research has thrown light on the turtle's fascinating life cycle. After hatching on the beach of the lagoon the baby turtle undertakes the most dangerous journey of its life, a dash for the water. If it's lucky enough to avoid being eaten by a vagrant dog or a bird, or being gobbled by an awaiting fishy predator, it will be swept away by the waves and carried far from its birthplace. Once it becomes strong enough to make way against the ocean currents the turtle starts to feed closer to shore and turns omnivore, with a liking for the sea grasses of shallow waters. Sexual maturity comes at 8-10 years and the female then heads back to the place of her birth. In order to escape both the heat and possible predators she hauls herself up on the beach at night and digs a nest in the sand and deposits her clutch of ping-pong ball eggs. The eggs hatch two months later and the cycle starts all over again. Mayotte's turtles are now under the protection of the Department of Agriculture and Forestry and the two most important nesting sites on the island, the beaches of Moya, on Petite Terre, and of Saziley, on Grande Terre, are under 24-hour surveillance. On other beaches members of a voluntary association watch over egg-laying turtles and help to prevent poaching.

Whales and Dolphins

Numerous species of **whales**, large and small, can be observed both inside and outside the lagoon, making Mayotte a largely undiscovered place for whale-watching from the end of June to the end of November, when they arrive to calve before returning to the Antarctic. Among the species you can expect to see are 25-30 ton **humpback whales** (*Megaptera novaeangliae*), whose 13-ft long (4 m) pectoral swim fins are the biggest of any whale, the **melon-headed whale** (*Peponocephala electra*) – an 8 ft (2.5 m) pygmy whale often mistaken for a dolphin – and the rare cachalot, or **sperm whale** (*Physeter macrocephalus*), the largest of the toothed whales and monsters which average 49 ft (15 m) in length and weigh up to 45-50 tons.

Sharing the waters with these cetaceans are their smaller relatives, the **dolphins**, many of which can be spotted in the lagoon all year round. Common are the **bottlenose** dolphin (*Tursiops truncatus*), the agile and exuberant **spinner** (*Stenella longirostris*), the pantropical **spotted** dolphin (*Stenella attenuata*), and **Fraser's** dolphin (*Lagenodelphis hosei*), which is usually seen in pods of at least a hundred, often with melonheads and other dolphins. Another visitor is the timid and rarely seen **humpback dolphin** (*Sousa chinensis*).

Rarities

The marine mammal that gave rise to the old stories of mermaids might, with a great deal of luck and patience, be seen grazing in the seagrass meadows of the lagoon. This is the **dugong** or sea cow (*Sirenia)*, which has been hunted close to extinction but is occasionally spotted feeding among the mangroves.

Excursions

Eco-tourism operators offering whale, dolphin, turtle, and even lemur-watching excursions include:
Biocéan: tel/fax 61 22 63.
Les Naturalistes de Mayotte: tel/fax 62 29 48; e-mail naturalistes.mayotte@wanadoo.fr.
Megaptera: Mamoudzou (tel 61 23 15; fax 61 17 21), whale-watch specialists.
Sea Blue Safari: Mamoudzou (tel/fax 61 07 63).
Terre d'Asile: Ilô Bouzy (tel 61 03 30; fax 61 05 57).

SPORT AND RECREATION

Sports and recreational activities on Mayotte fall into the usual land, sea, and air categories, but with a natural emphasis on the second option. The island does not have the range and choice found on, say, Mauritius or Réunion, but what there is on offer is peerless. Whether you intend to hike or ramble, dive or fish, sail and swim, take to the air, or simply go sight-seeing to soak in the tranquillity of island life we recommend that you seek local guidance to make the most of your choice.

Tour operators offering such excursions include:

Mayotte Vacances: 7 Place du Marché, Mamoudzou (tel 61 25 50; fax 61 25 55).

Mayotte Aventures Tropicales: tel/fax 61 19 68.

Siri za Maoré: Ouangani (tel/fax 62 30 87).

Hotels can also usually organise diving trips and guides for hiking and rambling excursions, and some of the larger ones have their own watersports centres. Small operators are popping up in odd corners of Grande Terre who tend to specialise in half and full day outings to one or other of the 20 islets dotting the lagoon around the island.

DIVING AND SNORKELLING

There's good snorkelling and scuba-diving around all the islands of the Comoros archipelago but Mayotte boasts the finest dive sites because of the incredible coral reefs which have built up around it, geologically the oldest of the islands. The diving compares favourably with the better known Maldives, Seychelles, and the islands of Polynesia, especially in two exceptional sites, the **Passe Longogori** through the Pamandzi reef south of Petite Terre, and better known to the diving fraternity because of its shape as *Passe en S*, and within the 7,809 acres (3,160 ha) of the **Saziley Park Marine Reserve**, off the south-east tip of Grande Terre.

The area of the 'S' break in the reef has been a proclaimed marine reserve since 1990 and it is demarcated by half a dozen yellow buoys, **strong currents** in this area call for diving experience.

The **Saziley reserve** is great for all levels of scuba and snorkelling proficiency and has within its confines the attractive little *Ilot de Sable Blanc* ('White Sand Isle') with its own adjoining coral reef system where you might see such wonderfully coloured fish as demoiselles, parrotfish, Moorish idols, clownfish, emperors, trumpet, angel, trigger, unicorn, butterfly and surgeon fish, sand perch, goatfish and devilfish. There's an underwater trail at Saziley and you can get a free booklet guide (in French) from the Fisheries and Marine Environment Division at the Department of Agriculture and Forestry (DAF) in Mamoudzou (tel 61 12 82; fax 61 35 13; e-mail daf.spem.mayotte@ wanadoo.fr). Saziley Park also covers nearly 1,235 acres (500 ha) of the Saziley headland onshore, with a choice of some fine beaches and pleasant walks. There are lots of other good diving spots, such as **Pamandzi islet** off Dzaoudzi, and snorkelling off **Longoni Beach**, but you really need local advice on sites as there are stretches of reef in the lagoon still to recover from the devastation caused when cyclone El Niño ripped through the region in the 1990s and raised the temperature of the water sufficiently to kill off large quantities of coral-building polyps. The notorious crown of thorns starfish (*Acanthaster planci*) also contributes to the problem, as it feeds on polyps struggling to regenerate. One of the reasons for the blanket ban on the collection of shells is that some species of shellfish prey on this menace.

One spot that is a must for all divers and snorkellers is off **N'goudja beach** in the south-west, in front of the resort hotel of Jardin Maoré. Any time of the day you'll find huge turtles grazing on the sea grass in depths of 5-10 ft (1.5-3 m) and it's quite a thrill to swim among them and see how turtles in their true element are nothing like the ponderous beasts seen on land. N'gouja also offers scuba enthusiasts a choice of deep, shallow or drift dives, inside the reef, on it or outside it, or on one of the many drop-offs. Visibility is usually pretty good, and depending on which side of the reef you are you can expect to see **groupers**, **sharks**, **morays**, **leopard rays**, **dolphins**, and in the right season (see *Flora and Fauna*) pods of visiting **whales**.

No one is allowed to spearfish or take anything out of the sea, so you'll see lots of shellfish and other marine life around. Whale-watching is a growing attraction the world over and the Fisheries and Marine Environment Department, aware of its importance to eco-tourism, has drawn up a charter laying down strict rules for the observation of whales in the lagoon. The rules apply equally to dolphins and dugongs and explain how to approach all these marine mammals in safety and with respect for them, how close to go and how long to stay in their vicinity. The charter has been drawn up in collaboration with whale-watch specialists and eco-tourism operators *Megaptera* (see *Flora and Fauna*). You can get a copy of the charter (in French) from DAF (see above).

DIVE CENTRES

There are six recognised diving centres on Grande Terre and one on Petite Terre.

On Petite Terre:

Le Lambis: Boulevard des Crabes, Dzaoudzi (tel 60 06 31; fax 60 08 46), dives from FF200.

On Grande Terre:

Aqua Diva: Mamoudzou (tel 61 18 59; fax 61 20 18), dives from FF220.
Lagon Maoré: (tel 60 14 19; fax 60 15 19) based at the resort hotel of Jardin Maoré at N'goudja beach, dives from FF250.
Maji Club: Mamoudzou (tel 61 02 19; fax 61 22 40), dives from FF220.
Mayotte Lagoon: (tel/fax 62 15 42) at Trévani on the north coast, dives from FF200.
OK Corail: Mamoudzou (tel/fax 61 22 63), dives from FF200.
Sud Explo: (tel/fax 62 01 92) based at Bandrélé and Chirongui, dives from FF220.

All the dive centres have their own boats, catamarans or rubber dinghies, and all staff are fully qualified, largely with NAUI, PADI, CMAS, and CEDIP diplomas. CEDIP, the European Committee of Professional Diving Instructors, is not so well known to British, US and Australian divers as the other qualifications. For more information e-mail cedip.antibes@wanadoo.fr or contact Pierre Gauvin in Mamoudzou (tel 61 18 59/61), or David Lecornu (tel 62 26 19; fax 62 26 19). Dives are usually organised for 9am and 2pm. You can hire gear and get air fills at all the dive centres without a problem. There is no recompression chamber on Mayotte, but this is not a problem as dives with local operators start at 16 ft (5 m) and don't get to decompression stage diving.

The **best time** for diving in Mayotte is during the southern winter (June-October) when the water is clear, breezes are constant and there are whales inside the lagoon and lots of large pelagic fish such as **dogtooth tunny**, **kingfish**, **barracuda** and **wahoo** outside the barrier reef to add interest and excitement to your dive. By contrast, the sea is calm and warmer in the southern summer months

(November-April) and this is the season when many species of fish are in their reproductive cycle. There can be a difference of anything up to 13 ft (4 m) between high and low water.

Mayotte Croisieres offers diving trips and cruises on its 57 ft (17.5 m) catamaran *Turquoise* for a maximum of 8 people. Contact through *Mayotte Vacances*, in Mamoudzou (tel 61 25 50; fax 61 25 55; boat tel 00873-76200 6815, or fax 00873-76200 60817).

Alternatives

Non-divers who want to explore below the surface are catered for by the *Visiobul*, a glass-bottomed semi-submersible, which will allow you to view the undersea world in comfort (tel 60 00 05).

FISHING

The waters are teeming with fish and local fishermen take about 3,000 tons a year out of the lagoon alone. There are regulations, however, and if you plan to fish without local help you should ascertain what they are from the fisheries service (tel 61 12 82; fax 61 35 13).

For big-game and deep-sea angling contact Christian Gougeou, at **Pêche au Gros** (tel 61 04 61), or Serge (tel 62 14 38), or one of the charter/tour companies, which can take you trolling for marlin, swordfish, barracuda, yellowfin tuna (October-May) and other gamefish, and also take you **sailing** or **cruising**.

Charter Companies

All these also offer excursions and a variety of watersports:

Arnaud Païnatan: Hagnoundrou, on Bouéni Bay (tel/fax 62 00 89), he'll take you out in a pirogue to catch calamari between 4.30pm and 6pm for FF160 for two.

Centre Nautique Loc'Action: Mtsahara (tel 62 23 39; fax 60 53 51), also hires out sea kayaks for FF300 a day.

Le Jardin Maoré: N'goudja (tel 60 14 19; fax 60 15 19).

MAT: Hamouro (tel 61 19 68).

Mayotte Aventures Tropicales: tel/fax 61 19 68.

Mayotte Vacances: tel 61 25 50; fax 61 25 55.

Mayotte Lagoon: tel/fax 62 15 42.

Siri za Maoré: tel/fax 62 30 87.

You can usually hire a boat for the day in any of the coastal villages for around FF400. One possibility is *Chez Raza*, (tel 60 52 36) which is ideally situated at Hamjago in the north-west facing the islands of Mtsamboro and Choizil. You can buy any fishing, sailing or diving gear you might need from *Pêche and Yachting* at 43 Place Mariage, Mamoudzou, which can also organise half-day and day excursions (tel 61 03 41). As a rule of thumb expect to pay FF800-1,500 (£74/$111) for a half-day fishing expedition for two anglers and FF300-900 if you are joining a joyride excursion to one of the islets, such as Ilot Mtsamboro in the north, or Ilot de Sable Blanc in the south.

HIKING

Whatever else you pack if you are planning to hit the trail without a local guide you'll need a good map – an IGN 1:25,000 is best (see *Maps and Guides* p.183) – long, lightweight clothes, a hat, sun-cream, pocket torch, a flask or water bottle, and water purification tablets. You will not find drinkable water anywhere in the bush. You should also make sure you are up to date with your anti-malaria tablet intake. There are 11 recognised hiking trails and these will take you to almost every corner of Grande Terre.

Hiking Trails:

Route	Time	Distance	Grade
Mamoudzou to Koungou	4 hours	5 miles (8 km)	easy.
Koungou to Dzoumogné	6 hours	9 miles (15 km)	easy.
Dzoumogné to Mtsamboro	6 hours	6 miles (10 km)	difficult.
Mtsamboro to Mtsangamouji	6 hours	6 miles (10 km)	medium.
Mtsangamouji to Chiconi	6 hours	10 miles (16 km)	easy.
Chiconi to Miréréni	7 hours	7 miles (12 km)	medium.
Miréréni to Saziley	7 hours	9 miles (15 km)	easy.
Saziley to Bandrélé	5 hours	6 miles (10 km)	easy.
Bandrélé to Tsararano	8 hours	9 miles (15 km)	difficult.
Tsararano-Vahibé to Mamoudzou	4 hours	12 miles (19 km)	medium.
Vahibé to Mamoudzou	3¹/₂ hours	6 miles (10 km)	easy.

The Department of Agriculture and Forestry (DAF) in Mamoudzou has produced a guide to the trails (tel 61 12 82; fax 61 35 13). If they are out of stock (not unlikely) the Comité du Tourisme might be able to let you have a photocopy. For more information about hiking trails, guides and interpreters contact the Comité du Tourisme in Mamoudzou (tel 61 09 09; fax 61 03 46; e-mail comite-du-tourisme-mayotte@wanadoo.fr); *Kombas Tours* (tel 61 10 38); or any one of the tour operators detailed earlier. *Siri za Maoré*, in particular, specialises in guided trekking, as does *Oulanga na Nyamba* (tel/fax 62 13 14).

OTHER ACTIVITIES

Swimming and Surfing
Most of the best beaches are on the east side of Grande Terre. The protective reef means that virtually all the island beaches are safe for swimming, but useless for surfing. The only spot recommended for surfing by locals is off Moya beach, on the east side of Petite Terre – which can also be highly dangerous for swimmers.

Aerial Trips
You can get a bird's-eye view of the islands by taking to the air with *Mayotte ULM* (tel 60 01 37) at Pamandzi Airport, on Petite Terre, where the aeroclub can offer you a microlight flight for sightseeing, shooting videos and taking photographs, as well as the chance to parachute or sky-dive. A short flight costs FF220 (£20/$30), while a more extensive one over Mamoudzou and the Passe en 'S' in the outlying coral reef is FF350. *Les Ailes Mahoraises* (tel 60 12 71) also operates from the airport and offers a 55-minute light plane flight for three around Mayotte for FF850.

Golf

You have to be a dedicated golfer to swing a club in the heat and humidity, but if that's what floats your boat you can contact Mayotte's only golf course, the *Golf Club les Ylangs* at Combani (tel 61 29 38).

Opening Hours. Shopping and office hours: Monday to Saturday 8am to noon, and 3pm to 5pm. On Fridays most Muslim shops and businesses close at 11.30am in preparation for the weekly prayers at the mosque.

GIFTS AND SOUVENIRS

As late-comers to the business of tourism Mayotte has not yet built up a tacky souvenir and curio industry, and while this makes it difficult to shop for mementoes it does mean that those you do find are usually worthwhile examples of traditional craftwork and genuine echoes of island life. Look out in particular, for carved woodwork, gold and silver jewellery, musical instruments, and household utensils and products which make ingenious use of plaited palm leaves and bamboo. By the side of the road in rural areas you'll find small children selling enormous dried seed pods, nearly a metre long, which are popular with tourists in search of the unusual. The main market in Mamoudzou, near the ferry terminal, is worth a visit if only for its vibrancy, colour and smells – pleasantly aromatic and otherwise. You might find the odd curio among the plastic suitcases and tin plates, but for the genuine article you should visit one of the several co-operatives and *artisanats*, or craftwork associations, around Petite and Grande Terre.

Two things you can buy at the market are bundles of dried **vanilla sticks** and the lengths of the **colourful cotton cloth** the Mahorais women wear as chic wraparound clothing. Opposite the market is the Agricultural Co-operative, which among other products sells **coffee** grown on the island. You can also buy small flasks of **ylang-ylang** perfume oil here, although it's usually cheaper at the rural distillers producing it from this intensely fragrant yellow flower. Mamoudzou is also the place to buy T-shirts with island motifs, at shops in the rue du Commerce and the Place Mariage; books and postcards from *La Maison des Livres Librairie*, on Place Mariage; unusual and potentially valuable Mayotte postage **stamps** (see *Communications*); and attractive 35 x 24 inch (90 x 60 cm) colour **posters** from the Department of Agriculture and Forestry in Place Mariage featuring whales, turtles, dolphins, fish, and ecological themes. They cost FF15-20 each and you can buy them every Wednesday and Friday morning. At the other end of the scale is the filigreed gold and silver **jewellery** made by craftsmen in Mamoudzou, Pamandzi, Labattoir, Sada, and Mtsapéré. They offer a wide range of superb bracelets, rings, collars, chains, earrings and pendants to choose from at prices you can bargain down. Jewellers also deal in a variety of **semi-precious stones** from Madagascar.

Mayotte **vanilla** is regarded as the best produced in the Indian Ocean. Travelling around Grande Terre you'll find excellent vanilla at the co-operative in **Coconi**, on the road between Dembeni on the east coast and Sada on the west, and in nearby **Chiconi** at the *Co-operative de Vanille de Mayotte* (tel 62 03 69). Not far away is Sohoa, a coastal village noted for its **pottery**. At Sada, there's a *Maison de l'Artisanat* selling **embroidery**, **jewellery**, **basketwork** and **spices** (tel 62 26 81). South from Sada, at Poroani on Boueni Bay, is a village arts and crafts association (*l'artisanat*) which is worth a visit if you are interested in traditional **musical instruments**. Here you'll find *dzendzé* (like a sitar), *gaboussi* (three-stringed guitar), *tambours* (drums), and *m'cayamba* (a seed-filled raffia rattle). If these are not on sale at the association ask where the man who makes them can be found. Another local craftsman supplies the association with *pilons*, or pestles, a traditional wooden board game called *m'ra* and model pirogues. Again, they'll direct you to the craftsman if they are out of stock. Other local craft articles on sale are plaited **palm-leaf bags**, hats and mats.

Further north, in the centre of the island between Combani and Bouyouni and near the *Retenue collinaire* water reserve, is an ylang-ylang estate owned by famous French *parfumeur* Guerlain. You can visit this 35-acre (14-ha) estate, but you should contact the office first (tel 62 40 57; fax 62 12 37). From the flowers of the 1,800 ylang-ylang trees on his estate, Guerlain produces 220 lb (100 kg) of pure floral essence a year for his own blenders in France and for Chanel. You can buy 20 ml bottles, nearly a fluid ounce, of this essential oil for FF50. The estate also sells packs of vanilla sugar. On Petite Terre at Dzaoudzi, 'Au Royaume des Fleurs' (see *People* p.169) sells floral and traditional beauty products (tel 60 26 47).

Some other places to shop for souvenirs:
Art Magique: Labattoir, Petite Terre (tel 60 05 75).
Artisanats de Mayotte: 54 Route Nationale, Pamandzi (tel 60 00 68).
Ouhayati: Place du Marché, Mamoudzou (tel 61 52 33).
Oujouzi wa Maoré: 17 Boulevard des Crabes, Dzaoudzi.
Pamandzi Nouroulhairia: 147 Route Nationale (tel 60 20 36).
Quartier Artisanal: rue de l'Eglise, Mamoudzou (tel 62 13 88).
Senteur d'Ylang: 115 rue du Commerce, Mamoudzou (tel 61 71 71).

CRIME

This is happily of a petty nature, but as tourist numbers grow so do levels of theft, prompted largely by ostentatious displays of apparent wealth, such as visitors draped with camera equipment hauling out wallets stuffed with large-denomination banknotes. Local authorities advise visitors to Mayotte to observe a few simple precautions. If you are driving a hire vehicle do not lock it when you park, but do not leave anything of value visible on the dashboard or on the seats. This is sound Gallic logic as it's better for would-be thieves to open a door rather than smash a window. There have been no reports of muggings or crimes of violence against visitors, but it is still wise to act as though you might be the exception and take normal precautions when moving around (see also p.80).

DRINK, DRUGS AND THE LAW

Drink

Islam forbids the use of alcohol to the faithful, so you are unlikely ever to see a Mahorais staggering around the worse for wear, nor will you find them propping up bars. Assume that the ones you do see downing a beer are Christian converts.

Drugs

Drugs are another matter. The Prophet Mohammed never placed a prohibition on relaxants such as cannabis – marijuana and hashish. These drugs are illegal, but the police concern themselves only with trafficking and are not interested in locals using them for recreational purposes. Talk to them and they will tell you a story they vouch is true. During a routine check in a village they found a cupboard stuffed with 'bananas,' big fat rolls of *bungi* (cannabis). The owner was hauled before the local magistrate on a charge of trafficking. The man pleaded not guilty, saying that the drug was for his personal use. He was sentenced to three years imprisonment after the prosecutor told the Bench that with the enormous amount involved, the accused could never expect to live long enough to smoke it all. He was 98.

THE LAW

Law and order are the responsibility of the normal police force in Petite Terre, Mamoudzou and the larger towns; in the villages and rural areas the national gendarmerie, squads of military police, keep tabs on everything. Both forces are usually helpful, at least to visitors. At a pinch you could turn for help to a member of the French Foreign Legion stationed on Dzaoudzi – they're the tough-looking ones in camouflage wearing too-small berets and oversize black boots. Offenders who are Muslim have, in some cases, a choice of the penal code by which they wish to be judged. The French Code Napoleon is the basis of the legal system enforced in Mayotte. However, in Muslim civil cases, such as those concerning land, property, marriage, divorce, and succession, those involved can ask for their case to be heard by a *cadi*, or Muslim judge. As well as being a religious leader in the community, the *cadi* is also a civil servant. Non-Muslim visitors who fall foul of the law in Mayotte have no such choice and will be tried as though they had committed the offence in France.

Help and Information

TOURIST INFORMATION CENTRES

The main tourist office is the *Comité Territorial du Tourisme de Mayotte* at rue de la Pompe, Mamoudzou, behind the SNIE supermarket on Place du Marché. It's a few minutes' walk from the ferry. Open Monday to Friday 8am to 4.30pm and Saturday 8am to 11.30am (tel 61 09 09; fax 61 10 18; e-mail comite-du-tourisme-mayotte@wanadoo.fr). There is also a small tourist information kiosk at the ferry terminal in Mamoudzou (tel 61 41 71), and one outside the airport at Pamandzi (tel 60 09 68).

MAYOTTE TOURIST OFFICES AND REPRESENTATIVES ABROAD

You should be able to get information from a French Tourist Office.

Australia: French Tourist Bureau, 25 Bligh Street, Sydney NSW 2000 (tel 2-9231 5244; fax 2-9221 8682; e-mail french@ozermail.com.au or ifrance@internetezy.com.au).

Britain: French Tourist Office (Maison de la France), 178 Piccadilly, London W1V 0AL (tel 020-7491 7622; fax 020-7493 6594; e-mail piccadilly@mdlf.demon.co.uk).

Canada: French Tourist Office, 1981 Avenue McGill College, Suite 490, Montréal Quebec H3A 2W9 (tel 514-288 4264; fax 514-845 4868; e-mail mfrance@passeport.com or mfrance@attcanada.net).

France: Maison de la France, 20 Avenue de L'Opéra, F-75041 Paris Cedex 01 (tel 1-42 96 70 00; fax 1-42 96 70 71); and Comite Regional du Tourisme Riviera Cote d'Azur, 55 Promenade des Anglais, Nice Cedex 1.

Germany: Französisches Fremdenverkehrsamt, 47 Westendstrasse, D-60001 Frankfurt am Main (tel 69-580121; fax 69-745556).

Italy: Maison de la France, Ente Nazionale Francese per il Turismo, Via Larga 7, I-20122 Milan (tel 02-5848 6566; fax 02-5848 6222; e-mail: entf@enter.ut).

Japan: French Government Tourist Office, Landic no 2 Akasaka Building, 10-9 Akasaka 2-Chome Minato-Ku, Tokyo 107 (tel 582-5164; fax 505-2873).

Netherlands: French Tourist Office, Prinsengracht 670, NL-1017 KX Amsterdam (tel 20-627 3318; fax 20-620 3339; e-mail: fra-vw@euronet.nl or informatie@fransverkeersbureau.nl).

South Africa: French Tourist Office, 196 Oxford Road, Illovo 2196, PO Box 41022, Craighall 2024 (tel 11-880 8062; fax 11-880 7772; e-mail: runint@frenchdoor.co.za).

Switzerland: Maison de la France, 2 rue Thalberg, CH-1201 Geneva (tel 732-8610; fax 731-5873; e-mail mdlfgva@bluewin.ch).

United States: French Government Tourist Office, 444 Madison Avenue (between 49 and 50th Street), 16th Floor, New York, NY 10022 (tel 212-838-77800; fax 212-838-7855); 9454 Wilshire Boulevard, Suite 715, Beverly Hills, CA 90212-2967 (tel 213-271-6665; fax 213-276-2835; e-mail fgto@gte.net); 676 North Michigan Avenue, Chicago, Illinois 60611-2819 (tel 312-751-7800; fax 312-337-6339; e-mail fgto@mcs.net).

USEFUL INFORMATION

Time Zone. Mayotte is three hours ahead of GMT, two hours ahead of Paris in winter and one hour in the European summer.

Electrical Appliances. Power supply is 220 volts AC, but double check the voltage of your hotel before plugging in electrical appliances. Plugs are mainly European round two-pin. Carry a multi-pin adaptor.

Weights and Measures. Like France, Mayotte adheres to the metric system of weights and measures.

Useful Telephone Numbers

Air France/Air Austral: tel 60 10 52 or 61 10 52.
Police: Dzaoudzi (tel 60 12 85); Mamoudzou (tel 61 12 22).
Gendarmerie: Dzaoudzi (tel 60 10 48); Mamoudzou (tel 61 12 16).
Emergencies: tel 61 00 37 or 61 04 14.
Central Hospital: tel 61 15 15; Doctors (tel 61 02 43 and 61 02 03).

Dr Lesoin: Mamoudzou (tel 61 04 ,22).
Dr Devieux: Sada (tel 62 47 00).
Physiotherapists: L Dumazer, Mamoudzou (tel 61 01 58); Mr and Mrs Coppée, Pamandzi (tel 60 30 68).
Acupuncture: Petite Terre (tel 60 31 73).
Dentist: Marc Moisset, Pamandzi (tel 60 20 58).
Fire Brigade: tel 18
Customs Service: Dzaoudzi (tel 60 10 14).
Port Captain: for emergencies at sea (tel 60 10 33).
Palais de Justice (tel 61 11 15).
Grand Cadi (tel 61 15 21).
Post Offices: Pamandzi (tel 60 10 03); Mamoudzou (tel 61 11 11 and 61 1102); Kawéni (tel 61 11 18).
General Council: Administration (tel 61 12 33).
Préfecture: tel 60 10 54 or 61 10 95.
Department of Agriculture and Forestry (DAF): tel 61 12 82; fax 61 35 13.
Crédit Agricole: tel 61 12 00.
National Institute for Statistics and Economic Studies (INSEE): Mamoudzou (tel 61 36 35).

PUBLIC HOLIDAYS

FESTIVALS

If you are there at the right time you'll see some cultural events, festivals, competitions and races on Mayotte that you'll see nowhere else in the Indian Ocean. Most are seasonal, few have fixed dates. Check with the tourist office in Mamoudzou or pop into the *Centre Mahorais d'Animation Culturelle* (CMAC) on the rue de l'Hôpital. This cultural centre is open Monday to Friday from 10am to noon and 3pm to 5pm.

On 14 July at *La Course de Pneus à Mamoudzou* you'll see a competition in which children race tyres by striking and guiding them with pieces of wood. *La Mahoraid* is like an Iron Man contest, with different feats to be completed. This is organised by the Ministry of Youth and Sports. Competitors must paddle a dug-out pirogue from Mamoudzou to Dzaoudzi – best time for the mile (2 km) is 25 minutes – followed by a foot race of 13 miles (21 km) from Mamoudzou to Dzoumougné which climbs to 4,921 ft (1,500 m). The best time for this is 2 hours 24 minutes. Next comes a 6-hour mountain-bike relay race and the event ends with a tyre race. For more information contact Jeunesse et des Sports in Mamoudzou (tel 61 10 87).

In October/November, around the onset of the rainy season, comes *La Fête du Cocotier* (Coconut Festival) (tel 62 06 69), a rural shindig in the south of the island at Mronabéja, which includes a tree-climbing competition, palm frond plaiting, opening and grating coconuts, and a final cooking contest. *Le Wadaja* is a dance performed by rural women in the dry season to give thanks for the harvest. Their dance around a mortar sees some intricate choreography with the wooden pestles they use to pound rice and other cereals. Strictly for young men of opposing villages are *Le Tam-Tam Boeuf* which is an island version of a Spanish corrida, but an event that ends without the killing of the bull, and the *murengué,* an evening of island-style boxing bouts.

Mayotte celebrates both Muslim and European public holidays on which businesses and shops are closed (see also *Religious Festivals* in *Comoros: Practical Information* p.263).

PUBLIC HOLIDAYS

New Year's Day	1 January
Easter Holidays	March/April
Ascension Day	1 June
Bastille Day (1789)	14 July
Assumption Day	15 August
Christmas Day	25 December

EXPLORING MAYOTTE

TOURIST ATTRACTIONS

Petite Terre

The crater lake of **Dziana Dzaha**, the beach at **Moya, Dzaoudzi**, with its French colonial ambience, Foreign Legionnaires, and old **Préfecture**.

Grande Terre

The **Musée de la Mer** with its coelacanth and shell collection, and the colourful Mahorais **market** near the ferry terminal in Mamoudzou. The **northern peninsula**, for its views of offshore islands, the paradise islands of **Choizil** and **Mtsamboro**, the **Guerlain ylang-ylang estate**, near Combani, the Mahorais bush city of **Sada**, the west coast beaches at **Moutsumbatsu** and **Solou, Bouéni Bay** and **Mt Choungui**. The beach and lagoon at **N'goudja** for giant green turtles and indigenous forest lemurs, the intricate embroidery of **Kani-Kéli**. The turtle and marine sanctuary at **Saziley** and its **Ilot de Sable Blanc**, and the **giant baobab** at Bandrélé.

Exploration of Mayotte is best done by breaking it up into readily digestible chunks – which is not difficult in a territory only 24 miles (40 km) from top to bottom and 12 miles (20 km) at its widest point and the best place to start is with the smallest.

PETITE TERRE

This little island comprises two communes, **Labattoir**, the main commercial centre, and **Pamandzi**, where the international airport is located. The road from the airport passes in front of the **Cimetière de Sandavangeu**, a shady cemetery enclosing the tombs of former governors, French soldiers killed in the Madagascar expeditionary war, and that of Henry de Balzac, younger brother of French novelist Honoré, who died here in the early days of colonisation. The administrative centre Dzaoudzi used to be a separate 10-acre (4 ha) rocky islet linked to Petite Terre only by a sandy stretch, uncovered at low water and a favourite spot for crabs. The French turned this into a permanent paved causeway in 1850 and called it the Boulevard des Crabes. They also made Dzaoudzi the capital, before moving it to Grande Comore in 1962 and upsetting all the local traders. Petite Terre's main hotels and restaurants are situated along this pleasant boulevard, some fronted by small beaches. The **Faré beach** is a favourite with topless *wazungu* (white) sun worshippers; the terrace of the hotel-restaurant **Le Rocher** is a particularly pleasant gathering place with a panoramic view. As the Foreign Legion of Mayotte (DLEM) base is at the end of the Boulevard you'll find lots of bored members of this elite force drinking in the bars and talking about the good old days when there were lots of (or more) wars and revolutions. Dzaoudzi is known to locals simply as *le rocher* ('the rock') and is the historical heart of Mayotte, as it was from here that the colonial administration ruled France's domain and spread its influence throughout the region. There is still a colonial air about the rock, with its scattering of grand residences, government buildings and its *Préfecture*, the old garden residence of Mayotte's past governors. This was built in 1881 to plans drawn up by Gustave Eiffel, the man who designed France's most famous landmark, which probably accounts for all the metal girders and beams used in its construction. Behind the building is a brace of ancient cannons ranged for enemies who never came.

There's not a great deal to see on Petite Terre once you have wandered around the streets of down-at-heel Labattoir and Pamandzi, but before you move on to much more attractively endowed Grande Terre you should take a *taxi-brousse* to a couple of worthwhile spots. Make sure the driver knows where you want to go as some of them will refuse to chance their often decrepit vehicles on badly eroded stretches of road outside the communes and, at best, will leave you to pant up the last bad stretch on your own. A 10-minute drive from Labattoir is the lake of **Dziani Dzaha**, lying in an old volcanic crater and looking quite like sinister green pea soup. Even so, it is sacred to the Mahorais and the subject of local legends. The water is supposed to be useful in the treatment of skin problems, although from the crater rim at 338 ft (572 m) it's a long way down the steep slope to collect a sample.

Moya Beach is also on the east coast and not far away as the crow flies, but you have to double back on your tracks almost to Labattoir to get there. The beach is virtually unprotected by the reef that makes bathing safe at most other Mayotte beaches and the sea can get quite rough here. Nonetheless, it is a popular weekend picnic and sunbathing spot for lots of French expats and their families. At one end of the main beach, over a small rocky promontory, is a sheltered sliver of beach the locals recommend for *une bronzette intime*, or a quiet spot to get an all-over tan. To the south and dominating the landscape is *La Vigie* a 666 ft (203 m) hill. It's an easy walk or drive to the top for excellent views.

To the west of the crater lake there's another beach area called **Badamiers**, but it's not marked on the IGN map, which is just as well as it's a let-down after the Moya beaches and suffers from its proximity to rubbish dumps and various unsightly installations. On the way to Badamiers is an archaeological site called **Bagamoya** (Swahili for 'I left my heart'), which has yielded pottery and other artefacts indicating a 10th century Shirazi Arab settlement.

GRANDE TERRE

MAMOUDZOU

If there's anything you need, anything you have forgotten to bring, before starting out to explore this small but diverse island Mamoudzou is the place to get it. Apart from this the bustling little capital itself has little to offer in the way of interesting sights outside its commercial activity. There are no echoes of the winding Arab medinas and narrow streets that characterise the main towns of Mayotte's neighbouring islands in Comoros. Mamoudzou is an intriguing blend of French high-rise and pavement Africa, giving way to wide, dusty streets and wattle and daub palm-thatched huts once out of town. Jutting out into the straits separating Mamoudzou and Dzaoudzi is

Pointe de Mahabou, where public gardens provide local joggers with paths around the **tomb of Andriantsouli**, the sultan who ceded Mayotte to France for a mess of pottage (see *History* p.165). This is a pleasant place to enjoy the view of the lagoon and its tiny islands and cogitate on the fact that there is no cemetery for whites on Grande Terre because, according to an enigmatic French expat, 'white people don't die here'. The gardens close at 6pm. The rocks slightly to the north of the inter-island ferry route are known as *les Quatre Frères*, after the four brothers legend says were turned to stone for preferring fishing to praying in the mosque.

Nearby, off the rue Mahabou, is the remarkable little *Musée de la Mer*, which is run by the Fisheries and Marine Environment Service (tel 61-1282, fax 61-3513, e-mail: daf.spem.mayotte@wanadoo.fr) and whose fascinating exhibits deserve more space and better presentation. The museum is open Monday to Thursday from 7am to 3pm, and Friday from 7am to noon. It has a splendid collection of rare shells and corals, a variety of fish from around Mayotte, including the mounted heads of huge black marlin, parrotfish, dorade, and mérou. The pride of the exhibits

MAMOUDZOU-GRANDE TERRE

1 Tourist Office
2 Market & Taxis
3 Le Caribou
4 Air Austral
5 Post Office
6 Mayotte Cultural Centre (CMAC)
7 Police
8 Hospital
9 Musée de la Mer (Sea Museum)
10 Tomb of Andriantsouli

is a 161 lb (73 kg) **coelacanth** (*Latimeria chalumnae*), the prehistoric fossil fish that came back from the dead to astound the scientific world in December 1938 when it was first found off East London in South Africa. The Grande Terre specimen was caught in 1991 in 23 ft (7 m) of water off the south of the island by a fisherman identified only as Mr Renard. As far as we know, this find has never been accorded any international recognition in reports of discoveries of the coelacanth popularly known as 'Old Fourlegs' – a fish thought to have become extinct some 70-million years ago. Until Mr Renard's catch, Mayotte's only link with this fossil fish was that an 82 lb (37 kg) specimen (*Malania anjouanae*), caught off the nearby island of Anjouan in December 1952, was flown from Dzaoudzi to South Africa, a flight that nearly caused an international diplomatic incident. For more about this read *Old Fourlegs: The Story of the Coelacanth* by JLB Smith (1956, Longman, Green) and *A Fish Caught in Time* by Samantha Weinberg (1999, Fourth Estate, London), a riveting account of a very fishy tale.

THE NORTH

You can quite easily cover the northern third of Grande Terre in a day, with lengthy stops, by car from Mamoudzou by way of crowded Koungou, the island's deep-water port of Longoni, Bouyouni, Dzoumonyé on the east coast, up to Handréma and Mtsahara in the north, opposite the islands of Choizil and Mtsamboro, and down through the western coastal villages of Acoua and Tsingoni. From there you can take the cross-island route back to Mamoudzou by way of central Combani.

An alternative route from Combani is to detour north to the **Guerlain ylang-ylang estate** for an interesting walk among the gnarled trees whose flowers and the oil they yield are the delight of all the top perfumiers of Europe (see *Gifts and Souvenirs*). At least 441 lb (200 kg) of ylang-ylang flowers have to be distilled to produce $1^3/4$ pints (1 litre) of the flowers' essential oil, and this Guerlain enterprise produces about 220 lb (100 kg) of essence a year. Ylang-ylang trees on this estate are 60-70 years old and still producing commercially useful flowers. The best floral oil, like the best olive oil, comes from the first pressing, or six-hour distillation.

To carry on north past the estate to rejoin the coast at Bouyouni you definitely need a 4x4 vehicle to tackle the marshy *piste*, or rough trail, through thick jungle. If you are not equipped for this you should continue from Combani on the road to Vahibé, although the hardy can probably do the **piste hike** in about three hours. En route, at Vahibé, you can also stretch your legs up a path to the summit of **Mt Mtsapéré** at 1,877 ft (572 m) the highest point in the north. Vahibé is a centre for the cultivation and distillation of ylang-ylang and at the entrance to the village is an *alambic*, one of the moonshine-type stills used to extract the essential oil. On the upper north-east coast a couple of pleasant **hiking trails** start at Dzoumonyé, one which will take you to the west coast village of Mtsamboro by way of the dominant northern peak **Dziani Bolé** (1,549 ft/472 m), and another which brings you to Acoua, through the magnificent **forest reserve** of Machiroungou where you'll see lots of *makis* and birds. If you are motoring, north of Handréma between the road and the sea is an area known in Mahorais as *Maji Anyouni*, the 'Water of Birds' which, depending on the season, is worth a visit. Where the road doubles back on itself to head down the west coast you'll find a footpath which takes you out on to the final narrow peninsula of Grande Terre. From the **beacon** here you'll get a splendid view of the offshore islands and, looming on the horizon, Comoros neighbour Anjouan.

CENTRAL

From the Combani-Vahibé road to Passamaïnty south of Mamoudzou you have a choice of a short outing down to Dembeni and then across the island again through the rural villages of Tsararano, Coconi, Barakani, Chiconi, to Sada on the west coast. Vanilla-scented **Chiconi**, with its **ancient mosque**, is an old Shirazi village and the finer features of the people hint at an ancestry more Arab than African. Sada is a bush city of about 9,000 people and is regarded as being truly representative of the Mahorais people and their culture. It is also renowned for the delicate filigreed silver and gold jewellery made here, its wooden sculptures and its wild straw hats. The inhabitants are noted for being proud and clever, and Sada does indeed have more craftsmen and provides more of the island's civil servants than the rest of Mayotte. Interesting to visit, and photograph, but not for long; there is no sanitation in the modern sense of the word. If you want to take photographs of any Mahorais make sure you first have their permission, as many of the more rural still have the old lingering Muslim doubts about their image being captured.

WEST COAST

On the upper north-west coast you have a choice of trips to the offshore islands of Choizil and Mtsamboro, which has its own micro-climate and boasts the only orange groves in Mayotte. The town of the same name on the coast was the ancient capital of Mayotte. A stop at Mtsamboro will enable you to enjoy the popular **local pastries** and allow you to visit **two ancient mosques** and the **ruined tombs** of the *M'Chambara*, the old kings of Mayotte when this village was their capital.

About 12 miles (20 km) down the coast, past Acoua, is an isolated little beach called **Moutsumbatsu**. To reach it from the main road entails a 30-40 minute walk, but it's worth the effort. The beach at **Soulou**, by contrast, attracts hordes of people at the weekend, but its main attraction is the lovely **waterfall** which plunges 26 ft (8 m) directly on to the beach when the tide is out. This is great for showering off the salt after a swim in the lagoon.

The road follows a picturesque coastal route until Tsingoni, which has the remains of the **oldest mosque and graveyard** on Grande Terre. From Tsingoni the road veers inland to Combani, before reaching the coast again at Chiconi and Sada. A short detour north from Chiconi is the village of Sohoa, which has a pleasant little beach populated by goats and chickens and a pottery co-operative, Cap Hairi, marketing naïve local handiwork. The road hugs the coast again from Sada around the huge bay of Bouéni, with Chirongui at its head. Out in the bay you'll see the islet of Caroni, noted for the savour of the little oysters that cling to the roots of its mangroves. From Chirongui one road turns inland to cross the island's narrowest point to join the east coast road. Continue around at Bouéni Bay and you enter the extreme southern region. Dominating the landscape is the bald basaltic cone of **Mt Choungui**, an ancient volcano. A secondary road branches off to Choungui from the coast road, from where a short but **stiff one-hour hike** will take you to the summit at 1,949 ft (594 m).

THE SOUTH

On the southern toe of Grande Terre is the **baobab-shaded beach** regarded by many as the finest in Mayotte. This is on the lagoon at N'goudja, where the Jardin Maoré hotel resort has virtually staked a claim to its length. Sealife abounds here and even with only *palmes, un masque et un tuba* (fins, mask and snorkel) you can marvel at the underwater scene and swim among **giant turtles** (see *Flora and Fauna* and *Sport and Recreation*). Nearby **Kani-Kéli** is worth a halt to look at the delicate *récélé* embroidery and the Muslim *koffiah* skull caps for which the village women are renowned. You can also start a **3-hour hike** here on an alternative route to the top of Mt Choungui. From here it is an easy hour's drive back to Mamoudzou, unless you branch off to the **green turtle sanctuary** of Saziley to enjoy the Marine Park and its underwater trail, or the beaches and walks onshore. Enter the reserve near Mtsamoudou. From the end of the road it's a 30-minute walk. Within the marine reserve is the *Ilot de Sable Blanc* (White Sand Isle), better known to the Mahorais as *Mtsanga Tsoholé* because its sand is like white rice. This little coralline islet, along with those of Choizil in the north-west, is a must-visit outing. You'll find fishermen on the beach at Mtsamoudou who, for a small fee, will be happy to paddle you out to the islet in a dug-out pirogue.

THE EAST

An easy 20-minute drive from Mtsamoudou is the village of Bandrélé. Stop on the outskirts at **Musicale Plage** ('Musical Beach'), which takes its name from the celebrations held here by the local fisherfolk after a particularly good catch. There's **good snorkelling** not far offshore. Stop also to admire one of the island's oldest and largest baobabs by the side of the road near Bandrélé. Offshore to the north is *Ilot Bandrélé*, which is a popular weekend picnic venue for *wazungu* from Mamoudzou. Two **hiking paths** start at Bandrélé which will take you through a humid forest reserve to the summit of Mayotte's highest mountain, **Mt Bénara**, at 2,165 ft (660 m). If you don't want to retrace your steps you have a choice of several trails down, along one to Tsararano and Dembeni to the east, and a shorter path to Miréréni in the west. Allow 6-8 hours for the walk whichever way you go.

Along the coastal road is Hajangoua, a village noted for the giant freshwater prawns which you can watch local youngsters fish out of the nearby river by means of a curious little lasso tied to a bamboo stem. All the way along the RN2 coastal road back to Mamoudzou is a succession of pleasant little **beaches** all perfect if you want to Robinson Crusoe the days away. From either Tsoundzou, Passamaïnty or Mtsapéré it's a short boat trip out to **Ilot Bouzi**, off Mamoudzou, where the waters offer good catches of calamari (squid). There is a lively **lemur population** and the remains of an old leper colony hospital on the island.

Comoros

Mosquée du Vendredi,
Old Dhow Port, Moroni

GEOGRAPHY

Wedged in the northern part of the warm Mozambique Channel between the north-west tip of Madagascar and the east coast of Africa lie the four islands of the Comoros archipelago, but the crescent flag of the Federal Republic of the Comoros flies over only three of them. The fourth island, Mayotte, remains a French possession, although the Republic's territorial claim to its neighbour remains an uneasy question mark over the area. The islands are the visible summits of an undersea volcanic ridge, whose explosive activity over millions of years first created **Mayotte** (*Maoré*), then in succession the islands of **Anjouan** (*Ndzuani*), **Mohéli** (*Mwali*), and **Grande Comore** (*Ngazidja*), geologically the youngest of the four.

Grande Comore is the largest and most westerly island, lying 188 miles (303 km) from the coast of Mozambique, with the seat of government in Moroni, the Comoros capital. Grande Comore has an active volcano, Mt Karthala, rising to a height of 7,746 ft (2,361 m) above sea level. The smallest of the islands, Mohéli, is 28 miles (45 km) to the south-east of Grande Comore, and has a central mountainous spine topping 2,556 ft (790 m). Anjouan is about 25 miles (40 km) east of Mohéli, and is the nearest to Mayotte, 44 miles (71 km) distant. The central peak on mountainous Anjouan is Mt Ntingui at 5,072 ft (1,575 m). The three islands have a total surface area of 718 sq miles (1,860 sq km) – roughly three times the size of the Isle of Man or two-thirds the size of Rhode Island – made up of Grande Comore 442 sq miles (1,145 sq km), Anjouan 195 sq miles (505 sq km), and the smallest, Mohéli, 81 sq miles (210 sq km). The capital towns of Anjouan and Mohéli are Mutsamudu and Fomboni respectively.

Topography

Geologically speaking, the relatively recent emergence of the three islands from the ocean deep means that they have not yet had the time necessary to develop the extensive outlying coral reefs like the fabulous one surrounding Mayotte. Reefs are sketchy by comparison and diving sites, for instance, are somewhat limited. Best places for reef are off Mohéli and its offshore islets of Nioumachoua and at odd

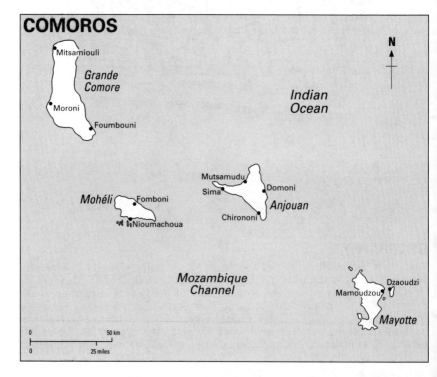

spots along the coast of Anjouan from Chironi in the south to Bimbini in the north-west. Out in the Mozambique Channel, about 12 nautical miles (22 km) south-west of Grande Comore, is Banc Vailheu, which is a superb undersea mount and coral reef teeming with all forms or marine life, and a first-class dive site by any standard. Anjouan is regarded as the most scenic of the three islands, with high forests watered by numerous rivers, lakes and waterfalls; fertile Mohéli, also well wooded and watered, is the least developed and therefore the least spoilt; Grande Comore has forest-clad Mr Karthala, but no rivers or streams of any consequence in its 37 mile (60 km) length, as rainfall simply drains away through its porous mantle of volcanic soil. Beaches along the 211 miles (340 km) of coastline, whether they are pebble stretches, white or black lava sand, are a delight that draw the sun worshippers. There are lovely isolated nooks on all the islands, although on Grande Comore the two up-market hotels have naturally bagged the best beaches and made them their private domains. Overall lies an invisible but fragrant blanket compounded of the scent of ylang-ylang flowers, cloves, cinnamon and vanilla from the plantations that flourish everywhere and are the life-blood of Comoros.

CLIMATE

Like everywhere else south of the equator, the seasons in Comoros are the opposite of those in the northern hemisphere. Summer, the hot, wet season, lasts from November to April, when humidity can be unpleasantly high and daytime temperatures can reach 86-90°F (30-32°C). The highest temperatures and humidity occur in March and April and November and December; the lowest temperatures are experienced from July to September. January has the heaviest rainfall and tropical storms are common. September-October is usually the lowest rainfall period, although it can rain at any time. Rainfall and temperature can vary from island to island during any month and even vary on an island due to differences in topography, but generally the central, higher areas of an island are often cooler and more moist than the coastal regions. Winter, the cool dry season, is vaguely from May to late October, and this is the **best time to visit** the Comoros. During the summer months the warm *kashkazi* winds blow from the north-west. During the dry season the cool *kusi* trade winds blow from the south-east. The Comoros islands lie within the Indian Ocean cyclone belt and periodically, usually every few years, they take a battering from violent winds sweeping across the region. Sea conditions for diving are generally best between March and November.

Average Temperatures

January	81°F	(27°C)
February	81°F	(27°C)
March	79°F	(26°C)
April	79°F	(26°C)
May	77°F	(25°C)
June	75°F	(24°C)
July	74°F	(23°C)
August	74°F	(23°C)
September	74°F	(23°C)
October	75°F	(24°C)
November	79°F	(26°C)
December	79°F	(26°C)

Average Rainfall

January	14 inches	(351 mm)
February	12 inches	(306 mm)
March	11 inches	(285 mm)
April	12 inches	(308 mm)
May	10 inches	(265 mm)
June	10 inches	(248 mm)
July	9 inches	(235 mm)
August	6 inches	(166 mm)
September	3 inches	(75 mm)
October	5 inches	(132 mm)
November	4 inches	(101 mm)
December	12 inches	(301 mm)

Irrespective of heat, humidity or rainfall the busiest times in Comoros are December to January, the southern hemisphere holiday season, and July to September, during the winter season.

HISTORY

Being situated at what turned out for centuries to be a maritime crossroads in the south-west Indian Ocean certainly didn't make for a peaceful history for the islands the ancient Arab seafarers first called *Djazaïr el Kamar* or Islands of the Moon. Whether they really meant *Kumr*, or 'The Burning One,' because of the active volcano on the main island, is still open to debate, but either way the Arabic was eventually corrupted to Comoros. Early Arab traders initially found the islands of the archipelago uninhabited, although a good case is made out for touchdown much earlier by Malayo-Polynesian wanderers who left more concrete evidence of their arrival in nearby Madagascar after epic sea voyages of more than 6,000 miles (9,656 km). King Solomon's merchant fleets are also credited with exploratory visits and in local legend even the king himself is regarded as an early visitor with his consort, the Queen of Sheba. The Comorians themselves, however, make light of the conflicting cross-currents of history swirling around their islands and believe that the first inhabitants were *jinnees*, or spiteful spirits. The Arabs established a number of small settlements on the islands, starting with Anjouan, and used them as convenient refreshment halts and outposts for the conversion of infidels to the teachings of Islam, the new monotheistic religion sweeping down coastal eastern Africa during the 7th century from the Middle East. The Shirazis from Persia became the dominant influence in Comoros between the 15th and 16th centuries, entrenching Islam and linking the islands with their strongholds on the coast of present day Tanzania, especially the ancient entrepot of Kilwa, and with Zanzibar, a link still holding firm to this day.

Once the redoubtable Portuguese broached the sea route to India and the east round the Cape of Good Hope in the late 15th century the historical path of Comoros took a different course as the cross met the crescent and northern Arab interests came under pressure from adventurers of Europe's maritime nations pushing up from the south. By 1527, when the Comoros islands first appeared on a European map, they were already acknowledged to be prosperous regional trading centres under the dozen or so Sunni Muslim sultanates established by the Shirazis to control the exports of spices, rice, ambergris and slaves to the markets of East Africa and the Middle East. Records of the time mention trade links with countries as far away as Japan. By the early 17th century the trade in black slaves dominated all other forms of island commerce and the struggle for control of this lucrative market was the start of the internecine squabbles and wars that characterised the long reign of the motley sultans and eventually brought about their ruin.

The late 17th and early 18th centuries saw Comoros, especially well-watered Mohéli and Anjouan, become a favourite stamping ground for some of the most infamous English and French pirates of the day, among them Captain William Kidd, Captain 'Long Ben' Avery, Davey Jones, Thomas Tew, Captain Edward England and Olivier le Vasseur, the French corsair known as 'The Buzzard'. When they weren't fleeing for their lives the islanders apparently reacted to the invasions of the period with the fatalism of their religion; some learnt to sing lewd pirate shanties and others even adopted the names of British aristocratic families used as nicknames by the pirates. The black pirates of Madagascar who followed them towards the end of the 18th century were not so jolly. These, the Sakalava, depopulated large areas of the islands with their ruthless slaving raids until troubles at home forced them to flee Madagascar and settle down on Mayotte and Mohéli. French colonial rule eventually put an end to all slave trading activities and paved the way for the Comoros islands to become pawns in power games going on in the chancelleries of Europe during the scramble for overseas possessions.

The French were already well established in southern Madagascar and on the island of Nosy Bé when the opportunity arose in 1841 for them to plant the tricolore on Mayotte (see p.165). This proved to be the thin end of the edge. By 1886 France had placed all three other islands under its protection, neatly side-stepping a half-hearted British attempt to establish an official presence in Comoros in 1846 and later countering the covetousness of the Germans eyeing the islands from East Africa. By 1912, the last sultanate had been dismembered and France officially proclaimed the Comoros colonies. The archipelago then became a province of the French colony of Madagascar and was administered from there until 1947 when, a French overseas territory, its administrative ties with its giant island neighbour were severed and it set about learning to run its own affairs, under French tutelage. In a referendum held in 1958 Comorians voted overwhelmingly to stay French and by 1961 a constitution was in place destined to lead to internal self-government. All seemed set for a peaceful, rosy future. There was then no hint that where the early development and history of Comoros had been a riotous Sinbad the Sailor affair, with distinct Byzantine and later Machiavellian overtones, three of the islands were soon to become a political and economic bad joke in the region.

POLITICS

Not for nothing has Comoros been wittily dubbed Cloud Coup-Coup Land – an apt reference to the fact that since unilaterally declaring independence and breaking with France in July 1975 the islands have been convulsed by nearly 20 coups and attempted coups, the first of which deposed the first Comoros president only a month after he took office. Leading up to this were 14 years of increasing Comorian frustration and turmoil, stirred from afar in Tanzania where Comorians announced their struggle for independence with the launch of the *Mouvement de la Libération Nationale des Comoros (Molinaco)*. The *Parti Socialiste des Comoros (Pasoco)* joined the fray in 1968, attracting students and other young people who in that year mounted a mass demonstration in Comoros which was put down by the French with undue severity, using the French Foreign Legion. Discontent continued to simmer and burst out again in a pro-independence riot in Moroni in late 1973 during which the Chamber of Deputies was set on fire. A year later France bowed to the inevitable and held a referendum on the independence issue at which 95% of the voters on Grande Comore, Anjouan and Mohéli supported independence. The majority of the voters on Mayotte opted to stay French. Before the French could even get around to considering their withdrawal and the orderly transfer of power in Comoros, Ahmed Abdallah, leader of one of the major political parties, proclaimed the independence of Comoros on 6 July 1975 in a move he described as 'a regrettable necessity'. Four weeks later, on 3 August 1975, he was ousted from power in a mercenary-assisted coup in which he was replaced as leader of the new island nation by an unstable firebrand called Ali Solih, whose main mission in life seemed to be to emulate the excesses of the Red Guards during Communist China's Cultural Revolution by destroying the traditional and social fabric of Comoros to build a new revolutionary society. Solih and his special militia of uncontrollable 14-year-olds managed to destroy plenty during his reign, including 135 years of government archives and the island's economy. To exacerbate the growing problems France, while formally recognising the independence of Comoros, minus Mayotte, had pulled out all its technicians and advisers and suspended all its aid programmes, which accounted for more than 40% of the Comoros national budget. Riots in Madagascar against the Comorian community in Mahajanga led to nearly 17,000 Comorians fleeing back to their homeland in 1976 and the following year, in April 1977, the volcano on Grande Comore, Mt Karthala, erupted to pour lava down to the coast, leaving several thousand people homeless.

The stage was set for the re-entry of latter-day pirates, the mercenaries of French-born soldier of fortune Colonel Bob Dénard. This veteran of wars, revolution and secessionist movement from Indo-China to the Congo landed with 50 of his dogs-of-war – known as *Les Affreux*, or 'The Dreadful Ones' – on Itsandra Beach, north of Moroni, on 12 May 1978 and overthrew Ali Solih and his minions to the cheers of the populace. On 29 May Solih was killed 'while attempting to escape'. Deposed former president Ahmed Abdallah returned from exile in Paris and was soon holding the reins of sole executive power again. Abdallah rewrote the Constitution to proclaim the Federal Islamic Republic of the Comoros, restore Islam as the state religion and entrench himself for a six-year term as president. Abdallah also announced a 12-year ban on political parties, guaranteeing his re-election in 1984. In 1982, Comoros became a one-party state, with Abdallah's *Union Comorienne pour le Progrès (UCPD)* naturally the only party active. A couple of failed coups punctuated Abdallah's consolidation of power, the most publicised occurring in 1983 when a former Comorian ambassador to France, Saïd Ali Kemal, was arrested in Australia while trying to recruit mercenaries to overthrow his former ally. Abdallah called on his old friend, Bob Dénard, again to return to Comoros and stiffen the presidential guard with French and Belgian mercenaries. Dénard was happy to oblige and also became deeply embroiled in Abdallah's business ventures. It was no secret that Abdallah placed his personal enrichment well ahead of national interest when deciding economic policy. Several more coup attempts were ruthlessly squashed during a period when Comoros became a client state of the various foreign governments and international organisations whose loans and aid programmes vainly tried to plug the holes in the economy. By 1988, Abdallah's last full year in power, 80% of annual public expenditure in Comoros was funded by external aid and imports of staple rice took 50% of all its export earnings. Abdallah was busy setting up the constitutional framework to ensure his life presidency when, on the night of 26 November 1989, he was assassinated in his residence, *Beit el Salama* ('House of Peace'). A few days later Dénard and his mercenaries staged a coup and replaced the provisional president with Saïd Mohamed Djohar, giving Comoros its third president in as many days. This was too much to swallow even for France and South Africa, the two main supporters of Comoros, and on 15 December Dénard was forced to surrender to French forces and flown out to house arrest in Pretoria. He returned to France in February 1993 to face charges implicating him in the shooting of Abdallah but was exonerated by a judicial enquiry. Comorian pressure subsequently saw Dénard and his mercenary aide brought to trial in Paris in May 1999 for the president's murder, but a jury found them not guilty.

Following Dénard's departure from the political scene elections in March 1990 confirmed Saïd Mohamed Djohar as president for a six-year term, briefly interrupted in August that year by one Ibrahim Ahmed Halidi who used a by now time-honoured coup to declare himself president for two days. Djohar survived another coup in September 1992 and hung on to power until September 1995, when the irrepressible Dénard paddled ashore on Grande Comore with a band of 30 mercenaries and replaced Djohar and his government by joint presidents Saïd Ali Kemal and Mohamed Taki Abdulkarim. Once again the French winkled out Dénard and his men and flew them back to France. An abortive coup later, Abdulkarim was re-elected president in December 1996 to be succeeded in office after his death from apparent heart attack in November 1998 by Mohamed Tadjidine Ben Saïd Massounde, who was ousted in a bloodless coup by Comoros Army Chief-of-Staff Colonel Assoumani Azali on 30 April 1999. Fed-up diplomatic representatives of foreign embassies on Grande Comore boycotted the ceremony at which Azali installed himself president. Azali claims he seized power to restore law and order, deteriorating since separatists on the islands of Anjouan and Mohéli seceded from the federation in 1997, leaving Grande Comore the only member. The Organisation of African Unity (OAU) has been trying to broker an agreement to salvage the Comoros federation but it's an uphill battle. OAU members seem to have become reconciled to the political carnival atmosphere of this tiny member nation. The military coup of 1999 was, for example, regarded by South Africa as nothing out of the ordinary and 'just the normal way of Comorian elements doing their thing' according to the Department of Foreign Affairs. Nobody had been arrested, tourists were safe and there were no plans for evacuation. Even the deposed president was relaxing at home. The one remarkable thing throughout this amazing succession of coups and rebellions is that tourists continued to enjoy their sun-blessed vacations, generally unaware that anything untoward was happening.

One tip from a dedicated island watcher: If the radio unaccountably switches from normal Comoros reggae rhythms to classical music get ready for an announcement that the government has been overthrown.

THE ECONOMY

Comoros is one of the world's poorest and least developed nations. This small multi-island state has no mineral wealth and no natural resources other than those derived from the surrounding ocean. In the decades since independence in 1975 government corruption and mismanagement, coupled with political chaos and collapsing prices for the few agricultural commodities the islands do produce, has left the economy terminally fragile. The islands are surviving on international aid hand-outs and loans. External debt is running at well over $200-million, not a huge amount in global terms, but heavy enough where annual gross domestic product (GDP) is $400-million and annual imports – 90% rice – cost five to six times the amount brought in by exports. Between them France and the US take more than 80% of Comoros exports, with Germany and the rest of Africa well down the trading league. France is the major source of imports, followed by South Africa, Kenya, Madagascar, Singapore, and Japan. France also provides the direct budgetary support critical to the government's day to day operations. More than half of the national annual budget is spent on food imports and less than 10% of the active population is formally employed. The wage-earning labour force is small and numbers fewer than 7,000, including 5,000 government employees. Civil servants go on strike from time to time, usually because they haven't been paid for months on end. Farming on small land holdings, subsistence fishing, and petty commerce make up the daily activity of the rest of the population.

Imports. Rice and other foodstuffs, cement, petroleum products, consumer goods, and transport equipment.

Exports

Vanilla, ylang-ylang, cloves, copra, and coffee. Although the quality of the land differs from island to island, most of the widespread lava-encrusted soil formations are unsuited to agriculture. As a result, most of the inhabitants make their living from subsistence agriculture and fishing. Agriculture, involving more than 80% of the population and providing 40% of GDP generates virtually all foreign exchange earnings. Services including tourism, construction, and commercial activity make up the rest of the GDP. Comoros is the world's leading producer of essence of ylang-ylang, used in the manufacture of perfume. It also is the world's second largest producer of vanilla. Other potential cash crops are pepper, cardamom and fruit. Demand for vanilla, ylang-ylang, and copra has shrunk considerably as many former importers now manufacture or import synthetic substitutes. Plantations engage a large proportion of the population in producing the island's major cash crops for export. As extensive land holdings remain in the hands of foreign companies and the traditional ruling elite, land for subsistence agriculture to produce the staples making up three-quarters of the islander's diet – coconuts, cassava, bananas and rice – is inadequate to meet the needs of the ordinary islander. The fishing grounds are rich in marine life, but this sector remains relatively underdeveloped. There is a small-scale manufacturing industry, but this is hampered by the cost of transport and shortage of raw materials. The main activities include sawmills, facilities for processing vanilla, cloves and copra, a printing plant, a soft drinks bottling plant, and plants for plastics, food products, and clothing. The government is struggling to upgrade education and technical training, to privatise commercial and industrial enterprises, to improve health services, to diversify exports, to promote tourism, and to reduce the high population growth rate. There is speculation that the move by bilateral creditors to ease the debt burden of Africa's poorest nations may benefit Comoros. The country lacks the infrastructure vital to its further development. Some villages are not linked to the main road system or at best are connected by tracks usable only by 4x4 vehicles. The island's ports are rudimentary, although aid has resulted in the construction of a deep-water facility at Anjouan. Despite improvements only small vessels can use the quays of Moroni on Grande Comore. Ocean-going vessels must lie offshore and be offloaded by smaller boats. During the cyclone season this can be a dangerous business and makes ships reluctant to call. Most freight for Comoros is first sent to Mombasa or Réunion and trans-shipped from there.

Tourism

Although the various governments have had high hopes for increased tourism, the unstable political situation (see *Politics*) has put the brakes on the type of development necessary to cope with any major tourist influx. The main potential for tourism is based on the scenic attractions of the islands, the rich Islamic cultural heritage, and the variety of marine life. Tourism has not grown much since 1995. Plans to boost the sector's performance were frustrated by a failed coup in late 1995 and the violence associated with the secessionist movements in mid-1997. This put a crimp in efforts of travel companies in Europe and other countries to promote Comoros as a holiday destination. Interestingly, South African vacationers tended to ignore the shenanigans in the islands and continued to spend their rands there. They still do, although with international interest picking up again they are rubbing shoulders with increasing numbers of continental visitors.

'Old Fourlegs'

One odd little factor which has had economic consequences for Comoros is a fish which was thought to have been around 400-million years ago and became extinct on earth about 70-million years ago. This is the intriguing fossil fish, the coelacanth (*Latimeria chalumnae Smith*), dubbed 'Old Fourlegs' by South African ichthyologist Professor JLB Smith when he revealed to a startled scientific world a specimen trawled up off the South African coast near East London in December 1938. For the next 14 years Professor Smith doggedly sought what he believed was the real home of this remarkable fish, a possible evolutionary link between sea and land vertebrate life. He wrote that the Comoros was a 'great treasure house of fish life' and this is where 'Old Fourlegs' popped up again. On the evening of 20 December 1952 off Domoni, Anjouan, a local fisherman hauled into his outrigger *galawa* an 82 lb (37 kg) fish all the fishermen had known for years as *gombessa*. It was not long before Professor Smith, alerted by *Radio Cocotier* ('Radio Coconut Palm' or bush telegraph), was on his way to collect it in a South African Airforce Dakota, placed at this disposal by the then Prime Minister, Dr DF Malan. Prof Smith was overjoyed and named the new coelacanth specimen *Malania anjouanae Smith*. The lucky fisherman was also overjoyed; he got himself a reward equal to five year's pay for a catch all fishermen regarded as definitely poor eating. After being invisible for millions of years the coelacanth now started to appear in catches throughout the islands.

Within two years a further eight coelacanths had been caught, 21 were caught in 1960, 26 in 1962. By 1987 more than 140 had been caught and a lucrative trade had developed with scientific institutions and natural history museums all over the world which paid the Comoros government huge sums for specimens of the fossil fish. By the time the government was presenting them stuffed or frozen to visiting heads of state and other visiting dignitaries there was growing international concern that 'Old Fourlegs' might this time really be on its way to extinction. The market was by now saturated and no respectable institution was available to buy coelacanths, so its value to the Comoros fiscus declined. The last known local specimen caught off Anjouan in 1985 can now be seen on display at the Musée des Comores in Moroni, on Grande Comore. The Convention on International Trade in Endangered Species (CITES) placed the coelacanth on its endangered list in 1996. Since then coelacanth communities have been found off Madagascar and in 1998 a 64 lb (29 kg) specimen was caught off North Sulawesi, Indonesia, where coelacanths are well known to local fishermen as *Raja Laut* ('King of the Sea').

THE PEOPLE

Population figures and total surface area of the islands indicate that with 786 people to the sq mile (303 to the sq km) they should be bursting at the seams. In essence they are, although you'd never notice this as more than a third of the 565,000 people living in Comoros are settled in the main towns and urban areas. Grande Comore is the most heavily populated island, with around 250,000 people, although its east coast is sparsely populated. Anjouan, with around 1,100 people to the sq mile (425 to the sq km), is the most densely populated.

Nearly 90% of the islanders share Arab-African origins, but over the centuries there has been a leavening of Malay, Persian, Malagasy and European influence which has resulted in an ethnic blend of attractive, laid-back and hospitable men and women, whose idea of a good time seems to be a dance that never ends. The population is growing by nearly 4% a year, with a fertility rate of 6.8 children for each woman. Some 20% of the men believe in Muslim polygamy and have up to four wives. Nearly 70% of all Comorians are under the age of 30. Life expectancy is only 58 years: 54 for men and 59 for women. About 48% of the population is literate.

The pervasive Arab influence in cultural and everyday life can be seen in everything from architecture to the way the men and women dress. The women generally wear *chiromanis*, brilliantly coloured and patterned wraparound lengths of cotton. The fundamentalist Muslim practice of keeping women heavily veiled is no longer followed and saw its final demise during the presidency of Ali Solih, who grabbed power in a coup in the mid-1970s (see *Politics*) and banned face covering and other feudal Muslim traditions. Solih was shot not long after he told a public gathering that he was God, but the purdah veil never caught on again. No matter how poor they might be Comorian women believe they are not fully dressed unless they are wearing the intricately filigreed gold and silver rings, chains and other jewellery for which the islands are famous. No matter how photographically tempting they might appear, never take a photograph of a woman without first asking her permission. It's also good form to offer a token payment afterwards. Comorian men wear the sensible and comfortable *kanzou* a long cotton nightie-like shirt, over trousers. An embroidered Muslim skull-cap, the *yamatso* or *koffiah* is *de rigueur.* The further away from Moroni you get the more likely you are to be watched or followed by local people, who have an unquenchable curiosity about *wazungu* (Europeans) and rarely see them outside the capital or the confines of a tour vehicle. This is where your grasp of *Shikomoro* will come in handy (see *Languages* p.224).

WOMEN

Violence against women in Comorian society is rare, although cases do occur and are reported to medical authorities and to police. Women can seek protection through the courts in cases of violence, but in reality problems are usually addressed within the extended family or at rural village level. Men have the dominant role in society, and few women hold positions of responsibility in government or business. Although women have the vote, there are no women in the legislature or in the Cabinet. Social discrimination against women is most apparent in rural areas where women do most of the farming chores, as well as raising children and running the household. This allows them fewer educational and employment opportunities. By contrast, change in the status of women is most evident in the island towns where growing numbers of women are a recognised part of the labour force and generally earn the same, or similar, wages to men. While legal discrimination exists in some areas, inheritance and property rights do not, in general, disadvantage women. For example, the house that the father of the bride traditionally provides for the daughter on her marriage remains her property in the event of divorce or separation. The government is constitutionally committed to protecting children's rights and welfare, but population pressure and poverty levels oblige some families to offer their children for work in the homes of other, better off people. These children, often as young as seven years of age, usually work long hours as domestic servants in exchange for food and shelter. A lack of inspectors to monitor the situation means that the legal rights and welfare of children are not strictly enforced, although in common with all other island societies in the south-west Indian Ocean children are often pampered to the point of being idolised. As one village elder put it *l'enfant est roi* ('the child is king'), and cases of reported child abuse are rare in Comoros.

LANGUAGES

It's difficult enough for travellers to cope with a foreign, incomprehensible, language without the added complication of discovering that many words are happily spelt in a variety of ways and that the same language has a completely different name in different parts of the same country. This is the linguistic situation in Comoros, but the seeming puzzle is really quite easy to unravel with a bit of patience.

The lingua franca of the islands is Comorian, which in essence is a local dialect of the Swahili spoken on the coast of East Africa, a language itself a form of kitchen Arabic largely developed during the old days of the African slave trade. It's estimated that 50%-60% of the Swahili vocabulary is derived from Arabic, and as it was originally written in Arabic script the placing of the vowels, and even the vowels used, is often a matter of conjecture. This is the reason for the different spellings today once words are written in the Roman script: Ndzuani and Nzwani for Anjouan, for instance. Comorian itself remains basically the same language on all the islands of the archipelago, but takes the name of the island where it is spoken. Comorian, also known as *Shikomoro*, becomes *Shingazidja* on Grande Comore, *Shinzwani* on Anjouan, *Shimwali* on Mohéli, and *Shimaoré* on Mayotte. The Shikomoro names of the islands are, of course, Ngazidja, Ndzuani, Mwali, and Maoré. The vocabulary of the Comorian language has been enriched over the centuries through their contacts with other trading nations and words of Portuguese, English, Persian, Indian, Arabic and French origin have gone into the melting pot with those of Madagascar and the African mainland.

If all this is still as clear as mud, don't worry, you can get by with French (or Arabic – these being the Republic's two official languages) and you'll find even English is spoken in some areas as a result of the years Comoros was a magnet for South African holidaymakers denied access to most other places in the region because of their government's racial policies. Be careful, though, when you venture your French. There is still an undercurrent of hostility in places to France and things French and it wouldn't be wise to spout French where the most popular graffito seems to be the equivalent of 'Down with France'. Like people the world over Comorians respond warmly to anyone attempting to converse with them in their own language, and a simple greeting is better than nothing.

Try some of the following for size (pronounce as written):
Salaam aleikum – the polite universal Muslim hello, meaning 'Peace be with you'. Backpackers might like to memorise *Salaam aleikum. Kwezi, gomanzou nibaki da mi na mdu* ('Peace be with you. I would like to stay with someone, please).

USEFUL WORDS AND PHRASES

English	Comorian
Hello	Jeje
How are you?	Habari gani?
I am well	Ndjema
Goodbye	Kwaheri ya kuonana
Yes	Aiwa
No	Siyo
Thank you	Marahabha
Day	Mtsana
Tonight	Uku vani
Night	Uku
Yesterday	Jana
Today	Leo
Tomorrow	Meso
Where is ...?	Wapi/ndahu...?
Post office	Poste
Mosque	Maukiri/masjid
Boat	Markabu/djahazi
Bus	Bisi
Bicycle	Bisikleti
Motorcycle	Moto
Where is the taxi rank?	Wapi kituo cha motokaa ya kukodi?
Where is the beach?	Wapi mtsangani?
How long will it take	Muda gani?
How much is this?	Hii ngapi?/ryali nga?

What is your name?	Jina lako nani?
Excuse me	Uniwie radhi
I don't understand	Tsisielewa
Eat	Houla
Food	Chahoula
Where is the toilet?	Sho sha havi?

You can get by with even these few words and phrases and unless you are a linguistic whizz there's not much point in learning to say *Nitsofanya jeje ata niswaswili...?* ('How do I get to...?') if you don't understand a word of the reply. The key here is to make the effort.

RELIGION

One of the major imports by Comoros throughout the year is cement. The bulk of it goes to build, extend or repair the hundreds of mosques whose minarets pierce the skyline everywhere you go in the islands. Virtually the entire population of Comoros is Muslim, but the islanders' version of Islam's precepts is not the fanatical one of Iran, the source of the islands' majority faith, although fundamentalism is now appearing with the return of young students from the sterner Muslim countries of Libya, Sudan, and the Gulf States to the north. The religion taught by the Prophet Mohammed is practised in a tolerant fashion, and the further away you are from Grande Comore the more tolerant it seems to become. In Mohéli, for instance, it is not unknown for the palm wine to flow freely when villagers celebrate something, anything, with music and a knees-up. An estimated 98% of the people are adherents of the Sunni Muslim branch of Islam, the rest are Catholics. The Shirazi Arabs who brought Islam to the Comoros came via East Africa from what was then Persia. They were Sunni Muslims adhering to the legal school of Muhammad ibn Idris ash Shafii, an 8th century Meccan scholar who followed a middle path in combining tradition and independent judgment in legal matters. A Comoros legend tells of seven Shirazi brothers who set sail in seven ships, landed on Ngazidja and Ndzuani, and established colonies in the 15th century, dividing the former island into 11 sultanates and the latter into two. They extended their rule to Maoré and Mwali. The Shirazi built the first mosques and established Islam as the religion of the islands. They also introduced stone architecture, carpentry, cotton weaving, the cultivation of a number of fruits, and the Persian solar calendar.

Since then the religion has been reinforced in island life by the tradition of sending small children for religious instruction for several hours every morning, when they recite suras from the Koran in Arabic, a language hardly anyone speaks. Muslims believe that their daily lives should be guided by this holy book of Islam. One of the first things the late President Mohamed Taki Abdulkarim did on taking office in 1996 was to reinforce the ban on alcohol for believers and to lay down the law on 'immodest dress'. These strictures remain in force today. He also established a new legal code consolidating French and Muslim law (*shariah*). While the Comoros constitution prohibits discrimination based on religion or religious belief it establishes an Ulamas Council to advise government and administration on whether Bills, ordinances, decrees, and laws conform to the principles of Islam. However, the government allows non-Muslims to practise their faith, and Christian missionaries work in local hospitals and schools, but are not allowed to proselytise and look for converts. The Constitution provides for equality before the law without discrimination based on race, religion, or religious belief and while the government generally respects these provisions, it discourages the practice of religions other than Islam. As a visitor you should always respect Muslim customs and practices. One of the more important is that when you visit a mosque you should be appropriately dressed and you should take off your shoes before entering. Women should not enter mosques, and men should not enter unless accompanied by a Comorian.

NATIONAL ANTHEM AND FLAG

The national anthem of Comoros is *The Union of the Great Islands*, set to music by Kamildine Abdallah and Saïd Hachim Sidi Abderemane. You'll really make friends and influence people if you can get your tongue around the words in the following local Comorian dialect:

I beramu isi pepeza
i nadi ukombozi piya
i daula ivenuha
tasiba bu ya i dini voya trangaya hunu Komoriya
Narikéni namahaba ya huveindza ya masiwa
yatru wasiwa Komoro damu ndzima
wasiwa Komoro dini ndzima
Ya masiwa radzali wa ya masiwa yarileya
Mola neari sayidiya
Narikeni ha niya riveindze uwataniya
Mahaba ya dine na duniya.
I beramu isi pepeza
rangu mwesi sita wa Zuiye
i daula ivenuha
zisiwa zatru zi pangwi ha
Maoré na Ndzuani, Mwali na Ngazidja
Narikeni namahaba ya huveindza ya masiwa
I beraba ya huveindzor ya masiwa.

English

The flag is flying,
Announcing complete independence;
The nation rises up
Because of the faith we have
In this our Comoria.
Let us always have devotion
To love our Great Islands,
We Comorians are of one blood,
We Comorians are of one faith.
On these islands we were born,
These islands brought us up.
May God always help us;
Let us always always have the firm resolve
To love our fatherland,

Love our religion and the world.
The flag is flying,
From the Sixth of July;
The Nation rises up
Our islands are lined up.
Maoré and Ndzuani, Mwali and Ngazidja,
Let us always have devotion
To love our Great Islands.

Comoros has had almost as many national flags since independence as it has had coups and changes of government. What all have had in common, however, is the white crescent of Islam on a green field dotted in constellations of varying shapes with four stars representing the four main islands of the archipelago – Grande Comore, Anjouan, Mohéli, and Mayotte, the French territorial collectivity claimed by Comoros. In late 1996 the flag was changed to include the word *Allah* in Arabic in the top-fly corner and *Mohammed* in the bottom hoist corner. The use of the national flag on any commercial item, especially clothing, is considered inappropriate or, at worst, insulting, so don't be tempted by any T-shirts emblazoned with the flag.

FURTHER READING

Malyn Newitt's *The Comoros Islands: Struggle Against Dependency in the Indian Ocean,* is out of print, but it should be fairly easy to find a second-hand copy or request it from your local library.

Last of the Pirates: the Search for Bob Dénard, by Samantha Weinberg (1994, Jonathan Cape, London) is an account of French mercenary Colonel Bob Dénard, who poked his finger into a number of coups and revolutionary situations on the African continent and in the Comoros islands.

A Fish Caught in Time is Samantha Weinberg's enthralling account of the search for the coelacanth, eventually found in Comoros (1999, Fourth Estate, London).

Old Fourlegs: The Story of the Coelacanth by Professor JLB Smith (1956, Longman, Green). The earlier account by the South African scientist who first alerted the world to the fact that this fossil fish had come back from the dead. If you don't read anything else you should read Prof Smith and Samantha Weinberg.

The Sea Fishes of Southern Africa, by Professor JLB Smith (1965, Central News Agency, South Africa).

Birds of the Indian Ocean Islands, by Ian Sinclair and Olivier Langrand (1998, Struik Publishers, Cape Town).

Marine Turtles in the Comoros Archipelago, by J Frazier (1985, North-Holland Publishing Co, Amsterdam, Oxford, New York).

Historical Dictionary of the Comoro Islands, by Martin and Harriet Ottenheimer (African Historical Dictionaries, No 59).

PRACTICAL INFORMATION

BY AIR

Yemen Airways, the national carrier of Yemen, is the only airline flying to the Comoros from Europe – and they are all non-direct routes. You can fly from Paris to Sana'a on a Monday, flying time 6 hours and 50 minutes. From Sana'a there is a flight to Moroni on Tuesday, flight time 4 hours. From Rome you can fly to Sana'a on a Tuesday, flying time 5½ hours, and then from Sana'a to Moroni on a Saturday. The other more complex option is to fly from London to Cairo on a Wednesday, flying times 5 hours. From Cairo you can fly to Sana'a on a Friday, flying time 6 hours 50 minutes, or a Monday, and eventually from Sana'a to Moroni on a Tuesday – a whole week to reach your destination. Otherwise you can reach Comoros via Johannesburg – there are two flights every Sunday, flying time 3 hours. It's advisable to check the flight schedules with the Yemen Airways office in Sana'a (tel 1-27-6456; fax 1-20-1821) or in Johannesburg (tel 11-484 4222; fax 11-484 6111).

THE BEST ROUTE

The best way to get to the Comoros, however, is probably from London to Paris, then by Air France to Réunion or Nairobi, and then by Air Austral to Comoros. Six airlines operate flights with varying frequencies to Réunion from France. They are Air France (9 weekly flights), AOM (daily flights), Air Liberté (4 weekly flights), Corsair (3-6 weekly flights), Aerolyon (1 weekly flight), and Jet Ocean Indien (6 weekly flights). The non-stop flight to Réunion takes 11 hours or up to 13 hours with stops en route. There are also flights from Lyons, Marseilles, and Toulouse on certain days and periods of the year. Prices depend on travelling dates, and there are often attractive promotional fares.

You can also fly Air Mauritius from London (Heathrow and Gatwick), Manchester, Paris, Brussels, Frankfurt, Vienna, Geneva, Zurich, Milan, Rome, Munich, Mumbai, Melbourne, Perth, Hong Kong, and connect to Moroni. Other major airlines serving Mauritius include Air Europe, Air France, Air Austral, Air India, Air Madagascar, Air Seychelles, British Airways, Cathay Pacific, Singapore Airlines, Condor, South African Airways, Air Zimbabwe, and Kenya Airways.

There is no direct commercial air service between the US and Comoros, but travel can be arranged via London, Paris or Johannesburg as Air France, American Airlines, British Airways and Virgin all have routes to these destinations from major US airports.

Other Routes

If you opt for a stop-over in Africa or another Indian Ocean island on your way to

Comoros you can connect to Moroni as follows:

From Kenya: *Air Austral* flies into Nairobi every Monday and has one weekly flight to Comoros every Tuesday.

From Madagascar: *Air Madagascar* flies from Antananarivo to Moroni on a Friday, and from Mahajanga to Moroni on a Sunday.

From Mauritius: *Air Mauritius* flies to Comoros twice a week, every Tuesday and Friday, and returns to Mauritius from Moroni on a Monday and Thursday.

From Réunion: *Air Austral* flies to Moroni, Grande Comore, every Monday, Thursday and Saturday. The flight takes about 2½ hours. Air Austral has two flights a week from **Mayotte** on a Monday and Thursday. There are flights from Comoros to Mayotte, on Tuesday and Thursday; to Réunion on Tuesday, Thursday and Sunday.

From South Africa: *Air Austral* has two weekly flights to Réunion, on Thursday and Sunday, and usually increases its frequency during August, December and January. *Interair* has a one flight a week, on Sunday, from Johannesburg to Moroni. For more information, contact your travel agent or get in touch with the airlines.

AIRLINES SERVING COMOROS

The general sales agent in Comoros for both *Air Austral* and *Air Mauritius* is Ario, PO Box 1285, Route Magoudjou, Moroni (tel 73-3144; fax 73-0719). The office is open Monday to Thursday from 7.30am to 2.30pm, Friday from 7.30am to 11.30am, and Saturday 7.30am to noon.

Air Austral: 2 rue de l'Eglise, F-92200, Neuilly (tel 1-92 01 33; fax 1-92 01 37).

Contact address in Comoros: rue Magoudjou, Moroni, Grande Comore (tel 73-3144; fax 73-0719).

Contact address in Mayotte: Air Austral, Dzaoudzi, Petite Terre (tel 60-1052; fax 60-0387; e-mail agence.issoufali@wanadoo.fr); Air Austral, Place du Marché, Mamoudzou, Grande Terre (tel 61-3636; fax 61-1053; e-mail mayotte@air-austral.com). Open Monday to Friday from 8.30am to 12.30pm and 1.30pm to 4.30pm, Saturday 8.30am to 11.30am.

Contact address in Réunion: 4 rue de Nice, St Denis Cedex (bookings tel 1-90 90 90; fax 1-90 90 91); Roland Garros International Airport (tel 48-8020); St Pierre, 14 rue Archambaud (tel 96-2696; fax 35-4649; e-mail saint-pierre@air-austral.com); Pierrefonds Airport (tel 96-8020; fax 96-8019).

Air France: 119 Champs Elysées, F-75384 Paris Cedex 08 (tel 1-42 99 23 64).

Contact address in Britain: 1st Floor, 10 Warwick Street, London, W1R 5RA (tel 0207-474 5555; Website www.airfrance.fr/).

Contact address in Kenya: International House, Mama Ngina Street, Nairobi (tel 33-3301; fax 33-5867).

Contact address in Mauritius: Air Mauritius Centre, Rogers House, President John F. Kennedy Street, Port Louis (tel 212-2666; fax 211-1411).

Contact address in Mayotte: see Air Austral addresses above.

Contact address in Réunion: 7 Avenue de la Victoire, St Denis (tel 40 39 00); Reservations (tel 40 38 38, fax 40 38 40).

Contact address in South Africa: Oxford Manor, 196 Oxford Road, Illovo, Johannesburg (tel 11-880 9039; fax 11-788 5440).

Contact Address in USA: 120 West 56th Street, New York, NY 10019, USA (tel 1-800-237 2747 reservations).

Air Liberté: (also agent for British Airways) Parc d' Affaires SILIC, 67 rue de

Monthléry, Rungis (tel 1-49 79 23 00).

Contact address in Réunion: 13 rue Charles Gounod, St Denis (tel 94 72 00, fax 41 68 00).

Air Madagascar: Société Nationale Malgache de Transport Aériens, 31 Avenue de l'Indépendance (tel 20-22-22222; fax 20-22-33760; e-mail airmad@dts.mg).

Contact address in Comoros: Travel Service International, Bâtiment DHL rue Oasis, Moroni (tel 73-3044; fax 73-3054).

Air Mauritius: Air Mauritius Centre, Rogers House, President John F. Kennedy Street, Port Louis (tel 207-7070; fax 208-8331; e-mail: resa@airmauritius.com); SSR International Airport (tel 603-3030; fax 637-3266).

Contact address in Britain: 49 Conduit Street, London W1R 9FB (tel 020-7434 4375; fax 020-7439 4101); and Room 3067, Terminal 2, Manchester International Airport, Manchester M90 4QX (tel 0161-498 9909; fax 0161-437 6069).

Contact address in Madagascar: Ario, 77 Lalana Solombav Ambahoaka Frantsay, BP 3673 Antsahavola, Antananarivo 101 (tel 20-23-5990, fax 20-23-5773).

Contact address in Réunion: Corner Charles Gounod and Alexis de Villeneuve Street, 97400 St Denis (tel 94-8383; fax 41-2326; e-mail: airmauritius@wanadoo.fr).

Contact address in USA: 560 Sylvan Avenue, Englewood Cliffs, New Jersey 07632 (tel 201-871 8382; fax 201-871 6983; e-mail: airmkusa@concentric.net).

AOM (Aire Outre Mer): Bàt 363 BP 854, F-94551 Orly Aérogare Cedex (tel 1-08 03 00 12 34).

Contact address in Réunion: 7 rue Jean Chatel, St Denis (tel 94-7777; fax 20 07 16).

American Airlines: 4200 Amon Carter Boulevard, MD 2644, Dallas Fort Worth Airport, Texas 75261, USA (tel 1-800-321 2121; website wwwr3.aa.com/).

Contact address in Britain: 45-46 Picadilly, London, W1V 9AJ (tel 0208-572 5555).

British Airways: Waterside, PO Box 365, Harmondsworth, UB7 0GB (tel 0208-759 5511; website www.british-airways.com).

Contact address in USA: British Airways can be contacted anywhere in the US on freephone 1-800-AIRWAYS.

Interair: (Head Office in South Africa) Ground Floor, Finance House, Ernest Oppenheimer Road, Bruma Lake Office Park, Bruma, Johannesburg (tel 11-616 0636; fax 11-616 0930).

Contact Address in Britain: Buckingham Palace Road, London 0SW1 9TA (tel 020-7707 4581; fax 020-7707 4165).

Airport

Hahaya International Airport is 15.5 miles (25 km) from the centre of Moroni, about a 30-minute drive. The airport is situated on the west coast of the island. An airport tax of 9,000 Comorian francs (£12/$25/FF120) is applicable on departure and this tax must be shown on the ticket. Buses and taxis run to the town in 30-50 minutes. Airport facilities include left luggage facilities, open 6am to 6pm; and a post office. Available for international flights is a bar and light refreshments, open 6am to 6pm. Avoid official-looking people at the airport claiming to be tourist information officers, they're touting for business for various hotels. It is unlikely you'll find any genuine tourist information officers hanging around the airport. Don't allow anyone to carry your luggage for you at the airport or you might never see it again.

BY SEA

There is a limited inter-island ferry service between Mayotte and Comoros (see *Mayotte: Getting Around* p.183) and the islands are connected to Madagascar by regular ferries and to Mombasa, Kenya, Mauritius and Réunion by irregular cargo ship services. You might be able to get a berth on a ship sailing from Mombasa or Zanzibar to Madagascar and drop off at Grande Comore or Anjouan on the way, but don't bank on it. It is usually easier to find a cargo ship from Mauritius, Réunion or Madagascar, if you are prepared to hang around the ports.

The **Mediterranean Shipping Company (MSC)** of Geneva is a privately owned shipping line which is the fourth largest container carrier globally. MSC vessels call at 174 ports through 81 main direct and 55 combined weekly liner services and the company maintains agencies and offices all over the world. The company runs regular services to the Mascarene islands.

In Australia the head office of MSC (Aust) and the cruise office of Mediterranean Shipping Company Travel are at Level 8, 155 George Street, Sydney, New South Wales (tel 2-9252 1111; fax 2- 9252 1258/1448).

In France contact MSC France SA, 23 Avenue de Neuilly, F-75116 Paris (tel 1-5364-6300; fax 1-5364-6310); and the cruise office MSC Croisieres Sarl, 59 rue Beaubourg, F-75003 Paris (tel 1-4804-7620; fax 1-4804-5165); and Centre Havrais de Commerce International, Quai George V, F-76065 Le Havre (tel 23-274 6800; fax 23-274 6810).

In Madagascar contact the head office of MSC Madagascar SA, 72 Avenue du 26 Juin 1960, Analakely, Antananarivo 101 (tel 20-22-32130; fax 20-22-30188; e-mail mscmad@dts.mg).

In Mauritius MSC can be contacted at 5th Floor Rogers House, 5 President John F Kennedy Street, Port Louis (tel 202-6818; fax 208-5045; e-mail msc@rogers.intnet.mu).

In Réunion contact MSC France SA, 49 rue Evariste de Parny, Le Port Cedex (tel 42-7800; fax 42-7810).

In South Africa you can contact MSC Holdings at MSC House, 54 Winder Street, Durban 4001 (tel 31-360 7911; fax 31-332 9277); and MSC House, Duncan Road, Table Bay Harbour, Cape Town (tel 21-405 2000; fax 21-419 1546). The general sales agent for MSC cruises is Starlight Cruises at Starlight House, 1 Wessels Road, corner 5th Avenue, Rivonia 2128, Johannesburg (tel 11-807 5111; fax 11-807 5085; e-mail starlite@yebo.co.za).

In the **USA** the head office of MSC (USA) is at 420 5th Avenue (at 37th Street), 8th Floor, New York, NY 10018-2702 (tel 212-764-4800; fax 212-764-8592).

You could also try La Ligne Scandinave (SEAL), BP 679, Antananarivo 101 (tel 20-22-22356; fax 20-22-33902; e-mail sealtana@dts.mg). Yacht clubs in Durban and Cape Town, South Africa, are worth scouting during the yachting season from April to November, as this is when lots of members head for the Indian Ocean island cruising grounds. Royal Cape Yacht Club, Cape Town (tel 21-421 1354/5; fax 21-421 6028; Royal Natal Yacht Club, Durban (tel 31-301 5425; fax 31-307 2590); and Point Yacht Club, Durban (tel 31-301 4787; fax 31-

305 1234).

The *Baraka-Belinga* line sails from the Comoros to France. *Norwegian American* runs Arabian Sea cruises from Genoa to Mutsamudu, Anjouan. For sailings to Europe contact the Direction Générale du Tourisme et de Hotellerie in Moroni (tel 74-4242/3; fax 74-4241).

TOUR OPERATORS

A to B Tours: 205 Winchester Road, Basingstoke, Hampshire G21 8YH (tel/fax 01256-351979).

Africa Extraordinaire: Cottney Meadow, Old Park, Bradley, Ashbourne, Derbyshire DE6 1PL (tel 01335-372170; fax 01335-327171).

Comet Travel: 21 Newman Street, London W1P 4DD (tel 020-7437 7878; fax 020-7636 3907).

Elite Vacations: Elite House, 98-100 Bessborough Road, Harrow, Middlesex HA1 3D7 (tel 020-8864 4431; fax 020-8426 9178).

Hayes and Jarvis: 152 King Street, London W6 0QU (tel 020-8741 9932; fax 020-8741 0299).

Jules Verne: 10 Glentworth Street, London NW1 5P4 (tel 020-7616 1000; fax 020-7723 8629).

Sunset Faraway Holidays: 4 Abbeville Manor, 88 Clapham Park Road, London SW4 7BX (tel 020-7498 9922; fax 020-7978 1337).

Tana Travel: 2 Ely Street, Stratford-Upon-Avon, Warwickshire CV37 (tel 01789 414200; fax 01789-414420).

Union Castle Travel: 86-87 Camden Street, Kensington, London W8 7EN (tel 020-7229 1411; fax 020-7229 1511).

Wexas International: 45 Brompton Road, Knightsbridge, London SW3 1DE (tel 020-7589 3315; fax 020-7589 8418).

TRAVEL SAFELY

Both the UK Foreign Office and the US State Department have travel information offices which provide regularly updated free advice on countries around the world (see p.48 for their contact details).

Red Tape

ENTRY REQUIREMENTS

PASSPORTS AND VISAS

To enter Comoros your passport must be valid for at least 6 months after date of entry and you will need an onward ticket – don't be surprised if the authorities hold your onward tickets while you're visiting. Except for Comorian and French nationals, a visa is required. This can be issued by diplomatic representatives of Comoros in your home country, but as there are not many of these around visas are usually obtained on arrival at Hahaya International Airport from an immigration officer and are issued for stays of up to 45 days. Maximum fee is CF15,000 (£18/$27), other visa fees depend on length of stay. The fee is payable in either German marks, Swiss francs, pounds sterling, French francs, or US dollars. You will need an application form, which is provided at the airport, a valid passport, the fee (payable in cash only), and two passport-size photographs for an exit permit, which costs another CF500 (£0.62/$0.92) and is required by every visitor. If you are staying at one of the Sun International hotels, the cost of the visa is usually included in your holiday package price. Visas are not required by transit passengers continuing their journey by the same or first connecting aircraft, provided they hold valid onward or return documentation and do not leave the airport. For more information or applications contact the Direction Générale d'Immigration at Hahaya International Airport on Grande Comore. You should also be aware that entry to Anjouan and Mohéli may not be covered by the visa you obtain when you arrive on the island of Grande Comore. For instance, access to Anjouan, Comoros second largest island, requires prior permission from authorities on that island, which unilaterally declared itself independent in 1997.

HEALTH DOCUMENTS

You do not need any vaccination or health certificate for Grande Comore, although you must supply an international vaccination certificate if you are arriving from a yellow fever area. Tetanus and rabies vaccinations are recommended if you intend to travel in rural areas.

CUSTOMS REGULATIONS

The following duty-free items are allowed for all persons over the age of 17 years:

400 Cigarettes, or 200 cigarillos, or 100 cigars, or 500g of smoking tobacco
One litre of any alcoholic beverage of more than 22 proof, or 2 litres of wine
75 cl of perfume for personal use
Gifts up to CF5,000 (£6/$9) in value

Do not take in more than the duty-free allowance as customs officials can either confiscate your goods or charge whatever duty they feel like. There is no restriction on the amount of foreign currency you can bring, and there are no restrictions on cameras or film, as long as it is for personal use. Mercenary involvement in past coups and revolutionary activities has made the authorities hypersensitive to arms and weapons in any shape or form. One result of this is that you will not be allowed to bring in a diving knife, or any knife with a blade longer than 4 inches (10 cm) and, as spearfishing is prohibited, no spearguns. Also prohibited are weapons and ammunition, radio transmission equipment, plants and soil.

Customs officials can be unpredictable, so if you are taking in any scuba-diving equipment it's best to fill in a baggage declaration form on arrival to obviate any problems when you want to take your gear out again.

CAUTION

Finally, don't be tempted to take out any coral, turtleshell or sea shells when you leave. Comoros implements a strict ban on the collection and trade in these, mainly endangered, products and any you have will be confiscated if found and you'll undoubtedly also face a stiff fine.

COMOROS EMBASSIES ABROAD

France: Embassy of the Federal Islamic Republic of the Comoros, 20 rue Marbeau, F-75116 Paris (tel 1-4067-9054; fax 1-4417-7296/9188). It is open from 10am to 4pm Monday to Friday.

United States: Mission and Embassy of the Federal Islamic Republic of Comoros, Second Floor, 336 East 45th Street, New York, NY10017 (tel 212-972-8010; fax 212-983-4712). This office also deals with enquiries from Canada.

Comoros does not have diplomatic or tourism representation in Australia, Britain or Canada.

What Money to Take

The basic currency is the Comorian Franc (written as CF) made up of 100 centimes. Notes are in denominations of CF10,000, 5,000, 2,500, 1,000, 500, 100, 50 and 25. Coins are in denominations of CF20, 10, 5, 2 and 1, and 20 centimes. The Comoros franc is part of the French Monetary Area and French Francs (FF) may also be in circulation and are usually accepted as legal tender throughout the islands. It is advisable to take some French francs in cash, which is accepted everywhere, and the rest of your funds in FF or sterling travellers cheques. US dollars are, of course, almighty everywhere. It is hopeless to try to change Comorian money back into an international currency once you have left the country, although you can re-convert it before you leave if you have the bank slips proving you changed it while you were there.

Exchange Rates

The Comoros exchange rate is dictated by that of the French franc, to which it is tied as part of an agreement concluded in 1978, which brought Comoros into the franc zone. This gives the currency a stability and strength that it would lack if its value was dictated solely by the strength of the national economy, which is poor. Along with other countries of the franc zone, the Comoros was affected by the devaluation of the French currency in January 1994. The Comoros government, however, insisted that the devaluation of its franc should be only 33% and not 50% as elsewhere. This was allowed in 1995 and the exchange rate became fixed at CF75=FF1.

Exchange rates (mid 2000) were:

Europe	Euro 1 = CF496
UK	£1 = CF792.4
France	FF1 = CF75.75
Germany	DM1 = CF254
USA	US$1 = CF525
Canada	Can$1 = CF355
South Africa	R1 = CF75
Australia	A$1 = CF304

Banks and Banking

There are branches of the Banque Internationale des Comores (BIC) on all three islands. The bank in Moroni is near the central post office and is your best bet to change traveller's cheques (tel 73-0243; fax 73-0349).

Hours. Banks are open Monday to Thursday from 7.30am to 1.30pm and on Friday from 7.30am to 11am.

Credit Cards and ATMs

International credit cards are not the financial 'Open Sesame' they are in most other countries of the world. There is limited acceptance of most but check with your credit card company before you leave home for details of merchant acceptability and other services which may be available. The main hotel group on Grande Comore, Sun International, accepts credit cards and will cash travellers cheques, but at a heavy commission. They will not advance cash against your credit card.

Tipping

Gratuities of any kind were unknown in Comoros until tourists started to arrive. Tipping is still not widespread outside the main hotels, but naturally always gratefully received. Tip about 10% in restaurants and taxis if you are happy with the service.

BEFORE YOU LEAVE

Malaria is endemic and there are occasional outbreaks of cholera in rural areas; while cholera cannot be contracted person to person and there are no reported cases of visitors being infected, it is best to go prepared. Immunisation offers protection against some of the diseases doing the rounds. In general, immunisations are available for many of the more severe infections, for example cholera, yellow fever and polio. It is not yet possible to immunise against many of the less severe but more common diseases, such as traveller's diarrhoea. You should ensure that you are up to date with the immunisations recommended for your journey and, ideally, allow 6-8 weeks to undergo a full course of immunisation. To find out which immunisations are recommended contact your doctor or attend a travel clinic. In the UK you can obtain a Health Brief from the Medical Advisory Services for Travellers Abroad (MASTA), which can be taken to your own doctor or to a British Airways Travel Clinic (see *Madagascar: Health & Hygiene* p.54). Yellow fever immunisation is mandatory for entering some countries and you will not be allowed in without a certificate. Cholera immunisation used to be a mandatory requirement for entry into many countries, but this is no longer the case.

All travellers are advised to be up to date with their tetanus and polio immunisations. Depending on where you are going, MASTA recommends immunisations for polio, typhoid, tetanus, hepatitis A and B, yellow fever, cholera, and rabies, and provides the following guidelines.

Cholera

Immunisation with the old injected vaccine against cholera is not considered appropriate for most travellers as it offers poor protection, although where it is known that border officials may demand a cholera certificate it is wiser to be in possession of one. The newer oral cholera vaccine provides significant protection against cholera and is well tolerated. Anyone who might be exposed to uncertain water and food hygiene should consider immunisation with the oral vaccine. Immunisation, however, does not absolve you from following recommended food and water hygiene practices, such as drinking safe bottled, boiled or treated water only, and being careful of fruit and vegetables that cannot be peeled or cooked. Do not eat raw seafood, as the cholera bacterium has been shown to survive for extended periods in sea water.

Malaria

Precautions are advised as there is a risk of malaria throughout the year. Resistance to chloroquine has been reported and the recommended prophylaxis is mefloquine, although expert advice should be obtained before leaving home from a doctor or a travel clinic. It is important to realise that the tablets you should take can vary, because in some parts of the world the malaria parasite is resistant to certain drugs. Antimalarial tablets do not provide 100% protection and ideally you should avoid bites of the mosquitoes that spread malaria. You should start taking your tablets one week (2-3 weeks if taking mefloquine) before you enter a malaria area and you should continue taking them for one month after you leave the last malarial area.

Polio

This is an oral vaccine usually given on a lump of sugar. It is a simple and safe protection against the poliomyelitis still prevalent in some tropical and developing countries.

Rabies

Pre-imunisation against rabies should be considered by travellers going to areas where rabies is endemic, who are staying for considerable periods of time or are at particular risk. The immunisation can be life-saving, but any traveller who is bitten or licked by a potentially rabid animal must seek medical advice, as the vaccine will then definitely require boosting.

Tetanus

This is a disease found throughout the world and is potentially life-threatening. A booster dose is given as a single injection.

Typhoid

This disease is caused by contaminated food and water and leads to high fever and septicaemia. Three vaccines are available for protection against typhoid: the older monovalent vaccine, a new injected single-dose vaccine, and a live oral vaccine. Immunisation is usually advised for those going to areas where the standards of food and water hygiene are low.

Viral Hepatitis

Hepatitis is an infection of the liver caused by viruses which do not respond to antibiotics. As there is generally no effective treatment for most viral infections prevention is of paramount importance. Although there are many different types of hepatitis, the two commonest forms are hepatitis A, and hepatitis B. Both are relatively common in less developed parts of the world.

Hepatitis A. Short-term protection against this water-borne viral disease is offered by a single injection of immunoglobulin. A vaccine is now available which provides protection for 10 years.

Hepatitis B. This is a potentially fatal disease and is acquired by contact with contaminated body fluids, especially blood. Contaminated or unsterile medical equipment is a common source of infection, usually in lesser developed countries where disposable medical equipment may be re-used. It may also be sexually transmitted. In general, Hepatitis B is acquired in much the same way as the human immunodeficiency virus. The incubation period is 2 to 6 months. An effective vaccine is available against this form of hepatitis.

Yellow Fever

This is a viral illness for which there is no cure, but there is an effective vaccine which will prevent it. The vaccine, if properly administered, provides solid immunity against the disease for 10 years. Travellers immunised against yellow fever are issued with an internationally recognised vaccination certificate for inspection by immigration officials. The international health regulations concerning yellow fever control are strict, and unvaccinated travellers may be denied entry, or even face quarantine.

MEDICAL SERVICES

Bear in mind that in all cases prevention is better than cure, and is a definite bonus in a place such as Comoros, where medical facilities are poor and only the most basic treatment is available. In order to ensure even this medical care you should be covered by comprehensive health insurance, as there is no reciprocal health agreement with the United Kingdom. Any treatment you get from a doctor or hospital usually has to be paid for immediately in cash. As recently as 1998 the World Bank approved a US$8.4 million loan to Comoros to improve the health status of the population by reducing the number of deaths from infectious diseases, including malaria. The money was to be spent on improving health care facilities and services; upgrading mosquito control activities; and improving medical staff skills by providing training for health sector personnel. More than 80% of all Comorians live within 3 miles (5 km) of a health facility, but the poor quality of these facilities and poorly trained staff deter most of them from seeking health care. Less than half of the population ever visit a doctor, despite the high levels of infectious diseases. There is roughly one doctor for every 20,000 people. There are several pharmacies in Moroni and two at Mutsamudu, Anjouan. The nearest place with medical facilities of recognised world standards is Mayotte, and you should head for this French outpost in a real emergency.

EVERYDAY HEALTH

Reports vary as to where and whether the water that comes out of the tap is safe to drink in the islands. Err on the side of caution and drink only bottled water. Refuse any bottle that comes with the cap seal broken. It's best to avoid ice cubes, unless they come with your drink in one of the two up-market hotels on Grande Comore. The worst water comes out of the taps in Anjouan. As local milk is unpasteurised, it should be boiled before use, and you should exercise care when eating fresh salads and uncooked fruit, as well as mayonnaise. It is advisable to eat only well-cooked meat and fish served hot. Stomach upset is the most likely affliction when travelling, so carry something such as Imodium tablets to deal with any discomfort.

HEALTH HAZARDS

DIVING

No one wants to ruin a good dive in a perfect spot by dwelling on the things that could go wrong and create problems or even a life-threatening emergency, but the wise scuba-diver is the one who is prepared for every situation. Let's face it, diving can be a serious health hazard, but problems can be minimised if suitable precautions are taken. Recognising symptoms of trouble and knowing how to deal with emergencies is essential. Diver efficiency can be affected by a number of elements, including weightlessness, anxiety, restriction of movement and vision, carbon dioxide build-up, nitrogen narcosis ('Rapture of the Depths'), alcohol, and drugs. These and other factors can impair memory, reasoning power and manual dexterity, but such problems can be offset to some extent by pre-planning dives to minimise mental effort.

Barotrauma ('Squeeze')

This is caused by tissue damage in the ear, sinus or dental cavities brought about by uncontrolled alteration of pressure in air spaces in the body during descent or ascent. **Precautions**. Avoid diving until effects of sinus or bronchial infection or nasal obstruction have cleared. Observe controlled descent and ascent procedures. Do not dive for four weeks after a dental extraction. **Symptoms**. Pain and bleeding; pain increasing with depth, diminishing with ascent, persisting afterwards. If ear drum bursts, vertigo and nausea. **Treatment**. Treat for shock and obtain medical help immediately.

Rupture of Lung Tissue

In uncontrolled ascent, lung tissues may rupture as trapped compressed air expands. One of the following may then happen:

Acute emphysema. **Symptoms** are pain, voice change, fullness of throat, coughing up blood, and sometimes face or neck puffiness. **Treatment** administer oxygen.

Pneumothorax. **Symptoms** are chest pains, shortness of breath. Urgent surgery may be necessary.

Air Embolism

Symptoms are pains in chest, dizziness, slurred speech, collapse, unconsciousness. Professional medical assistance is urgent. As **first-aid**, place diver on his left side with head lower than feet. Administer oxygen. Rush to nearest recompression chamber.

Nitrogen narcosis ('Rapture of the Depths')

When compressed, as in the compressed air supplied to divers, nitrogen dissolves in the body and effects the brain. **Precautions**. Significant effects should be watched for by diving buddy from 66 ft (20 m) down, but can occur as early as 43 ft (13 m). **Symptoms**. Impairment of reasoning, memory and physical co-ordination; light-headedness; hallucinations; eventual unconsciousness. **Treatment**. Terminate dive and return to surface at prescribed rate. There are no after-effects.

Decompression Sickness ('Bends')

Decompression sickness is caused by the release into the blood and tissues of excess nitrogen which has been gradually dissolved under pressure. Decompression stops on way to surface allow excess nitrogen still in solution to be eliminated gradually. **Precautions**. Plan dive so that you know what the decompression stops are and adhere strictly to the schedule. Carry emergency oxygen supply. Avoid heavy exertion after dive. Ascent between stops must be uniform and as close as practicable to 59 ft (18 m) a minute. **Symptoms**. Pain in joints; weakness or paralysis of limbs; dizziness; skin itch; shortness of breath; coughing; visual disturbance; tingling, numbness and mottling of skin; unconsciousness. **Treatment**. Administer 100% oxygen at high flow rates on return to surface (but not underwater). Treat for shock. Obtain medical assistance immediately. Nothing to eat or drink until medical assessment. Take diver to nearest recompression chamber immediately; **do not** put diver down again. If affected diver is to be transported by aircraft, do so only in a pressurised aircraft cabin. Do not dive again for 24 hours if you have dived below 131 ft (40 m) or fly in an aircraft within 12 hours of completing such a dive. Remember that there are definite risks in diving below 79 ft (24 m), or breathing two tanks of air a day at a depth of 49 ft (15 m) or more, or both. Find out before you go where the nearest recompression chamber is located and what emergency procedures and transportation exist to get you to it. In the case of Comoros the nearest 'pot' is in Durban, South Africa. Emergency air evacuation, chamber treatment and hospitalisation can be extremely expensive, so make sure your medical insurance is sufficient in both type and amount of coverage. Retain all receipts for medical treatment for proper claim documentation when you get home.

DIVING AND FLYING: CAVEAT

One last word of advice about diving and flying. Diving and jet travel, in that order, can bring about decompression sickness and for the travelling diver there is a simple rule to follow: don't fly in a jet for at least 12 hours – ideally 24 hours – after a scuba dive. It's the excess nitrogen remaining in the diver's system after a dive that causes, or at least increases, the chances of decompression sickness if further decompression (flying) occurs, and pressure reduction does occur in modern jets. It's easy to see then that a diver's stored nitrogen – from a recent dive plus the body's normal amount – can become excessive and cause decompression sickness as the aircraft attains cruising altitude and atmospheric (cabin) pressure decreases. No matter how long or short your holiday, put the heavy (and deep) diving days in the middle. Squeezing in one last dive before catching the flight out is clearly unwise and the risk can be considerable. Use the last day for shopping, sight-seeing, or local culture appreciation. If you must dive then make it a relaxing snorkelling outing.

CLOTHING

What to Wear and When

As Comoros is an Islamic country it is advisable to adhere to certain of the local customs, specifically with regard to women travellers. Revealing clothing, shorts, slacks and sleeveless dresses should not be worn away from resort hotels. It is advisable for women to dress relatively conservatively when sightseeing around the islands. Light cool clothing should be worn during the day in both summer and winter. A jacket and tie may be required for hotel restaurants and the casino in the evenings. The up-market hotels specialise in theme dinners and evenings and visitors are advised to pack clothing for these special events, for example, pirates' evening, tropical evening. Take a sweater for evenings and the higher elevations all year round. In the rainy season you'll need an umbrella and a light, maybe plastic, raincoat. Dress is informal and smart casual for dinner at tourist hotels such as *Le Galawa* and *Itsandra Sun*. A light jacket or sweater might be necessary in the cool season, otherwise sleeveless is adequate.

MAIL

There are post offices in all the main towns. They are generally open Monday to Thursday from 7am to noon and from 3pm to 5pm, Friday from 7am to 11.30am, and on Saturday from 7am to noon. Expect mail to Europe to take at least a week. Post offices are usually crowded and this is where usually polite and reserved locals become a pushing and shoving mass. Use your elbows.

TELEPHONES

If you want to make an outgoing international call through the international operator – dial 10 to get the operator – be prepared to have your patience tested. To check an island number there's a good telephone directory, which will also give you call and postal rates. The directory also covers Mayotte. To telephone Comoros from outside the islands you must dial the international access call followed by the Comoros country code, which is 269.

Telecommunications links in the Comoros are not completely reliable and are very limited, although the islands are now linked to satellite services and there is direct dialling for international calls. Don't expect to communicate easily back home via phone, fax or e-mail, and don't be surprised if the telephones don't work on holidays and weekends. There is a public fax office in Moroni behind the main post office. Outgoing calls should be made through telephone offices or a hotel switchboard as public telephone boxes are few and far between. You can, however, buy telephone cards (*telecarte*) to use in public call boxes. There are no readily accessible e-mail facilities. The country is served by a sparse system of radio relay and high-frequency radio communications stations for inter-island and external communications to Madagascar and Réunion. There is an inter-city high frequency radio and microwave radio relay and international high frequency radio. In an emergency you can try the telephone and fax facilities available at *Le Galawa Beach* and *Itsandra Sun* hotels, but as communication is via satellite, this can be a very expensive option. First check the rates with the hotel switchboard. France Telecom has given the islands access to the Internet, but very few people seem to have the equipment, the money, or the desire to hook up.

MEDIA

Radio and Television

The government-controlled radio station Radio Comoros is the only national radio station. An opposition station called Radio Tropique leads a chequered existence and it has been closed down a number of times by the government. Islanders can tune in to broadcasts from Mayotte Radio, as well as from French TV. BBC World Service and Voice of America are easy to pick up, although frequencies change from time to time.

Newspapers and Magazines

There are no English-language newspapers. The two main weekly papers are *Al Watwan* (state-owned) and *L'Archipel* (independent). The Comoros Constitution does not provide for freedom of the press, but small independent journals do exist along with the semi-official *Al-Watwan*. Independent newspapers often criticise the government, and even *Al-Watwan* has been known to publish commentary critical of the government. Books and foreign newspapers are available from *La Maison du Livre and Nouveautés* in Moroni.

Maps and Guides

Maps of the islands of the Comoros archipelago are not easy to find, and when you do succeed in finding them they are invariably ancient. Luckily, not all that much changes in this part of the world, except for governments. For UK dwellers the London bookshop Stanford's, at 12/14 Long Acre, Covent Garden is the place to try (tel 020-7836-1321; fax 020-7836-0189; e-mail sales@stanfords.co.uk; www. stanfords.co.uk). The French Institut Geographique National (IGN) series

Archipel des Comores covers the archipelago, one 1:50,000 scale map to each island. They cost £8.95 each. Stanford's doesn't always have them all in stock, so you can contact IGN direct at 136 bis, rue de Grenelle, 75700 Paris Cedex, France (www.ign.fr/), write for them to DGTPUH, BP 12, Moroni, Grande Comore, RFI des Comores, or you can buy them in Moroni when you get there, from the Nouveautés bookshop. You should also look for Éditions Baobab's *Archipel des Comores* which also has useful street maps of Moroni, Mutsamudu, and Fomboni. Alternatively, write to Editions Baobab, BP 575, Moroni, Grande Comore, RFI des Comores, to see if they are still handing them out free of charge.

Also free is the only local directory in English (and French), which you might pick up in Moroni from the tourism office, the Direction Générale du Tourisme et de l'Hotellerie (tel 74-4242/3; fax 74-4241). This directory is useful for its list of hotels and diving contacts.

BY AIR

Getting around the islands by air is problematic and depends on when you are in Comoros, as the political situation is always fluid and relations between, for instance, Grande Comore and Anjouan are, unlike the weather, changeable. At the time of writing (mid-2000) the Organisation of African Unity was trying to get the islands of Anjouan and Mohéli to return to the fold of the Federal Islamic Republic, from which they half-heartedly seceded in 1997. After Anjouan and Mohéli seceded the then president, Mohamed Taki Abdulkarim, severed air and sea links with the rebel islands, although travellers could still go there from Grande Comore, but only by way of French Mayotte. Since then this ban has been rescinded and there's an on-off situation. Even though the three islands are politically and governmentally at loggerheads inter-island communication goes on, whether it's official or not.

There's an airfield on each island. On Grande Comore it's at Hahaya, on Anjouan at Ouani, and on Mohéli at Djoiézi, about 2 miles (4 km) east of Fomboni. Airlines flying between islands of the archipelago also seem to come and go in the blink of an eye, and to date nearly half a dozen have tried to make a commercial success of these routes before falling by the wayside. Two airlines now ply the routes. These are **Comores Aviation** (1 Avenue de la Ligue des Pays Arabes, Moroni, Grand Comore; tel 73-3400; fax 73-3401) and **Comores Air Services**. Comores Aviation seems the most together operator, and uses two 17-seater planes to connect all four islands of the archipelago.

Comores Aviation Timetable

On **Monday**, the airline flies from Moroni to Anjouan at 9.30am and then on to Mohéli at 10.10am; and from Moroni to Mohéli at 3pm, returning to Moroni at 5pm. The flight to Anjouan takes 25 minutes, and to Mohéli 20 minutes.

On **Tuesday**, there is a flight from Moroni to Anjouan at 3pm, Anjouan to Mohéli at 4pm, and Mohéli to Moroni at 5pm.

On **Wednesday** it leaves Moroni for Mohéli at 8.30am, then on to Anjouan at 9.10am, returning at 10am; and Mohéli to Moroni at 10.35am, returning at 11.30am. There is also a flight from Mohéli to Mayotte at midday; Mayotte to Mahajanga, Madagascar, at 1.10pm, returning to Mayotte at 2.30pm, and back to

Mohéli at 3.45pm. You can also fly from Mohéli to Anjouan at 4.30pm, returning at 5.15pm.

On **Thursday** it does the Moroni to Mohéli route at 10am, Mohéli to Anjouan at 10.40am, Anjouan back to Moroni at 11.30am; and Moroni to Anjouan at 3pm, returning to Moroni at 5pm.

On **Friday** you can fly from Moroni to Mohéli at 9am, Mohéli to Anjouan at 9.40am, Anjouan to Mohéli at 10.20am and Mohéli to Moroni at 11am.

Finally, on **Saturday** it's Moroni to Mohéli at 8.30am, Mohéli to Anjouan at 9.10am, Anjouan to Mohéli at 9.45am, Mohéli to Moroni at 10.30am and Moroni to Mohéli at 11.30am.

There are no flights on a Sunday. Check with Comores Aviation for any changes to the schedule.

BY ROAD

The bush taxi (*taxi-brousse*) is the transport workhorse of the islands. These are usually canopied Peugeot pick-up utility vehicles which stop to collect and drop off passengers on request. The only other wheeled transport available is from **Tourism Services Comores**, which operates minibuses, or hire vehicles. For details of minibus services and special minibus excursions contact the tourist office in Moroni (tel 74-4242/3; fax 74-4241).

BY SEA

There are ports at Fomboni, Moroni, and Mutsamudu and if the inter-island ferry service is working on the day you want to travel these are where you'll disembark. Access to Anjouan, the subject of an independence dispute, requires prior permission from authorities there, or you risk being refused permission to land. A number of small motorised and sailing ships carry passengers between the islands, but the only way to make use of these is to be on the spot at the port and enquire around. There are usually notices pinned up at the port in Moroni listing services and sailings. The most reliable ferry service is the one which operates throughout the archipelago and Madagascar from Mayotte (see *Mayotte: Getting Around* p.183). A boat can be especially useful to get around Mohéli, where the road system is, to say the least, rudimentary. Local fishermen are usually glad to oblige and will hire you their *galawa* outrigger and their services for a reasonable daily fee. This is never set and will rely on your bargaining skills.

DRIVING

Licences

An international driving licence is required by visitors who want to drive a vehicle in Comoros. You must be 21 years or older, and you must have your licence with you at all times while driving.

ROADS

As in France and Mayotte, you drive on the **right-hand side** of the road. There are about 466 miles (750 km) of roads on the islands, about half tarred, but as in most underdeveloped countries they are narrow and not kept in very good condition. They are badly lit at night so exercise extreme caution when driving after dark. Hire a 4x4 vehicle if you are planning to drive in the interior of Grande Comore, or in the islands of Anjouan and Mohéli, especially in the rainy season.

Fuel

Petrol costs about CF480 (£0.60/US$0.87) a litre, but as the largest island, Grande Comore is only 37 miles (60 km) from top to bottom you shouldn't use much fuel for outings.

VEHICLE RENTAL

To hire a car in Comoros you must be 21 or over and have an international driving licence, which you must have held for at least one year. The same conditions apply to any additional driver. The rental cost is quoted in French francs and is payable in advance, plus insurance excess and petrol. Only Avis and American Express (Amex) charge cards are accepted. Car hire companies offer a vehicle delivery and collection service, but at a cost of about FF70 (£6/US$9), and all vehicles are hired on an unlimited kilometre basis. A Suzuki Jeep will cost you the equivalent of £49-£52/US$72-77 a day, and a small Peugeot from £50-£57.

You can hire a vehicle on arrival at Hahaya International Airport, Grande Comore, through *Avis Rent A Car*, which is open Monday to Sunday from 8am to 5pm (tel 73-3044; fax 73-3054). You can also hire Avis vehicles from the *Le Galawa Beach Hotel*, Mitsamiouli (tel 73-8118; fax 73-3054); and at *Itsandra Hotel* (tel/fax 73-3044). Both these hire facilities are also open Monday to Friday from 8am to 5pm. Avis also offers a chauffeur-driven service which costs an extra FF120 (£12/US$) a day on the standard rental rate (tel 73-8118; fax 73-8132). Avis operates a breakdown recovery service and you should discuss details of this when you hire a vehicle.

Tropic Tours and Travel in Place de Badjanani, Moroni, also hire out vehicles at more competitive rates (tel 73-0202; fax 73-1919). On Mohéli you can try the *Hotel Relais de Singani* (tel 72-0249), and on Anjouan the *Hotel Al-Amal* (tel 71-1580), but the islands are so small and the roads either so bad or non-existent it's better to rely on bush taxis, or walk.

HAZARDS

The main hazards, as everywhere in the Indian Ocean, are free-roaming children and domestic animals. Of the island's road system less than half has recognisable topping, so surfaces can be testing for drivers and potentially dangerous in the rainy season.

Comoros receives only a few thousand tourists a year and while this has a preservative effect on the islands it also means there is a narrower range of accommodation for visitors. South African-based hotel group Sun International owns the only up-market tourist hotels on Grande Comore – the *Le Galawa Beach Hotel and Casino*, on the dry, north-west coast, with a budget option of its adjoining *Maloudja Beach Bungalows*, and the *Itsandra Sun Hotel*.

Le Galawa Beach: Box 1027, Moroni (tel 78-8118; fax 78-8251). 15 miles (25 km) from the airport, is set on the edge of a bay at Mitsamiouli, which once formed part of an ancient Arab Sultanate. It is the only luxury hotel on Grande Comore. All its 182 bedrooms are air-conditioned and overlook lush, tropical gardens and two of the prettiest and safest beaches, as well as some excellent diving sites. Every morning the sun rises from the volcano behind and sets in the sea in front, making for wonderful photographic opportunities. Superb cuisine is combined with daily theme evenings, and there is excellent live entertainment, complemented by a popular casino. Two dining rooms serve breakfast, lunch, dinner and afternoon teas while the *Bahari* restaurant serves a la carte lunches. There is also a pool bar in the middle of the pool, access by two bridges, a beach bar, and a casino bar. The hotel can organise vehicle rental and offers a full laundry service. Take detergent with you to wash drip-dry garments and save on the bill. A mini-club organises daily entertainment for children 2-12 years. A baby-sitting service is also available at a nominal fee. Book 24 hours in advance. Cots and highchairs are available. Sports facilities include two floodlit tennis courts, volley-ball, table tennis, soccer, darts, water aerobics, and petanque (bowls). There is no charge for sailing, canoeing, paddle-skiing, snorkelling, windsurfing, water-skiing, or pedaloes, although you pay extra for scuba-diving, deep-sea fishing, parasailing, cruises, and glass-bottomed boat trips.

Maloudja Beach Bungalows, 300 yards along the beach from Le Galawa, is simply furnished and situated on one of the most beautiful beaches on the island at the heart of a former coconut plantation. If you opt for this budget accommodation you can use all Le Galawa's facilities. There is no telephone and no television, you never have to dress up, and it's perfect for the Robinson Crusoe lifestyle.

The *Itsandra Sun Hotel* (tel 73-2316; fax 73-2309) is perched dramatically on top of a cliff about 4 miles (7 km) north of Moroni, with a postcard view across the Indian Ocean. The hotel has a private cove beach and provides comfortable, friendly and personalised service. This hotel has no sporting or leisure facilities, although there is a casino with slot machines. This is the hotel used by most visitors with business to attend to in Moroni.

For more information contact:

Sun International Indian Ocean Central Reservations: Poste Restante Poste de Flacq, Mauritius (tel 401-1000; fax 401-1111).

Contact Address in Britain: Badgemore House, Gravel Hill, Henley-on-Thames, Oxfordshire RG9 4NR (tel 01491-411222; fax 01491-576194).

Contact Address in France: 12 rue de Castliglione, F-75001 Paris (tel 1-4261-2266; fax 1-4286-8985).

Contact Address in Germany: Feldbergstrasse 8b, Oberursel D-61440 (tel 60171-57071; fax 06171-54149).

Contact Address in Italy: Via Ippodromo 58, I-20151 Milan (tel 02-4820 5000; fax 02-4820 2322).

Contact Address in Spain: Glorieta Marques de Vadillo 6 4° 1, E-28019 Madrid (tel/fax 91-460 6447).

Contact Address in United States: 1415 East Sunrise Boulevard, Fort Lauderdale, Florida 33304 (tel 954-713-2500; fax 954-713-2083).

Other, less grand, hotels on **Grande Comore** include:

Hotel La Grillade: (tel 73-3081; fax 73-3268) on the beachfront road Boulevard de la Corniche, about a mile (2 km) from the centre of Moroni, charges about FF280 per person a night. The hotel will collect you from the airport for an additional charge of FF67, and can organise treks up Mt Karthala and tours of the island.

Hotel Coelacanthe: tel 73-2575.
Hotel Karthala: tel 73-0057; fax 73-0274.
Hotel Les Arcades: tel 73-2847; fax 73-2846.
Moifaka Studio Hotel: tel 73-1556; fax 73-0382.

Pensions offer the cheapest accommodation. Three to try are:

Pension Zilimadjou: tel 73-1696.
Pension Barakat: tel 73-0436.
Pension Kohinoor: tel 73-2808.

Accommodation on Anjouan

Hotel Al-Amal: Mutsamudu (tel/fax 71-1580).
Moya Beach Hotel: at Moya (tel 71-1433).

Accommodation on Mohéli

Hotel Relais de Singani: Fomboni (tel 72-0249). On the beach facing the Mohéli Marine Reserve is a tiny complex of 10 bungalows for rent. For more information contact Jean-Marc Heintz, general manager and chief pilot of Comores Aviation (1 rue de la Ligue des Pays Arabes, Moroni; tel 73-3400; fax 73-3401). The postal address is BP 1674, Moroni, RFI des Comores.

If you are not on an all-in package holiday bear in mind that your hotel bill will be swollen at the end of your stay by a CF1,000 (£1.24/$1.83) a night bed levy claimed by the government. This applies to both adults and children.

Budget Accommodation

Unless you are really prepared to rough it, budget travel is recommended only for the truly stoic and unsqueamish. This is an extremely poor country, one of the poorest in the world, and facilities are everywhere basic in the extreme. Although there are no **camping** sites or facilities, there are no restrictions on pitching a tent and you can camp anywhere. Beach huts or *paillotes* dotted along the coast of Grand Comore are available through the agency *Indian Ocean Exhibition* in Moroni. Guest houses are a further option, but they don't advertise and are difficult to find. To locate one, check with the tourism office in Moroni or, probably better, strike up a conversation with a waiter at one of the main hotels. There are simple shelters (*gites*) on the slopes of Mt Karthala which you can use to overnight in while you tackle the climb.

Eating and Drinking

CUISINE

Comorian food would be fairly bland without the range of assertive sauces that accompany everything from the popular battered fried bananas to chicken barbecued over an open fire. Every household has its own speciality sauce, calling on various spices and chillies, and so does every island. On Grande Comore expect plenty of the island's famed nutmeg; on Mohéli they prefer the taste of vanilla and black peppercorns; on Anjouan – renowned for its volcanic goat stew – you'll get plenty of chillies, as well as cinnamon and cloves, in your sauce. Bananas grow wild throughout Comoros and, with rice, are a staple of all poor families, which means most households. Comoros used to be self-sufficient in rice but now has to import most of its requirements. There are two reasons for this: one is the rapidly expanding population, the other the short-sighted economic policies of President Ahmed Abdallah during his reign in the 1980s. The president ignored World Bank advice to impose tariffs and domestic taxes on imported rice and joined with vanilla growers in resisting international pressure to turn over vanilla-producing land to corn and rice crops for local consumption. President Abdallah's import-export firm was heavily involved in vanilla exports, as well as in the importation of Far Eastern rice at three times its price at source.

As this is a Muslim country pork is taboo; beef, being largely imported from Madagascar and mainland Africa, is expensive and therefore not common; sheep wear the wrong coats for the tropics and don't thrive, so don't expect local lamb chops or mutton legs; goat and chicken are the usual offerings for meat eaters, supplemented by a bewildering variety of fish and seafood from the bountiful waters around the islands. Parrotfish, grouper, marlin, shark and tuna are popular. If you are not put off by the suckers on the tentacles, octopus with chilli sauce is a dish to remember; if you are, you might consider the less in-your-face squid, which has a similar taste and texture. Another treat is langoustine in vanilla sauce or, less expensive, fish or chicken cooked in the coconut cream the islanders use to give a velvety lift to any dish, even plain rice. At a pinch, you can get a curry or even a plate of couscous. All this, of course, relates to food eaten by Comorians at home and that dished up in typical island restaurants. There are not many of these and the few there are tend to attract none but the most gastronomically adventurous.

For slap-up meals there's really only one place and that's *Le Galawa Beach Hotel* on Grande Comore (tel 78-8118; fax 78-8251), where you don't have to be a resident to tuck into their wonderful buffet dinners. Their restaurants and casino are the only facilities you can use if you are not staying there, or at the hotel's Maloudja Beach bungalows. As there are few local restaurants the hotel has perfected the art of the theme evening with Comorian cuisine on the menu every Thursday. Snack on taro roots before tucking into the catch of the day prepared in cassava leaves, or a briyani with island spices. Other theme nights feature such enticements as freshly caught dorado served with tomato and chilli sauce, prawns from Madagascar, calamari in lemon juice, parrotfish wrapped in banana leaves, and smoked marlin. There are also French and Italian menus at gastronomic evenings. The hotel is also renowned for its luxurious picnic baskets, available for guests going out hiking, diving, or sailing.

If neither up-market dining nor venturing into a dubious Comorian eaterie appeals, the middle path is to eat in the dining-room or restaurant of a local hotel, but choice here is limited. On Grande Comore check out the menus at the *Hotel les Arcades* (tel 73-2847; fax 73-2846); the *Hotel Karthala* (tel 73-0057; fax 73-0274); and the *La Grillade* restaurant on Boulevard de la Corniche (tel 73-3081; fax 73-3268). On Anjouan, the *Moya Beach Hotel* (tel

71-1433), is noted for seafood and fish dishes, which must be booked in advance if you are not a resident. In Mutsamudu try the *Hotel Al-Amal* (tel/fax 71-1580), and the *La Paillotte Restaurant*, which is on the beachfront road near the Hotel Al-Amal, and has a reputation for serving up some of the best food in Comoros.

Fruitarians will have no problem following their regimes on the islands, so long as they especially like coconuts, pineapples, mangoes, and other exotic tropical fruits. Remember that the long, fat bananas are bland and used for cooking, and that the smaller, yellow variety are the sweet ones. Vegetarians can ask for any meal minus the meat and will find that plenty of leafy greens are used in salads, with vegetables as accompaniments. Island tomatoes are particularly luscious. Long French loaves are still baked fresh every day in Moroni, Grande Comore, in Mutsamudu, Anjouan, and in Fomboni, on Mohéli. Comorians are fond of sticky, sweet pastries and, if you also have a sweet tooth, you'll find a good selection stuffed with spiced fruit in the area around the Volo-Volo market on Grande Comore.

DRINKING

Comoros should effectively be a nation of Muslim teetotallers, with both religious and official governmental sanctions in place against the use of alcohol. As mentioned elsewhere (see *Crime and Safety* p.248) it's an offence for visitors to give, sell or offer alcohol to a Comorian, but this prohibition doesn't seem to take into account the case of a Comorian buying it, or making it, for himself. This being so you'll see locals slipping into nondescript stores and shacks doubling as bars and beer halls. As with most other things on the islands tolerance is the key word. Beer is the most popular (legal) drink, but it's expensive as it is all imported, mainly as Castle lager from South Africa. Decent wine is even more expensive as this is also imported, from France and South Africa. Ditto spirits. Fruit juices are the islands' saving grace for the purse or wallet-watcher, made from a welter of delicious fresh tropical fruit – but decline the ice cubes for health reasons. As all travellers know, where you find palm trees throughout the world you find some sort of local knock-out drop made from the fermented sap. In Comoros, lax Muslim villagers favour palm wine and they produce a brew that can blow your socks off. If you try it, cancel the rest of your day.

Entertainment

For visitors who enjoy an evening's lubricated relaxation the main source is *Le Galawa Hotel*, on Grande Comore, which boasts three bars, a casino, film shows and slide presentations, a live band, with dancing every night, and live entertainment, including displays of Comorian dancing in the restaurant or on the beach. Comorians love to dance and this is their main form of entertainment in a country where the only cinema in the capital, Moroni, has closed down and where, in the rural areas, television is unknown and the nearest thing to a night-club is a palm frond shack illegally selling palm wine. The islands of the archipelago have absorbed a variety of cultural and musical influences from East Africa, the Arab states of the Middle East, Madagascar, and southern India. As a result there is a remarkably wide range of musical styles. Musicians in the islands have been combining traditional sounds and themes in a modern idiom to produce some fascinating music. Traditional instruments used include gongs, drums, tambourines, rattles, oboes, zithers, and five-stringed lutes. Shirontro is a well-known singer and instrumentalist from Anjouan. A CD you might enjoy is *Comores: Musiques traditionnelles de l'ile d'Anjouan.* You can buy it in Comoros, or if it's sold out, you can order it from Inedit in Paris (tel 1-4544 7230). Other island favourites are Halid and Abou's CD called *Tsass*, and Abou Chihabi's *Folkomor Ocean.*

Casinos. *Le Galawa Sun*, Mitsamiouli (tel 73-8118/9; fax 73-8251); *Itsandra Sun Hotel*, Moroni, has a slot casino (tel 73-1316/2232).

FLORA AND FAUNA

FLORA

Rainforests the world over are rapidly coming under the axe, with dire results for their delicate eco-systems. The deforestation of Comoros is also under way, but at a slower pace and it is still possible to wander through the tropical rainforests on Grande Comore, Mohéli and Anjouan and marvel at **giant ferns** and 66 ft (20 m) **cycad palms, camphor, takamaka** and **wild fig trees**, in lush vegetation harbouring several varieties of **wild orchids** and other dazzling flowers.

The rainforest on Mt Karthala is a belt halfway up the volcano's slopes, before it thins out into stunted tree cover and heathland. As the most densely populated of the islands (see *People* p.222) Anjouan's eco-system is the one most under pressure in Comoros. Villagers practising the age-old slash and burn technique to clear more land for food crops and to gather wood for fuel are having a serious impact on indigenous forests. In the 15-year period to 1986 alone Anjouan lost 73% of its natural forest, and more than half of Mohéli's also vanished. There's still enough left for them to recover if the government takes a firmer stand on the issue, but island ecology is not exactly at the top of any political agenda. One previously unconsidered result of haphazard deforestation which might jog the state's elbow is the effect it is having on watersheds and soil stability. In 1925, Anjouan had 45 permanent rivers; in 1992, only 11 still ran. As the soil erosion worsens with unregulated deforestation some rivers run red with eroded soil which is carried out to sea to sink in a smothering blanket over the coral reefs. This is something that is gaining notice as the reefs and the waters around them are the designated number one playground for the tourists the government is striving to attract. The wonderful fragrances that scent the air almost wherever you walk come largely from cultivated spices such as cinnamon, cloves, ylang-ylang, coffee, and vanilla, as well as a variety of introduced garden plants and flowers which thrive in their foster homes, among them jasmine, honeysuckle, lemon grass, gardenia, and roses.

FAUNA

Animal life in Comoros is not abundant, but it does have several species which are either unique to the archipelago or rarely found elsewhere. The famous **coelacanth**, a fish once thought to be extinct, is very much alive in Comorian waters, **Livingstone's flying fox** is found nowhere else in the world, and several varieties of insects, butterflies and more than a dozen bird species are unique to the islands. Sadly, many of these species are now threatened with extinction.

Over the centuries settlers, traders and other visitors have let loose a number of animals on the islands which, although not indigenous, have adapted to the point where they are now an accepted part of the local fauna. The brown lemur and the mongoose lemur, or *maki*, were early imports from Madagascar. Genet and civet cats, elephant shrews and the mongoose were later arrivals. The mongoose was let loose to kill off poisonous snakes, a job it did with such efficiency that today there are only a few harmless snakes left on the islands. Other common reptiles are chameleons, lizards and gekkos.

THE COELACANTH

It's been called the greatest fishing story ever told. It covers several decades and countries, beginning in South Africa in 1938 with a find hailed as the most significant zoological discovery of the century, and continuing to this day on Comoros. The creature that caused the scientific stir was the coelacanth, a fish known from the fossil record to have swum in ancient seas at least 400-milion years ago, but likewise thought to have become extinct some 70-million years ago. The excitement started when a fish unlike any even seen before was brought into East London by a trawler and given to the local museum. It proved to be what was soon known as a 'fossil fish' and 'Old Fourlegs' because of its stumpy leg-like fins – the first recognised coelacanth. No one knew at the time that fishermen in Comoros had been pulling these 5 ft (1.5 m) prehistoric fish they called *gombessa* live from the waters around Anjouan and Grande Comore for a long time. They were not prized in any way and were regarded as poor eating. Eventually news of a second coelacanth came to ears of the international scientific community. In 1952, one was hauled up from the depths off Anjouan and since then Comoros has become the coelacanth capital of the world. So many have now been caught, dissected and analysed that their evolutionary role is no longer the mystery it was in 1938, when it was thought by some to be the 'missing link' in the evolution of land vertebrates. Coelacanths live at depths of 492-1,312 ft (150-400 m) off steep, rocky shores, so it's unlikely you'll ever spot one while you are snorkelling or scuba-diving. To get up close to one of these intriguing fossil fish on Grande Comore go to the Musée des Comores, the Centre Nationale de Documentation et Recherche Scientifique (CNDRS), in Moroni (tel 73-3990), where they have a specimen caught in 1985, or to the boathouse at the Island Ventures dive centre, Le Galawa Beach Hotel, at Mitsamiouli. Their coelacanth was landed in 1995.

FRUIT BATS

Three kinds of fruit bat are found in Comoros. Two of these are the related **Livingstone's flying fox** (*Pteropus livingstonii*) and the **Comoros flying fox** (*Pteropus seychellensis comorensis*); the third is the entirely nocturnal **Comoros roussette** (*Rousettus obliviosus*), which takes its Latin name from the fact that it was never seen, and thus forgotten.

Livingstone's flying fox is the largest and rarest of these bats. Apart from the fact that this monster has a wingspan of up to 5 ft (1.4 m), you can't mistake its round 'Mickey Mouse' ears. It weighs around 247 ounces (700 g) and has a characteristic slow wing-beat when flying, they glide frequently and also soar on thermals. They live in upland forests on the islands of Anjouan and Mohéli, roosting in steep sided valleys and are rarely seen at low altitudes. The major threat to Livingstone's flying fox is the loss of the upland forest that provides roosting and food. All roosts sites are either in or close to natural forest. These fruit bats feed on a wide range of food items and loss of forest habitat not only reduces the total amount of food available throughout the entire year, but may also result in periods when key food items are absent. Livingstone's flying fox does not adapt well to secondary forest and cultivation, unlike the common Comoros flying fox. Since 1925, more than 80% of the Anjouan upland forest has been destroyed, and bat roosting sites have been particularly hard hit.

The Comoros flying fox is smaller and more common than Livingstone's flying fox. It is found on all the islands. It has a wingspan of about 3 ft (1 m) and weighs about 16 ounces (450 g). They can be easily distinguished by their yellow head and shoulders, pointed ears and narrow wing profile. It roosts from sea level up to 2,625 ft (800 m), and roosts of 500 to 2,000 bats have been counted.

The Comoros roussette is much smaller than either of the other two bats. It weighs about 2 ounces (45 g) and has a wingspan of 1.5 ft (0.45 m). Little is known about the ecology of this bat, which has been caught in forests on Grande Comore, Mohéli and Anjouan.

If you would like more information about these misunderstood animals contact **Action Comores**. This is a voluntary conservation organisation working in the islands with the primary objective of helping to alleviate environmental problems through scientific research, direct conservation and environmental education. Action Comores has visited the Comoros every year since 1992 (c/o Will Trewhella, The Old Rectory, Stansfield, Suffolk CO10 8LT; e-mail Will.Trewhella@Nottingham.ac.uk).

MARINE TURTLES

Comoros is home to a large population of green turtles (*Chelonia mydas*), which have breeding sites on the southern coast and on Mohéli's offshore islets. Ecologists say the importance of this area for green turtles has not yet been fully recognised, although the establishment of Mohéli's marine park is a concrete step. The catching and slaughtering of turtles is still widespread, even though they are officially protected. The marine turtle is as fast and elegant in the sea as fish, whales and penguins, but on land it is clumsy and slow, and this is where females are at the mercy of turtle hunters when they come out of the sea to lay their eggs. Between December and March each year large numbers of female turtles lay their eggs on Mohéli. Nesting mainly occurs at full moon, which makes breeding females doubly vulnerable to human poachers. The turtles are found by the tracks they leave in the sand to and from their nests. This makes it easy to find and empty the nests of eggs or to catch a turtle on the beach. Green turtles, which can weigh more than 220 lbs (100 kg), are immobilised by overturning them. As they are too big to fit into traditional outrigger pirogues the turtles are butchered on the beach and only the meat and eggs are taken away.

BIRD WATCHING

The Comoros islands shelter more than 20 endemic birds, most of which you'll find on Grande Comore. That's not a lot in birding terms but a total of about 54 bird species should get twitchers' juices flowing.

Grande Comore

Endemic birds are the **Comoro pigeon, Karthala Scops owl, Comoro cuckoo-roller, Comoro drongo, Comoro thrush, Comoro bulbul, Humblot's flycatcher, Comoro cuckoo shrike, Kirk's white-eye, Karthala white-eye, Comoro brush warbler, Comoro green sunbird**, and the **Comoro fody**. All of these can be found on Mt Karthala, but an overnight stop on the upper slopes is necessary if you want to spot the Karthala Scops owl and the Karthala white-eye. The owl is common in forests near ruins on the open grassland area known as La Convalescence. Search for the white-eye in the forests and heathland on the way to the summit of the volcano. You are most likely to find the Comoro drongo, least common of endemics, on the way to the volcano crater from the village of Kourani, to the south.

Mohéli

Endemic birds are the **Comoro blue vanga, Benson's brush warbler**, and the **Comoro green pigeon**. From Fomboni, take any trail leading to the island's distinctive forested ridge. Each time the track forks, follow the higher path. The three local endemic birds are easy to see.

Anjouan

Endemic birds are the rare **Anjouan Scops owl**, and the **Anjouan sunbird**. The sunbird is common, and can be seen just about everywhere. The little brown owl is more elusive. Take a bush taxi from Mutsamudu to Dindi, near Tsimbeo, where the steep, forested slopes above Dindi and the area around Lake Dzialandzé are the best places to spot the owl, which is an inquisitive creature and can often be heard calling during the day, a long drawn-out whistle. It's best to take a local guide who knows both the area and the bird, known locally as *bandanga*. Bird-lovers who can read French should carry a copy of *Les Oiseaux des Comoros* by Michel Louette (1998, Musée Royal de l'Afrique Centrale, Tervuren).

NATIONAL PARKS

There are only two national parks in the Comoros, one a marine reserve for the protection of sea turtles and other marine life around the little island of Mohéli. Visits can be arranged from Nioumachoua on Mohéli. The other national park is also a marine reserve. It is situated off the shore at Le Galawa Beach Hotel, on Grande Comore.

SPORT AND RECREATION

DIVING

There are plenty of opportunities for the visitor who wants to do more than simply soak up the sun on a dazzling beach. Without doubt, the premier sporting attraction is scuba-diving. There's not much fringing coral reef around the islands, but what there is is usually in top-notch condition as the Comoros has not (yet) experienced the tourist boom of many of the neighbouring Indian Ocean island states. The real diving, therefore, is done over steep and even vertical drop-offs in water temperatures averaging around 81°F (27°C) and visibility of up to 55 yards (50 m). The **best time to go** for all-round diving is between April and November.

You don't have a choice when it comes to island dive operators and centres. Luckily, the only commercial dive centre is run by highly qualified English and French-speaking operators who know what they're about and can look after divers from snorkellers and beginners to latter-day Cousteaus. The operation run by *Island Ventures* is a PADI Gold Palm 5-star dive centre, situated at *Le Galawa Beach Hotel* on the northern end of the island and offering boat diving to more than 30 different sites, including the long-range wall and off-shore dives for which the Comoros is famous. A single dive costs FF230 (£21/$31). PADI and NAUI scuba training courses ranging from the Discover Scuba Diving Course through to Speciality Courses (environmental, wreck, photographic and night diving) are offered. A PADI diving course costs FF500 (£46/$69), an open-water course FF2,500, and an advanced open-water course FF1,700 (£158/$236). There is a surcharge of FF150-300 for long-range dives. The centre has 28 full sets of scuba gear as well as a selection of wetsuits ranging from extra small to extra large. Fins and masks are also available for hire. To hire scuba gear you'll pay FF65 (£6/$9). There is no charge for wetsuit hire. Speciality diving courses include wreck diver and deep diver (FF1,775 each), night diver (FF1,445) and naturalist and photographic diver (FF1,115).

There are two types of diving in Comoros, one on shallow, gently sloping reefs, consisting mainly of hard corals with gullies, cracks and overhangs, where you will see vast schools of smaller reef fish and plenty of interesting reef life that divers, especially photographers will enjoy – **leaf-fish**, **frogfish**, **stonefish**, **scorpionfish**, **lionfish**, and **nudibranchs**. The hard corals are magnificent and areas of reef are carpeted in short purple-blue soft corals.

The second type of diving is off the wall. Most wall dives entail a boat ride of an hour or two. **Dolphins** frequently escort the boat to the dive. **Giant tuna**, **sharks**, **mantas**, **sailfish**, **marlin** and **whale sharks** are possible sightings. For all dives proof of certification is necessary. Open-water qualification is fine for most dives; advanced diver qualification is necessary for Banc Vailheu.

THE BEST DIVE SITES

Some great dive sites off Grande Comore include:
Banc Vailheu: This is undoubtedly the premier dive site in the Comoros. A 2¹/2-hour boat trip from the dive centre will bring you to this underwater seamount 32 nautical miles (59 km) from *Le Galawa Beach Hotel* and 12 nm (22 km) off

Moroni on the western side of the island. The seamount rises from 6,562 ft (2,000 m) to a mere 33 ft (10 m) from the surface. The top is flat and the north and western edges form a sheer drop-off which runs for miles. From 66 ft (20 m) it becomes a vertical cliff dropping down to unplumbed depths. Visibility here is outstanding and a gentle current pulls you along the wall. Small shallow caves with large black coral trees punctuate the sheer drop. Giant dogtooth, tuna, sharks, schools of rainbow runners and kingfish are often encountered and mantas, whale sharks and hammerhead sharks are occasionally seen. Clownfish, enormous honeycomb morays and snow-white stonefish inhabit a pristine coral garden of hard and soft corals on the wall at 66-33 ft (20-10 m). A safety stop is done gently drifting along at 10 ft (3 m). This is a full-day, 2-tank excursion, with lunch served on board.

Hahaya Wall: A 60-minute boat ride from the centre brings you to Hahaya Wall, a true wall dive with the drop-off starting only 33 ft (10 m) from the shore. As this site is on the sheltered western side of the island, the numerous table and other hard corals are in excellent condition. Angelfish, butterflyfish, parrotfish, and schools of goldies abound. Gorgonian fans and amphora sponges dot the steeply sloping and at times sheer reefwall. Large gamefish are often spotted. A safety stop can be enjoyed in the shallows on top of the wall, exploring for geometric morays, stonefish and other reef creatures. The current is usually gentle and ideal for a drift dive.

Masiwa Wreck: This 243 ft (74 m) North Sea fishing trawler was sunk as an artificial reef in 1991. It was used by Colonel Bob Dénard to smuggle his mercenaries into the Comoros in 1978 to overthrow the Marxist government of Ali Solih. The wreck lies on the sand 125 ft (38 m) below the surface and can be dived between 39-115 ft (12-35 m). Large fish such as barracuda, tuna and bonito are often sighted, and living in the wreck are numerous lionfish, moray eels, and a brindle bass. A school of batfish usually hovers around the masts. Hard and soft corals are colonising the wreck. A certified wreck diver may do a penetration dive into the holds and superstructure. The wreck is also used for a wreck speciality course by the dive centre. The **Masiwa Wreck** has an interesting history. After the coup the old trawler was used to ferry supplies between the islands. On one such trip the steering mechanism broke and it was left anchored off Mohéli. In 1980 a tropical storm washed *Masiwa* on to the reef where it lay abandoned until staff of Island Ventures found it 10 years later. They towed it to the northern tip of Grande Comore (where their dive centre is located), and sank it to form an artificial reef in a depth of 79 ft (24 m). A subsequent storm pushed the wreck into deeper water, where it now rests on sand at between 39-115 ft (12-35 m).

Other dive sites:

Treasure Cove: Beginners but also enjoyable for qualified divers.
Depth: 33-49 ft (10-15 m).
Situation: Five-minute boat ride from the hotel boathouse.
Description: Mostly hard corals, very large mushroom. Tropical fish in abundance, as well as tame trigger fish.

Coral Gardens: Beginners and qualified divers.

Depth: 33-69 ft (10-21 m).
Situation: Five-minute boat ride east of hotel.
Description: Abundance of hard corals and tropical fish.

Masiwa Reef: Qualified divers only.
Depth: 82-128 ft (25-39 m).
Situation: 10-minute boat ride north-east of the hotel.
Description: Superb corals. Undulating topography. Prolific shell and fish life.

Tsada Beach: Beginners and qualified divers.
Depth: 33-49 ft (10-15 m).
Situation: 10-minute boat ride east of the hotel.
Description: Sandy bottom dotted with coral bommies, or isolated coral clusters. Rays, turtles and lionfish are often seen.

Msanga Drift: Qualified divers only.
Depth: 33-89 ft (10-27 m).
Situation: 20-minute boat ride east of the hotel.
Description: Fingers of lava covered with soft purple corals, surrounded by white sands and coral bommies. Large schools of tropical fish.

Oasis: Qualified divers.
Depth: 66-82 ft (20-25 m).
Situation: 10-minute boat ride west of the hotel.
Description: Vast area of sand with pebbled area covered with anemones, large bubble corals. Abundant shell life, morays, scorpionfish, parrotfish and octopus.

Mosque: Beginners and qualified divers.
Depth: 16-49 ft (5-15 m).
Situation: 15-minute boat ride from the hotel.
Description: Corals, tropical fish, plenty of scorpionfish and a large, tame, honeycomb moray eel.

Shrine: Qualified divers only.
Depth: 59-79 ft (18-24 m).
Situation: 10-minute boat ride north-east of the hotel.
Description: A feast of corals.

Lac Salé: Qualified divers only.
Depth: 16-82 ft (5-25 m).
Situation: 25-minute boat ride east of the hotel.
Description: Fingers of lava covered with plate coral. Large variety of moray eels. Turtles often sighted.

Parrot Point: Qualified divers only.
Depth: 33-82 ft (10-25 m) on the edge of a drop-off.
Situation: 35-minute boat ride east of the hotel.
Description: Fantastic dive with a wide variety of life, including manta rays, large reef and game fish, as well as turtles.

Njamba: Qualified divers only.
Depth: 33-82 ft (10-25 m).
Situation: 40-minute boat ride east of the hotel.
Description: Excellent drift dive with a large variety of big fish.

Chamoni: Qualified divers only.
Depth: 33-115 ft (10-35 m).
Situation: 2-hour boat ride south-east of the hotel. There's a surcharge for this
    excursion, which includes food and drink for two meals, as departure is before
    breakfast and returns at 4.30pm. Two dives are done on this outing, with a
    picnic lunch on Chamoni beach.
Description: Feast of plate corals on lava flows and fantastic fish life.

Aquarium: Beginners and qualified divers.
Depth: 33-59 ft (10-18 m).
Situation: 10-minute boat ride west of the hotel.
Description: Sandy bottom covered with coral bommies. Abundance of tropical
    fish, electric rays, eels and octopus.

Ingambwe: Qualified divers only.
Depth: 66-82 ft (20-25 m).
Situation: 10-minute boat ride west of the hotel.
Description: Abundance of marine life, including scorpionfish, stonefish, moray
    eels and a variety of shrimp.

Fassi: Qualified divers only.
Depth: 33-82ft (10-25 m).
Situation: 15-minute boat ride.
Description: Fingers of coral extending into deep water with scattered coral
    bommies. Scorpionfish, stingrays, electric eels and a variety of moray eels.

Castle Rock Bommies: Beginners and qualified divers.
Depth: 16-82 ft (5-25 m).
Situation: 30-minute boat ride south of the hotel.
Description: Several outcrops of hard and soft corals. Plenty marine life,
    including eels, lionfish, scorpionfish and rays. Excellent for photography.

Beneath the Castle: Qualified divers only - Multi-level.
Depth: 33-99 ft (10-30 m) and beyond.
Situation: 30-minute boat ride.
Description: 45 degree sloping sand wall with several outcrops of coral, sponge
    bowls and a 16 ft (5 m) wall.

Abyss: Advanced divers only - Multi-level.
Depth: 16-128 ft (5-39 m).
Situation: 45-minute boat ride south of the hotel.
Description: A wall beginning at 82 ft (25 m), dropping into the unknown. Divers
    drift along the Gorgonian-covered wall and then slowly ascend a lava boulder
    plain and a shallow wall abundant with tropical fish.

Black Coral Cave: Qualified divers only - Multi-level.
Depth: 16-82 ft (5-25 m).
Situation: 45-minute boat ride south of the hotel.
Description: Beautiful coral reef, with plenty of hard corals. This reef is close to shore and drops off dramatically to 59 ft (18 m), with a small cave filled with black coral. A finger of lava encrusted with magnificent coral formations extends into the depths.

President's Palace (dived only with special permission from authorities) Qualified divers only - Multi-level.
Depth: 16-128 ft (5-39 m).
Situation: In front of the government buildings in Moroni. A 45-minute bus ride from the hotel.
Description: Shore entry with a 109 yard (100 m) swim. There are beautiful hard and soft corals, anemones and plenty of fish life. Varying topography with caves and a drop off.

Coelacanth: Qualified divers only - Multi-level.
Depth: 33-128 ft (10-39 m).
Situation: In front of the *Coelacanthe Hotel*, Moroni. A 45-minute bus ride.
Description: Shore entry, with the drop-off only 16 yards (15 m) from the shore. Large plate corals, huge bowl sponges and anemones. Hard and soft corals.

The Big Blue: Advanced divers only.
Depth: 115 ft (35 m).
Description: A true blue drift dive.

These dive sites have been recently opened up by Island Ventures:
Sponge: An advanced dive about 20 minutes from the boathouse on the western side of the island. A basic wall/slope dive. Dive limited to 98 ft (30 m) but it slopes down much further. Nice dive with the possibility of seeing game-fish such as kingfish, tuna and barracuda.
   Fisherman's Alley: A shallow dive with maximum depth of 49 ft (15 m). A 10-15 minute boat ride. Lots of such smaller fish as paperfish, pipefish, and nudibranch.
   Through the Castle: Very shallow dive, about 25-30 minutes boat ride. Lots of swim-throughs, overhangs and boulders. Lots of the smaller fish life, but an exciting dive. Highly recommended.

Island Ventures offers a sail-away dive package on a 3-cabin, 6-berth catamaran to dive the uninhabited islets around Mohéli, 50 nautical miles (93 km) south of Grande Comore. The diving here is generally better and the marine life more prolific than that close to the main island. For more information contact Ronnie Bogatie or Mandy Latimore at Island Ventures head office in Johannesburg, South Africa (tel 11-285 2513; e-mail diving@wlh.co.za).

FISHING

Deep-sea angling for big-game fish is a relatively new sport in the Comoros, which is good news for enthusiasts as the waters have still to be unlocked by the pros who are already hooking records in Seychelles and Mauritius. Fishing is best from mid-September to the end of May, when the waters teem with **barracuda, wahoo, dorado, Job, tuna, bonito** and **kingfish**. Gamefish such as **marlin** are best found between November and May, **sailfish** between January and June. The best operators, with fully equipped boats, are on call through *Le Galawa Beach Hotel*. Fun inshore fishing can be enjoyed by joining local fishermen in their dug-out *galawa* outrigger canoes. Sail-boats and canoes are available to hire around the port areas of Grande Comore, Anjouan and Mohéli, but if you fancy this option it's advisable to also hire a fisherman to guide and help you as the currents around some parts of the archipelago are extremely tricky.

OTHER WATERSPORTS

Aqua-sports are usually included in a package holiday, and you can enjoy water-skiing, snorkelling, canoeing, paddle-skiing, pedaloes, sailing and windsurfing free of charge if you are staying at one of the major hotels. You pay extra for motorised watersports such as parasailing, snorkelling and scuba-diving boat cruises. For the less energetic there are sunset and champagne cruises, short island cruises by catamaran, one-hour glass-bottom boat excursions, and sailaway packages, one of which includes a shopping expedition to Moroni (see *Shopping*).

HIKING AND SCRAMBLING

Hiking is like any other activity in Comoros – to get the best out of it you really need a guide. Even if most of the maps available were not inadequate for walkers it is still quite difficult to find your way around as a directional signboard seems to be rarer than a coelacanth.

The obvious goal for any serious hiker is the beckoning topmost rim of Mt Karthala, the volcano whose 7,746 ft (2,361 m) bulk dominates the centre of the island. Mt Karthala is still active, and last erupted in 1977 when it erased most of the west coast village of Singani, but left enough volcanic ash for the locals to level and turn into a popular football field. Main hiking routes to the summit start from M'vouni village and Boboni, south of Moroni. Best time to climb the mountain is between April and November, when the slopes are dry. Super-fit hikers have done the climb in a single day, 5 hours up from Boboni and 7 hours down to M'vouni, but this is not recommended. Allow for an overnight camp at the summit. You'll have to trek in your tent, bed and other equipment if you don't hire a guide – CF20,000 (£25/$36) a day – and/or porter.

Rather than haggle and hassle when you get to the mountain hire a guide and a porter at the village of Bomboni or sign up for an organised guided climb in Moroni at the *Mt Karthala Hotel*, or at *Le Galawa Beach Hotel*, where you'll find a **Karthala Expedition** on offer from Tourism Services Comores (TSC), who will get you up and down, with an all-found camp at the summit. Tents, sleeping bags, food and drinks are provided. You depart early from Le Galawa Beach Hotel and drive to M'vouni village at the foot of the volcano. Head for the top, with light snacks and refreshment on the way. You'll reach the top after a strenuous 7-8 hour walk. Tramp around the rim and view the fascinating crater with its green sulphurous lake. Your guide and porters will pitch the tents. A bonfire will warm you up as the sun sinks and freshly barbecued food will help to restore your energy levels. This tour is only for the extremely fit and energetic. Cost of the expedition is open to negotiation and depends on how many hikers sign up for the trip.

TSC can also arrange to take you on walks to the **Three Craters** – Lamnavaliya, Chaine du Dragon and Lac Salé – the **La Grille Rainforest** in the north, a 6-hour halfway-house trip up the volcano to the **Karthala Rainforest** at around 4,921 ft (1,500 m). As well as wild orchids you should also see many of the endemic birds of Grande Comore flitting around the rainforest.

Mohéli is an easier place for the solo hiker to get around. There's not so much ground to cover – the island is 30 miles x 11 miles (48 km x 18 km) – and there's a busy network of bush taxis to take you to starting points and pick you up when you've completed your day's walk. The sulphurous crater lake of **Dziani Boundouni** at the centre of the island can be reached on a day walk from the capital, Fomboni, and other walks will take you through woods and among plantations and waterfalls. Visitors, however, are advised to check the latest travel advice from an official organisation, such as an embassy (or the State Department or Foreign Office websites see p.48), before embarking on a trip to either Mohéli or Anjouan.

Mountainous Anjouan is tough walking territory but the effort is repaid by the island's wealth of lakes, rivers, waterfalls, and forested areas. A good day's stretch from Bambao on the east coast, or alternatively, from the capital Mutsamudu, or Pomoni on the south coast, will take you to the summit of the highest peak on Anjouan, **Mt Ntingui** at 5,233 ft (1,595 m). The route from Bambao will take you half-way up past the crater lake of **Dzialaoutsounga** and a little higher past Lac Dzialandzé. The stiffest hike on the island is from **Lac Dzialandzé** back to Mutsamudu and it is almost impossible to do this without a local guide to break trail. The *Hotel Al-Amal* in Mutsamudu is the best place to find a guide, as it's the best place to find out just about anything else on Anjouan.

Opening Hours: Shops are generally open from 8am to noon and 2pm to 4pm Monday to Thursday; 8am to 11am on Friday; and from 9am to 1pm on Saturday.

GIFTS AND SOUVENIRS

Shopping in the old Arab-style markets and medinas of Moroni is a colourful and exciting experience. It can also be expensive, unless you are a seasoned haggler. It's a good idea to pinpoint the type of souvenirs or gifts you like early on in your stay, find out in which village they are made and then wait until you visit the place in your wanderings. This way you'll not only find a better choice, but the prices will have scaled down considerably. If you don't find the rural craftsmen who make what you fancy you can always go back to the markets at the end of your holiday. The old market in the ancient Mtsangani quarter down from the Post Office in Moroni is a good place to start, even if its only to enjoy the bustle and admire the stalls full of exotic spices, fruits, island vegetables, chillies, coffee and rice. You'll also find a wide selection of *chiromanis*, the colourful cotton lengths Comorian women wear with such flair. These are good buys and weigh next to nothing. You'll also find them at other markets, such as the Mtsangani bazaar, and the enormous new Volo-Volo market, on rue Magoudjou, about a mile (2 km) north of the centre of Moroni. Comoros is famous for its intricate gold and silver jewellery, at prices well below those of First World countries. The skills of the Comoros craftsmen who make the delicate jewellery is legendary and you'll find some of the best around the Friday Mosque, near the port. Almost as renowned are the wood-carving skills of the artisans on Grande Comore and Anjouan. Take a bush taxi to Mitsoudjé, about 7 miles (11 km) south of Moroni, to see them at their craft and buy some of their work. Carvings and furniture in *takamaka* wood and rosewood are made at Domoni, on Anjouan. You can also buy games boards made of ebony and coconut palm wood and something that will really puzzle your family and friends, a wooden coconut-peeling chair. Look out for carved and inlaid woodwork. Good examples are chests, panels, *portes-croix* (lecterns), Koran covers, model dug-out *galawa* outrigger canoes, and, if you can afford to buy one and ship it home, the intricately carved Arab doors which are a feature of houses in countries on the old Arab trade routes south from Zanzibar.

Anjouan is known for its interesting raffia dolls, which you can also buy on the other islands, Mohéli for its beautifully embroidered Muslim headwear, the *koffiah* and the *yamatso*, and Itsandra village on Grande Comore for its prayer mats and basketry. Other things to look out for in the shops and markets are embroidered Arab slippers, pottery, incense holders, and exotic spices, such as bundles of cinnamon quills, vanilla, cloves, peppercorns, and nutmeg.

Don't leave without a sample bottle of ylang-ylang oil, used to make French perfume and one of the reasons it is so expensive. You can usually buy this essential oil at your hotel, but rather get it at source where it's cheaper and has the bonus that you'll probably be able to see how the oil is distilled from these fragrant greenish-yellow flowers. Good places to try are Salimani, down the west coast from Moroni, on Grande Comore, Bambao, in the eastern hills of Anjouan, and on the large estates at the eastern end of Mohéli.

If you want to be sure of finding all the right little nooks and crannies of the shopping maze in and around Moroni you might like to take the Tourism Services Comores (TSC) Half-Day Shopping Moroni tour. Visit Moroni, the capital and main trading centre and the typical colourful market at Volo-Volo with its spices and varied souvenirs from Madagascar and Comoros. Walk in the Medina, the old quarter of Moroni, where the call to prayer is heard five times a day from the old Friday Mosque. The mosque was built in 1427, but the minaret was completed only in 1912. You can admire the old dhow port, opposite the mosque, before shopping for the beautiful locally crafted gold and silver jewellery, and other souvenirs and curios. This tour costs CF11,886 (£15/$22) for adults and CF5,547 (£7/$10) for children under 12. You can contact TSC through Le Galawa Beach Hotel (tel 78-8118; fax 78-8251), or the Itsandra Sun Hotel (tel 73-2316; fax 73-2309).

CRIME

Comoros is regarded as an extremely safe country for tourists and the incidence of serious crime is rare. There are tourists who never leave the admittedly magnificent *Le Galawa Hotel*, the country's sole resort hotel, unless it is for a one-day guided bus tour of the capital, Moroni. The adventurous visitor, however, needs to be sensible and realise that young people living in one of the world's poorest countries are not unnaturally tempted by flashy displays of apparent wealth. Petty thieves have their hands chopped off in most Islamic countries, but this extreme form of legal disapproval is not practised in Comoros and petty crime is common. Pick-pocketing, purse snatching, and various types of scams are the most common forms of crime in crowded market areas, beaches and parks. Even during the worst of the political disturbances during coups and other changes of government the main holiday area in the north of Grande Comore has experienced few problems, although visitors are always cautioned to remain vigilant and consult their hotel management before travelling elsewhere on the island. This also applies to the islands of Anjouan and Mohéli, which have experienced tense ongoing rivalry between political factions since early 1997 when these islands seceded from the Comoros Republic. Foreign residents and visitors have not been targeted during outbreaks of civil disorder, but you should avoid political rallies and street demonstrations and maintain security awareness at all times. While the country's troubles seldom affect visitors it's always a good idea to check out the travel advisories put out by the Foreign and Commonwealth Office in the UK and those of the US State Department (see p.48). Bear in mind, though, that these, quite rightly, are always ultra-sensible and cautious. (see also p.80)

DRINK DRUGS AND THE LAW

Drink

It is illegal to drink alcohol in public, and an offence, as well as an insult, to sell, offer, or give alcohol to a Muslim Comorian. There are no restrictions on visitors drinking alcohol, but you should confine this to your hotel bar – if there is one – or imbibe discreetly. Where religious practice is more lax, such as on Mohéli, you might be offered locally tapped palm wine. Do not underestimate its potency, but make sure it's strained through a sieve before you gulp it down.

Drugs

An anti-drug brigade has been formed to assist the 500-strong local police force as Comoros authorities are concerned about the growing trafficking of narcotics in the archipelago, specifically the trafficking of cocaine and heroin from South Africa, Tanzania and Madagascar. Drug dealers are reportedly concentrating on the Comoros islands because of the lack of anti-drug legislation and lax border controls. Drugs dealt in locally – cannabis, Mandrax, Methaqualone and various other drugs in tablet form – are bought not only by 'fringe' people as previously thought by the authorities. A government spokesman says: 'Information available clearly shows that this is no longer a problem of degraded youths, but indeed a real national scourge'. Local adolescent drug users prepare themselves mixtures made up of local plants such as khat and datura, which grow in the wild on the islands. Official reports even note the use of crushed anti-mosquito spirals and aspirin, mixed with ordinary tobacco, as a mind-altering concoction. The anti-drug brigade accuses the authorities of providing little support for its crusade and, in fact, of apparently condoning the trade. Local cannabis is known as Comorian

Gold and, along with hashish from Zanzibar, is widely available on the streets.

The Law

If all this sounds appealing to recreational drug users, bear in mind that foreigners arrested on drug-related charges can expect to go to jail, and local prisons are noted for their lack of proper sanitation, overcrowding, inadequate medical facilities, and poor diet. The Constitution of Comoros does not specify a time limit between arrest and appearance before a magistrate. There are few lawyers in the country, making it difficult to obtain legal representation, and the government does not provide free legal counsel.

TOURIST INFORMATION CENTRES

The tourist office in Comoros is the *Direction Générale du Tourisme et de l'Hotellerie*, BP 97, Moroni, Comoros (tel 74-4242/3; fax 74-4241). You could also try *Cordev Marketing* in Johannesburg, but their information is based largely on that provided by Sun International hotels on Grande Comore. Contact Cordev at 13 Hawthorne Drive, Dalecross, Sandton, Johannesburg, PO Box 784932, Sandton 2146, South Africa (tel 11-783 2070; fax 11-783 4760).

FOREIGN EMBASSIES AND CONSULATES

Australia. Represented by its embassy in Kenya, Riverside Drive, PO Box 39341, Nairobi (tel 44-5034; fax 44-4617).

Britain. Staff are resident in Madagascar and the British Embassy in Antananarivo deals with enquiries relating to the Comoros islands (Lot 11, 1 164 Ter, Alarobia Amboniloha, Antananarivo; tel 20-224-49378; fax 20-224 9381; e-mail ukembant@simicro.mg). Open Monday, Tuesday and Thursday, GMT 4.30am to 9am and 9.30 to 1.30pm, Wednesday from 4.30am to 9.30am, and Friday 4.30am to 11am. There is also an office in Toamasina represented by Seal Tamatave (tel 20-53-32548/69; fax 20-53-33937; e-mail sealtmm@bow.dts.mg). There is also a British Consulate in Moroni, PO Box 986, Moroni (tel/fax 73-3182).

Canada. The Canadian High Commission in Tanzania deals with enquiries relating to the Comoros islands, 38 Mirambo Street, Garden Avenue, Dar es Salaam, PO Box 1022, Dar es Salaam, Tanzania (tel 51-1128317/7; fax 51-116896). The Canadian Embassy in Kenya also represents Comoros, Comcroft House, Haile Selassie Avenue, PO Box 20481, Nairobi, Kenya (tel 214804; fax 216485).

United States. The US closed its embassy in Moroni in 1993 and is now represented by a non-resident ambassador in neighbouring Mauritius. The US embassy in Mauritius is at Rogers House, President John F Kennedy Street, Port Louis (tel 208-2347; fax 208-9534).

DISABLED TRAVELLERS

There is no evidence of discrimination in Comoros against the disabled in the provision of education or other services, but nor is there any legislation in force, or pending, concerning accessibility to public buildings or services for people with disabilities. There is thus no information regarding access and facilities for disabled travellers, but given the nature of the country, it should be assumed that few or no facilities exist. Sun International advise that only the reception and gift shop areas of their hotels are inaccessible for disabled and guests in wheelchairs. Once past these areas disabled/wheelchair guests have complete access to all other facilities at the hotels. There are same-level pathways; ground floor rooms are recommended as there are no specific rooms for the disabled.

USEFUL INFORMATION
Time Zone. Comoros is three hours ahead of GMT, eight hours ahead of Eastern Standard Time, 7 hours behind Australian Eastern Standard Time, and one hour ahead of South Africa.

Electrical Appliances
Electricity is generated by diesel engines, making it among the most expensive in the world, and power cuts occur in Moroni from time to time, but with little or no effect on tourist areas. Power supply is 220 volts AC, at 50 cycles Hertz. European two pin plugs are common, but in the Sun International hotels the South African three-prong plugs are used. In the hotels, adaptors are available, but we recommend that you take your own.

Useful Addresses and Telephone Numbers
Police: Grande Comore (tel 17); Mohéli (tel 72-0137); Anjouan (tel 71-0200).
Hospital: Grande Comore (tel 73-2604); Mohéli (tel 72-0373); Anjouan (tel 71-0034).
Ario: general sales agent for Air Austral and Air Mauritius, BP 1285, Route Magoudjou, Moroni (tel 73-3144; fax 73-0719).
Banque Internationale des Comores (BIC): tel 73-0243; fax 73-0349.
Comores Aviation: 1 rue de la Ligue Des Pays Arabes, BP 1674, Moroni (tel 73-3400; fax 73-3401).
Ministère de l'Intérieur: tel 74-4666.
Tropic Tours: part of highly efficient MauriTours in Mauritius, Place Badjanani, Moroni, Grande Comore (tel 73-0202; fax 73-1919).

PUBLIC HOLIDAYS

FIXED DATES
New Year's Day	1 January
Labour Day	1 May
OAU Celebration Day	25 May
Independence Day	6 July
Christmas Day	25 December

RELIGIOUS FESTIVALS

Muslim festivals are timed according to local sightings of the various phases of the moon and this means the dates change. During the lunar month of Ramadan in the first quarter of the year Muslims are obliged to fast between sunrise and sunset and normal business hours are interrupted. Many restaurants are closed during the day and there may be restrictions on smoking and drinking. As a mark of respect you should not eat, drink or smoke in public during Ramadan. Disruption of business and shopping hours can extend into the following period of Eid-al-Fitr, when the new moon appears to signal the end of the Ramadan fast. This is the biggest celebration in the Islamic calendar.

March	*Eid-al-Kebin*	Feast of the Sacrifice, in honour of Abraham.
April	*Muharam*	The Islamic New Year.
April	*Ashoura or Ashura*	Day honouring martyr Imam Hussein.
June	*Mouloud or Maoulida*	Celebration commemorating the birth of the Prophet Mohammed.
October	*Leilat-al-Meiraj* or *Miradji*	Marks the ascension of Mohammed to heaven.

Comoros also celebrates the following major Islamic holidays when shops may, or may not close.

January	*Lailatul-Baraat.*
May	*Zil Hajj* (Day of Haj).
August	*Rabi-ul-Akir.*
August	*Gyarwin Shareef.*
December	*Miraajun-Nabi.*

EXPLORING COMOROS

GRANDE COMORE (Ngazidja)

Grande Comore, the largest of the three islands of the Federal Islamic Republic of the Comoros is the only one with any recognisable tourist facilities, although even these are still largely at an embryonic stage. If you plan to visit the islands of Anjouan and Mohéli – and you should – you'll undoubtedly have to make your arrangements with operators from this, the main island and seat of government. Grande Comore could be a natural template for most other volcanic islands of the Indian Ocean as like them it has one major coastal road circling the island, two roads which actually cross from east to west, along with a couple which are indeterminate and tail off into tracks or nowhere, and a central volcanic massif which is full of ancient craters and, in this case, a real livewire volcano which is reputedly, at a mile in diameter, the largest active crater in the world. The interior of Grande Comore is virtually *terra incognita* to most visitors and calls for a fair measure of fitness, stickability, and time to penetrate and enjoy the central highlands, which is why if you're short on time you should consider taking one of the organised tours on offer.

MORONI

This, the capital, can rightfully claim to be one of the oldest settlements in the southern hemisphere, especially if there is truth in the legend that King Solomon and the Queen of Sheba were the first tourists to visit nearly 3,000 years ago. Moroni was founded by Arab merchants and retains an intriguing air of its early days, similar to the Arab-Swahili culture of the maritime trading hub Zanzibar and the East African coast with which it is linked. The real flavour of this era is found in the *medina*, or Arab quarter of the town, in Mtsangani, Badjanani, and the old port area around the **Mosquée du Vendredi**, the Friday Mosque.

Moroni has a rich architectural tradition with balconied Arab-style buildings in a maze of narrow streets, alleyways and hidden courtyards, many with beautifully carved ornate wooden doors bearing the geometric and floral designs of Zanzibar's famous doors. Many are studded with the spikes that echo Zanzibar's more tempestuous days when huge spiked door bosses were used to prevent elephants being used as battering rams on them. In the **Iman Shafii quarter**, which bears the name of the founder of the branch of Islam to which local Sunni Muslims belong, there's an Arab inscription carved in stone and dated 1332. On **Badjanani Square**, the Friday Mosque bears the date 1437, although the smaller mosque on the Mtsangani side of the square said to be much older. In Mtsangani, not far from this mosque, is the **blue wooden portal** of what is said to be the oldest house in the medina, and is probably 15th century. Houses in the Arab quarter are usually two to four stories high. Most are without electricity and use candles and paraffin lamps. The medina streets are so narrow you must explore on foot. This is the quarter where you'll find **silversmiths' workshops**.

In the heart of the medina is the **Zawylani Mosque**, whose fretted design reveals a vast green prayer hall. Across the street is the Koranic school for young girls where, squatting on carpets, they learn to memorise verses from the Koran in Arabic. On the seafront is one of the oldest lighthouses in the Indian Ocean, built by Sultan Saïd Moussa in 1487 to guide in the trading dhows at night. In the **boatyard** near the Friday Mosque you can watch men building wooden sailing boats whose design has barely changed since the early days of the seagoing Arab traders.

At the **Musée des Comores**, the Centre Nationale de Documentation et de Recherche Scientifique (CNDRS), you can tour the exhibits on your own or hire an English-speaking guide. Guides also speak French, Italian, and German. Natural history displays feature butterflies and a specimen of the famous coelacanth, birds, butterflies and fish. There are also creative displays of Comorian culture, explaining island traditions, rituals, local behaviour, and daily

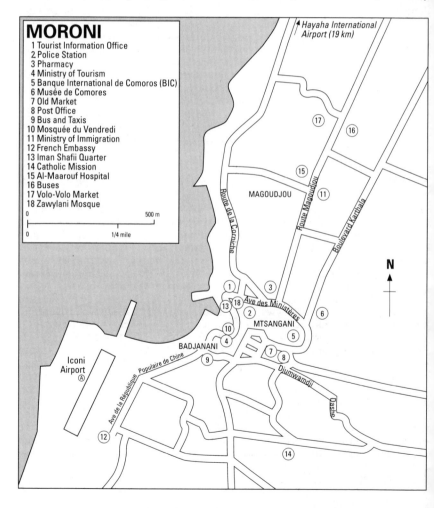

MORONI

1 Tourist Information Office
2 Police Station
3 Pharmacy
4 Ministry of Tourism
5 Banque International de Comoros (BIC)
6 Musée de Comores
7 Old Market
8 Post Office
9 Bus and Taxis
10 Mosquée du Vendredi
11 Ministry of Immigration
12 French Embassy
13 Iman Shafii Quarter
14 Catholic Mission
15 Al-Maarouf Hospital
16 Buses
17 Volo-Volo Market
18 Zawylani Mosque

0   500 m

0   1/4 mile

Hayaha International Airport (19 km)

MAGOUDJOU

Route de la Corniche

Route Magoudjou

Boulevard Karthala

Ave des Ministères

MTSANGANI

BADJANANI

Iconi Airport

Populaire de Chine

Ave de la Republique

Djumwamdji

Dashe

N

life. The museum also has displays tracking the eruptions of Mt Karthala. The museum is open Monday to Thursday from 8am to 1.30pm and 3pm to 5.30pm; Friday from 8am to 11am; and Saturday from 8am until noon.

Far away in the US the names of the islands and the town of Moroni have sparked questions among followers of the Church of Jesus Christ of Latter-day Saints. In the *Book of Mormon* there is reference to the angel Moroni, son of

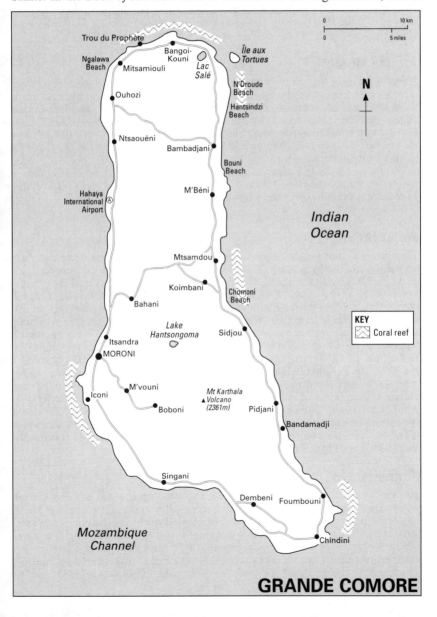

GRANDE COMORE

Mormon, and a hill called Cumorah. There is speculation about the possible relationship between these Mormon names and those of Comoros. The name of the town and the name of the islands naturally pre-date Joseph Smith and his *Book of Mormon*, but whether the relationship between the names in the book and those in the islands is coincidental or there is some historical relationship between the two is the question exercising US Mormons. Some believe Joseph Smith might have heard of Moroni and Comoros since American whalers were visiting the archipelago in the early part of the 19th century. The names were probably known in the north-eastern US at the time Smith had the vision that established the Mormon Church.

Around Moroni

About 4 miles (6 km) north of Moroni is the fishing village of **Itsandra**, which was once the capital of the island. All that remains of this ancient glory are the ruins of some **16th century tombs**, a **sultan's palace**, and five-sided **fort** in thick vegetation. The village has 200 yards of fine white beach, which is where Colonel Bob Dénard stormed ashore with his mercenaries on 12 May 1978 to overthrow the crazed Ali Solih (see *Politics* p.218). The *Itsandra Sun Hotel* is about 2 miles (3 km) north of the village.

Inland north of Itsandra village is **Ntsoudjini**, a quaint walled settlement where the main attractions are a 14th century **mosque** built by Grand Sultan Wakandzou and the 18th century **tomb** of Sultan Fumnau.

MITSAMIOULI

The second largest settlement on Grande Comore has the longest stretch of beach on the island. You can watch fishermen putting out to sea in their *galawas* early in the morning and even spend the day fishing with them for a small fee. Women wade in the shallows and fish with nets they call *chiromani*, driving fish into them by smacking the water with sticks. The Sunday market is an attraction with its array of fresh produce, cloth and other goods. The *Le Galawa Beach Hotel* is on Grande Comore's most impressive stretch of sand, the **Ngalawa Beach**, regarded as the finest on the island. If you are not resident at the hotel you'll have to fork out CF5,000 (£6) to use the beach. A short hike north of Mitsamiouli is the **Trou du Prophète** ('Hole of the Prophet'), a tiny bay which local legend asserts was once the landing place of Muslim Prophet Mohammed. What is more certain is that pirates did some careening and carousing on the sheltered quiet white beach in the 17th century. At **Bangoi-Kouni** village, 3 miles (5 km) east of the hotel, you can see the **Mosquée Miraculeuse**, (the Miracle Mosque) which, locals will assure you, was built overnight by magical forces. There are also some old Shirazi tombs nearby.

Further Afield

Heading east is the salt lake crater of **Lac Salé**, which exhibits some unusual properties. Apart from the fact that its waters – if you can get down there – are reputedly a sure cure for skin ailments, they also change colour remarkably throughout the day. Early in the day the water is a deep, sulphurous, green, which becomes blue as the day wears on. Between July and October it can go brown or even white. Local legend (yes, another one) has it that an old village lies submerged in the depths of the lake. Apparently the inhabitants refused food and shelter to a Muslim holy man who had arrived to warn them of an impending volcanic eruption. One family did offer him hospitality and was deservedly saved when the village vanished a few nights later into what is now Lac Salé.

This legend has an interesting spin-off for visitors, especially backpackers. Devout Muslims are now supposed to offer food and shelter to strangers to avoid the same fate. Many nowadays follow this ancient injunction – but usually there's a modern price tag attached. Another myth is that no stone thrown from the rim of the crater will ever reach the water, but will be repelled by some mystic force. More concrete and interesting is the large colony of fruit bats which you can watch glide in and out of the trees above the lake.

THE EAST COAST

Grande Comore's eastern seaboard is the least populated and the wildest coast, bearing the brunt of the Indian Ocean's trade winds. There's more to see on the west coast, but the east is still well worth visiting, if only for its wonderful beaches. Voted the best of them, from the north down, are the beaches at **N'Droude**, **Hantsindzi**, **Bouni**, and **Chomoni**. Heading down the east coast from Bangoi-Kouni, about 2 miles (3 km) from Lac Salé, is the eroded volcanic ridge of the **Chaine du Dragon**, a jagged peninsula which is all that remains of a crater which erupted and destroyed itself 600 years ago. It's on the map as Goula'ïvouani and is a regular tour stop. From this dragon's backbone you can look out to **Ile aux Tortues** ('Turtle Island'), a lovely little islet you can walk out to at low water. If you paddle out between December and March you'll probably see the nesting green turtles which give the islet its name and, with luck, you might even be there when eggs hatch and baby turtles emerge to scamper for the safety of the sea.

The beaches at **Bouni** are a fair hike out from the village, so try to flag a bush taxi if you are not on an organised tour. The beaches are protected by a coral reef, which means safe bathing. A curiosity at **Mtsamdou** village on the way south to Chomoni is a 500-year-old hollow baobab, the largest on Grande Comore, which is so enormous that it once served as the local lock-up for wrongdoers.

Chomoni

Wedged between high cliffs the coral beach at Chomoni is a great spot for all-over tanning. Chomoni itself is a scruffy coastal settlement favoured for some reason by well-heeled Comorians. More importantly it's near the crossroads of the island's only three main roads. The mountain road that winds inland from here to Ntsoudjini, Itsandra and Moroni on the opposite coast is a truly glorious drive through forests and hill meadows. On this road is **Koimbani**, where you can see the ruins of a 15th century **Arab palace** that belonged to a famous and uncommonly fat sultan. To trek to the ancient volcanic craters and other sights around Koimbani you'll need a local guide as you'll have to do some off-road bundu bashing.

Foumbouni

Grande Comore's third largest community, is noted for the pottery produced by local craftspeople and there are several craft shops on the hill behind the town where you can judge their artistry for yourself. There's a 17th century **fort** on the outskirts offering good views from its ruined walls and north of the town, at Bandamadji, are several 16th century **tombs**, supposedly of Portuguese seafarers.

THE SOUTH COAST

From **Chindini** at the south-eastern tip of the island, you can look across the 31 miles (50 km) stretch water to the island of Mohéli, and you might persuade a local fisherman to sail you across in a motorised *galawa*. There's a pleasant bathing beach on the western outskirts of town, with the bones of an old shipwreck within paddling distance offshore.

Singani village's claim to fame is that it was engulfed by a swathe of boiling lava from Mt Karthala in 1977. From the rebuilt village you can walk up this lava highway, which has already sprouted a forest of young trees. About 4 miles (6 km) up the coast road through plantations of ylang-ylang is **Mitsoudje**, a place noted for its accomplished wood carvers and a good place to buy excellent souvenirs.

ICONI

The fishing village of Iconi, 4 miles (6 km) south of Moroni was the capital of the island in the 17th century. The tall cliff wall of the crater of Ngouni to the north is known to Comorians as the 'Cliff of the Faithful Wives.' They were certainly brave. Two hundred of them hurled themselves from the top when their lofty hiding place was discovered by the raiding Sakalava slave traders from Madagascar who had murdered most of their husbands. There's a difficult path to the top if you want to peer down from the ruins of the Citadel at the spot where they committed mass suicide. There is also a good view of Moroni from the top. A more recent tragedy is remembered on the southern side of Iconi by a plaque fixed to a bullet-pocked wall. This marks the spot where, in 1978, members of President Ali Solih's infamous Youth Brigade shot down local men who had protested about his anti-religious decrees. Like its successor as capital, Iconi also has its **Mosquée du Vendredi**, with an imposing square minaret. Other places worth a look are the **Palais de Kaviridjeo**, built in the 16th century for sultans from Anjouan, and another ruined palace called **La Fortaleza**, whose name – Portuguese for 'fortress' – indicates early island links with these adventurous seafarers.

THE CENTRAL REGION

From Iconi or Moroni you can trek to **M'vouni** and **Boboni**, starting points for the trail up to the mist-shrouded summit of Mt Karthala. Boboni is a remote rainforest settlement on the lower slopes of the volcano and lies at the end of a bone-shaking mud and rock switchback track. M'vouni, at the foot of the mountain, is the easier launch pad for the start (see *Sport and Recreation* p.258). Mt Karthala has poured out lava in 12 major eruptions since 1857. The biggest was in 1918 and the most recent in 1977. The major part of Grande Comore is dominated by the bulk of the volcano; the north by a rocky plain known as **La Grille**. This highland plain rising up to 3,281 ft (1,000 m) above sea level offers trekking trails to a series of peaks and extinct craters.

The road inland from **Ntsaoueni** takes you to the village of **Maoueni**, from where a network of walking trails leads up through rainforest and over to the east coast. Before you branch off from Ntsaoueni take a look at the oldest mosque in the Comoros, the **Mosquée Dalao** probably built early in the 14th century, and the pink **Mosquée Djumbe Foumou** from the same period.

EXCURSIONS

More than 90% of all visitors to Comoros make use of organised tours to see the full range of attractions offered by the Islands of the Moon. If you'd like to check out this hassle-free option and have your exploring organised for you by local experts, guides and interpreters, Tourism Services Comores (TSC) are the land excursion specialist partners of *Le Galawa Beach Hotel*, and the *Itsandra Sun Hotel*, which is where you can contact them. Here's a sample of what TSC can offer.

Perfume Island Tour

In Mitsamiouli, the second largest town, you visit the ylang-ylang distillery which produces the basic essence for luxury perfumes, before touring the historical monuments and sultan's fort and palace at Itsandra village. In Moroni, guides take you to the historical and literary museum and, at Badjanani, the Great Friday Mosque and the port area, then on to the fishing village of Iconi. Next halt along the south coast is at Singani village to view Mt Karthala volcano and the lava flow from its last eruption in 1977, then Chindini beach for swimming, sunbathing and a picnic lunch. To Chomoni after lunch where solidified black lava contrasts with the powder-white sandy beach. At Mtsamdou village, you'll see the 500-year-old baobab tree. View the Chaine du Dragon at Goula'ïvouani, and an impressive natural display of lava rocks. Last stop is at the extinct crater lake of Lac Salé. This tour costs about CF18,225 (£23/$33) for adults and CF10,301 (£13/$18) for children under 12, including picnic lunch.

Moroni-Chomoni

For the same price this full-day tour takes you to Moroni in the morning, with ample time to visit the national museum, the old Arab quarter of the town, the sultan's palace at Iconi and the ramparts at Itsandra. You then drive inland over the foothills of Mt Karthala past dramatic lava flows to Chomoni beach on the east coast for a swim, sunbathing and a picnic lunch or barbecue. In the afternoon to the north of the island, driving along the east coast to visit Lac Salé salt crater lake. You can also stop to buy vanilla and exotic spices at the village of M'beni before returning to the hotel.

Three Craters Nature Walk

This tour takes you to three interesting sites with different characteristics, each one with stunning panoramic views. The **Lamnavaliya Crater** 328 ft (100 m) deep, offers a bird's-eye view of the northern coastline. Climb up the **Chaine du Dragon**, a natural volcanic rock phenomenon created by an eruption. From the top, you'll get a clear view of Turtle Island, off the north-east coast. Walk around the rim of the **Lac Salé**, and enjoy a refreshing drink while you watch the sun sink behind the mountain range. This excursion is especially recommended for the energetic. Comfortable shoes should be worn. The tour costs CF11,886 (£15/$22) for adults and CF5,547 (£7/$10) for children under 12.

La Grille Rainforest

For the same cost this tour takes you through the town of Mitsamiouli where, according to legend, seven Shirazi princes landed in the 15th century and established sultanates on the islands. Then to Maoueni village at 3,281 ft (1,000 m) amid tropical vegetation. Walk in the rainforest and a deep valley with its dense cover of indigenous trees, and delicate wild orchids. Transport is by bush taxi. Comfortable walking shoes are recommended.

Karthala Rainforest

Drive to M'vouni village at the foot of Mt Karthala volcano. Walk up the slopes to an altitude of 4,921 ft (1,500m) through plantations of guavas and bananas, then through takamaka, wild fig, and camphor trees sheltering a variety of wild orchids. This is a 5-6 hour walking expedition and is recommended only for people in good physical condition. A picnic lunch is provided. The tour costs CF27,734 (£35/$50) for adults, including picnic lunch. No children are accepted on this tour.

Throughout the islands you'll notice unfinished dwellings, built usually to roof level and then seemingly abandoned. These are the houses Comorian parents start to build when a daughter is born and completed as a gift to her when she gets married. In the case of an eventual separation or divorce she is thus never left homeless. On the other hand, a Muslim with the permissible four wives has a choice of four roofs over his head.

ANJOUAN (Ndzuani)

Anjouan is shaped like a roughly chipped arrowhead pointing south-east towards the black sheep in the Islamic family, French Mayotte. Hankering after the same metropolitan benefits, Anjouan seceded from the island republic in 1997, but as France has no intention of being lumbered with another poverty-stricken island Anjouan is undoubtedly on the path back, along with sister secessionist island Mohéli, to the federal fold under a dispensation offering local administrators more say in their own affairs. This is the brief background to the situation that makes travel between the three islands problematic but by no means impossible. Fishing craft criss-cross between them unhindered, ferries and ships from Mayotte and Madagascar serve the ports of Grande Comore and Anjouan, making holes in Anjouan's 'spice curtain.'

The island was the first in the archipelago to be settled, probably because it was well wooded and watered, prime requisites for early seafarers. In the 17th and 18th centuries the islanders were the, often unwilling, hosts to a string of British privateers and pirates, who knew the island as Johanna. It was in Anjouan Bay that French corsair Olivier le Vasseur captured the British merchantman *Indian Queen* only to lose her later on the reefs of Mayotte while readying her for a fresh piratical expedition. The pirates were just one more eddy in the tide of people and races whose descendants are now regarded as the most attractive of all the islanders. When a Comorian man decides to marry they say he first checks out available bride material on Anjouan.

MUTSAMUDU

The capital and port of Anjouan, on the north coast, Mutsamudu is a ramshackle place founded in 1482 and a conglomeration of old Arab houses in the usual maze of narrow streets which characterises any *medina* in the Indian Ocean. **Whales**, known as *baleen*, are regular visitors to the bay and the island is one of only two places where you can see the **rare** king-size bat, **Livingstone's flying fox**. The other place is Mohéli (see *Flora and Fauna*). Your nose will lead you to the clove sorting warehouse at the port but, as the hills rise sharply behind Mutsamudu, you have to climb some steep steps to reach the **Citadel** built in 1860, whose cannon once commanded the approaches to the port. The cannon with their graven French fleur-de-lis and British crown are still there. The haul up the stairs to the old building is worthwhile for the seagull'-eye views over Mutsamudu. Behind the Citadel is a French Catholic **church** built in the early 20th century. There's an **aromatic market** near the town square where, as well as spices and local produce, you'll find the famous Anjouan raffia dolls for sale. The black pebble beaches are disgustingly polluted and don't warrant a glance, but a short walk from the town is the pleasant waterfall of **Dziaucoundré**.

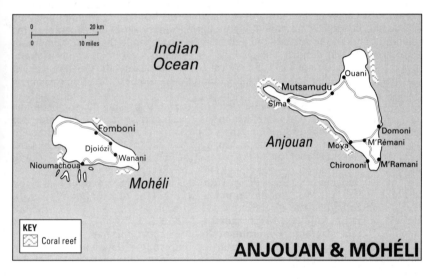

AROUND ANJOUAN

About 4 miles (6 km) away from Mutsamudu is **Ouani**, which is where you land at the island's airport if you haven't hopped over by ferry or *galawa*. Between the two are the overgrown ruins of an old **Arab palace** and a **French colonial fort** but just as interesting are the **freshwater springs** welling up among the pebbles of the nearby beach. The water has a tonic water flavour and locals say it's good for indigestion. Anyone interested in stronger stuff will find houses along the road selling potent palm wine. It's said to be the best drop in the islands. From Ouani the road turns sharply inland to the east coast town of

Bambao. The road bypasses one of the island's best beaches at **Hayoho**, which you can get to only after a 5-mile (8 km) slog from Bambao or, more easily, by boat. Dominating features of the town are the white 19th century palace of Sultan Abdallah, the **Bambao Mtsanga**, and a distillery which has been busy since 1880 producing essential oils of ylang-ylang, frangipani, geranium, orange flower and other exotic fragrances. You can tour the distillery and buy its products at bargain prices.

Domoni

Six miles (9 km) south of Bambao, is the old capital of Anjouan and you can still see the original houses built in those early days by the Shirazi Arab settlers who came from Persia. There are more than the usual number of interesting old mosques in the town, but the ostentatious white and gold tomb of assassinated President Ahmed Abdallah, who was born here, is the major attraction for visitors. The lavish mausoleum was inexplicably a gift from the government of Communist China to the family of this devout Muslim leader. Domoni is famed for the carvings of its craftsmen, whose extraordinary skills are apparent in the splendid doors of the sultan's old palace at Bambao, while the local womenfolk are noted for their delicate embroidery. The town has a further claim to fame. In the waters off Domoni in 1952 a local fisherman, Ahamadi Abdallah, caught the first coelacanth recorded in the Comoros and focused the attention of the scientific world on Anjouan.

From nearby Papani the road crosses the island, bypassing the southernmost tip of Anjouan, which you can reach only by bush taxi or on foot. This side trip will bring you to some unspoilt beaches, such as the one at **Chirononi**, although the finest beach on the island is at **Moya**, where the cross-island road hits the west coast. A coral reef provides protection here for relaxed bathing and snorkelling.

The River Lingoni comes down from the heights near **Pomoni** and you can take a pleasant walk uphill through a little village to **Lingoni Waterfall**. Trails lead inland in the direction of **Mt Ntingui** at 5,233 ft (1,595 m), the highest point on Anjouan, **Mt Trindrini**, (4,836 ft/1,474 m), and the crater lakes of **Dzialandze** and **Dzialaoutsounga** (see *Sport and Recreation* p.274). Further along the coast road is **Sima**, a picturesque village sited high on a palm-covered hill which, after Domoni, is the oldest settlement on the island, as is evidenced by one of its three mosques standing on the foundations of another dating back to the early 14th century. Sima is the centre of Anjouan's **clove** production and the overpowering scent is everywhere, as are the drying buds. You can buy spices at rock-bottom prices in the local **bazaar**. The road back to Mutsamudu, about 12 miles (20 km) away, forks at Sima and leads 3 miles (5 km) to **Bimbini**, a fishing village on the north-west prong of the island. The village has an unsavoury reputation among conservationists as a popular dish for locals there is turtle meat. The meat and eggs of the officially protected green turtle (*Chelonia mydas*) are commonly sold in the village market and the fact that turtle meat is even cheaper than vegetables indicates that a plentiful, if illegal, supply is being brought in from the turtle grounds of nearby Mohéli. The local turtle population of Anjouan has already been effectively wiped out.

MOHÉLI (Mwali)

This island, the smallest of the three, is definitely for the young – or the young at heart. It is virtually without mod cons and it's Coral Island and Treasure Island all rolled into one. It is one of the most beautiful little islands in the Indian Ocean, one of the most neglected and arguably the least developed. The people are the closest in the archipelago to their African ancestral roots and the least strait-laced. For interior-bashing, and camping for any length of time, food and water and anything else required should be packed in. Don't forget to take a torch. There's a circular road around the island, closely following the coast before bisecting the bottom south coast bit in the obligatory cross-island stretch.

Privateers and Pirates

In the mid-17th century, long before France staked its claim, faraway British monarch Charles I of England, in trouble with his Virginian investments and in need of ready cash, sent a small company of men to Mohéli under Captain Quail with a commission to 'Range the world over and make prize of any ship not belonging to a country having a formal treaty of alliance or peace with the King of England below the equatorial line'. They favoured Mohéli as their base. From it they preyed on passing merchantmen and eventually returned to England loaded with booty but minus the good Captain Quail, who died in the course of lining his monarch's pockets.

Mohéli was a favourite stamping ground for Indian Ocean pirates, corsairs and privateers in the 16th and 17th century and on the seaward side of **Mbatse**, between Fomboni and Domoni, are ruins from that boisterous freebooting era. There's also talk of treasure buried on Mohéli by French corsair Bernadin Nageon de L'Estaing.

FOMBONI

Mohéli's capital is Fomboni, a nondescript settlement of coral brick houses and palm thatched huts, with a jetty where incoming boats berth when the tide's in and an uninspiring beach where you land when it's low water. Visible on the island's central elevated spine, **Mledjélé Ridge** behind Fomboni, is its highest point, 2,592 ft (790 m) **Mt Koukelé**, which is flanked to the east by second highest peak 2,510 ft (765 m) **Mt Kibouana**. Bush taxis can be found parked near the market on the northern side of Fomboni, ready to take you to the other side of the island where the best beaches are to be found, or anywhere else you want to go. You'll also find the immigration office and police station here. Above the beach near the taxis local shipwrights can sometimes be seen building and repairing traditional dhows and outriggers. Nearby are some old **Shirazi Arab tombs** across from a **Christian cemetery** which holds, among other neglected graves, the remains of French trader Francois Lambert, an ordinary enough name for an extraordinary man. Lambert, a Mauritian ship owner, enjoyed a protracted and passionate romantic affair with Mohéli's ruling Malagasy Sultana Fatima in the mid-19th century which set he and his British partner William Sunley up as owners of extensive plantations and, through a series of Byzantine machinations, finally resulted in Mohéli's becoming a protectorate of France in 1886. Sunley shares the cemetery with Lambert.

Near the harbour is the crumbling **palace** built by Fatima's father, Ramanetaka, who wrenched the sultanate from ruling Anjouan in 1830.

AROUND MOHÉLI

Mohéli is bursting with fertility and if you ramble out into the heights you'll walk among forested hills and dales full of ylang-ylang, coffee, cocoa plantations, crops and pasture land. Escapee pets originally from Madagascar have bred in the forests to give them resident populations of mongoose and crowned lemurs. From the local airport at **Djoiézi** the road heads south to the village of **Wanani** where it forks. In the south are **Itsamia** and **Iconi**. Between them are pleasant walking trails around **Lac Dziani Boundouni**, near the south-eastern toe of the island. Like Lac Salé on Grande Comore this piercing blue crater lake is reputed to cure virtually all ailments. Itsamia beach is a mess, and so is the sea here, but things get better for beach lovers as the track swings through Iconi to rejoin the road that takes you to **Sambia**, site of Mohéli's best beach, where an inshore reef protects bathers and snorkellers. If you should be in Iconi on a Friday evening you could be there for a **seafood slap-up** and some palm wine drinking leading to a night of unbridled animist partying unrivalled and envied throughout the more staid sister islands.

Behind Nioumachoua (see below), forest trails lead up to waterfalls in the bush on the **Chiconi River**. There's a succession of beaches along the unspoilt coastline from **Miringoni** to **Chiconi** and **Domoni**, then comes a green turtle nesting beach at **Kavé Houani**, after which you're on the way back to Fomboni with a nod on the way at M'batse to the shades of King Charles I and his faithful subject, Captain Quail.

NIOUMACHOUA MARINE RESERVE

The goal of the visitor is, or should be, the south coast's Nioumachoua Marine Reserve. The hamlet of the same name is the gateway to this marine gem, established after marine biologists from South Africa's JLB Smith Institute of Ichthyology – named after the famous coelacanth man – produced a hefty report on conservation proposals in the late 1980s for the government of Comoros. This laid down guidelines for the conservation of four endangered animals or groups: Sea turtles, coral reef communities, the dugong, or sea cow, and the coelacanth. The report also proposed a series of small and large marine reserves with different levels of protection for natural resources, formulated in such a way that the rights of traditional fishermen were respected. The Nioumachoua reserve is the only one since proclaimed, apart from a small marine sanctuary off Ngalawa beach on Grande Comore, which was created after agitation from *Le Galawa Beach Hotel* and its active dive centre.

The Mohéli marine reserve encompasses part of the south-west coast of the island and the Nioumachoua group of offshore islets, which includes **Kanzohi**, **Chandzi**, and **Ouénéfou**, once a leper colony and now a favourite nesting place for green turtles. Fishermen will ferry you out to the islets, but you'll need to stock up on food and water if you plan to camp for a few days on idyllic Ouénéfou, and if you want to enjoy some excellent scuba-diving you'll have to lug in your own gear. Snorkelling is a lighter weight option.

Offshore islands are not inhabited and the entire reserve area is beautiful and relatively unspoilt. The reserve has a large population of rare **Livingstone fruit bats** (*Pteropus livingstonii*), **coral reefs** in excellent condition and, most notably, is a breeding ground for the densest population of green turtles in Comoros. Studies of the migratory habits of marine turtles in the region show that Mohéli could well be the breeding hub for a much larger area.

INDEX

Abdallah, Ahmed (Com)   218, 274
Abdulkarim, Mohamed Taki
    (Com)   219, 225
Acoua (May)   209
Action Comores (Com)   251
aerial trips (May)   199
AIDS (Mad)   56
AIDS (May)   179
airfields (Mad)   64
airfields (Com)   242
airlines (Mad)   0
airlines (May)   0
airlines (Com)   0
airports (Mad)   45
airports (May)   175
airports (Com)   230
alcohol (Mad)   74
alcohol (May)   19
alcohol (Com)   225, 261
Alliance Francaise (Mad)   130
Ambalavao (Mad)   125
Ambataloaka (Mad)   135
Ambatoharanana (Mad)   137
Ambinanibe River (Mad)   148
Amboasary Sud (Mad)   150
Ambodifotatra (Mad)   158
Ambohimanga (Mad)   123
Ambondro (Mad)   135
Ambositra (Mad)   124
Ambovombe (Mad)   149
amphibians (Mad)   103
Ampijoroa (Mad)   142
Anakao (Mad)   146
Analakely (Mad)   120
Analamanga (Mad)   120
Analamera Special Reserve (Mad)132
Andasibe National Park (Mad)   155
Andilana Beach (Mad)   135
Andohahela National Park (Mad)150
Andraikiba (Mad)   124
Andranovory (Mad)   145
Andriantsouli (May)   165

Andringitra Strict Nature Reserve
    (Mad)   126
ANGAP (Mad)   111
Anjanaharibe Sud Reserve (Mad)   133
Anjohikely (Mad)   142
Anjouan (Com)   272
Ankarafantsika (Mad)   142
Ankarana Special Reserve (Mad)   132
Ankify (Mad)   134
Antaimoro paper (Mad)   125
Antalaha (Mad)   156
Antananarivo (Mad)   120
Antoetra (Mad)   125
Antongil Bay (Mad)   156
Antsirabe (Mad)   124
Antsiranana (Mad)   130
Avenue of the Baobabs (Mad)   143
aye-aye (Mad)   92, 156
Azali, Colonel Assoumani (Com)   219

Badamiers (May)   207
Badjanani (Com)   265
Bagamoya (May)   207
Baie de Sainte-Luce (Mad)   149
Baie des Courriers (Mad)   131
Baie des Dunes (Mad)   131
Baie des Forbans (Mad)   158
Baie des Sakalava (Mad)   131
Bambao (Com)   260, 273
Bambao Mtsanga (Com)   274
Banc Vailheu (Com)   215, 253
Bandamadji (Com)   269
Bandrélé (May)   211
banga (May)   168
Bangoi-Kouni (Com)   268
banks (Mad)   51
banks (May)   178
banks (Com)   235
baobabs (Mad)   90
baobabs (May)   193
baobabs (Com)   269
bats (Mad)   101

bats (May) 194
bats (Com) 230
Bay of Ampasindava (Mad) 133
Beaches (Mad) 135
Beaches (May) 162
Beaches (Com) 215
Berenty Private Nature
    Reserve (Mad) 150
Betampona (Mad) 109
Betsiboka River (Mad) 20, 140
Beza-Mahafaly Special
    Reserve (Mad) 148
bilharzia (Mad) 57
Bimbini (Com) 274
birdlife (Mad) 103
birdlife (May) 193
birdlife (Com) 252
Bombetoka Bay (Mad) 140
Bouéni Bay (May) 210
Bouni (Com) 269
Bouyouni (May) 209
Bush House Private Reserve
    (Mad) 154
bush taxis (Mad) 68
bush taxis (May) 184
bush taxis (May) 243

camping (Mad) 71
camping (May) 188
camping (Com) 246
Canal des Pangalanes (Mad) 154
Canyon des Singes (Mad) 147
Cap Miné (Mad) 131
Cape Faux (Mad) 148
Cape St Marie Special Reserve
    (Mad) 148
Caroni islet (May) 210
Castors Shore (Mad) 137
Caverns of Anjohibe (Mad) 142
Caves of Sarodrano (Mad) 146
caving (Mad) 142
Centre Culturel Albert Camus
    (Mad) 129
Centre Culturel Arabe Lybien
    (Mad) 130
Centre Culturel Indonésien
    (Mad) 130
Chaine du Dragon (Com) 269
chameleons (Mad) 101
Chandzi (Com) 276

Charles I (Com) 273
Chiconi (May) 210
Chiconi River (Com) 276
Chindini (Com) 269
Chirongui (May) 210
Chirononi (Com) 274
Chiroroni (Com) 214
Choizil (May) 209
cholera (Mad) 57
Chomoni (Com) 269
Chutes de la Mort (Mad) 155
Cirque Rouge (Mad) 141
Citadel (Com) 273
Cliff of the Faithful Wives (Com) 270
coelacanth (Mad) 88
coelacanth (May) 208
coelacanth (Com) 221, 250
Combani (May) 209
Coral (Mad) 136
Coral (May) 181, 194
Coral (Com) 233
coups (Com) 217
Crater Lake of Tritriva (Mad) 124
crater lakes (Mad) 124
crater lakes (May) 135
crater lakes (Com) 162
craters (Com) 259
credit cards (Mad) 52
credit cards (May) 178
credit cards (Com) 235
crocodiles (Mad) 102
Crown of Thorns (May) 196
currency (Mad) 50
currency (May) 178
currency (Com) 234
Darwin, Charles (Mad) 91
Dembeni (May) 210
Dénard, Col. Bob (Com) 218
dinosaurs (Mad) 116
disabled travellers (Mad) 83
disabled travellers (Com) 262
diving centres (Mad) 136
diving centres (May) 197
diving centres (Com) 253
Djamandjary (Mad) 135
Djohar, Saïd Mohamed (Com) 219
Djoiézi (Com) 276
dolphins (May) 195
dolphins (Com) 253
Domoni (Com) 274

drugs (Mad)   81
drugs (May)   202
drugs (Com)   261
dugongs (May)   195
dugongs (Com)   276
Duke University Primate Center
    (Mad)   113
Dzialandze (Com)   274
Dzialaoutsounga (Com)   259, 274
Dziani Boundouni (Com)   259
Dziani Dzaha (May)   162, 207
Dziani Bolé (May)   209
Dziaucoundré waterfall (Com)   273
Dzoumonyé (May)   209

elephant bird (Mad)   87
ethnic groups (Mad)   30
excursions (Mad)   123
excursions (May)   184, 195
excursions (Com)   270

Famadihana (Mad)   38
Faré beach (May)   206
ferry services (May)   175, 183
ferry services (Com)   231, 243
festivals (Mad)   75, 84
festivals (May)   171, 204
Fianarantsoa (Mad)   125
Fiherenana River (Mad)   146
fishing (Mad)   137
fishing (May)   198
fishing (Com)   257
Fomboni (Com)   278
Forest of Miary (Mad)   146
Fort Dauphin (Mad)   149
Fort Rova (Mad)   141
fossa (Mad)   88, 92, 102
fossils (Mad)   116
Foulpointe (Mad)   153
Foumbouni (Com)   269
free maps (May)   183
free maps (Com)   242
French Foreign Legion (May)   162
French Foreign Legion (Com)   218
Friday Mosque (Com)   265

gay travellers (Mad)   82
Giant jumping rat (Mad)   102
golf courses (Mad)   130
golf courses (May)   200

Grande Mariage (May)   168
Grotte d'Andrafiabe (Mad)   132
Grotte des Portugais (Mad)   147
Guerlain (May)   201

Hajangoua (May)   211
Handréma (May)   209
Hantsindzi (Com)   269
Haute Ville (Mad)   120
Hayoho (Com)   273
Hell-Ville (Mad)   135
hira gasy (Mad)   75
HIV AIDS (Mad)   56
HIV AIDS (May)   179
hot springs (Mad)   124
humpback whales (Mad)   157
humpback whales (May)   193

Iconi (Com)   270, 276
Ifaty (Mad)   146
Ihosy (Mad)   145
Ilafy (Mad)   123
Ilakaka (Mad)   147
Ile aux Nattes (Mad)   157
Ile aux Tortues (Com)   269
Ile St Marie (Mad)   156
Ilot Bandrélé (May)   211
Ilot Bouzi (May)   211
Ilot de Sable Blanc (May)   196
Ilot des Portugais (Mad)   149
Ilot Madame (Mad)   158
Ilot Mtsamboro (May)   210
Iman Shafii quarter (Com)   265
Isalo Massif (Mad)   147
Isalo National Park (Mad)   147
Isoraka (Mad)   120
Itsamia (Com)   276
Itsandra (Com)   268

Jardin d'Essai et Parc Zoologique
    d'Ivoloina (Mad)   153
Jardin des Amours (Mad)   141
jet-lag (Mad)   54
jewellery (Mad)   78
jewellery (May)   200
jewellery (Com)   268

Kaleta Park (Mad)   150
Kani-Kéli (May)   211
Kanzohi (Com)   276

Katsepy (Mad) 141
Kavé Houani (Com) 276
kayak safaris (Mad) 156
Kemal, Saïd Ali (Com) 218, 219
King Solomon (May) 164
King Solomon (Com) 216
Kirindy Forest (Mad) 143
Koimbani (Com) 269
Koungou (May) 209

La Fortaleza (Com) 270
La Grille (Com) 270
La Grille Rainforest (Com) 259
La Vigie (May) 207
Labattoir (May) 206
Laborde, Jean (Mad) 24, 121, 123
Lac Anony (Mad) 149
Lac Dzialandzé (Com) 259
Lac Dziani Boundouni (Com)259, 276
Lac Salé (Com) 259, 268
Lac Vert (Mad) 155
Lake Ampisabe (Mad) 154
Lake Anosy (Mad) 120
Lake Lanirano (Mad) 149
Lake Ravelobe (Mad) 142
Lambert, Francois (Com) 275
Lamnavaliya (Com) 271
leeches (Mad) 60
lemurs (Mad) 92
lemurs (May) 193
lemurs (Com) 276
Les Quatre Frères (May) 208
Libanona Beach (Mad) 149
Libertalia (Mad) 130
Lingoni waterfall (Com) 274
Lokara Peninsula (Mad) 149
Lokobe Reserve (Mad) 134
London Missionary Society (Mad) 33
Longoni (May) 209

M'Chambara (May) 210
Machiroungou (May) 209
Mahajanga (Mad) 140
Mahambo (Mad) 154
Maintirano (Mad) 143
malaria (Mad) 58
malaria (May) 180
malaria (Com) 236
Mamoudzou (May) 207
Manafiafy (Mad) 149

Mananjary (Mad) 154
Manakara (Mad) 154
Manambolo River (Mad) 108, 143
Mananara National Park (Mad) 155
Manangareza (Mad) 154
Manangotry rainforest (Mad) 150
Mandrare River (Mad) 150
mangroves (Mad) 91
mangroves (May) 93
Manjakatompo Forestry Station
   (Mad) 124
Mantadia National Park (Mad) 105
Mantasoa (Mad) 123
Maoueni (Com) 270
Marine Museum (Mad) 33, 196
Maroantsetra (Mad) 0156
Marodokano Mosque (Mad) 134
Marojejy National Park (Mad) 133
Masoala National Park (Mad) 156
Masoala Peninsula (Mad) 155
Mayotte Comité du Tourisme
   175, 199, 202
Mbatse (Com) 275
medina (Com) 265
mercenaries (Com) 218, 219
Michelin train (Mad) 67
millipedes (May) 181, 194
Miréréni (May) 211
Miringoni (Com) 276
Mitsamiouli (Com) 268
Mledjélé Ridge (Com) 275
Mohéli (Com) 275
Montagne d'Ambre National
   Park (Mad) 131
Montagne des Francais (Mad) 131
Moramanga (Mad) 155
Mormons (Com) 267
Morombe (Mad) 85
Morondava (Mad) 143
Moroni (Com) 265
Mosquée Dalao (Com) 270
Mosquée Djumbe Foumou (Com) 270
Mosquée Miraculeuse (Com) 268
Moutsumbatsu (May) 210
Moya (Com) 274
Moya Beach (May) 207
Mozea Akiba (Mad) 141
Mt Bénara (May) 211
Mt Choungui (May) 210
Mt Karthala (Com) 258

Mt Kibouana (Com) 275
Mt Koukelé (Com) 275
Mt Maromokotra (Mad) 132
Mt Mtsapéré (May) 209
Mt Ntingui (Com) 259, 274
Mt Passot (Mad) 135
Mt Trindrini (Com) 274
Mtsahara (May) 209
Mtsamboro (May) 209
Mtsamdou (Com) 269
Mtsangani (Com) 260, 265
Mtsapéré (May) 211
Musée d'Andafiavaratra (Mad) 122
Musée d'Art et Archéologie (Mad)122
Musée de l'Académie Malgache
    (Mad) 122
Musée de la Gendarmerie (Mad)155
Musée de la Mer (May) 208
Musée des Comores (Com) 250, 267
Museum of Antandroy Culture
    (Mad) 150
Musical Beach (May) 211
musical instruments (Mad) 76
musical instruments (May) 201
musical instruments (Com) 249
Mutsamudu (Com) 272
MV Mpanjakamena (Mad) 154

N'Droude (Com) 269
N'goudja (May) 196, 210
Namorona River (Mad) 118, 125
national parks (Mad) (Com) 107, 252
Ngalawa Beach (Com) 268
Nioumachoua Marine Reserve
    (Com) 276
Nosy Bé (Mad) 133
Nosy Bihento (Mad) 156
Nosy Boraha (Mad) 156
Nosy Fàly (Mad) 133
Nosy Komba (Mad) 135
Nosy Lonja (Mad) 131
Nosy Lulangane (Mad) 142
Nosy Mangabe Special
    Reserve (Mad) 156
Nosy Manja (Mad) 142
Nosy Mitsio (Mad) 136
Nosy Sakatia (Mad) 135
Nosy Satrana (Mad) 146
Nosy Tanikely (Mad) 136
Nosy Tsarabanjina (Mad) 136

Nosy Ve (Mad) 146
Ntsaoueni (Com) 270
Ntsoudjini (Com) 268

Octopus tree (Mad) 90
Onilahy River (Mad) 146
orchids (Mad) 91, 157
orchids (Com) 249, 259
Ouani (Com) 273
Ouénéfou (Com) 276

Palais de Kaviridjeo (Com) 270
palm trees (Mad) 88
palm trees (May) 193
palm trees (Com) 249
Pamandzi (May) 206
Parc Botanique et Zoologique
    de Tsimbazaza (Mad) 122
Passamaïnty (May) 209
Périnet (Mad) 105, 155
phonecards (Mad) 63
phonecards (May) 182
photography (Mad) 80
photography (May) 210
photography (Com) 222
Pic St Louis (Mad) 149
Pic Boby (Mad) 126
pirate cemetery (Mad) 158
Pirate's Island (Mad) 157
pirates (Mad) 57
pirates (May) 164
pirates (Com) 217
Pointe de Mahabou (May) 208
polygamy (Com) 222
Pomoni (Com) 274
population (Mad) 30
population (May) 167
population (Com) 222
pottery (May) 200
pottery (Com) 269
pousse-pousse (Mad) 68
prostitution (Mad) 81

Quatre Frerès (Mad) 137
Queen of Sheba (May) (Com) 216
Queen Ranavalona I (Mad) 24

Radama I (Mad) 24
raffia dolls (Com) 260, 273
Ramanetaka Palace (Com) 276

Ramena Beach (Mad)   131
Ranohira (Mad)   147
Ranomafana National Park (Mad)125
Ratsiraka, Didier (Mad)   26
River Lingoni (Com)   274
Rova (Mad)   120
royal tombs (Mad)   122
Russian graves (Mad)   133

Sada (May)   210
Saiadi Botanical Park (Mad)   149
Sakaraha (Mad)   145
Sambava (Mad)   133
Sambia (Com)   276
sapphires (Mad)   147
Saziley Park Marine Reserve
   (May)   196
scorpionfish (May) (Com)   181, 253
seasickness (May)   180
sifakas (Mad)   93
Sima (Com)   274
Singani (Com)   270
snakes (Mad)   103
Soavita (Mad)   126
Sohoa (May)   200, 210
solar eclipse 2001 (Mad)   84
Solih, Ali (Com)   218
Soulou (May)   210
spiny desert (Mad)   90, 145
St Augustine (Mad)   146
St Augustine's Bay (Mad)   145
St Mary's Island (Mad)   156
stamps (May)   182
steam locomotives (Mad)   67
stonefish (May) (Com)   181, 253
Sultana Fatima (Com)   275
Sunley, William (Com)   275

taboos (Mad)   39
Taolagnaro (Mad)   148
tenrecs (Mad)   102
tide table (May)   183
Toamasina (Mad)   152
Toliara (Mad)   145
Tomb of Abdallah (Com)   274
Tomb of Andriantsouli (May)   208
Tomb of King Baba (Mad)   146
tombs (Mad)   38, 145
tortoises (Mad)   103
tour operators (Mad)   47, 81

tour operators (May)   176
tour operators (Com)   232
tourism (Mad)   29
tourism (May)   167
tourism (Com)   221
trails (Mad)   147, 156
trails (May)   199
trails (Com)   270, 276
Tranovato (Mad)   149
Travellers tree (Mad)   89
Trou du Prophète (Com)   268
Tsararano (May)   211
Tsaratanana Strict Nature
   Reserve (Mad)   132
Tsiafajavona (Mad)   124
Tsimanampetsotsa (Mad)   109
Tsingoni (May)   209
tsingy (Mad)   21, 132, 143
Tsingy de Bemaraha (Mad)   143
Tsingy de Namoroka (Mad)   109
Tsiranana, Philibert (Mad)   25
Tsoundzou (May)   24
turtles (Mad)   103
turtles (May)   194
turtles (Com)   251

underwater trail (May)   196
University Museum (Mad)   146

Vahibe (May)   209
Vangaindrano (Mad)   134
vanilla (Mad   28
vanilla (May)   167
vanilla (Com)   220
vegetarians (May)   189
vegetarians (Com)   248
Vezo (Mad)   145
Vichy French (Mad)   25, 131
Volo-Volo market (Com)   260

Wanani (Com)   276
water (Mad)   55
water (May)   179, 191
water (Com)   238
whales (Mad)   157
whales (May)   195
whales (Com)   272
Windsor Castle (Mad)   131
World Wildlife Fund (Mad) 112, 115

ylang-ylang (Mad)   134
ylang-ylang (May)   167
ylang-ylang (Com)   220

Zafimaniry (Mad)   78, 125

Zafy, Albert (Mad)   27
Zahamena (Mad)   109
Zawylani Mosque (Com)   266
Zombitse National Park (Mad)   148

Vacation Work publish:

	Paperback	Hardback
The Directory of Summer Jobs Abroad	£9.99	£15.95
The Directory of Summer Jobs in Britain	£9.99	£15.95
Supplement to Summer Jobs in Britain and Abroad *published in May*	£6.00	–
Work Your Way Around the World	£12.95	–
The Good Cook's Guide to Working Worldwide	£11.95	–
Taking a Gap Year	£11.95	–
Taking a Career Break	£11.95	–
Working in Tourism – The UK, Europe & Beyond	£11.95	–
Kibbutz Volunteer	£10.99	–
Working on Cruise Ships	£10.99	–
Teaching English Abroad	£12.95	–
The Au Pair & Nanny's Guide to Working Abroad	£10.99	–
Working in Ski Resorts – Europe & North America	£10.99	–
Working with Animals – The UK, Europe & Worldwide	£11.95	–
Live & Work Abroad - a Guide for Modern Nomads	£11.95	–
Accounting Jobs Worldwide	£11.95	–
Working with the Environment	£11.95	–
Health Professionals Abroad	£11.95	–
The Directory of Jobs & Careers Abroad	£11.95	£16.95
The International Directory of Voluntary Work	£10.99	£15.95
The Directory of Work & Study in Developing Countries	£9.99	£14.99
Live & Work in Scotland	£10.99	–
Live & Work in Saudi & the Gulf	£10.99	–
Live & Work in Japan	£10.99	–
Live & Work in Russia & Eastern Europe	£10.99	–
Live & Work in France	£10.99	–
Live & Work in Australia & New Zealand	£10.99	–
Live & Work in the USA & Canada	£10.99	–
Live & Work in Germany	£10.99	–
Live & Work in Belgium, The Netherlands & Luxembourg	£10.99	–
Live & Work in Spain & Portugal	£10.99	–
Live & Work in Italy	£10.99	–
Live & Work in Scandinavia	£10.99	–
Panamericana: On the Road through Mexico and Central America	£12.95	–
Pacific Coast Passenger: Mexico to Canada by Train, Boat & Bus	£12.95	–
Travellers Survival Kit: Scottish Isles	£11.95	–
Travellers Survival Kit: Oman & the Arabian Gulf	£11.95	–
Travellers Survival Kit: Mauritius, Seychelles & Réunion	£10.99	–
Travellers Survival Kit: Madagascar, Mayotte & Comoros	£10.99	–
Travellers Survival Kit: Sri Lanka	£10.99	–
Travellers Survival Kit: Mozambique	£10.99	–
Travellers Survival Kit: Cuba	£10.99	–
Travellers Survival Kit: Lebanon	£10.99	–
Travellers Survival Kit: South Africa	£10.99	–
Travellers Survival Kit: India	£10.99	–
Travellers Survival Kit: Russia & the Republics	£9.95	–
Travellers Survival Kit: Eastern Europe	£9.95	–
Travellers Survival Kit: South America	£15.95	–
Travellers Survival Kit: USA & Canada	£10.99	–
Travellers Survival Kit: Australia & New Zealand	£11.95	–

Distributors of:

	Paperback	Hardback
Summer Jobs USA	£12.95	–
Internships (On-the-Job Training Opportunities in the USA)	£17.95	–
Green Volunteers	£10.99	–

Vacation Work Publications, 9 Park End Street, Oxford OX1 1HJ
Tel 01865 – 241978   Fax 01865 – 790885

Visit us online for more information on our unrivalled range of titles for work,
travel and adventure, readers' feedback and regular updates:
www.vacationwork.co.uk